MANAGEMENT OF TEACHING SKILLS IN PRIMARY SCHOOLS

Encyclopaedia of Primary Education Series

MANAGEMENT OF TEACHING SKILLS IN PRIMARY SCHOOLS

Edited by

B.V. Verghese

ANMOL PUBLICATIONS PVT. LTD.

NEW DELHI - 110 002 (INDIA)

ANMOL PUBLICATIONS PVT. LTD.
4374/4B, Ansari Road, Daryaganj
New Delhi - 110 002
www.anmolbooks.com

Management of Teaching Skills in Primary Schools

First Edition, 2002

ISBN 81-261-1051-1

PRINTED IN INDIA

Published by J.L. Kumar for Anmol Publications Pvt. Ltd., New Delhi - 110 002 and Printed at Mehra Offset Press, Delhi.

Contents

Preface

'Teaching skill' is the most important quality of a teacher. It is acquired, sharpened and updated for making teaching emphatic. So it is necessary for a teacher to equip oneself with essential teaching skill—particularly at primary school level—where the foundation of a pupil is shaped and moulded in proper way.

Here in this book a number of core issues like—assets for teaching, placement of subject matter, a model for teaching, strategies of learning, activity method of teaching, working with a coursebook, think for yourself, teaching of social studies, magnets and their properties, the energy of electricity, new developments in elementary school training, opportunities for ICT in teaching mathematics etc. are given elaborate treatment.

I am grateful to all the scholars whose writings and fruits of painstaking research are cited or substantially made use of in this book. I am also thankful to all my friends and colleagues who have assisted me while preparing the manuscript. Last but not the least, I am grateful to Mr. J.L. Kumar, Managing Director, Anmol Publications Pvt. Ltd., New Delhi for undertaking the publication of this work.

—B.V. Verghese

1

Assets for Teaching

No matter how long you have been preparing for teaching or how extensive your experiences with children, you will be a rare individual if you do not face your first opportunity to take full-time responsibility for a class with some trepidation. Will my pupils like me? Will they work with me? Will I be able to help them learn? How satisfied will I be that I have chosen wisely in deciding upon teaching as my life's work? These are the kinds of questions that all beginning teachers ask themselves.

It is often said that teachers are born, but it is the rare individual who seems, from birth, to have a gift for working with children. It is perhaps closer to the truth to say that teachers are developed. Experiences from early childhood—with other children, with your parents and other adults, with everyday events—have combined to make you the person you are today. Throughout your years in the elementary and secondary school, your teachers have contributed to your store of knowledge, to your skills, to your ability to think, and to your attitudes toward your chosen profession. Academic courses at college have deepened your understanding of the cultural heritage and the world in which you live. Professional courses have developed and clarified your insights into your responsibilities as a teacher. You bring this accumulation of attitudes, knowledge, skills, and insights with you as you step inside your own classroom for the first time.

Student teaching and your first years on the job are late steps in the long process of preparing to become a teacher. You need have few apprehensions about your ability to take these steps successfully if you have been building toward them wisely—heeding the counsel of these persons who know you best—and capitalising upon the available opportunities for growth. There is, however, much to be learned in this, your first venture in full-time responsibility for a group of boys and girls. Whether or not your chosen profession offers all the satisfactions for which you have hoped depends, to a large extent, upon you. Are you aware of your own assets? You will want to capitalize upon them in your work with boys and girls. Have you made a clear-eyed, objective appraisal of your potential liabilities? You must be prepared to compensate for these in your classroom work. How well do you know yourself? What must you do to make yourself a successful teacher?

WHAT PERSONAL ASSETS DO YOU BRING TO THE CLASSROOM?

You will bring to the classroom your innate personal equipment and what you have been helped to make of it over the years of livine—physical stamina, intellectual ability, special talents, personal appearance, vioice. For no two people is this personal equipment the same. None of the extensive research concerning the characteristics of an effective teacher has uncovered a definite patternof talents and capacities that results automatically in success on the job. You do not, therefore, have to make yourself into a different person in order to become a good teacher. What is important is that you learn to use your unique personal equipment as effectively as possible in the interests of the maximum growth of the boys and girls under your care.

How do you appraise your physical stamina? Teaching can be exhausting. The most rigorous combination of college classes, committee chairmanships, and a part-time job rarely equals the physical demands of the classroom. There will be few opportunities during the school day to relax completely. There will be no half-day off to rest unless serious illness demands it. You will probably be on your feet for longer periods than those to which you have been accustomed. Even with conscientious efforts to encourage active participation on the part of your pupils, you will be making more use of your voice than ever before. There will be as much "required" reading as was ever demanded by a full schedule of college classes. You will be repeatedly exposed to colds, influenza, mumps, measles, chicken pox.

People differ in their physiological requirements. Even though you have received a clean bill of health in a recent physical examination, it is important to identify just what your own physical limitations are. Are you a person who needs more than the usual amount of sleep in order to be fresh, bright, and cheerful? If so, it might be well to take another look at your college programme and extra-class activities. It is far better to postpone an elective course or to resign from a committee than it is to drag yourself into the classroom day after day fatigued by midnight study or long hours in committee sessions. Do you know your own nutritional needs? The days that you try to teach after an inadequate breakfast or lunch can become unbelievably long and weari-some. How long can you keep going without a chance to relax? A few teachers seem to be human dynamos whodraw strength from the stimulation of an active group of youngsters, but most find that they cannot operate at full power all day long. The typical elementary school schedule does not allowmany free periods away from the children, but you can, for their sake as well as your own, learn to plan a programme in which there is an appropriate alternating of active and quiet work—periods in which you are giving active leadership to the entire group and work sessions where you can talk with youngsters individually, times when you need to be on your feet and times when you can sit for a few minutes. It is not an indication of weakness to recognize one's personal need for such adjustments. Teaching ceases to be fun if the physical demands of the classroom become unbearably heavy.

If you are a person whose physical resistance tends to be below normal you should take particular precautions to avoid the fatigue that often insites trouble. You will soon find that your teaching will lose its effectiveness for your pupils and its satisfactions for you if it is interrupted by a series of absences for illness. Consult your family physician if necessary, for appropriate medical advice. Plan your personal living to provide the rest and relaxation consistent with the professional job you have to do.

But is a hermit-like existence all that you can anticipate when you begin to teach? By no means. The old adage that a change is as good as a rest has sound psychological foundations. Every teacher needs to make sure that he does not allow his preoccupation with professional responsibilities, challenging and stimulating though these may be, to cut him off from other types of activities which he finds personally satisfying. Certainly you will need to arrange your schedule so that you are not harassed by more demands than you can handle. Work for balance in your activities. Broadly interpreted, health is emotional as well as physical. Do not sacrifice completely your recreational and social life. Children deserve to be working with teachers who have buoyancy, enthusiasm, and a zest for living.

How flexibly do you deal with new ideas? A candid analysis of classroom activities indicates that there are dozens of times a day when the quality of pupils' learning depends upon their teacher's ability to sense the implications of a situation quickly and accurately. Your boys and girls will become confused at the most unexpected points; you will have to set them straight. They will phrase their question? vaguely and leave you wondering exactly what they mean. They will grasp only part of an explanation and arrive at conclusions incomprehensible to anyone not intellectually agile enough to follow their reasoning. They will contribute anecdotes from their out-of-school life that can have major bearing upon then classroom work if you but sense the relationships. They will ask an appalling number of questions, many of which appear only distantly related to the immediate topic under discussion. You will have to decide how to deal with these.

Not all people can think with ease and facility on their feet. Some see the far-reaching ramifications of a situation instantly; others need time to marshal their thoughts. Some grasp what another person is trying to say from a minor cue; others must have the point fully spelled out. Some can follow several threads in a discussion at once: others become confused when they try to deal with more than one idea at a time. You are not likely, during you: student-teaching experience, to make many fundamental changes in the way you think. You can, however recognize your own characteristic wins of teaching to new ideas. Once you are aware of these you can prepare more intelligently for the classroom situations you will inevitably face.

Whether you think quickly or slowly on your feet, you owe it to your pupils to make careful plans. Experienced teachers never neglect this, even though they are going over much the same ground for the umpteenth time. Teaching is far more complicated than merely getting along companionably with a group of boys and girls and answering their questions glibly. You must make each minute count. The more skillfully you learn to think through every detail of the work on which you are about to embark, the better prepared you will be to handle your pupils' questions and comments in ways that will result in maximum growth. Experienced teachers will tell you that their planning is usually much more thorough than merely mapping out a single course of action. They plan alternate illustrations upon which they may draw if the ones they first use prove inadequate. They identify points at which pupils might become confused and plan how to give more help if it seems to be needed. They think about the applications to out of school life that their pupils are likely to make and the relationships to previous lessons that they may identify. No matter how adept you are in handling emergencies, you will be a more skillful teacher if you learn to prepare yourself for the unforeseen.

But suppose you are a person who needs time to grasp the full implications of a new idea or to sense the importance of a question. If this is true, you would do well to recognize the fact and to come to your classroom carefully prepared to use techniques that will give you a chance to catch your breath. You will contribute far more to the development of accurate information and clear thinking if you are prepared to say frankly to your boys and girls, "Let's not guess; we'll need to look that up," than you will by vague acceptance of an incorrect fact of an illogical conclusion. Likewise, you will stand a much better chance of helping the pupil who is confused if you will question him until you are sure you have understood his difficulty than you will by launching into a hasty explanation that misses the point.

On the other hand, you may be a person who enjoys the matching of wits in a good argument. In this case, you would do well to take a second look at the way you handle new ideas. You may recognize in yourself a tendency to respond too readily—to jump to a conclusion regarding what a pupil is trying to say without hearing him out, to advance a solution to a problem without giving the child who is in difficulty a chance to think, to pull the entire class off on a tangent because of the implications you happen to see in a question, to be impatient with the youngster who thinks slowly. If you have a tendency to make snap decisions, it may be important for you, also, to develop techniques that will give you time to think about the implications of the situation you face.

Nothing is more satisfying to a teacher than to watch boys and girls acquire new skills and concepts. Your first classroom situation is the time and place to discover the detail with which you, yourself, must prepare, in order to guide their learning competently. It is your opportunity to develop the techniques you need to manage the give and take of class discussion effectively.

What impressions will your personal appearance convey? "I'm not sure that older children will listen to me. Some of them will be taller than I am." "Won't a man my size frighten fourth-graders?" "I feel so odd asking sixth graders to sit down. After all, I don't look much older, myself." Children give their respect and their love to teachers of all ages, sizes, and shapes. What you reveal about yourself through your dress, your grooming, your voice, and your manner makes the difference. If a petite young woman adopts a very youthful dress and hair style and tries to joke and tease like a ten-year-old, her pupils are apt to respond in kind. If her clothing, hair style, and manner suggest maturity, she will be regarded as an adult.

If a large man gives the impression from his dress and grooming that he is engaged in manual labor and uses a blustering voice and manner, his pupils may be intimidated. If he wears the clothing they associate with professional people and his manner is gentle, they will turn to him readily. First impressions are important. Before you step into your new classroom, give some thought to your personal appearance.

What should you wear? If you think back to your own school days you will realize that you noticed your teacher's clothing. You looked forward to the days when Miss Simpson wore a dress which you particularly admired or when Mr. Jones donned a tie that was your favourite. On the other hand, you may also remember at least one occasion when you were so fascinated by a teacher's jangling bracelet or the extreme style of her dress that you could scarcely keep your mind on your work. Bright colors, attractive and youthful styles, and costume jewelry belong in today's classrooms.However, although you would act deny your pupils the fun of seeing you dressed for a tea (or for a picnic) once in a while, you should for the most part, choose garb suited to the activities in which you will be engaged. You will need to be active in playground games, to help mix paints, to stretch to write on the blackboard, to kneel to work beside a youngster. This calls for attractive, informal business attire and comfortable, well-fitting shoes.

You will want to pay particular attention to your dress the first day YOU arrive. It is a wise precaution to dress attractively but conserva-lively until you have an opportunity to ascertain the custom in your particular school. (For women this means hose, and for men a coat and tie. even in warm weather.) For your first few days in the classroom you would not choose your most youthful garb. Certainly, doming that identifies you immediately, as a college student (socks, saddle shoes, athletic sweaters, or whatever is the current campus craze) is inappropriate, even though you are merely walking down the hall to the laboratory school which you have visited countless times. Above everything else, choose for your first day the costume in which you feel most at ease and poised. Use your dress to contribute to your feelings of competence and security.

If you expect your boys and girls to appearwith clean hands, minicured nails, combed hair, and clean clothing, you can do no more than set them a good example. Good grooming is, perhaps, partly a matter of habit, hut it conveys to others a definite impression about the way you regard yourself. So, in the case of women, does the choice of cosmetics. You may not possess a large wardrobe, but you can at least make sure that your boys and girls will be working with someone who is fastidious about personal cleanliness, who is conservative in the use of cosmetics, whose clothing is spotless; and whose ,shoes are polished.

Have you listened to your voice lately? Your pupils are a captive audience. If you speak too rapidly to be easily understood, lisp, employ a harsh, shrill voice, or speak in monotonous tones, you are creating an annoyance which they must endure day after day. Perhaps even more important, the quality of your voice can have a definite effect upon your pupils' behavior. If you sound competent, assured, and secure they will accept your leadership: if you sound uncertain, dubious, and hesitant, they are likely to feel doubtful. If the edge in your voice indicates that you are becoming increasingly tense and irritated, their behavior may reflect your irritation. You can arouse them to a fever pitch by the excitement in your tone or you can help them to become relaxed and calm by your serenity. Few of us can appraise our own voices accurately. In fact, it is a common experience not even to recognize one's own voice in a recording. Seek help in evaluating the quality and volume of your voice and in eliminating undesirable mannerisms. Many a teacher has discovered that with a little practice he can make a decided improvement in his ability to use his voice effectively in achieving his purposes in the classroom.

"Yes," beginners sometimes say, "I know how to dress, but how shall I *behave* if I want the children to respect me?" The personality to which your boys and girls will be responding is made up of many things—voice, posture, dress, grooming, poise, assurance, friendliness. You cannot don a new personality as you would a new costume. You can, however, be your normal, competent, adult self. From your vantage point, the gap between your age and that of your pupils may seem negligible, but from theirs it is very great indeed. If you are so unwise as to try to adopt the mores and manners of your pupils in order to be accepted by them, they will recognize that your behavior does not ring true and Will respond accordingly. Dress like the adult you are; speak with the assurance of your twenty-odd years of living; walk, stand, and sit with poise. Have confidence in your own leadership ability and you will convey this confidence to your boys and girls.

HOW BROAD IS YOUR ACQUAINTANCE WITH YOUR CULTURAL HERITAGE?

You have chosen a profession that calls for depth and breadth of understanding. You will be responsible for helping pupils to grow in understanding their world. Yours will be the challenge of opening to them the doors to creative expression—literature, art, music, drama, dance. You will be helping them to gain command of problem-solving skills—reasoning; communicating, observing, listening, calculating. You will be providing the experiences they need to develop physical coordination and skill in games. You will be the one to help them grow in their ability to work cooperatively with their fellows.

A total of some sixteen years in school (and some twenty years of living) no matter how wisely invested, has taken you only a short way along the road toward becoming an educated person—a road which you have obligated yourself to travel for the remainder of your life. As you begin to think about guiding the growth of the boys and girls under your care, it is appropriate to inventory your cultural accomplishments. What have you to offer? What are the resources at your command to help yourself grow as your pupils grow?

Where are the strengths in your academic background? Not until you face thirty or more eager youngsters—be they five, eight, or a dozen years old—will you have any notion of the extent to which your academic background will be taxed. Children will respond to the subject matter you are trying to teach with questions that explore the most minute details. They will push logical discussions to conclusions; you have never dreamed of. Nor will your pupils' zeal for information be confined to the topics listed in the course of study. They will bring their outside world to school. Eager voices will report on last night's television production. Grubby hands will present you with leaves to classify, snakes to name. Young scientists will come bearing their latest ventures in developing miniature rockets. Budding musicians will ask for help in transcribing a new song to paper.

What has been the pattern of your college work? Where do your strengths lie? Even in areas in which you are well schooled, you may find, yourself turning for further information to a variety of technical and nontechnical resources, but here, at least, you have depth of background upon which to draw. Do not count, however, on teaching only those subjects in which you feel most secure. Your pupils have a right to expect guidance from you no matter what direction their interests take. Where is your background the most limited? At these points you would be well advised to embark early upon an extensive reading programme. Do not count on keeping only a page ahead of your class. Their questions will not fall into such an orderly pattern. Read your pupils books first. These will acquaint you with the background materials from which their questions will come. Do not, however, stop at this point. The simplified statements in children's texts have a host of meanings back of them. You will have to read carefully at the adult level if you are to enrich and expand upon these materials. It is not uncommon for teachers to say that they have never learned as much about a topic as they did the first time or two that they taught it. This is your time in grow. Make the most of it.

How good is your grasp of the basic generalisations and problem-solving techniques of the various subject fields? Even if your major has been geography, you are not likely to have mastered the details of topography, climate, and ways of living for every country to which you and your pupils may have reference. If, however, you have learned to think as a geographer thinks, you will have some basic principles to guide you as you and your pupils begin to read about an unfamiliar land. You will not know all the answers to the question that alert second graders can pose about living things, but if you have learned to think clearly and objectively you can help then to discover many answers for themselves. Your sense of historical perspective should alert you to glaring errors of fact and point the direction for further reading. Your grasp of the principles of science should allow you to indicate the general direction of an answer to a pupil's question even as you plan with him for further reading or for experimentation. You bring as a major strength to your classroom your grasp of basic principles and your ability to think logically within the boundaries of a subject field.

How well do you know available resources? Your pupils will think no less of you if you propose that you and they stop to search for an answer. They have a right to expect, however, that you will be able to turn to appropriate resources. One of your first steps upon entering your classroom should be to survey the available teaching aids—texts, reference books, globes, maps, pictures, models. Marshal your own resources, too. You possess college texts and notes that can be helpful. Besides, you have access to library facilities. If you are near your college campus you will have, in your professors, expert help to which you can turn. You bring ten more years of intellectual maturity to a problem than do your pupils. Given a chance to catch, your breath overnight, you can at least put yourself in a position to give intelligent leadership as your pupils plan how to explore a topic with which you are relatively unfamiliar. One of the challenges of teaching is to help your pupils grow in their ability to solve problems. You need not be able to supply all the answers yourself if you can direct them to the resources which will help them to find the answers for themselves.

What special talents and training do you bring to the classroom? Beginners who feel reasonably competent in their ability to give leadership in areas where it is possible to go to the library to locate the necessary information often feel much more hesitant in attempting to give guidance in areas such as art, music, or creative writing. It is a rare individual who brings to the classroom exceptional talent and special training in every area in which he is expected to guide the growth of a group of boys and girls. You may be inclined, at first thought, to say modestly that you have no real talent at all. Actually, this is equally rare. Some persons would even say that the individual who is completely lacking in talent does not exist, although they would acknowledge that in many cases potential ability has been given little chance to develop. Perhaps by the standards of the Metropolitan Opera. Broadway, or the National An Gallery, your talents are modest. Nevertheless, you will have something special to contribute—a good sinking voice, skill in games love of poem, a flare for dramatics, talent in arranging flowers or planning bulletin boards. Pupils deserve the stimulation that comes from their teacher's special enthusiasms. It is important that you recognize the points at which you can make a unique contribution to their lives.

Need your pupils have less stimulating programme than they deserve in areas in which you have no unusual interests or abilities? This will not happen if you recognize your deficiency and take steps to compensate. Undoubtedly your professional courses in college have equipped you with techniques which you can use to release your pupils' creative abilities in fields where you, yourself, are not particularly talented or in which you are not an exceptional performer. A choreographer, for example, does not have to be a talented dancer. The director of a play probably is not a gifted actor. Yet each of these makes a vital contribution to those who have special talents and gifts. Do not hesitate to use the skills and abilities which you have, limited though 'they may be, to develop special talents in your boys and girls. The most important talent you possess is your ability to guide children—your skills in helping them to set goals, in freeing them to undertake new ventures, and in helping them to evaluate their own performances.

It is possible, and very exciting, to learn while your pupils learn. If you put your mind to it, it is not very difficult to acquire enough skill to be able to use your piano once in a while. As you and your youngsters work together to develop a play, you will discover that your sensitivity to the elements of a good dramatic production will increase. Your skill in oral reading will improve rapidly if you work at it. You should expect that your first experiences in taking full-time responsibility for a classroom will make a marked contribution to your professional insights and skill. If you are truly interested in becoming an effective teacher, use these experiences to contribute to your personal growth as well.

How broad is your general experience background? Your college preparation is only a small part of the total breadth of preparation you bring to the classroom. The reading you have done, the jobs you have held, the trips you have taken, the longer life you have lived—all these and more are assets not to be taken lightly. City children will be enthralled with tales of life on the farm. Your contacts with foreign students at college can help enrich discussions of other lands. Your summer work experiences may allow you to speak with authority in areas where your pupils have limited background. Beginning teachers are sometimes reluctant to talk about themselves and their livers, but you have, in the wealth of your experiences, an important means of cloting your pupils reading with reality. In appraising your assets for teaching, count on your background of experience.

You will not be the only one in your classroom with a wealth of experience to offer. It is not uncommon for a teacher to find himself in a situation where many of his pupils have traveled more extensively than he. Nor is it uncommon for creative children to have developed special interests and talents far beyond their teacher's level of attainment. What help can you be in such situations? You can utilize your teaching skill to enable the youngster with the special background to make his unique contribution to the group. Your most effective role may be that of guide—one who comments on interesting and important contributions and keeps the discussion pointed toward outcomes that are worth while. If you are an intelligent listener, your general experience background and your additional years of living will enable you to achieve profitable learnings for all.

You would not be meeting your full obligations to boys and girls if you were not, right now, making plans to extend your own experiences. At least, you can find time for the daily paper, a weekly news magazine, the programmes on television most likely to broaden your understandings, an occasional travel magazine. It may be far more important for your pupils' total growth to take time for such enriching experiences than to collect and grade that extra set of papers. In the longer view, begin to weigh a summer of travel against a summer in college classes. Or, if your travel has been extensive, weigh another trip against employ-ment for the summer.

Teachers cannot afford to live in ivory towers. You owe it to your pupils to be able to acquaint them with history, the arts, the scientific advances that are part of their cultural heritage. You have an obligation, also, to help them explore the realities of the world around them. This yon cannot do unless you, yourself, are closely in touch with that world.

HOW DO YOU MEET PROBLEMS OF EVERYDAY LIVING?

Teaching is a profession calling for mature ability to make decisions. You will be entering into many new kinds of relationships with people—pupils, colleagues, supervisors, parents. There will be complex class-room activities to coordinate. You will have reports to file and a variety of other administrative details to handle promptly and systematically. There will be days when everything goes smoothly and days when one emergency arises after another. How well prepared are you to meet the problems of this complex new environment?

Beginners bring to their classroom work varied backgrounds of experiences in handling difficult situations and making decisions. Some will have been fully responsible not only for their own personal lives but for managing a home as well. Others will have lived under the family roof with parents ready and willing to be consulted whenever a problem arises. Some will have learned from a series of successful attempts to assume responsibilities in home, school, and college that the most complicated task usually works out satisfactorily. Others may have grown to doubt their ability to make a sound decision when faced with even the simplest problem. Most feel more competent in some areas than they do in others.

Your own attitude toward your competence as a person will make a difference in the way in which you approach your responsibilities as a teacher. It is only human to be optimistic and resilient in areas in which we feel secure and to tend to become panicky, discouraged, and perhaps defensive if difficulties arise in situations in which we already have some doubts regarding our ability. Experiences stretching back to early childhood have taught you to react as you do to the problems, you face. You will not relearn new ways of behaving overnight. You can however, identify the situations which, for you, pose the most difficult hurdles. Self-understanding is a first step toward more mature behavior.

Where are your strengths in working with people? The fact that you have chosen teaching as a profession indicates that you find satisfaction in working with people. Not until you begin to teach, however, are you likely to realize just how many types of human relationships a teacher is expected to handle competently. Children may view you as a purveyor of information, an aid in solving problems, a friend, a counselor, a parent substitute. Parents may look to you for advice and counsel or may regard you as a public servant whose methods, dress, and manner can be openly criticised. You will be pan of a team—a member of the school faculty with definite obligations to those who have administrative responsibilities. You will be a colleague, sharing with other persons joint responsibility for the welfare of boys and girls. You will be a learner looking to persons with supervisory re-sponsibilities who will help you grow. Some roles you will be well equipped to handle; others may be roles in which you have had little experience; stillothers may represent roles about which you have developed anxieties. Take a look, before you begin to teach, at your areas of strength and your areas of inexperience in working with people.

What have been your relationships with children? Some beginning teachers bring broad and varied experiences with children to their classroom work; others have had only limited contacts with boys and girls. What has been your experience in working with youngsters?—companion? playmate? playground leader? It is not unusual for beginning teachers to discover that they must learn new ways of behaving in order to assume leadership in the classroom. Are there youngsters with whose background you are not familiar? The middle-class teacher for example, often has to make an extra effort to understand the values, attitudes, and behavior of the youngster from the lower class. Are you aware of differing attitudes toward certain types of children?—some to whom you are likely to be drawn? some you are apt to mother? some you tend to reject? It is a rare teacher who does not find that he has to guard against a tendency to accept from some children behavior that he would not accept from others. Learning to work with and to understand children takes time. You will bring much to the lives of boys and girls through your youth and your generous desire to be of help. You can make your contribution even more significant if you are sensitive to the points at which your present skills and understandings are the most limited.

What have been your previous relationships with adults? Have you been in a variety of situations under democratic leadership where older persons treated you as a colleague? If so, you are well prepared for your role as a member of a school faculty. Not all young people however, have had this experience. Have older persons tended to make your decisions for you? This may mean that you have some lessons to learn in carrying your share in cooperative relationships. Are you, by any chance, still struggling with an adolescent urge to prove to your elders that you are completely competent without their help? or with an adolescent feeling that grown-ups really don't understand and the less shared with them the better? It will be difficult for supervisor to assist you unless you, yourself, can change such attitudes. Have you been accustomed to having the spotlight at home?—to being given lavish praise for a job well done? to having an atentive audience whenever you speak? Your colleagues will welcome you as one with interests similar to their own, but they will not assume that you need any special recognition. You will be an asset to a school faculty with your new ideas, your eagerness to learn, your enthusiasm. Before you assume your responsibility as a teacher, analyze your ability to work with others on a professional level.

How effective are your skills as a group member? Even persons who have had a number of years of experience with children have not always had the opportunity to develop the skills they require for classroom leadership. It is important for you to know the areas in which you may need more experience. Have you worked with large groups? There are techniques for giving leadership to a class of thirty or more that are not of as crucial importance if one is working with a group of five or six. Did your experience with large groups call for democratic planning, or were you merely giving ordered? If the latter, you may have some discussion skills to develop. Can you operate as the resource person or the harmoniser in situations where someone else has the leadership? This is an important technique in working with pupil committees. Have you have experience in adjusting your leadership skills to the age group to which you are now assigned? If not, do not he surprised to find that you have some additional lessons to learn. Learning to teach is, in large measure, a matter of learning to work with groups. This is your year to examine, test out, and refine your skills.

How readily do you assume leadership responsibilities? You are stepping into a situation where your pupils will be looking to you for leadership—in approaching a new problem, in situations involving behaviour, in emergencies. They sense reluctance and hesitation readily. Have you tended to stay in the background, hoping that someone else will act? If so, this is a behaviour pattern you will have to overcome from your first day of school. Do you hesitate to say anything which implies criticism of another person lest you lose his friendship? In the classroom you must learn to speak frankly when pupils disregard agreed-upon rules. Are you, on the other hand, someone who goes ahead impulsively and thoughtlessly? This can sometimes result in decisions that disregard the feelings of others.

You are about to have some challenging experiences in defining and learning how to accept an effective leadership role. You can make a marked contribution to your own growth by learning to evaluate yourself in action.

How skillfully do you handle complex situations? Teaching is not an easy task for someone who dotes upon calmness and order. The very fact that thirty or more individuals are looking to you for guidance, for leadership, and for a friendly expression of interest in their concerns makes it inevitable that there will be days when your attention is demanded in a dozen directions at once. Furthermore, if you meet individual needs, there will be aspects of your programme where your boys and girls work on independent projects or in small groups. As if this much confusion were not sufficient, there will be records due in the office, announcements to make, special events for which your care fully planned programme must be adjusted. Can you handle a multitude of demands with calmness and good humour?

In spite of your most thorough preparation, some days will be confused. There will inevitably be situations causing you to revise your carefully laid plans. Do you become flustered when you must make adjustments? Irritable with your pupils or your colleagues? You can prepare yourself to some extent for such days by learning to consider ahead of time just how your plans might best be adjusted if an emergency arises. You can also, for the sake of your colleagues, your pupils, and your own nervous system, learn to recognise the situations most likely to cause your temper to become frazzled and to take whatever steps are most helpful in restoring your serenity. It is sometimes far wiser, on the day when it seems that one more ounce of confusion can not be borne, to switch to a quiet work period than to proceed with an activity as planned.

How methodical are you? You are joining one of the most creative professions, but it is also a profession in which there must be meticulous attention to detail. You will not be able to stroll in late in the morning to take a few extra minutes to wind up a discussion if your class is due in the library, to hand in records and reports to the office at your convenience. There will be attendance records to maintain accurately cumulative records to keep up to date, your own grade book to keep systematically. If you and your pupils are not going to waste time, you will need to see that books are in order, supplies are stored neatly, desks and notebooks are well-organised. Effective teachers are good classroom administrators. Reliability is one of their important characteristics.

Promptness, orderliness, and reliability are, in part, habits. Yet the person who has not developed these traits may be revealing something more basic about the way he handles his problems. If you are a person who is never quite on time, who never quite completes all the details of the task for which you volunteer, who always ends up in eleventh-hour confusion, it might be well to ask yourself why. Are you, without realising it, putting off the jobs in which you don't quite feel secure? Are you late partly because you are reluctant to face a new situation? Does working in disorder and confusion provide you with a convenient excuse for not doing the job well? Do you tend to put your energy only on those things you consider important, disregarding the needs of others? Whatever your answer, you are now in a situation where many people other than yourself will be inconvenienced by your shortcomings. If your value your professional reputation, you will be will advised to set up a firm work schedule to guarantee that your responsibilities will be met promptly and methodically.

How objective are you when things go amiss? Perfectionists usually have an unhappy time in teaching. The very nature of your responsibility in trying to give leadership to thirty lively youngsters makes it inevitable that some things will go wrong. Your pupils will misunderstand you at the most unexpected places. They will forget information that seemed to be completely mastered yesterday. They will ask question to which you do not know the answers. The more complex the project you undertake, the greater will be the possibilities for trouble. An objective understanding of these inevitable sources of confusion will make your work easier.

How good is your sense of humour? You cannot work week after week with a roomful of live-wire youngsters without some very amusing occurrences. Sometimes one pupil will upset the entire class; sometimes you will make the error. It will be tragic, indeed, if you view such episodes as evidence of your ineffectiveness as a teacher or as proof that your pupils are uncooperative and disinterested. Your year will be much more satisfying if you come to your work prepared to enjoy the humorous entanglements in which you will inevitably find yourself.

How sensitive are you to the needs of others? Not all of the disruptions in your day will be of your own making. Billy may be so enthralled by his new baseball glove that he completely ignores your arithmetic assignment. Your entire group may vent upon you their resentment of the rain that prevented their trip to the park. One of your colleagues, with his mind upon his own teaching, may forgetfully take your time in the visual-aids room. Your principal or your cooperating teacher may ask for the reports he needs without regard for your plans for the evening. You will have to learn to view these as normal occurrences in a situation where people must work together, not as personal affronts or attempts to throw as many barriers as possible in the way of your doing a good job.

Can you take responsibility for your own mistakes? It is important for a teacher to develop depth of insight into the motives of others and generosity toward their inadequacies. It is equally important for him to accept responsibility for his own errors—to look frankly at his short comings. The administrative organisation of almost all school system today is developed upon the assumption that teachers want to improve. In your student-teaching experience, your cooperating teacher will be expecting to help you to analyze your lessons and to develop more effective teaching techniques. As you step into your first position, you principal and probably a supervisor will be prepared to offer similar service. It will not be easy for them to help you if you cannot accept the fact that you may occasionally be wrong. Have you tried to analyze your reactions when you make a mistake? Do you typically try to justify your actions? blame someone else? become so upset that person who could help you spend all their time trying to reassure you? Have you learned to admit frankly that you did a poor job and to proceed cheerfully to figure out how to do it better the next time?

How patient are you? You have not joined a profession whose secrets can be acquired overnight. Some of the skills you will be trying to master are very complicated indeed. Unless you are a most unusual learner it will take time to coordinate the thousand and one techniques that must operate smoothly together, furthermore, just as you think everything is proceeding satisfactorily, some seemingly minor incident will cause the entire situation to take on a different aspect. He quickly do you become discouraged? Can you work toward a skill, day after day, even though it may take you weeks to master it?

How willing are you to take a chance? Teachers who want each to unfold smoothly under their complete control sometimes bar themselves and their pupils from experiences that can be highly stimulating and educationally challenging. Are you going to be willing to try something new for the sake of your own growth as well as that of your pupils, or will you feel compelled to protect yourself from possible failure by staying with the routine and the familiar? There will probably never again be as much help available to you as there is during your student-teaching experience and your first few years on the job. This is your chance to learn from the mistake you make. Are you sufficiently secure in your own feelings of competence to profit from it?

WHAT ARE YOUR ATTITUDES TOWARD YOUR CHOSEN PROFESSION?

Do you have a clear understanding of the social significance of your profession and of the contribution it can make to our present social order? Just how do you view your role as a teacher? Your attitude toward the profession of teaching will have a major influence upon the ways in which you approach your classroom responsibilities. What you believe about your function as a teacher will condition the steps you take to prepare yourself as a contributing, worthwhile member of the profession. How seriously have you thought about these matters?

How do you view the social significance of your profession? The school is an institution which society has established to meet one of its needs. As such it is always close to the people and will at one time or another be subject to criticism. The articles and books you have read, your contacts with schools and teachers, the opinions of other persons — all these have helped to build your attitudes and beliefs about teaching. Have you tried to think through carefully just what you believe and feel about your chosen profession?

Why did you choose to become a teacher? Did you see in teaching an opportunity to make a vital contribution to the lives of boys and girls and through them do your share in developing our democratic ideals and in preserving our cultural heritage? Did you choose to teach because you like to help people and find the warmth of their response satisfying? Is teaching a second choice, elected reluctantly because you were not able to complete the work in some other specialised field? Is it merely an extra string to your bow, a guarantee of an income if plans for marriage and a family do not work out? Perhaps you are saying honestly that there was a bit of all these influencing your decision. This may well be true, but which one predominates now?

What is your attitude toward professional education? Do you regard teahcers as members of a corps of competent persons equipped with specialised skills and knowledge or have you tended to deprecate professional training — to regard teaching as "largely common sense"? If your attitude has been the latter, you may well find yourself having to rediscover, on the job, principles regarding how children learn which should have long been part of your professional equipment. Have you stopped recently to take stock of the professional skills, know how and Knowledge you will bring to your first classroom? These are to be valued highly as you make your initial contribution as a member of the teaching profession.

Each teacher takes into the classroom his expectancies regarding the roles he will play. He may see himself as a dispenser of information whose major major responsibility is to inspire his pupils to learn. He may view himself as a hero to his pupils—someone surrounded by an adoring group. He may act as a benevolent adult—someone who takes responsibility for pupils' welfare, does things for them. He may serve as a counselor and guide. The role or roles you assume depend upon many things—your previous experiences with teachers, the satisfactions you have found in your relationships with people, the roles your pupils expect of you. Whether or not you are conscious of the roles you a playing, they will have a decided effect upon the way you work with boys and girls. You would do well, as you plan for your first contracts with boys and girls, to take time to examine the concept of an "ideal" teacher which you will take into your classroom.

Teaching will achieve greater status as a profession as there is increased public recognition of the contributions teachers are making to the lives of boys and girls. This will come about, in part, as more and more teachers speak with assurance of the social significance of their work and demonstrate in action the quality of their professional competence. Will you be able to make a positive contribution?

How dedicated are you to the task of becoming an effective memberof your profession? Master teachers have never ceased to grow. In the zeal to give the most effective leadership in the classroom, they work constantly to develop a better understanding of boys and girls, better ways of helping them to learn, and broader insights into world affairs. They continually seek new ways of doing—new ways of enriching only the lives of their pupils, but, equally important, their own lives, too. They are contributing, members not only of the school community but also of the larger community—the home, the church, and an ever widening circle of personal and professional friends. In short, they are professional people—adjusted, alert, curious, ever anxious to improve. If you approach your first classroom experience with the same attitudes, this will be a most significant year for your over-all professional growth.

This book is based on the premise that you are anxious to learn that you want to improve yourself as a person and that you are read to become a professional individual who can make an effective contributton to the lives of boys and girls. It is organised around the major problems you are likely to meet as you grow into the profession of teaching. Its aim is to help you to think about these problems, not to provide you with ready-made answers. The truly competent teacher knows what he wants to achieve and why. This should be your goal as you embark upon your new venture.

USES OF TEAM TEACHING

During the 1950's and 1960's, the quality of education offered in the secondary schools has become of increasing concern to both professional educators and the lay public alike. As a result, many traditional approaches to learning, once secure in their acceptance by the educational profession, have been thrown open to question. Perhaps non-instructional tasks might be removed from the teacher's back. Possibly all learning does not have to be directed by teachers. Conceivably, greater emphasis on individual study might be fruitful in some situations. Maybe programmed instruction holds considerable implications for education in the future.

A particular irritation has been the limiting effect which many traditionally organised school systems have placed upon the teacher's time. The staggering load of a five-period day and 50-minute classes, topped not infrequently by three different subject-matter preparations and extracurricular duties, leave most teachers little time for improvement of their individual capabilities. Accordingly, structural variations which offered relief from these traditional limitations were eagerly welcomed.

In addition to an emphasis upon the structural reorganisation of the activities of the teacher and students within the school, a considerable ferment has been developing within the social studies. Not only have new approaches and organisations been urged for the course content of the disciplines traditionally 'offered in the schools (i.e. history, geography, political science, and economics), but also advocates have appeared urging inclusion of the behavioral sciences in the secondary school curriculum.

The publications which probably most encouraged consideration of team teaching, large and small group instruction, teacher aides, independent study, and flexible scheduling as a means of structural reorganisation were the three pamphlets prepared by J. Lloyd Trump: *Images of the Future. New Directions to Quality Education* and *New Horizons for Secondary School Teachers.* Shortly after these appeared, a flood of other articles began to appear in the professional journals. Since 1957, over 200 articles and books have been published on team teaching. By way of contrast, not a single article concerning the subject was listed in *Education Index* between 1955 and 1957.

It must be admitted that team teaching seems to mean various things in various places. Considerable diversity exists in terms of both methodological organisation and aims of instruction. It probably would not be an exaggeration to state that there are as many different types of team teaching as there are different school systems which utilize such teams. As observed in some situations, for example, it is merely take-turn teaching; here the true concept of teamed instruction seems completely lost.

Some characteristics are more commonly cited than others, however. Often flexibly grouped by ability, students are divided for various types of instruction into large classes for oral and visual presentations, and into smaller groups for discussion and debate. Frequently sessions are provided where students may study individually by themselves. The large classes usually number around 90 or more students: the smaller ones, 30 or less. Team members determine staff competencies and make assignments accordingly; they also determine the sequence and manner of the subject to be presented and, using their combined professional judgment, whether large groups, small groups, or individual study, will prevail during the time allotted to them.

What are the advantages of team teaching? Many have been suggested: Teachers will be able to pool their talents, thereby giving the student a far richer educational offering than they would otherwise experience. Unnecessary duplication can be minimised. Through combined teacher planning, and the variety of instructional situations provided, individual differences among students can be more adequately considered. The type of instructional presentation needed can be more closely matched to student interests, needs, and abilities. Differentiated instruction geared to differing student abilities can be more easily arranged. During individual study periods, able students or those students with special interests, can pursue their bent at their own pace and in greater depth than an ordinary classroom situation might allow. Teachers will be more free to plan, study, prepare, relax, and be creative.

On the other hand, a number of arguments both logical and psychological seem to offer themselves against such instructional arrangements:

First, the teachers as individuals. Are all teachers suited for team operations? Many prefer and, in fact, are more effective, when working alone. What about the unimaginative, the less flexible, those not willing or able to compromise? How about the timid and the insecure? Not every teacher is prepared, either academically or psychologically, to emerge from the isolated cave he has known for so long into more open cooperation with and comparison by colleagues and students which teams afford.

Secondly, the curriculum. Some subjects may lend themselves more readily than others to team organisations. Economics, for example, may need more tutorial assistance from the individual teacher than team situations may allow. It may be difficult to organize in large groups the less formally structured presentations, such as a problems course or the emphases that "inquiry" or "discovery" approaches might entail.

Thirdly, the facilities. Not all plants can handle team arrangements. Are there rooms sufficiently big for large group presentations? Is there sufficient space for individual study? Will enough rooms for small group discussions be available? Does the school schedule permit modification, considerable student movement, and frequent changes in room assignment and usage? Can team operations take place without disturbing other more traditionally arranged classes?

Fourthly, the administration. Is it one geared to change and susceptible to new ideas? Can it permit, even welcome, a less than permanently arranged staff and facility utilisation? Is it one willing to experiment— to revise and revamp, to tolerate ambiguity and open-endedness? Is it flexible?

Lastly, the students. Can all types of students benefit

from the various types of instructional arrangements inherent in team instruction? Certainly many things we have observed make us suspicious as to whether or lot teams are maximally effective with all ability levels. Large amounts of actual material presented without any chance for immediate feedback (as in large group lectures, for example) may be less effective with students of lesser ability than more conventional arrangements. Group cohesiveness may be minimal—a large number of students may have difficulty identifying with the large lecture groups and it seems quite likely that the small discussion groups may not meet frequently enough for any cohesion to take place.

Students of lesser ability may have trouble adjusting to the flexibility of schedule around which the team revolves -indeed, may, in fact, need more regularly spaced presentation and a more steady instructional situation. Such students may not be prepared to make effective use of the individual study periods so often programmed into team operations. It might well be questioned whether or not non-verbal students will benefit from the smaller discussion groups which are especially provided for in the team design.

It should be noted that team teaching, as presently described and designed, seems especially geared to middle-class students. What about those described as "culturally disadvantaged"? Their weakness in formal expression, and "paying attention;" their utilitarian orientation; their, emphasis upon immediate satisfaction of needs; their more ready response to visual and kinesthetic signals rather than oral and written stimuli; their basic anti-intellectualism; their proficiency in physical and motoric skills rather than mental problem solving; their lack of "test-taking skills;" their lack of reading material in the home, and their resultant reading weaknesses: their preference for spontaneous over structured situations; all these seem to prepare them for failure rather than success under current team teaching practices.

Whether this necessarily must be so is something else. If maximum provision for individual differences can be provided for within the team structure: if teams can be organised which are committed to experimentation and flexibility: if a variety of activities—not only intellectual, but physical as well can be provided; if presentations can be prepared which consider the cultural backgrounds of the students involved: if imaginative teachers can be employed to plan programmes to involve *all* the students within their charge; if less emphasis can be placed upon the traditional chronological content and more innovational programmes offered instead: then perhaps team teaching can be all that its advocates urge that it is. One observes, however, too many situations in which numerous of the aims of the social studies are being neglected. What essential skills, for example, are being developed where pupils meet in large groups every day, have little or no library research assignments related to the continual lectures, and seldom, if ever, are given the opportunity to discuss?

The essential question is this: Is team teaching more effective in producing learning than the traditional classroom arrangement of one teacher operating independently within an individual classroom? The only way we can answer this question is through research! What empirical evidence exists which supports team teaching as being more effective? Sad to say, such evidence is extremely slight.

The research journals, to say the least, are disappointing. Only one article on team teaching appears in *The Journal of Educational Research*, between January, 1960 and May, 1965.[1] No reports appear in the Cooperative Research Project

Bulletin of the United States Office of Education.[2] The vast majority of articles on team teaching have been collected in the January 1958, 1959, 1960, 1961, 1962, and May 1963 issues of *The Bulletin of the National Association of Secondary-School Principals.*[3] Each issue contains summaries of the experimentation undertaken by various school systems. Only some data on learning is given, however.

The Research Division of the National Education Association has published abstracts on team teaching, but only one of these is not a previous article taken from the *Bulletin.* The *Review of Educational Research* briefly deals with the topic in but a part of one issue, entitled "Curriculum Planning and Development.[4] The two issues of *Social Education* which have carried a review of research in social studies education contained no reference to experimentation with teaching teams.[5] We were able to locate only two dissertations' and one master's thesis.[6]

With few exceptions, the following quotation is typical of the subjective evaluations which appear:

1. Teachers who have worked on a team favour its retention and extension.
2. Students comment favourably on the flexibility and variety of method and materials used.[7]

Articles on team teaching which appear in the professional journals seem to be almost unanimously descriptions of: (1) how teachers and students who experienced a team teaching venture liked it, or (2) descriptions of pitfalls to avoid before embarking on such a venture. In the main, the reports center on a description of structural arrangements or methodological arguments. None specifically describe any attempts to evaluate empirically a difference in content mastery by students when team taught as compared with more traditional approaches.

Before wholesale acceptance of team superiority occurs, therefore, more carefully structured and controlled research on the learning achievement of pupils instructed by teaching teams as compared with more traditional approaches should take place. According to one definition, team teaching is "a type of instructional organisation involving teaching personnel and the students assigned to them in which two or more teacers are given responsibility, working together, for all or a significant part of the instruction of the same group of students.[8] It should be noted that according To this definition, organisation can differ as can the statement of objectives which the team proposes to accomplish. No one particular organisational structure is at present mandatory. What is essential is that one's aims are clear, that researchers carefully describe the particular structure under investigation, and that any extrapolation of research findings be applied only to team operation in the same manner. We have raised many queries about team instruction that demand investigation.

In short, let's look before we leap!

HOW TO PLAN FOR INSTRUCTION?

Once the teacher has made the overall decisions about course organisation and classroom management, he turns next to more specific tactics. With continuing attention to purposes, to the kinds of pupils he will have, to the principles of learning, and to the instructional materials available, he moves into two kinds of complementary planning. Initial planning concerns unit or longer-term arrangements and is followed by attention to daily lessons. The editors relieve strongly in the value of rigorous planning, both long and short term. Such preparation does not preclude considerable involvement of the pupils in many aspects of the direction of their own learning. Nor does it imply that a degree of flexibility should not be built into unit calendars to allow for emerging developments. Operating in a social studies laboratory situation with well-conceived unit plans, the teacher will usually find the combination of elements most conducive to learning for the largest number of students.

While the experienced teacher tends to have to give less time to both long and short term preparation than the beginner, there are very few teachers who can regularly bring off a truly fine lesson without careful thought and adequate plans. Well prepared, daily lessons that also link yesterday with tomorrow are basic to continuing instructional success. One of the inexcusable reasons for unhappy students rejecting studies is the too frequently experienced "off-the-cuff" attempts to teach.

In reading the following articles, review the arguments for planning in terms of larger blocks of time. What contributions will unit organisation bring to your instructional programme? How can you incorporate student involvement into the development of a weekly calendar? What are the essences of an effective daily lesson plan? How will planning be affected if you are moving into a team teaching or flexible schedule situation?

To be sure, history for today's student must be very different from that which his teachers have studied. "It should not only record the achievement of the past, but also try to find analogies applicable to the confused present."[9] And surely in its study we must find "devices for stimulating insight and imagination, for shaking the mind loose from the tyranny of conventional words, unexamined cliche's, and pleasantly familiar paths of thought."

Although the social sciences can contribute enormously to its study, history remains the integrating discipline *par excellence*. It seeks to order man's experience in some intelligible pattern so that both the past and the present can be more appropriately and pertinently interpreted. "A people who cannot look back to their ancestors cannot look ahead to posterity," and to destroy the historical perspective of our students is to deny them an understanding of their heritage. Part of that heritage is anthropological and sociological to be sure—but to sever the trunk of the social studies curriculum and to expect its branches to flourish is to render a disservice to those we teach.

One cannot be unmindful of the outstanding work of Bruner and of some of those working in curriculum who are attempting to adapt his ideas to the needs of the social studies for today's schools—but it is the element of cultism. of the neo-orthodoxy which is already apparent, to which one must strenuously object.

There may be need for curriculum modification, but there is a greater need for more effective teachers. There may be need for a unified curriculum, but there is a greater need for first understanding the principles around which such a curriculum may be organised. There may be need for students to appreciate the mode of thought and the procedures of the historian and the social scientist, but there is a greater need to examine critically the accumulated store of experiences of the human community. There may be need for the inductive approach, yet the deductive cannot be summarily abandoned.

The changes inherent in the incipient revolution in the social studies are welcome, but only to the extent that they encourage teachers to go on with the job of teaching, in the best way they can, man's message to man.

THE TEACHING OF SKILLS

READING SKILLS IN THE SOCIAL STUDIES

Generally, one is considered to be skilled if he possesses a high degree of competence in a trade, profession, a sport, or, in school, in a subject area. The student with skills is the one who is bright, superior, able to grasp information and insights with little apparent effort. On the other hand, we label as a "slow learner" the student who has few skills—and often consider it impossible for him to achieve proficiency in the use of the skills in the subject area. If this is so, we may as well surrender our efforts to teach the "slow learner," for truthfully, without skills, no one can succeed in the social studies.

"Slow learner" has become that convenient term by which educators describe any child who seems yearly to fall further behind in his efforts to master conventional subject matter. Most often, however, when a pupil is categorised as a slow learner, what is really meant is that he is a *slow reader*. There is nothing startling about the fact that some children read less capably than others. This has always been so, and as long as we continue to establish a norm that purports to represent the "average" reader, we will always have pupils who surpass the norm or lag behind it. Although there is considerable hesitation in admitting that we will inevitably have slower readers, no matter what we do in our schools, the truth is that a "norm" decrees by its nature that some must be slower than others.

The task of the teacher, therefore, is one of *raising the norm*, so that the slower reader of today is the equal of the better reader of yesterday. And this is not an unlikely promise, for studies in both the reading and social studies abilities of present-day pupils reveal that slower readers of this age, in great part, achieve and surpass the norms established by standard measuring instruments of 30 years ago.[11]

In the social studies, the slow reader suffers because of the all-too-prevalent, concept that a class must "cover" a certain amount of subject matter in an established number of weeks or months. The object of this article is not, however, to enter into a discussion of the nature of syllabi or the approaches to time allotments or emphasis upon the varied social studies disciplines. It is, rather, the censure of any orientation that provides Tip service to social studies instruction without an emphasis upon social studies skills and the methods of instruction in those skills.

Let us admit, first, that the *basic social studies skills are reading skills.* Social studies teachers pride themselves on the fact that in their classes, if in few others, their pupils do read. After all, the textbook must be consumed and research must be carried out by means of a variety of reference materials. Assignments are made for out-of-class reading from library sources as well as the textbook. Often the daily homework assignment is, "Read pages 41 to 44 and answer these questions. . . ." Yes, the social studies student reads, or at least tries to read and to understand what is expected of him. But how does the slow learner the slow reader- fare under this kind of reading programme? Is he being taught to read within the framework of the social studies?

More often than not, the reading difficulty that plagues the majority of slow learners has caused them to fall behind in their social studies, and it has convinced them that they *cannot* read better than they do—and that failure awaits them again each time they renew the attempt. What is more, it probably does, unless there is a structure in social studies teaching that combines improvement in reading skills with the development of specific social studies skills, knowledges, and concepts. If there are certain skills whose development is an obligation shared by the social studies, we must *consciously* plan for their development. Students do not learn skills by chance. Inherent in any skills programme is a fundamental concept: a skill must be taught, and it must be practiced, consciously and with effort.

In the 1963 NCSS Yearbook, *Skill Development in the Social Studies,* skills in which the social studies at least share responsibility for development are listed: locating and gathering information; organising and evaluating information; reading, speaking, and listening; interpreting pictures, graphs, charts, and tables. Going further, Eunice Johns and Dorothy Fraser emphasize that these skills must be taught *functionally* and in the *context of study;* there should be repeated opportunity to *practice* the skill: and that skills instruction, must move from the simple to the complex.[12]

We can heartily subscribe to all these suggestions and recognize the service they render in the development of social studies skills.

But let us be specific. The basic skill that leads to most others in the "shared" skills category is the ability of the student to find the *main idea* of a paragraph or section (or even a sentence). Without this ability, we can forget about our students being able to outline, summarize, or take notes effectively. Going further, all the skills involving critical thinking, substantiating opinions with proof, and supporting generalisations are based upon the ability of the youngster to determine the main, the important, the central thought of the spoken and written word. The ability to recognize the main idea and its supporting details is related to the ability to separate the relevant from the irrelevant.

But how often have we asked pupils to utilize these skills without having taught them, given opportunity for practice and reinforced them continually? Normally, a social studies teacher expects that the skills have been taught—by someone else in some other class. Even if they have been, a skill is not just taught; it must be practiced. This practice is necessary even for the student with a high intellectual capacity if he is to acquire the competence of which he is capable. The skilled carpenter and surgeon have practiced their arts after first having been taught them.

Do not think that the recognition of the main idea of a selection is too difficult for the slower reader. The frequency of error of our slower readers of junior high school age on standardised reading tests has been analysed and has revealed that questions requiring pupils to determine the main thought of a paragraph are answered correctly *must* often. There have been more correct responses for questions involving the selection of the main thought than for questions that test the ability to note significant details or the meaning of words in context. This is true whether the pupils were reading at a fifth- or tenth-grade level. The task of the social studies is to apply this skill as emphasised in the 1963 Yearbook, functionally and in the context of study.

I am not suggesting that the social studies teachers become teachers of reading exclusively. I am suggesting that in the social studies we should know the skills our students possess and ought to possess -reading skills, let's call them—and that the ability to use these skills is fundamental to their success in their studies. Let us examine a few practical applications of reading skills to the social studies.

The teacher begins by selecting a textbook passage about three paragraphs in length. He asks the students to read silently each paragraph in turn and to select the main thought of the paragraph. (What is the paragraph about?) Inquiry is then made as to trie reason for the selection. Members of the class are encouraged to comment on the choices of their classmates. (This kind of discussion will prove invaluable as students progress in ability and become concerned with the author's purpose in writing.) As a result of this procedure, the class will have selected three main ideas— three headings for a basic outline. Now the *reasons* for the selections of these important ideas are recalled; these are the details that support each of the headings. Thus, a simple outline has been developed, while subject matter has been learned. This kind of developmental process can be used again and again until it becomes part of the student's equipment whenever he is called upon to outline and summarize. Furthermore, how much better he can study and digest a new lesson on his own with this aid to learning available to him!

In performing a basic research assignment, students will build upon the process of making an outline. The shopworn project that requires a student to look for information in the library from some nebulous source and make a report with pictures and charts (to be finished in two weeks) must go! This kind of project is best entitled, "Frustrating the Slow Reader."

Rather specific materials must be known to the teacher and the students must be directed to them and instructed in their use. For example, students may read a specific article from a magazine, preferably one that the teacher has read, and submit five important ideas from the article. Then, in conference with the teacher or in a class situation, the reasons for the selection of these ideas may be discussed.

Logically, students will follow the lessons learned in class on the method of determining the important ideas. Now the article may be reread for supporting statements. The details are filled in and the outline for the report is made before the student moves on, in due time and with sufficient planning, to the more complex outline or summary.

What would you think when you observe such a scene as this in a classroom? The class secretary is at the chalkboard prepared to record the notes of the class discussion. After a few minutes in which the class suggests problems resulting from the introduction of machinery in the eighteenth century, the teacher asks the class to suggest the *main idea* of the discussion. The secretary dutifully writes the suggestion on the board. The teacher then asks, "What have we discussed that supports this idea?" As the class responds, the secretary writes the sub-topics in proper outline form. A glance at pupil notebooks reveals that on a series of successive lessons pupils have recorded notes with the labels of "main idea" and "sub-topic" next to the statements recorded. It does not require great wisdom to discern that this class is going to use this procedure in all their work.

In the process, content has not been forsaken. In fact, the important ideas of the passage have been made more memorable. It is not idle guessing to state that the student will probably retain such information for a greater length of time as well. For the student is not only practicing a skill, he is focusing on the important ideas and the use of the skill makes it possible.

The same emphasis prevails during the viewing of a film or in listening to a speaker. Listening is one of the "shared" skills. During the presentation, notes are recorded. Instead of an immediate discussion of the film or speech, which can become rambling in nature, it is most effective to have the students present the ideas they have selected from the notes they have just recorded. When these ideas are seen on the chalkboard, it will be obvious that there is considerable overlapping in wording; some are then condensed into a single idea, and the important ideas evolve. The message of the presentation is spotlighted through the important ideas presented, and the skill is being practiced functionally.

Stress on this technique during a talk will help to overcome a common criticism that students do not listen. Do we *direct* their listening? Do we check their listening skills by reading in short bursts and calling for a brief statement of the important idea of the selection? Do we afford the opportunity for youngsters to judge the relative importance of the speaker's words? The answer to these questions must be an affirmative, for most of us secure much of our information from the spoken word. Practice in listening is as important as practice in reading in the social studies. And, the intensity of the concentration is even greater, for there is no chance for the listener to refer to material already spoken. Just as we expect youngsters to look for clues and inferences in the written word, we hold the same expectation for them in the spoken word. Too often we have assumed that listening has taken place. We must be assured that it *has* taken place.

Hopefully, the traditional homework assignment of "Read and answer these questions" is on its way out with the slow learner. Quite honestly, this type of assignment does have for its purpose the elicitation of the important ideas of the reading assignment. But if we wish our youngsters to concentrate on the location of important ideas and facts, why don't we specifically ask them to do so. The assignment may just as easily read (and with greater value in its statement of purpose and development of skill): "Read pages 61 and 62. Select the main idea of the first paragraph; select the main idea of paragraphs 2 through 5." The approach has been altered but not the emphasis, and the skills practice may result in better understanding than the search for specific and unrelated items.

Instead of "Identity these words or terms," we can ask: "What word, in the second paragraph means the same as "growing in amount"? In the following paragraph as "route or road"? In the last paragraph as "journey to a holy place"? And the student might even be asked, after instruction in the skills of determining the meanings of words in context, to name the *clues that helped him* to tell the meaning of the word or expression.

Part of the task in improving skills, and perhaps the greatest part, is proving to the student that he can learn. He must succeed, and he will succeed as the instruction in skills becomes basic, specific, and continual. Even such an advanced skill as skimming for content can be taught to the slow, reader, once he is convinced that he can do it. The fascinating instrument, the controlled reader, can be so manipulated as to convince the youngster that he can read faster than he believes he can by starting him at a faster rate and then slowing the rate until he is able to read with understanding. He will find that he is reading with comprehension at a rate that he believed was beyond his grasp.

The ability to skim social studies materials can be demonstrated by this simple process. Students are asked to open their books to a page selected by the teacher (preferably one without sub-headings) and simply read the first sentence of three or four paragraphs. Then, they close their books. After the sentences have been written or paraphrased on the chalkboard (or have been previously prepared for the overhead projector) a pattern appears in these sentences. The class is asked what this page is all about. You may be surprised how well they can determine the topic being discussed and even give a tentative title for the passage. Most often, the leading sentences become headings for an outline of the passage and this understanding has accrued *before* the selection has been fully read. The reaction of students to this demonstration is evidence that here is a stimulus to intensive effort in the improvement of skills, for they have learned quickly and dramatically that they have the abilities that are useful, and that practice will sharpen them to a keen edge.

Students are expected to reason. This reasoning may involve the ability to make inferences from the spoken word or written materials. Allied with the inferential ability are the skills of drawing conclusions, forming hypotheses, and making generalisations and judgments. All of these are skills of the social studies, and they are important components of instruments used to measure reading ability.

Our teachers have developed a group of questions that they have come to term "collateral questions." Their purpose is to develop in youngsters the ability to infer, predict, and characterize people and events. For example:

> What would be a good title for this selection?
>
> From what you have read, would you guess that ....?
>
> As a result of this action, would you say that...?
>
> Reading between the lines, what do you think of the statement
>
> that...?
>
> What will probably happen when ... ?
>
> What do you think the result would have been if... ?

What word would you use to describe .. . ?
How would you characterize this person or event?

Of course, not all of these questions are posed in a single class session, nor are all of them adaptable for every lesson. But the possession by teachers of a fund of questions with specific purposes leads to the kind of thinking on the part of students that assists in the development of "thinking" skills. All of these are inherent in social studies instruction, and they would be used more often if there was an awareness of their purpose and their contribution toward the success we seek with our slow learners— and our rapid learners as well.

Unfortunately for our slower readers, new patterns in the social studies do not seem to take him into account. Emphasis on research materials has always required specific skills in the social studies. Now, there is an increasing emphasis on the ability to derive information from original documents. Curriculum planners have not faced squarely the problem of the slower reader in the "new emphasis." Quite honestly, new curricula will have little effect on any student who does not possess reading competence. There is little use in changing our areas of emphasis in the social studies without concerning ourselves with the most vital of means by which objectives are to be accomplished. It is certainly not in our interest to omit one-third of our students from the benefits of a new focus. There is an increasing need for the concern of *all* social studies teachers with the reading competence of *all* our students.

Herein lies a possible flaw in planning—unless adaptations are made individually by teachers everywhere. One can foresee the barriers placed before some of the youngsters when asked to read the Magna Carta, the Emancipation Proclamation, or a Supreme Court decision.

For what good is familiarity with a document if it cannot be read with comprehension? Yet, the opportunities for reading growth are more readily available to us in the new curricula than even before. The opportunities cannot be lost. They will not be if social studies instructional practices are a reflection of the inherent importance of reading skills and their application within the framework of the social studies. There is no doubt that, if reading improvement is going to take place, social studies teachers are going to be the primary source of the improvement.

This is not an attempt to be either comprehensive or definitive on the subject of reading-social studies skills. I have tried to convey my deep concern at the assumption by some that what we should be doing in this field is not our proper function. *All* our students need instruction in fund mental skills. Of particular concern is the success of our slower readers whose abilities can be harnessed within a structure that enables them to grow and succeed or who can be left to flounder and fail because they do not possess the necessary building tools. We are concerned with the need to "reach" the slow reader. Make no mistake such pupils can succeed, and the development of basic skills in both social studies and reading is a primary step in the process.

TEACHING WRITING THROUGH HISTORY

English is not a subject, like physics or geography or Latin. It is a universal skill, and every teacher of academic subjects should be in some degree a teacher of English.

One of the English teacher's strongest allies is the history teacher. There are all sorts of ways in which the history teacher can and should give training in writing. He may assign research papers, book reports, precis of documents, and formal arguments in matters of controversy. And his every test should require written answers.

Yet in hundreds of high schools the classes in history, civics. problems of democracy, and so forth, do very little writing, and in some none at all. A recent bulletin for teachers from a state board of education lists thirty-one separate "activities" which "the modern teacher of social studies" should promote in her "classroom laboratory." There are "planning activities," "reading activities," and "storing activities." There are "reporting and reciting" and "carrying out research," but no specific mention of writing.

Part of this lack of interest stems from the change from history to social studies. A generation ago the study of history in many schools was a meaningless round of learning dead facts and regurgitating them on paper. In justifiable rebellion against this profitless business came the idea that the study of man in society should concentrate on real problems, such as public housing or agencies for world peace, instead of the Kansas-Nebraska Act or the Tariff of 1816. Students should be trained in social skills, such as making oral reports and carrying on discussions.

Now, writing is not an obvious social skill. It is, in fact, a lonely business, and a person engaged in writing of necessity withdraws from the group. Indifference, even apathy toward writing is increasing. I have seen it argued in an educational journal that, while the ability to write may be a graceful accomplishment, in an audio-visual age it is no more necessary than playing the violin.

Another influence toward the abandonment of pen and paper is the so-called objective test, in which the candidate simply checks off the answers. There can be no question that objective tests have been refined until they are increasingly successful in their primary task of measuring achievement and predicting future success. The difficulty is that they have entered the classroom. Schools can purchase objective tests designed for any standard course or text. This relieves teachers of the burden of concocting their own questions and reduces correction to the purely mechanical process of checking off the right answers.

The results of the abandonment of writing have been appalling. In 1955 a College Board committee tried out simple essay questions on several hundred freshmen recently admitted to top-ranking colleges. At least 80 percent of the candidates failed, and about 40 per cent failed abysmally. They did not know how to analyze a problem, or how to relate what they knew to it, or how to hitch one limping sentence to another in ordered sequence.

Objective tests have little place in a properly run history course for academically competent students. They imply that knowing history is simply a matter of guessing the right answer, and they suggest that there are simple right and wrong answers to complex problems. Above all, they encourage teachers to evade their obligation to share with English teachers the duty of teaching effective writing.

With the increasing awareness that American education has slighted the gifted, there has been a return to written tests. All the tests given, for instance, in the Advanced Placement Programme of the College Entrance Examination Board are primarily written. So far, however, this programme affects only the ablest students in the strongest schools. Even in this privileged area there has been too little serious thought about what written tests should do. Here is a question asked in a famous Eastern preparatory school:

> Describe the four reasons for the Seven Years' War.

The first "the" gives this question away. The boy answering it has been taught that there are four official causes of the Seven Years' War and now is asked simply to hand them back. A question in history or social studies should be so designed that it encourages the candidate to write something approaching an essay. Furthermore, the answer should be judged for its quality as an essay, as well as for historical content.

Generalisations are fruitless unless supported. So essay questions should ask for facts, hard facts, but insist that they be related to the question. Students are tempted to parade what they remember, regardless of relevance. They should lose credit if they have not *aimed* the facts at the problem under discussion.

Some teachers, although agreeing that the essay question has its uses, fear that without testing on specific details students will not learn facts. Yet testing nothing but facts encourages the notion that they are important in isolation. A teacher can get across the idea that facts are vital only insofar as they have significance by the use of short written questions such as the following:

Explain the interrelationships between FOUR of the following pairs:

1. Lenin: Mensheviks
2. Poland: Danzig
3. Five Year Plan: Kulaks
4. Beer Hall Putsch: :March on Rome
5. Munich Conference: Self-determination

These keep emphasis on the generalisations which tie facts together, rather than on rote knowledge. Each is designed to produce a little essay, in which skill in written expression, judgment, and ingenuity count.

Effective essay questions do not just happen. They have to be devised with many factors in mind: what the students have studied in class and outside, how far advanced they are, how much time is allowed, just how much progress toward a new juxtaposition of material can be fairly demanded, whether the directions are clear and understandable.

Phrasing is immensely important. A certain element of challenge can release the floodgates and make a student write better than he thought he could. Consider these two questions:

> Explain the effects of the Emancipation Proclamation. Describe what you consider to be three principal causes of the War of 1812.

There is nothing especially wrong with these, but you can nudge the pupil toward setting up an argument rather than just retelling what he knows by presenting paradoxes:

> "The Emancipation Proclamation did not free a single slave." Is this true?
>
> Explain why the War for Seamen's Rights was opposed in maritime Massachusetts and supported in inland Kentucky.

It is easy to go off the track. Here is a former College Board question which turned out badly:

> How did Hamilton and Jefferson disagree on economic and political questions? Show why two political parties developed out of the conflict.

The trouble with this was that most candidates wrote not one essay but two, failing to tie together the two parts of the question. It would have been an improvement to have hitched them together in the question:

> "Out of the disagreement between Hamilton and Jefferson on economic and political questions developed two political parties." Explain this quotation.

It is important to remember that the way students are tested often de-termines how they will study. There is almost universal testimony from teachers that pupils will study less hard for an objective than an essay test if only because in the former there is always the hope of guessing the answer. But assume two equally conscientious students putting in equal time on the same material, one studying for an essay test and the other for an objective test. You will find that they are likely to tackle their reviewing quite differently. The objective test, with its many items a hundred responses an hour is standard tends to put emphasis on particular facts or concepts, so the student prepares as he might for a quiz-kid programme. The essay examination emphasizes the larger picture, and to do well the student must grasp the main ideas and relate details to them.

It is often a useful practice to give out essay questions in advance. If these are chosen with care, the students will usually study with more purpose than if left to their own devices. One could fairly well take care of the period of the 1920s in American history by telling a class that it will be asked to assess one or the other of the following quotations:

> "The business of America is business."
>
> Calvin Coolidge

> "America has evaded her responsibilities as a world power, and has retreated into a sullen and selfish isolationism."
>
> Woodrow Wilson

Essay questions usually involve exposition, but they

can also be used to stimulate the imagination. Each of the following questions has produced answers which revealed that some students could project themselves into the past and think in terms of a society alien in space, time, or culture:

> Assume yourself to be an Athenian peasant at the time of Solon and explain what the introduction of money had meant to you and your family.
>
> Assume yourself to be an Athenian gentleman of the fourth century B.C. miraculously transported by a time machine to America and endowed with the ability to speak English. Explain in a connected narrative your reactions to any THREE of the following: a dinner party, a professional wrestling match, a play. Congress.
>
> Assume yourself to be the Spanish ambassador to the court of Queen Elizabeth. Write a letter home, giving your impressions of the Queen and of her foreign policy.

The above questions were given out in advance so that the students could think out possible answers, but all the writing was done in a single class period, with no more notes than could be put on a single three by five inch card. Put under pressure, students write better than if they had time to polish.

This "you were there" type of question is especially valuable when it can be tied in with contemporary source material. Having already studied a period in texts, a class can get the feeling of the times by browsing through magazines of the period. The following question was designed to create awareness of that grim era when the democracies seemed helpless against the rise of totalitarianism:

> Assume yourself to be someone living during the period between the Munich crisis in September, 1938, and the fall of Poland in September, 1939, and give your opinion about the future of democracy.

This produced, among other characterisations, a Nazi waiter talking to an American newspaperman in a Munich beer garden: a Polish exile in a Paris bistro; and an ex-Communist, a young man who had joined the Communist Party during the Farmers' Holiday in 1933, while at the University of Iowa, and who was now, in September, 1939, writing to a former Comrade to explain why he had just resigned from the Party and was on his way to join the Canadian R.A.F.

The illustrations of essay questions given here have nearly all come from one school with a strong academic tradition and a selected student body. It may be argued therefore, that the training in writing and analysis suggested is beyond the reach of the general run of students. But surely we are increasingly aware that those able to profit by rigorous academic training need special attention just as much as slow and "exceptional" children. There are many high school teachers, too, who believe that the essay test can be used with great benefit for all students within the normal range of ability. In a number of high schools, essay tests are graded by the English department as well as the social studies department.

Practical objection to the use of essay tests may come from those who point out that essay testing will impose further duties on already burdened teachers. It cannot be done, at least not well, by a teacher with a pupil load of

180 to 200. meeting twenty-five classes each week and patrolling study periods, a home room, and the school cafeteria between times. The answer is to lighten the burden, even if it costs money. In *The American High School Today,* James B. Conant recommends that the pupil load of English teachers be limited to 100 pupils in order to allow for the correcting of weekly themes. If the social studies teacher should also require constant writing, his teaching load should also be limited.

The essay test is a major means, and a far too neglected one, of teaching a pupil "to learn to argue a case and weigh evidence, to seize the point at issue, to arrange his thoughts and marshal facts to support a theory, to discover when a statement is proved and when it is not, to reason logically and express himself clearly—in fact, to play the great game of the intellect."

ESSAY QUESTIONS

We live in an age when everything conspires to reduce that faculty of attention which is gained by close reading and accurate writing. Since people who can neither read nor write accurately all too often are people who cannot think accurately, no teacher of any academic subject can afford to neglect the first two R's. In history and social studies classes students need unremitting training in how to extract and retain knowledge from the printed page, and in how to read for connotation as well as sense. Equal attention should be paid to a variety of writing exercises: brief sum-maries or analyses of outside reading, research papers, class reports. This paper will consider a too frequently neglected aspect of this training—the essay test.

The author has yet to meet an independent school history teacher who did not impose written tests, and who did not at least pay lip service to their importance. But the picture is not entirely rosy. In a few schools teachers. seem still to be preparing for the College Board Examinations of the early '30's, in which candidates were asked to regurgitate chunks of undigested, fact in a series of twenty-minute "essays," starting with a pre-canned biography of Henry Clay, or Alcibiades, or Gladstone as the case might be. This preparation for an outmoded, highly mnemonic type of history is quaintly called "keeping up standards," and is applauded by self-dubbed "patriotic" societies, who fondly imagine that if students go through the learning processes of a generation ago they will also acquire the political and economic philosophy of Calvin Coolidge.

Even where historical training is on a much higher plane, it is apparent that often there has not been careful attention to essay testing. Consider these two questions, both given in good schools to students taking advanced placement courses in American History:

> Trace American nationalism from 1815 to 1877. Bring in social, economic, and cultural as well as political factors. (This was one of eight questions in two hours.)
>
> Explain why slavery was the principal cause of the Civil War.

On the face of it the first question is an impossible assignment, particularly in the time allowed, and can only elicit from the student a hurried mish-mash of vague, unsupported generalisation. The second question at least focuses on a point and demands an argument, but it suggests that there is an official interpretation of history, which the student had better learn as unthinkingly as he learns the dates of the Presidents. No, these won't do. If you call a lest an "essay test," you must see that the student is encouraged to write an essay, which according to the dictionary is a "literary composition analytical or interpretive in nature."

To illustrate, let us examine a run-of-the-mill question in American hisiory. Note the directions as well as the question itself:

Time: 50 minutes.

Directions: Write good English. You will be graded on:

1. organisation.
2. clarity and validity of general statements.
3. wealth of factual material related to the question.

Trace the connection between the slavery issue and political parties in the period 1840 to 1860.

What does the instruction, "Write good English" mean here? It means at least certain elementary virtues: well-constructed sentences, correct spelling and punctuation, avoidance of slang and abbreviations, attention to accurate expression. Unless these are insisted on all through the school, students will get the notion that they are simply idiosyncrasies of English teachers.

What does it mean that the candidate will be graded on "organisation"? Surely it strongly suggests an introductory paragraph of some sort. In this particular question one approach might be to contrast the situation in 1840 when both major issues were avoiding the explosive slavery issue like the plague, and the Whigs won by nominating a war hero who was alleged to live in a log cabin and drink hard cider, to the situation in 1860 when both major parties had broken apart over the issue, and when Lincoln's election was the occasion for secession.

How explain the change? A more obvious approach might be to start with the election of 1844, when slavery first began to obtrude in politics, and save I860 for the final paragraph. The important thing is that there should be a formal introduction which leads the reader into the question. Then the body of the essay should be arranged in some sort of logical sequence so that there is a *flow* of meaning. Each major point deserves a paragraph. To get the point across I tell students that if they don't know how to paragraph, at least indent every sixth to eighth line, and this may deceive the reader.

4. "The bourgeoisie are their -:- Monopoly own gravediggers."
5. "Religion is the opiate of -:- Christian Socialism the people,"

I have written elsewhere about this type of short question that it puts "emphasis on the generalisations which tie facts together, rather than on rote knowledge. Each (juxtaposition) is intended to produce a little essay, in which skill in written expression, judgment, and ingenuity count."

Essay questions take time to prepare, because so many factors must be considered what the members of a class may be expected to know, what they may he expected to infer from their knowledge, the time allowance, clarity of the directions, and exact expression in the question itself. More often than not, one is unsatisfied, but occasionally a question somehow emerges which stimulates the well-prepared and thoughtful to do. their best and at the same time penalizes the lazy and the glib. Such a question, more precious than fine gold, can be used year after year. One is this:

> How far do you agree with this statement: "Louis XVI could have led the French Revolution"?

This always seems to produce some superior answers. Perhaps this is because to do well the student must begin by defining two terms, "Louis XVI" and "French Revolution." Do you mean by "Louis *XVI*" the man himself timid, well-meaning, surrounded by contrary influences, the prisoner of Versailles, or do you mean someone else who might have held the position, a monarch with vision such as Queen Elizabeth or Henry IV? And what do you mean by "French Revolution"—simply the abolition of certain privileges, or the creation of a new order of society?

Incidentally, an excellent source of essay questions is the Advanced Placement Tests in American and European History, which may be obtained from the College Entrance Examination Board. While these are designed for superior students in college level courses, they suggest ideas which may be adapted for students of less maturity. The history examiners in the Advanced Placement Programme have succeeded brilliantly in devising tests which excite students to put their best foot forward, to write with verve and style.

While essay questions generally involve exposition or argument, they can also be used to excite the imagination. This can sometimes be accomplished by the "you were there" type of question. Among the first and best of these in my little treasure trove was one used for several years in an eighth grade class in ancient history:

> Assume yourself an Athenian peasant living at the time of Solon. Explain in your own words the effects of the introduction of money, and then of the Solonian reforms, on your life.

This type of question has special virtues when students can read contemporary documents in preparing for it. For instance, those given the question, "Assume yourself to be someone living in 1932, and explain how you would vote," were advised to browse through magazines of the period in order to get some feeling of a time almost as alien to them as the American Revolution. It also seems important that such a question be written in class, within a fixed amount of time. Limited to a single class period, knowing that they must finish somehow, they tend to lose their inhibitions. Sometimes they manage brilliantly. Note how quickly the status of the narrator and the historical sotting are sketched in the opening paragraphs of three answers to this question on the 1932 election:

> "Here I am slapping flies on the Capitol steps and sweating with a coupla thousand other guys in the same boat. We came here, us vets, 'cause we didn't know how else to get action. An" we ain't feeling too good about anything right now in the middle of July 19 and 32, and we ain't gonna feel any better if old man Hoover tries to kick us outta town the way they say he's gonna do...."

> "So you ask me how I'm going to vote this year? Well, I'll tell you, but first you ought to know about me, so I can explain my choice better. 1 used to work in a factory in Detroit up to a year ago. The plant used to produce auto parts, but it closed down. The big auto plants closed down too. Now I barely got a job. I got a wife and two kids to support, too Now I'm working for that banker's wife, Mrs. Couzens, as a gardener. It's a lousy job, but it pays $15 a week

> 18 Beekman Place.
> New York City,
> October 7, 1932

> Dear Nicky,
>
> Don't they teach you history at Groton any more? You asked some very foolish questions in your last letter. Of *course* your mother and I shall vote for Mr. Hoover this November. Mr. Hoover represents the Republican party, the party to which your family has always belonged and which acts in your family's interest. With God's help I think Mr. Hoover is perfectly competent to deliver the nation from its present difficulties.
>
> Franklin Roosevelt *used* to be a gentleman. I graduated when he was in the Fourth Form, and I remember him as a rather handsome boy, quite a good sailor.. . .

In these "you were there" questions, there often emerges some student of previously unsuspected talents who catches tire. Conversely that class of student often classed as "good"—the academic spigot who dutifully opens the cock and pours back what is poured in often does poorly.

In writing this article I have had the sobering experience of going over scores of old tests and being shocked at the shortcomings of many of them. Sometimes too much was packed in, so that the question resembled that mock debate subject once propounded in the Cambridge Union:

> *Resolved:* That this house, while approving the attitude of the First Lord of the Admiralty toward greyhound racing, supports a policy of unilateral disarmament, and believes that the salvation of the drama lies with the Liberal Party.

Sometimes I was guilty of the very sin I decried early in this article, that of asking students to hand back an argument: "Why is it natural that there should be more sympathy in the United States today for Moslem Pakistan than for Hindu India?" Often the wording was fuzzy or misleading. But such errors may be inevitable, because the fabrication of essay questions is an act of creation, and one's creative powers are seldom at a peak.

A final caution. Since essay questions are designed to induce acts of creation on the part of the pupil, he will vary in the quality of his responses he will "hit" a question one week and flub it the next. This must be accepted as a fact of life. If your principal aim is uniformity, you will use objective tests. But if you think it vital to train the student to write and to think you will give nothing but carefully framed essay tests, and hope that the average of many grades will somehow be a just measure of his achievement.

TEACHING RESEARCH TECHNIQUES IN THE SOCIAL STUDIES

Teaching the techniques of research is one of the major problems facing the social studies teacher. We know that skill in the research art is essential to all of our students; we know that the basic techniques must be "taught" and that the student must work at them if he is to master their use.

But this knowledge still leaves us with the problem of actually teaching the skills and techniques and this can be a problem to tax a Job.

How to teach these skills?

One effective method is to begin on the first day of school with the assigned textbook. This serves several admirable purposes, not the least of which is to familiarize the student with the text. Properly chosen text book problems can be used to teach the basic research skills and to build in our students a habit of following correct procedures. Once these basic skills become habit we can "introduce our scholars to a world wider than the textbook."[13]

And this is a point at which all of our carefully taught research techniques can collapse like a star that has exhausted its hydrogen.

Obviously, we cannot continue to teach research techniques by posing textbook problems. Sooner or later disenchantment will set in; sooner or later the young minds will want a more challenging task. What then?

Here we must recognize that, in the order of events, toddling comes first, then walking, then running. So, also, when teaching research skills. Our textbook problems constitute the toddling stage: our goal is the running stage during which we can pose real research problems for our students with some hope that they can be successfully completed. Before then, how-ever, we must pass through the walking stage during which we expand the research horizons of our charges. The problem, then, is to move our students form the toddling stage the textbook problems—into the walking stage, and, ultimately, into the running stage.

One way to do this is by a series of research projects that begin with a simple non-textbook task and move by graduated steps through a fairly complicated job. Each step should develop technique a bit more; each step should also reinforce the habits ingrained in earlier steps.

Such a series can begin with a dittoed copy of The Gettysburg Address and the question: What kind of man wrote this speech? The neophyte researcher will scan the Address and answer the question by listing all of the traits usually ascribed to Lincoln. When we ask "Precisely what words in the speech show that the author was kindly, humane, etc., The student will have learned a valuable lesson. This discussion should lead to the question of whether the written words is to be accepted as literally true and, if not, how do we determine if the written word simply says what the author thinks his audience wants to heart?

This lesson should not be a one-shot affair. It deals with the single most important technique of research and it must be learned well. A number of speeches should be dealt with in the same manner and a number of written works also.

From such assignments we can move our students, when individually appropriate, into the more complicated but still directed work:

> Using *The Dictionary of American Biography and T.A. Bailey, I Diplomatic History of the American People,* find out: (1) who was John Hay, and (2) what part did he play in our acquisition of the Panama Canal?

Using just the two sources we have listed, plus his textbook, the student will discover that Hay was a longtime Secretary of State around 1900 and that he negotiated the treaties that made possible the Canal; the student will also discover the provisions of the treaties. In short, he will have taken a step toward real research.

After a few such sessions, we can set out students—again when individually appropriate-a more difficult task involving the reading of two or more books and the organisation of the knowledge thus gained into a coherent pattern. For example:

> Read E.S. Osgood, *The Day of the Cattleman,* and W.P. Webb, *The Great Plains.* When you finish, write a brief paper explaining why the farmers were able to drive the ranchers out of most of the plains area.

When the student applies the techniques we have been teaching him all year to the two books assigned, he can write such a paper. Since the topic is not discussed as such in either book, he will be forced to think, select his material, to organise it in a sensible pattern, and, for him at least, discover a new truth. In sum, he will have done a piece of research that has value and is uniquely his.[14]

REFERENCES

1. Ken Giffin and John Waite Bowers. "An Experimental Study of the Use of Lectures to Large Groups of Students in Teaching the Fundamentals of Speech," *The Journal of Educational Research,* pp. 383-386. May 1962.
2. U.S. Office of Education. *Cooperative Research Projects. Bulletin 1961.*
3. "New Horizons in Staff Utilisation," *The Bulletin of the National Association of Secondary-School Principals,* vols. 42-47.
4. David R. Krathwohl, ed., "Curriculum Planning and Development," *Review oj Educational Research.* vol. 30, no. 3 (Washington. D.C.: American Educational Research Association, 1960).
5. *Social Education* 28:277-92, May 1964; 29.15 20, January 1965.
6. Jack R. Fraenkel, "A Comparison of Achievement Between Students Taught by a Teaching Team and Students Taught in Traditional Classes on a Standardised Examination in United. States History" (Master's thesis, San Francisco State College. 1965): William Nesbitt, "An Experimental Study of the Relative Effectiveness on Learning in Selected High School Subjects of the Conventional Methods and A Composite of Procedures Involving Modern Educational Media in Addition to Classes of Varying Sizes. Team Teaching, and Teacher Aides" Ph:D. diss. University of Texas, 1960): and Scott Thomson. "An Analysis of

Achievement Outcomes: Team Teaching and Traditional Classes." (Ed.D. diss. Stanford University. 1963).

7. Lloyd S. Michael, "Team Teaching," The Bulletin of the National Asociation of Secondary-School Principals, 47:36 63, May 1963.
8. "Judson T Shaplin. "Description and Definition of Team Teaching. " Shaplin and Olds. eds., *Team Teaching,* p. 6.
9. Thomas C. Cochran. *The Inner Revolution.* The Academy Library (New York: Harper and Row, 1964), p. 185.
10. *Ibid.*
11. J.R. O'Connor, "Social Studies Achievement. 1932 1962." *High Points.* 46: 46 50: March 1964. Scores achieved by 207 seventh- and eighth-grade children on the Metropolitan Advanced Reading Test, Form A. administered in January 1964, were compared with scores attained by the same children on the Metropolitan Advanced Reading Test. Form A. 1932. Whereas 142 pupils were "below grade" in reading based on the 1962 norms. 84 were below grade on the 1932 test. No children in either grade were more than one year below grade based on the 1932 standard.
12. Eunice Johns and Dorothy McClure Fraser. "Social Studies Skills: A Guide to Analysis and Grade Placement," in Helen McCracken Carpenter, ed., *Skill Development in Social Studies,* National Council for the Social Studies. 33rd Yearbook (Washington. D. C. 1963), pp. 310 Off.
13. James McGoldrick, "Research Starting With The Textbook," *Clearing House.* September 1961. The procedure outlined in the above paragraph is treated in some detail in the article in *clearing House.*
14. In "Comparative Reading Helps." *English Journal,* January 1961, I have described in detail a technique somewhat similar to the one used in this paragraph and the one proceeding; one of the major differences between the English Journal article and the assignment listed here is that the one in the English Journal uses novels

2

Placement of Subject Matter

American history is the only subject among the social studies that is studied by all American students in both elementary and secondary school. Further, the study of American history at both levels is required by the force of law. In many states such a requirement exists also for American government, and some states require some others of the social studies of all students in elementary or secondary school. But in general, while elementary schools or teachers may decide for themselves whether or not to include in their curriculum concepts drawn from anthropology, sociology, economics, or psychology, they must teach American history. The high school student may study civics, geography, economics, sociology, psychology, or the history of parts of the world outside the United States for a variety of reasons: the local school board may require the subject; the student may be interested in it; his parents may insist on it; the counselor may urge it; or it may be the only subject that the student thinks he can pass. One or more of these conditions may be true in the case of American history, but regardless of them or others, the force of law compels the study of American history.

The fact that the study of American history is required everywhere by state action in both elementary and secondary school should give some pause to the teacher, the supervisor, and other curriculum makers. The reasoning that brought the lawmakers to this determination must be a conditioning factor in the selection, organisation, presentation, and placement of American history in the curriculum. And that reasoning is clear. The lawmakers believed that knowledge of the history of this country is necessary to effective citizenship. That belief was set forth by Jefferson and others of the Founding Fathers. No other argument for the study of American history has been stated so frequently, so consistently, and so forcefully throughout the national period. Many other benefits should come to both the individual and society from the study of American history. Several of them will be referred to in this paper. They are not in conflict with the development of effective citizens, rather they support that development. However, common sense and wisdom, as well as a sense of duty, demand that we recognise that in the teaching of American history we are concerned not only with the pronouncements of historians and educationists, but also with a mandate from the American people as embodied in their governments.

PLACEMENT IN CYCLES

Let us discuss the placement of American history in the curriculum before we consider the other three matters assigned to this paper. One reason for so doing is the consideration just emphasised. Another is that the selection and presentation of subject matter (and perhaps its organisation also) must be viewed in the light of the maturity and previous knowledge of the learner. It is a commonplace that American high school graduates have studied the history of their country at three levels of instruction: the middle grades, the upper grades or junior high school, and the senior high school. Most often it is required in the fifth, eighth, and eleventh grades. The college student is likely to have a fourth course. As Professor Joseph Strayer has said, if school courses are taught properly, there should be no need for the college survey course. In fact, Princeton University did away with its general course in American history several years ago. But the three-cycle approach in the schools has much to recommend it, and probably no fundamental change should or can be brought about in the general practice of placement there. The importance and complexity of the subject are not to be gainsaid. Three years are not too long a time to devote to it, yet a three-year course at one level can hardly be conceived. The curriculum at each level has other essential concerns, and the study of American history can neither be delayed until adolescence nor completed before its onset.

The fifth-grader has gained enough knowledge and experience, both in and out of school, to profit from and appreciate the study of many aspects of his nation's history. Without such study he can hardly develop the sense of belonging that is necessary to his own stability and that of society. The eighth-grader has grown and learned enough to justify both a reconsideration of some of his earlier study of national history in the light of that growth and learning and an extension of his study into more complex matters. The eleventh-grader, nearly ready for college or the assumption of an independent role in society, can scarcely afford to forego earnest efforts to comprehend his relation to his developing land and people and their mutual dependence on one another and on other nations.

Agreements to expand or shift one of the cycles of American history into an adjoining grade may be successful, and substantial changes in emphasis may be brought about in one or more of the cycles, but the elimination of any of them is not to be feared or hoped for except for scattered or temporary experiments." The cycles are fixed by tradition and have popular support. It is difficult to get complete data about middle-grades offerings, yet American history is clearly there. It is listed as one of the most frequent fifth-grade offerings in each of six recent textbooks on the teaching of social studies in elementary school. And with few exceptions the arguments about it are not concerned with its elimination, but with emphases and the manner of its organisation. Some people have suggested the elimination of the junior high school course. But its place seems secure. Howard R. Anderson showed that in 1946-47 practically every American student studied United States history for at least two semesters in the seventh and eighth grades.[1] Grace S. Wright's report of last June for 1960-61 showed more students enrolled in United States history in the seventh grade, more than half a million more than in geography, and more ' than a million more than in either state history or something called simply "social studies." In 1960, Richard E. Gross and William V. Badger asserted in the *Encyclopedia of Educational Research* that, "there is greater unanimity throughout the United States on the desirability of this eighth grade offering than is true of any other social studies course or emphasis at any other grade level."[3] If there is an exception to their statement, it must be the senior high school course in American history. Here, again, Howard Anderson's report showed that practically ail high school students took a year of American history in 1946-47, and Grace Wright's report showed more high school students enrolled in American history in 1960-61 than the total number of eleventh-graders. Curriculum situations as firmly fixed as the three cycles of American history could not be eliminated easily even if large segments of the educational leadership did not support them. But many leaders do support them. And, beyond these arguments, one of the surest ways to bring the legislatures into the curriculum-making process could be to get a movement under way to reduce the emphasis on American history.

ORGANISATION OF CYCLES

The continuation of the *three-cycle approach* to American history requires that the cycles be planned so that there is no needless duplication among them. This is not to say that there will be no planned reuse of knowledge and skill gained previously. The cyclical approach, should demand the use of earlier learning to support new learning, reconsideration at *a more advanced level* of facts and ideas that are already somewhat familiar, and the development of new understanding and skill. The Committee on American History in Schools and Colleges, in 1944, made useful suggestions for differentiation among the cycles.[4] Despite the fact that its report is more than 20 years old, no more recent body of comparable stature has made significant additions to its proposals. The Committee recommended that differentiation be achieved through changing emphasis in central theme and in chronology, although all three cycles would give some attention to the whole period of American history. Thus in the middle-grades cycle the emphasis would be on how the people lived, and two-thirds of the time would be allotted to the period before the establishment of the government under Washington. The junior high school cycle would emphasise the growth of a free nation, with two-thirds of the time allotted to the century from 1776 to 1876. The senior high school cycle would emphasise a democratic nation in a world setting, with at least half the time devoted to the period since 1865.

American History in Schools and Colleges still makes much sense, and many teachers would improve their courses by adopting its proposals. The middle grades might well follow its recommendations. But too much has happened since 1944 for its proposal for chronological division between the two upper cycles to remain valid. At the least, the date for division in emphasis should be much later than 1865. More radical would be an outright division of the two cycles into courses dealing with distinct chronological periods. Several states are reported to be making plans for the junior high school course to stop with the Reconstruction and for the senior high school course to begin there, with only a brief review. One "illustrative desirable pattern" suggested in the "Social Studies in the Comprehensive Secondary School," a 1961 position paper of the National Association of Secondary-School Principals, would have the junior high school course stop in 1876 and the senior high school course begin there. Another such pattern in the same document would have the same kind of break between the two courses come in 1870. There is, in fact, a greater difference in content among the cycles than is often assumed. The authors of textbooks were shifting their emphasis throughout this century. By 1950, more than three-quarters of the typical text for the middle-grades cycle was devoted to social and economic matters, as was the major part of the typical text for the junior high school cycle. Only in the senior high school was more than half of the typical test given over to matters of politics and foreign affairs. Nevertheless, much needs to be done in many classrooms both to eliminate much unnecessary duplication between the upper two cycles and to give adequate treatment to the phenomenal and cataclysmic developments of the twentieth century. October finds too many senior high school classes still discussing the European backgrounds of the period of exploration. And far too many have not yet completed their study of the Civil War in March. Perhaps such matters can be remedied only when the senior high school course of study and textbook begin, as has been suggested, with the post-Civil War unit. Yet, no period or topic in American history can be taught without reference to others. Professor Strayer puts the case for the cyclical approach well. He says that American history can be divided into four periods that differ significantly in political, social, and economic development: colonial, early national, industrialisation, and emergence of a world power.

> A good deal can be done with the first two periods in elementary school and junior high school; the last two can be treated fully only in senior high school. This is not to say that nothing should be done with the twentieth century in the lower grades, or that a certain amount of repetition is undesirable. In fact, repeated coverage of a period with the introduction of new ideas and new materials is the only was in which a historical period can ever be fully understood. Nevertheless, the earlier periods should be emphasised in the lower grades and the later periods in senior high school.[5]

Aside from the unnecessary duplication that too often exists among the cycles of American history, such duplication between other subjects and American history should be avoided. This kind of duplication is often present, and it receives even less attention than that among the cycles. It takes place between state history and the junior high school cycle, which commonly are taught in successive years. In particular, the study of the Civil War in one year often can hardly be distinguished from that in the other. In some schools the Constitution is taught in almost identical fashion in the junior high school cycle of American history, civics, senior high school American history, and for the fourth time in twelfth-grade government or problems. The treatment of two World Wars and the complex world relations of the past half century is often very much the same in world history and senior high school American history. In these cases, as in the cycles of American history, it is desirable and necessary to use previous knowledge as a foundation for further learning, but it is wasteful to have outright, unplanned duplication. Such duplication can be avoided only when all social studies teachers are reasonably familiar with the entire twelve-grade program. And it must be said that this happy condition is a rare phenomenon in American schools. Even under it, the problems caused by overlapping of content between required and elective courses are difficult to solve, for the adjustment must be made largely in the elective courses, sometimes to their detriment. But where the overlapping is among required courses, careful planning can bring about true application of the sound theory behind the cyclical approach.

ORGANISATION WITHIN CYCLES

To open a discussion of the organisation of content within the cycles reminds one of a barrel of fishhooks. There are those who support a chronological and those who prefer a topical organisation. Some advocate approaching the matter through problems and some through social processes. Some believe that the task can be performed most effectively through teaching American history as a separate subject; some believe that the social studies should be formed into a single subject; some advocate combining the social studies with other subjects so as to bring about a core curriculum or a humanities course. Some advocate one of these approaches at one grade level and a different approach at another grade level. Some would use the same approach at all grade levels. The same arguments and counterarguments seem to be advanced by the most expert and the least expert, the most expert disagreeing among themselves on the same issues and in the same ways as do the others, but, presumably, for better reasons. On these matters, while there is strong feeling, there is little certain knowledge. In this situation, it hardly behooves the writer of this paper, or a supervisor, to dictate a specific form of organisation to a school or to a competent teacher. Yet some consideration of the arguments will be valuable to all curriculum makers.

Those who believe in a chronological organisation say that only such an approach can tell the story as it was taking place and can make it clear that an individual or group always is contending with many problems at the same time. It is countered that chronological history easily degenerates into a mere chronicle of names, dates, and events, many of which have no relevance to the present or the future. The proponents of a topical approach contend that it provides for study of the relevant and significant and that it allows the student to concentrate on a particular topic until he understands it well. The supporters of a social process approach use the same arguments, and add that organisation by social processes provides topics of importance to all people at all times and places. The advocates of a problems approach use all these arguments, and add a psychological one; namely, that learning takes place only when there is a problem to solve. Opponents of these approaches argue that their use brings about a loss in the advantages alleged for a chronological organisation, often leads to the omission of important matter, and introduces the bias of those who select the topics, processes, or problems to be studied. They say, further, that while there must be a problem in order for learning to take place, the problem may be simply the learning of important knowledge and skill, and that one of the tasks of the teacher is to create situations in which students solve that problem.

Those who support the organisation of the curriculum

into separate subjects say that these subjects have resulted from the best efforts of scholars and teachers to devise means for learning about society, that it is not efficient for students to study all of society at the same time early in their learning career, but that by successive study of various aspects of society from the point of view of various disciplines they will eventually be able to view it as a whole. The advocates of fused social studies or a core curriculum say that we live in a total society, not in a discipline, and that the curriculum should take account of that fact; that the boundaries between the subject are artificial: and that only through an interdisciplinary approach can the curriculum provide for meaningful study of the development and problems of society.

All of these arguments, and others that might have been given, have some validity. Yet, in our present state of knowledge about learning, none of them is conclusive. Sound planning or unsound planning, effective teaching or ineffective teaching, can be carried out under any of the proposals. The negative arguments will be useful to teachers and supervisors as warnings against weaknesses in any approach. Whatever organisational plan is adopted careful consideration of the others will be useful in evaluating it. If a chronological approach is used, checking the course of study against others organised by topics, processes, or problems will help in emphasising the relevant. If one of the latter three approaches is employed, checking against a chronological course of study will help guard against omitting matters of significance. And a word of caution is in order with regard to the meaning of "relevant" and "significant." It will not do to teach only those parts of American history that seem most relevant to the present. It is often true that nothing is older than yesterday's headline. Henry Johnson's test of enduring value is the fundamental test. What seemed relevant *then* to the people being studied may have as much relevance for the future as what seems relevant now to us.

Where American history is taught as a separate subject, it must be recognised that it may carry special burdens and obligations. To the extent that it is the only subject among the social studies to be required of all students, it must, as Strayer says, "carry most of the load of giving the students essential ideas about the nature of human society, and the skills and attitudes needed to deal with human problems." This is likely to be the case of the senior high school. In the junior high school and elementary school this load can be shared with whatever geography, world history, and state history are required. Fortunately, there are no rigid boundaries around any of the social studies. Historians, themselves, in their own scholarly endeavors, are finding it more and more necessary to be familiar with and to draw on the findings and procedures of other disciplines anthropology, economics, geography, political science, and sociology, as well as art, literature, music, and social psychology. Knowledge in these areas will be helpful to the curriculum maker and teacher of American history. The essays by scholars in the several disciplines continued in *The Social Studies and The Social Sciences,* in *High School Social Studies Perspectives,* and in *The Social Sciences: Foundations of the Social Studies* were designed to help those concerned with the curriculum and should be read by them.

Where the social studies are fused, or combined with other subjects, as is often the case in the middle grades and sometimes the case in junior high school, curriculum makers and teachers have a responsibility, not only to the laws and regulations of the state but also to the reasoning behind those laws and regulations, to see that American history is taught and its values gained. There is as little sense in correlating for the sake of correlation as there is in teaching history for the sake of history. Just as it is true that where American history is a separate subject it must be broad in scope, so where the subjects are combined, American history must have an important place, not only as incidental support for nonhistorical topics, but as history in the form of historical units and historical parts of units. The reason for organising instruction in American history is to facilitate the attainment, of our objective. The main objective is to help rear people who understand their society and their relation to it, and who have the knowledge, skill, and purpose necessary to make them effective members of that society as well as better persons.

SELECTION OF CONTENT

Consideration of the main objective provides guidance in the selection of content for school American history. The question to be answered is, What can these children or youth learn from the study of American history that will contribute most effectively toward the attainment of that objective?

The content must be such that the students concerned can learn it with a reasonable amount of effort. But this statement is helpful only in a negative way. There is so much content in American history that students could learn at any age that they have time to consider only a small portion of it. And, any tasks that we give them prevent them from undertaking others. Most middle-graders, and most high school students, can memorise a list of a hundred names, another of a hundred dates, and another of a hundred places. But probably teachers should not make such assignments. There are more important, more useful activities than memorising such lists. It is not that facts are unimportant; they are the principal materials required for the construction of useful generalisations. As William James said, no one sees further into a generalisation than his own knowledge of the details permits. But it is hard to make a significant generalisation out of the names of the capitals of the 50 states.

Good citizenship requires desirable action. Desirable action rests on sound attitudes. Sound attitudes must be based on intellectual generalisation and controlled emotion. These in turn must be achieved through facts and skill in getting and using facts. The study of American history should contribute to the development of all of these attributes. The content of school history should be chosen with a view to its contribution toward them.

Good citizens are loyal to their government. They seek, through the orderly processes of law, to perpetuate that which is good, and to change that which needs improvement. Through the study of their history they find examples of personal and social action, some of which they want to emulate and some of which bring shame. Even at the simplest level, knowledge of a common past is essential to lasting social organisation. This principle is followed by all social organisation. It is essential to a nation-state. To the question, why teach about Christopher Columbus, John Smith, William Bradford, George Washington, Thomas Jefferson, Abraham Lincoln, Robert E., Lee, George Washington Carver, Theodore Roosevelt, and Woodrow Wilson, one good answer is that is would be impossible to conceive of our country without them or a good American who does not respond warmly to them. The same could be said for the Mayflower Compact, the Maryland Act of Toleration, the Declaration of Independence, the Constitution, the Gettysburg Address, and the Four Freedoms. The case can easily be made for such examples as these, but they are not enough, and this case by itself is not complete.

The study of American history should provide a guide for social action. As a course of study is packed with specific facts, it becomes necessary that most of these facts are chosen because they support needed generalisations. And as the course becomes loaded with generalisations, it is necessary that they be supported by adequate details. Space does not allow for extended illustrations in this paper, but here is one.

There is general belief in this country that consideration of national origin, religion, and race has no place in the voting booth or the employment office. For this belief to be implemented, there must be action by citizens who respect officials and workers for what they are and do without regard to national origin, religion, or race. Such respect can be based on generalisation as well as on emotion. And the generalisation, to be well founded, must rest on specific facts.

Let us suppose that the junior high school teacher of American history is teaching a unit on the Westward Movement. Part of the unit is the story of the "Dark and Bloody Ground," the settlement of Kentucky and Tennessee before, during, and immediately after the American Revolution. It is an exciting story, and useful in many ways, only one of which concerns us here. Of course, the students will study persons and learn some names. By selection of materials, the teacher sees that his students learn more than the names and exploits of the people involved. The student will discover that Daniel Boone was a Welsh Quaker, that John Sevier was a French Huguenot, that James Robertson was an Ulster Scot, that Jost Heit was a German. Pietist, that Catholic Highland Scots and French, and men and women of English origin and varying faiths were involved. as well as Indians and Negroes. These details, and similar one from other episodes in other units, will go far toward helping children to establish a generalisation that moralising probably cannot establish: namely, that people of many differing national, religious, and racial origins worked together to build the nation. And it must be added, lest we grow too proud, there were good-for-nothings and blackguards of various origins who wrought damage as individuals and conspirators. These generalisations, it may be hoped, will contribute to right attitudes and desirable actions.

It may be charged that what has just been described is a perversion of history to a subject for undesirable indoctrination, that the teachers should 'let the facts stand for themselves." The answer to the charge is at least threefold. In the first place, no suppression or distortion of the facts was required to establish the generalisation. In the second place, the generalisations, attitudes, and action concerned have the support of the overwhelming majority of the American people and their curriculum markers, and the endorsement of every branch of our government. It would be a very different and unethical action for the teacher to seek to establish his own brand of politics or religion. In the third place stands a counter question: What facts are to stand by themselves? There is a myriad of facts about American history. A professional historian of the United States may, in the course of his training, take a survey course in American history and follow it with several specialised courses, one of which may be a course in the frontier in American history. These in turn may be followed by several year-long seminars, in one of which he devotes his full time to the settlement of the Shenandoah Valley. He emerges from the seminar knowing that he has dealt with only a small portion of the facts related to the settlement of the Valley and is thankful that the settlers there had no hostile Indians with whom to deal. After he has devoted a few years to the preparation of a specialised volume, he shudders at the thought of writing a school textbook that presumes to cover all of American history. He may undertake the task, but one of his major problems is to select the facts that will establish the big generalisations he considers vital. If any other curriculum makers, including teachers and supervisors, do not have the same problem, it is because they do not recognise it. There are too many facts about American history for those to be taught in one of several subjects taken by a student, during a single school year of 180 or 200 days, to stand by themselves. Either they will be selected in accordance with some principles, or they will be selected without regard to principle. In the latter situation, there is little reason for society to mandate the study of American history by all its young people.

The nature of the generalisations that this writer believes should make up the stuff of school history has been indicated in another place by a series, of questions. School history must treat of how people

> . . . met and solved, or failed to solve their many problems. How did they overcome, adjust to, or become overwhelmed by the physical characteristics of the regions in which they lived? How did they force nature to yield its riches, exploit these riches while yet conserving them, or lose the material basis of their society through failure to conserve? How, in modern times, has the dizzying pace of the acceleration of material progress become one of mankind's greatest problems and what sub-problems does that acceleration pose? What ways have men tried for organising their economic activity, and how well have they succeeded? What systems have been developed for governing people and with what sub-problems does that acceleration pose?

> What ways have men tried for organising their economic activity, and how well have they succeeded? What systems have been developed for governing people and with what success? Under what conditions has human liberty thriven or succumbed? How have men learned to work together peaceably to their mutual advantage? What causes have led them to conflict, and what means have they employed to eliminate conflict or its causes? What institutions have civilisations found necessary to their existence and strengthening? What forms have these institutions taken and what successes or failures have they had? What personal and societal values have people developed as guides to their activities? What means have people taken to bring up their young so as to preserve and enlarge their heritages?

Strayer suggests that at strategic points in a course in American history:

> . . .the student should be asked to consider the questions: What an American? How did these people view themselves? What did they believe were their greatest accomplishments and greatest failures? In what ways did they feel that they differed from other people?

And he suggests that the same sort of question be raised at the end of the course.

> What is an American? What do we think we stand for? What sort of a society and world do we want? How do we think we are going to get it? How has our past conditioned our present?

How can we make our present serve as a basis for the future we desire?

The answers to these questions have meaning for future social and personal action. The questions do not provide a basis for organising a course of study. But they will be of value in checking the adequacy of that course, and they should help in the selection of content for it.

3

A Model for Teaching

You've probably begun to read this material because you're either enrolled in an undergraduate general methods course or you're a teacher interested in updating your skills. Whichever position you're in, we want to put your mind at ease by describing an assumption we're making. As we write this material, we're assuming that while you've had experience with teaching—as we all have had as students, parents, aides, or tutors—you may not have done any formal teaching yourself. Based on this assumption, we're going to provide you with the background needed to launch you into further study of the teaching profession and to provide the basic tools needed to make intelligent decisions about planning teaching activities, performing or implementing those activities with children, and evaluating their success.

With this thought in mind, a basic theme of this text will focus on the process you go through and the kind of thinking you do as you study the material. We hope that when you have finished your study you will have conceptual or intellectual tools that will allow you to continue to grow as a professional throughout your career.

For those of you who have had formal experience with teaching, we hope this material will help make your work more systematic and will further assist you in making even better decisions about teaching.

Teaching Effectiveness

The education profession is at the most exciting and unique time in its history. Admittedly, it is under fire as a result of studies done by groups such as the National Commission on Excellence in Education (1983). However, the studies uniformly point out that teachers deserve higher salaries, better working conditions, and more prestige. Because of these studies and other factors, the public is finally becoming aware of the needs of the profession. Our view is that the future of education is brighter than ever before.

In addition to studies and public awareness, a substantial body of research literature is also exerting a prominent influence on educational decisions. This literature falls under a somewhat general category called *teacher effectiveness.* Simply stated, the research identifies what "good" or effective teachers do compared to what is done by those who are less effective. Historically, education has been very vulnerable to opinion, influenced by prominent thinkers, or at the worst, even whim. This is no longer the case. Because of this second theme we will cite throughout the text appropriate studies that document teaching effectiveness.

Now let's proceed to an introductory illustration of teachers in action.

THE TEACHING ACT

Because your background may be limited or may be quite informal, our first step in a systematic description of teaching begins with a brief look at the teaching act itself. To do this, let's look at three scenarios of teachers working in classrooms.

Examples

Scenario 1

Mrs. Shafer is a pleasant woman in her middle thirties who teaches at Plainview Elementary School. Plainview is an older school in a lower-middle-class neighborhood of Laqua, Florida. While the school is not new, the administration has kept the grounds and building very attractive. Everyone cooperates in keeping the small areas of grass from being trampled on and killed, and the paved and cemented areas are kept free from debris. There are no broken windows, and the water fountains and lavatories work well and smell fresh.

Mrs. Shafer's room has a high ceiling which makes it seem big, but she has grouped large boxes to make cubbyholes and privacy corners for her children. She asked for and received permission to paint designs and graphics (sayings or pictures such as rainbows) on her walls in addition to her use of several large bulletin boards for decoration.

Mrs. Shafer is presenting a unit in geography, and students have studied various geographic regions and their physical features. The children are now familiar with regions such as the American central plains, the Russian steppes, and the Argentine pampas; and the American Rocky Mountains, the Swiss Alps, and the South American Andes. They know how the regions are similar and how they differ. She now wants the children to understand the influence of geography on the people's life-styles and habits. She decides she will use pictures of people in different regions and will try to get students to compare the region with the appearance and activities of the people. She gathers her pictures and begins the lesson. She starts by showing a picture of some children playing in front of some grass huts.

"Look at the picture, everyone," Mrs. Shafer says smiling. "Tell me anything at all you see about the pictures."

"They're in Africa," Carol says immediately.

"Excellent, Carol, but how do you know that?"

"My dad is in the Navy, and we lived in Greece, and we took a trip to Africa, and we saw houses like those."

Jimmy's eyes open wide. '"You went to Africa? I've never been out of Laqua in my life."

Mike adds, "I've never been there, but I've read about it, and those children could live in India maybe 'cuz they don't wear many clothes in India either."

David is whispering and grinning at Billy as Mike is talking, and Mrs. Shafer gives him a stern look.

"What did we agree was one of our important rules, David?" Mrs. Shafer asks.

"We always respect others." David says quietly.

"And what is one way we do that?"

"We listen to what they have to say whether we agree or not, and then express our opinion when it's our turn."

"Very good, David," Mrs. Shafer says with a smile. "That's a good reminder for all of us. Now let's go on. What else do you see in the picture?"

The children continue describing what they see, and then Mrs. Shafer shows two Russian children playing with a sled in front of a mosque. Again she asks for a description of what the children see. She continues this process, showing pictures of Indian shepherds in Ecuador, and Bedouin tribesmen in Arabia. She asks the students to compare all of the pictures by showing similarities and differences. Finally she asks the children to summarize what they saw.

> "Well, people live in different places and their houses are different," Joan suggests.
>
> "Fine, Joan. Now, anything else?"
>
> "They dress different," Kim adds.
>
> "O.K."
>
> They're playing different games and stuff," Susan says.
>
> "Very good. What more can you say about what we've seen—people's houses, clothes, games they play, and so on?"
>
> "Well," Jimmy says somewhat hesitantly, "they're things about people."
>
> "Fine, and what things about people?"
>
> "Oh, how they live and everything."
>
> "Very good. So we're saving geography and climate affect people's lifestyles."

Mrs. Shafer goes into a discussion of Florida's climate, geography, and lifestyle and asks the children to compare that to how they would expect to live in northern Michigan or Minnesota.

After a number of comparisons are made, Mrs. Shafer announces, "Now, everyone, I have two short paragraphs that I want you to read. Then I want you to write four examples from the paragraph that show how geography and climate affect life-style."

The paragraphs she gives the children are as follows:

> Jose and Kirsten are two children about your age who live in faraway lands. Kirsten lives in

the mountains of Norway, which is quite far north. Jose lives on the flat plains of western Mexico where it is very hot and dry. Kirsten loves to ski and does so nearly every day in the winter. In the summer she and her brother put on light wool sweaters and go hiking in the mountains. They love to sit atop the peaks and look down over the valleys. In the evenings Kirsten's mother builds a fire, and everyone in the family reads quietly.

Jose loves to play just as Kirsten does. He swims every afternoon in a pond formed by a spring near his village. He becomes impatient because he has to wait until after the nap his mother takes every day at noon. The children go outside and play in the evening, enjoying the breeze that cools the village. They usually play until it is so dark they can't see.

Mrs. Shafer collects the students' papers and ends the class by saying she will introduce the idea of *culture* the following day and relate culture to geography and climate. She reviews the papers during her planning period and finds the following acceptable responses:

1. Kirsten skiing in the winter
2. Kirsten's family sitting and reading by the fire in the evening
3. Kirsten and her brother hiking in the mountains
4. Jose's mother napping every noon
5. Jose playing in the evening
6. Jose swimming in the afternoon

Scenario 2

Miss Adams works in a kindergarten classroom. She has her room arranged in sections. Today is Monday, so

Miss Adams arrives at school early to set up her room for the week. She changes her activities on a weekly basis and spends her Friday afternoons and Monday mornings getting them ready. This week she wants to put particular emphasis on manipulative skills and wants to be sure all of the children can perform tasks such as buttoning coats and tying shoes. In one corner she puts some flashlight bulbs in little holders, some dry cell batteries, and some wire. In another corner she places a large flannel board with different numbers of beans glued on it so children can match numerals such as 2 *or* 3 with the appropriate number of beans. She arranges similar activities in the other corners of the room.

As the children come in, Miss Adams asks them what activities they would like to choose and sends them each to a corner to begin. She then sits down on the floor with three boys to help them learn to tie the shoelaces on a large doll they've named Fred. Each day the children button Fred's shirt, tie his shoes, brush his teeth, and wash his hands after Miss Adams has taken him to the bathroom.

Jimmy is struggling to get Fred's shoe tied and appears slightly uninterested to Miss Adams. She feels his forehead, which appears to be warm, and immediately takes him by the hand down to the nurse's office. Jimmy is often ill, so Miss Adams is sensitive to his behavior when he appears listless.

As she returns, she sees Scott throw a beanbag at Lisa. Miss Adams admonishes him gently saying, "Scott, you're not supposed to throw the beanbag at Lisa; you're supposed to throw it so she can catch it."

"She threw it at me first."

"Did you Lisa?"

Smiling shyly, Lisa nods.

> "Throw it *to* each other and count to see if you can do it ten times each without missing."

Miss Adams continues working with groups of children until 11:30 when it is time for dismissal. She helps the children get safely on the bus and then goes back to her room.

Taking stock of her morning, she grins to herself as she recalls that David had improved significantly in tying Fred's shoes. She takes out a sheet that has the children's names on it and puts a check by David's name. She notices as she glances at the sheet that Bobby had trouble walking the balance beam and prepares a note for his mother suggesting some exercises he could do at home. With this done, she prepares for her afternoon class.

Scenario 3

Mr. Tyler is a history teacher in a large high school. He is working on a unit in group processing, and while his ultimate goal is for the students to understand the effects of group processing on democratic decision making, his particular interest in this lesson is to have his students learn to understand their own views more clearly and to learn to cooperate by making decisions in groups. To accomplish this, he splits the class into two groups and presents each group with a perplexing situation. The situation describes a shipwreck with some sick and injured people. The party is marooned on a deserted island, short of food and water fit for drinking. Fortunately, they're rescued but the ship can only handle part of the people in one trip. In all likelihood, many of the sick and injured won't survive the trip back to civilisation, but they'll surely die if left on the island. If the healthy are left until the second trip, many will die of starvation or thirst before the ship returns. He asks the students to discuss the issue during the class period, recording notes and decisions. Each group is to report the following day.

As the groups discuss the problem, Mr. Tyler listens and periodically raises questions if the students appear to drift away from the task at hand, or raises questions that aren't considered by the group.

The next day Mr. Tyler has the students discuss the process they went through, their feelings as they were involved in the discussion, and the bases for the decisions they made. As the year progresses Mr. Tyler makes short notes about each student describing the student's progress in working in group situations.

Analysis

We have described three teachers involved in activities with students at three different levels and in three different content areas. Let's analyze the three scenarios and see how they illustrate the framework we want to provide for later chapters in this book.

Teacher Emphasis

First let's look again at what the three teachers did. Mrs. Shafer wanted her students to understand the influence of geography and climate on life-style. Miss Adams had her children doing a variety of things; some worked with trying to light the bulb, some counted beans, and others worked on skills like tying shoes and buttoning coats. Mr. Tyler wanted his students to learn to cooperate in groups and involved them in a decision-making activity. We can see from the earlier examples that the differences among these three areas in many classrooms are those of emphasis rather than exclusion. For example, while Mrs. Shafer wanted her students to learn about the relationship between geography, climate, and life-style, she also viewed respect for others as important. She demonstrated this view when she reminded David and Billy to listen when Mike was talking. Also, in order to perform skills such as carpentry and hitting a tennis ball properly, knowledge of technique is required. All of this serves to show that the three areas—knowledge, skills, and attitudes—are closely interrelated and cannot be completely separated in any reasonable way.

All three of the areas are extremely important and should be emphasised as much as possible in schools. However, a discussion of the learning of knowledge, skills, and attitudes is beyond the scope of a single text, so we have chosen to emphasize the area of knowledge and information more than the others. The reason is simple. While skills and attitudes are important and are considered important by public school officials, relatively greater emphasis is placed on the acquisition of knowledge and the ability to think. For this reason we have chosen to concentrate on this area.

Based on the three scenarios, we see that students' learning can be more varied than we might expect at first glance. Mrs. Shafer's students were learning *information* or *knowledge* and how it can be used to explain objects and events that occur in the world. By comparison, many of Miss Adams's activities were related to *manipulative skills* such as buttoning Fred's coat and tying his shoes. Many other such skills are taught in schools—typing, carpentry, leatherwork, mechanics, and physical education skills in all the sports areas. Mr. Tylers activity was different from both Mrs. Shafer's and Miss Adams's. He wanted his students to acquire certain *attitudes* and *values,* such as cooperation, willingness to listen to a contrasting view, and respect for others.

So, we see now that students can learn much more than information in schools. Student learning can roughly be described as existing in three forms: (1) information and knowledge, (2) manipulative skills, and (3) attitudes and values.

Learning Environments

Let's look again at the three scenarios and see how the learning environments differed. Mrs. Shafer worked with her whole class, while Miss Adams worked with small groups and had learning centers set up. Mr. Tyler worked with two large groups. Adding one-to-one encounters to our list, the possible grouping arrangements appear as follows:

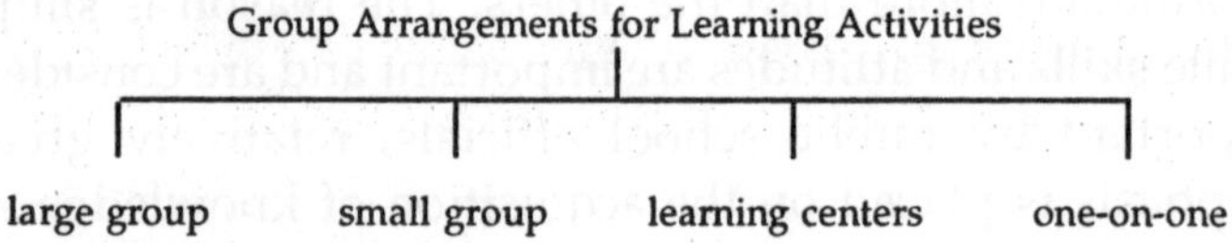

The material in this text is designed to be used with all group arrangements.

Other Influences on Learning

While the group arrangement affects the way children learn, many other factors influence what children take away from school. For instance, in Miss Adams's activity. Jimmy appeared listless, and it turned out that he didn't feel well. Health is certainly a factor that affects learning. Nutrition is another factor, and its importance, in addition to promoting general health, is evidenced by schools implementing breakfast and free lunch programmes for needy children.

Think for a moment now about the way Mrs. Shafer and Miss Adams their rooms to present them in the most attractive way possible. The physical environment has been shown to be an important factor affecting student learning of information and attitudes toward school.

Again, think about Mrs. Shafer's lesson. In discussing the picture of children playing in front of the grass huts, Carol reacted quite differently from because she had been to Africa and had seen live examples of huts and children similar to those in Mrs. Shafer's picture, while Jimmy had no frame of reference whatsoever. Mike's reaction was somewhere in between. He had no firsthand experience but was familiar with the ideas from pictures and stories. This all illustrates how background experience can affect what children learn. In the situation just described, Carol was certainly in the best position to derive the most benefit from the lesson because of her prior experience, while Jimmy was in the least advantageous position. Obviously, we as teachers cannot control students' backgrounds, but we can provide the most realistic examples possible, as Mrs. Shafer did, and promote as much student involvement as possible, again as Mrs. Shafer did. This illustrates the role of the teacher in influencing student learning, which brings us to the central theme of this text.

As you reflect on your role as a teacher in the schools, you see that as an individual teacher you can do little about the child's health, his nutrition, his outside experiences, or his emotional makeup. You can, however, significantly influence his learning by providing school experiences that promote thinking and by making learning as positive an experience as possible. This is what this book is all about. In succeeding chapters we will help you learn to plan, implement, and evaluate activities to promote as much student learning as possible. We will describe this process according to a three-step model or approach. This approach outlines the steps a teacher takes in developing any learning experience, and the majority of the remaining material in this text will be devoted to discussion and illustation of the three steps.

THE THREE-PHASE: APPROACH TO TEACHING

The model of teaching we are presenting is simple, and we realize curriculum development experts would include additional steps. However, the approach is understandable, practical, and workable in the planning of single lessons or units, and we have chosen it for these reasons.

The three basic steps in the three-phase approach to teaching are these:

1. The planning phase
2. The implementing phase
3. The evaluating phase

These three phases are sequential and interrelaled. In other words, a teacher, in developing any learning experience, first plans, then implements those plans, and finally evaluates the success of the activity.

In each of these phases effective teachers ask themselves a series of questions that are constantly kept in mind as the process develops. We are going to use these questions in our development of the remainder of the text. Keep this idea in mind and look now at each of the steps more closely.

Planning

All teaching begins with some kind of planning. At this point, a teacher asks himself:

"What do I want the students to know, understand, appreciate, and be able to do?"

The answer to this question will be the teacher's goal

The first step of the planning phase is the establishment of some kind of goal. This goal may be as mundane as keeping the students quiet for an hour or as lofty as developing students' moral or spiritual values. Whatever the intent, the establishment of some type of goal or purpose is the first priority in teaching.

You may wonder or ask yourself "What determines the goal?" Or, "From where does it come?" The answers to these questions can become very philosophical and we consider this issue in Chapter 2. In addition, a method for precisely stating teaching goals is described in Chapter 3.

Each of the teachers in our introductory scenarios established goals. Mrs. Shafer wanted her students to understand the influence of geography on life-style and habits, Miss Adams wanted her children to develop their manipulative skills, and Mr. Tyler wanted his students to work cooperatively in groups.

A second step in the planning phase is selecting a strategy and gathering the supporting materials. Mrs. Shafer wanted her students to discover the relationship between climate and life-style and attempted to accomplish this by showing pictures and asking questions. Her pictures were her supporting materials. Miss Adams chose as her strategy the simple procedure of practice with the doll being the supporting materials, and Mr. Tyler's strategy was to actually have the students involved in a group decision-making process. To accomplish his aim, Mr. Tyler needed no materials other than pencil and paper and the problem-solving situation. Chapters 2 through 5 are all devoted to the planning process.

Research evidence supports the value of the planning process. Peterson, Marx, and Clark (1978) found that teacher behaviors in the classroom depend on the plans teachers make. Clark and Yinger (1979) and McCutcheon (1980) both found that planning tends to give teachers confidence and security. For those of you who have not yet taught and are approaching the experience with understandable apprehension, the research results are encouraging. The implication for you is to plan carefully so that your feelings of uncertainty can be significantly reduced.

Implementing

Having determined the goal and selected an appropriate means to reach that goal, the teacher then must consider implementing that strategy. The teacher attempts in the implementation phase to accomplish the teaching goal through the selected strategy. The teaching activity in the implementation stage is the actual performance of the strategy the teacher has selected. Mrs. Shafer implemented her activity when she actually showed the pictures and asked the students questions. Miss Adams implemented her activity when she had the students practice on Fred, and Mr. Tyler was in the implementation phase when the students actually worked on making the group decisions. The implementation phase is simple to describe but may be much more difficult to perform. Essentially, this phase occurs when you actually do a teaching activity with the idea of reaching a pre-established goal. Interestingly, a surprising number of teachers do activities with little thought of what goal they're trying to reach. Mintz (1979), Peterson et al. (1978) and McCutcheon (1980) all found that teachers do not typically start the planning process with a consideration of goals but rather with a concern for activities, content, or materials. A goal for us in writing this text is for you as preservice and inservice teachers to make your planning, implementing, and evaluating of learning experiences for your students a systematic and considered process rather than a contingency or "seat-of-the-pants" approach. The research suggests that while planning and carrying out meaningful goal-oriented programmes isn't often systematically done, such action is possible and will be rewarded with positive results.

The question the teacher asks in anticipating the implementation of activities is "How will I get the students to reach the goal?" The answer to the question will be the teaching procedure, strategy, or technique that is used. Deciding the most appropriate method to use depends on the goal, the students' characteristics, the teacher's style, and other factors.

In addition to considering and implementing a teaching strategy to reach a predetermined goal, teachers must organize and manage their classrooms so the learning process can proceed smoothly. Management procedures range from something as simple as a word spoken to a student to complex procedures that require the creation of unique environments.

Mrs. Shafer was involved in classroom management when she gave David a stern look for whispering while another student was talking, and Miss Adams employed management procedures when she gently corrected Scott for throwing the beanbag at Lisa rather than to her. Additional management features were illustrated in the way Miss Adams arranged her room. Rather than having children organised in rows of semicircles, she had them in small groups working at stations.

As the anecdotes involving Mrs. Shafer and Miss Adams illustrate, classroom management and instruction are essentially inseparable. Without attending to the learning task, students cannot learn, and organising a learning activity invariably incorporates some management considerations on the part of the teacher. It is for these reasons that management of classrooms is included in our discussion of the implementing phase of teaching.

Evaluating

The third stage in the teaching act is evaluation. Here the teacher attempts to F gather information that can be used to determine if his teaching has been successful. This can be done in a number of ways including tests or quizzes or by noting students' reactions to questions or comments. Each of these methods can be used by the teacher in making decisions concerning whether or not the goal established in the planning stage was reached.

At this point the teacher is asking "How will I determine if the students know, understand, or appreciate the goal I have identified?" The answer to this question specifies the way in which the students' understanding will be measured and evaluated.

For instance, Mrs. Shafer gave the children an unfamiliar paragraph and asked them to identify illustrations of the relationship between geography and life-style in it, Miss Adams observed the children performing the manipulative tasks and checked the names of those who were successful, and Mr. Tyler observed the students and made notes regarding their progress in group situations.

In all these instances the evaluation procedures used by the teachers were chosen so as to be congruent with the established goals and the selected implementation strategies.

Summary

The scenarios in which the three teachers performed each of these phases can be summarised as follows:

	Planning	*Implementing*	*Evaluating*
Mrs. Shafer	Wanted students to know how lifestyle and geography relate. Selected pictures and planned discovery.	Had children observe pictures and discover relationship.	Gave children a paragraph and had them identify illustrations in it.
Miss Adams	Wanted students to develop manipulative skills. Decided on practice. Decided to use the doll.	Had students practice on the doll.	Observed students and checked their names on a check list.
Mr. Tyler	Wanted students to learn to work in groups. Chose a dilemma for groups to discuss.	Had students discuss the dilemma and arrive at group decision.	Observed students work in groups during the year.

Though described as three separate phases, the continuity and interrelationship of the phases should be emphasised. The goal that a teacher has for a particular group of students should determine both what is taught and how it is taught and should influence the manner in which the learning is evaluated. This relationship is shown in Figure 3.1.

Some of the relationships shown in Figure 3.1 are readily apparent while others may require some discussion. The effect of goals on implementation strategies and evaluation procedures is apparent in that the goal being taught influences how the lesson is taught and how the effectiveness of the lesson is measured. However, other relationships in the diagram may not be so apparent. Evaluation procedures also influence the goals chosen and the implementation procedures used. For example, if evaluation procedures show that the desired learning has not taken place, the teacher may wish to reconsider both the goals and the implementation procedures. Perhaps the goals were overly ambitious or inappropriate for the students. On the other hand, the teaching strategy may have been unsuitable for attaining the chosen goal. With feedback from one phase of the teaching act, the teacher can critically examine the effectiveness of the other components.

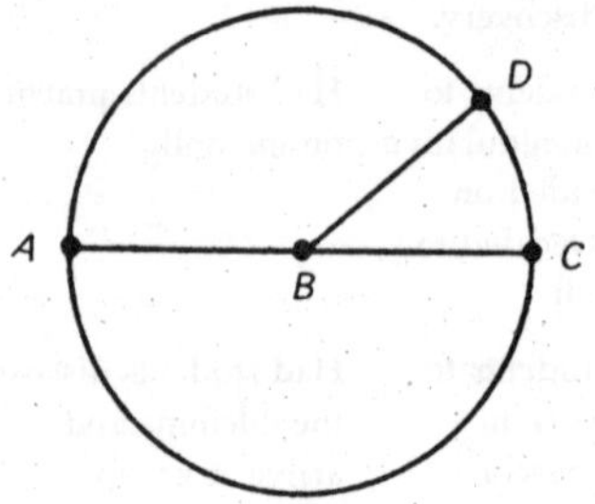

Fig. 3.1. The Three-Phase Approach to Teaching

The three-phase approach to teaching as described here is a sequentially related series of steps which proceed from the establishing of goals to a verification of the attainment of these goals. Stated another way, teaching is a logical operation in which goals are determined, attempts are made to reach those goals, and the effectiveness of those attempts are evaluated. Each of the steps can be identified with questions such as:

> "What do I want the students to know or understand?"
>
> "How will I get the students to the goal?"
>
> "How will I determine whether or not they know or understand what I have identified in the goal?"

Two major themes or goals will serve as structure for the text. The first is to develop in readers the mental tools needed to serve as a foundation for continued professional growth. The second is to describe and apply the results suggested by research in teaching effectiveness.

ORGANISATION OF THE TEXT

The material which follows has been organised into four units which are as follows:.

Unit 1: Planning
Unit 2: Implementing
Unit 3: Measurement and Evaluation
Unit 4: Directions

In an attempt to streamline the readability of the text, we have implemented a standard format that is used for each chapter. The format includes the following:

1. *Introduction.* An orientation to the material and a rationale for its inclusion in the book.
2. *Objectives.* A listing of the skills you will have upon the conclusion of the chapter.
3. *Content.* Materials which facilitate the objectives by providing explanations, descriptions, and examples.
4. *Exercises and Feedback.* Opportunities to practice the skills with explanations and answers provided. Feedback for all exercises is given at the end of each chapter.
5. *Summary.* Brief statements relating the work to the overall conceptualisation of the book.

As stated above, the first step to effective teaching is planning, and the planning phase begins with the identification of content areas. Turn now to Unit 1, where content analysis will be discussed in detail.

Education as it is currently practiced in this country is a combination of art and science. While research tells us in a systematic way about effective compared to less effective teacher behavior (the science of teaching), individuals must practice and apply what is known according to their own personality and to a certain extent their own intuition (the art of teaching). There is no one best way to teach, no *super strategy.* No programme of instruction or curriculum is any better or any worse than the individual doing the teaching.

This chapter and the ones to follow are based on this foundation. We are now beginning the second phase, *implementation,* of our three step model. Simply stated, you have identified one or more objectives and you are now prepared to help learners to reach the objective(s). The specific experiences and behaviors you design for students to reach or master an objective are called implementation. In a simple phrase, implementation is how *you teach.*

A cornerstone of any effective teaching technique is classroom questioning. It is a critical skill that can be used with any subject matter area, any grade level, and with any given teacher personality. It promotes involvement, enhances learning, requires little effort, and motivates the students. It promotes a shift from a teacher-centered to a student-centered environment while maintaining a teacher-led activity. Because of these factors, we will discuss questioning specifically in this chapter and will then describe how questioning skills can be incorporated into complete teaching procedures. Hopefully, after completing this chapter, you will have the background to begin forming a personal teaching style. Such development is an evolving process where the skills presented here are practiced, internalised, and incorporated into the strategies that follow. Finally, as the strategies are rehearsed and modified, the style develops.

We will begin our discussion with a description of question level followed by direction and will close the chapter with illustrations of questioning techniques.

Objectives

You should be able to accomplish the following objectives:

1. For you as a pre/inservice teacher to increase your understanding of low and high level questions so when given a case study you will identify each.
2. For you as a pre/inservice teacher to understand convergent and divergent questions so when given a scenario you will identify each of these questions.
3. For you as a pre/inservice teacher to understand questioning technique (redirection, prompting, probing) so that given a case study, you will identify each.

QUESTION LEVELS

Low Level Questions

The most frequently employed questions used in a teacher-led discussion are of a low level nature (Davis & Tinsley, 1967; Gall, 1970; Rogers, 1969). As pointed out in the discussion on the cognitive domain, the lowest or knowledge level requires the student to recall information that he has stored. Therefore, typically a low level response requires memorisation on the part of the student and requires no processing of information. The following are examples of low level questions:

> What are the three most common tools in a metal shop?

How much is 5 plus 5?
What is the Pythagorean theorem?
Who was the pacifist leader of India after World War II?
How do you spell *anonymous?*
What is one animal that has survived the prehistoric age?

Again, the simplest key to follow is that anytime you ask a student to. do no more than recall information such as terms, facts, names, and events, you have framed a low level question.

High Level Questions

We have suggested that low level questions require a student to merely *recall* information. These questions are important and valuable but we must help students give more complete responses and expand their thinking. This leads us to a discussion of *high level questions*. As discussed, the characteristic which separates a low from a high level question is that the latter requires a degree of intellectual processing on the part of the student while the former is limited to memorisation with the information being recalled upon demand.

We further pointed out that, regarding the cognitive domain, only the knowledge level is considered to be of a low nature. The remaining five levels (comprehension, application, analysis, synthesis, and evaluation) are all considered to be high level. The advantages of using high level questions were pointed out in a study by Hunkins (1969) in which the use of these questions resulted in an increase in higher levels of achievement with no decrease in the lower levels.

Simply stated, we are defining a high level question as

any question that requires the student to do more than recall previously learned information. Obviously, high level questions will vary in difficulty and demand placed on the student, but the key characteristic they possess is that they require more than mere recall. Researchers will vary to a certain extent in their definitions of high and low level. If you wish to read further on this topic, we refer you to Duncan and Biddle (1974). The primary issue, however, is not to be rigid in defining question level but rather to ask questions at a level appropriate for the learner and learning activity. Both low and high level questions are important.

Let's look now at an example.

> A teacher begins, "In looking at balance of power arrangements through history, we have seen most such arrangements rarefy last more than a few decades. Why do you suppose these arrangements collapse?" (pause) "Bob?"
>
> "I think the foreign policies of many countries are changing rapidly, and, as their goals change, the nations have to seek new alliances."
>
> "How does the United States seek out these alliances? Wanda?"
>
> "We try to find out who agrees with our position. This would include not only countries who would support us, but also those in need of our support."

By asking students questions beginning with phrases such as "why do you suppose" and "how does the United States seek," the teacher pushes the student beyond a rote memory exercise. Both students had to manipulate prior information and were therefore working at a high level.

Consider the statement "Give me an example, that we haven't previously discussed, of a simile." A student responding to this question must generate, on the basis of previous examples, a new example of the concept *simile*. This is an excellent and commonly asked high level question.

Another important high level question involves the ability to state an idea or definition in the student's own terms. An example is the question "Tell me in your own words what we mean by the statement, 'literature reflects the time and society of the authors.'" The answer to this question would likely be followed by the teacher asking for an example of an author, his work, and the characteristics of the society—another high level question.

A valuable discussion question of high level is the consideration of author motive, perspective or reference frame, as in this example: "We've read the column by William F. Buckley (a noted journalist). Where do you suppose Buckley is coming from in the column?" The discussion would involve consideration of his conservative orientation, probable motives, and basic philosophical stance.

An important additional high level question is one that requires the solution to a problem, such as "An item originally selling for $20.00 is marked 20% off. What is the sale price?" The solution to the problem requires a high level response. There is one caution we should mention, however. It is a quite common practice in math texts to include a series of problems identical to each other in form. The students solve each like they solved the first and the level of the task after the first problem is no longer high but, in fact, is merely recall of process. While this occurs more often in assigned work than in a questioning situation, it can occur in both and teachers think they are getting a high level response when the opposite is actually occurring. The solution is simple. Mix up the types of problems and students will be required to give high level responses in each case.

There are two other forms of high level questions which are easy to ask, quite easy to answer, and excellent for promoting student involvement. These are called *description* questions and *comparison* questions. The first type asks the learners to observe and describe an object or event such as an illustration, demonstration, map, graph, table, or statement. The description is initiated by the teacher making a directive such as the following:

1. "What do you notice here?"
2. Tell me about this."
3. "What do you see?"
4. "Describe the object in front of you."

This type of question offers an effective technique for promoting involvement, success, and depth of response. While it requires a simple and seemingly low level response, it calls into play the learner's experience, perception, and senses. It requires more than mere recall and we therefore define it as a high level question.

The second type, comparison questions, requires the learner to look at two or more objects, statements, illustrations, or demonstrations and identify similarities or differences between them. As students identify similarities, they are moving toward the establishment of a pattern that ultimately results in a concept or generalisation. For example, suppose students are shown the following three sentences:

1. She is quiet as a mouse.
2. He was as large as a mountain.
3. They ran as fast as the wind.

The question, "What is similar about the sentences?" requires the learners to identify patterns that ultimately specify the characteristics of the concept *simile*. For instance, the word as appears in each and a nonliteral comparison between two objects or ideas occurs in each.

Comparison questions are very effective high level questions in that they encourage students to process information. We will refer to description and copmparison questions in greater depth in the following sections:

EXERCISE 3.1

Read the following scenario and identify each teacher statement as being either a low (I) or a high (h) level question. Then check your answers with the ones given in the feedback section at the end of the chapter.

—— 1. "On the board are three lists of words I'd like for you to analyze for a minute." (pause) "What is special about the first two lists? Amy?" "All the words are alike."

—— 2. "Could you explain what you mean by 'are alike'?" "Well, they're all words that I would use to mean something good about somebody."

—— 3. "That's right. Does anyone notice anything else about these words? Bob?" "You could use one of them to mean the other."

—— 4. "Can you give me an example of this?"

"I could say, 'You are a very *competent* teacher,' or I could say, 'You are a very *skillful* teacher,' and, either way, I'd mean the same thing."

—— 5. "Good. Bob. So the terms in column one are more or less interchangeable with those in column two, right?"

There is general agreement shown by tumultuous applause.

—— 6. "What term do you use to designate this type of relationship?" There is no response.

—— 7. "O.K. Think back to your study of prefixes, suffixes, and root words. Can anybody remember the prefix that means same? Sally?" "*Syn-*"

—— 8. "Right. How about the one for *name?*" "*-Onym-*"

—— 9. "So, Sally, when you put them together you get . . ." "Synonym." ,

—— 10. "Very good. Can you find some relationship between the words in column one and those in column two? Bob?"

"Those in column two are synonyms of those in column one."

Amy adds, "And those in column one are synonyms of those in column two."

—— 11. "Yes. Now look at column three." (pause) "How do these words relate to those in the first two columns?" Amy doesn't respond.

—— 12. "O.K. Does *odious* mean the same thing as *pleasant?*" "No."

—— 13. "Does it mean the same thing as *agreeable?*" "No, it's the opposite of *agreeable.*"

—— 14. "O.K., Amy. Now, Bob, can you see another set of words in the column that has a similar relationship?"

"Yes. *ugly* means just the opposite of *pretty* and *attractive,* and *mean* is just the opposite of *kind.*"

—— 15. "So can someone state the relationship between the first two columns and the third? Sally?"

"Those in column three are opposites of those in columns one and two."

—— 16. "Good. Do you recall the word that expresses this relationship. Sally?" "Antonym."

QUESTION DIRECTION

Convergent Questions

Convergent questions are those that require *one correct answer*. In general, they are questions of fact or recall and are often of a low level, as described in the previous section. For example, the following are convergent questions:

1. What is 6 × 9?
2. What part of speech modifies a noun or pronoun?
3. A turtle is in what animal class?

4. What is the chemical formula for table salt?
5. What is the most populous country in the world?

Note in each of these that there is only one correct answer for each question and the answer requires recall of previously learned information.

An exception to this pattern would involve solutions for problems requiring application, analysis, or synthesis. For example, if you ask "I have four hundred feet offence and I want to enclose the maximum area in a four-sided figure. What should the dimensions be?" This is a very high level question but is still convergent in that only one answer to the problem is correct.

Divergent Questions

While convergent questions require one correct answer, divergent questions are just the opposite in that many different answers are appropriate. For instance, consider the following questions:

1. How are the beans alike?
2. What do you notice about the sentence "The gorgeous girl moved quickly to catch the attention of several men"?
3. Give me an example of a first class lever.
4. Give me one of the most significant dates in world history.

Notice that each of the questions can be answered in several ways. For example, in the first case, responses would be:

1. "All are sort of fat."
2. "They have seeds in them."
3. "Round."

4. "They have lines on them."

In the second example:

1. "It's a complete sentence."
2. "You are only inferring that the girl is trying to attract men."
3. "Both an adjective and an adverb appear in the sentence."
4. "There is a prepositional phrase in it."

The third:

1. "Screwdriver prying open a paint can lid."
2. "Crowbar prying up a rock."
3. "Scissors."

And the fourth:.

1. "1588—The defeat of the Spanish Armada."
2. "1215—The signing of the Magna Carta."
3. "1066—The Battle of Hastings."
4. "1776—The American Declaration of Independence."

Obviously, many more answers could be given in each case but the illustrations show how divergent questions can be used to promote student involvement by allowing a number of students to respond to the same question. Notice also that the level of divergent questions is high.

EXERCISE 3.2

Return to the scenario offered in Exercise 3.1 (page 113). Decide whether each of the 16 teacher statements is convergent (c) or divergent (d). Then check your answers with the ones given in the feedback section at the end of the chapter.

——	1.	——	9.
——	2.	——	10.
——	3.	——	11.
——	4.	——	12.
——	5.	——	13.
——	6.	——	14.
——	7.	——	15.
——	8.	——	16.

EXERCISE 3.3

As a review for both the level and the direction of questions, label the following statements as low level/divergent (l/d), low level/convergent (I/c), high level/divergent (h/d), or high level/convergent (h/c). Then compare your answers with the ones given in the feedback section at the end of the chapter.

—— 1. How is architecture influenced by culture?

—— 2. What were some of the possible economic motives of the U.S. which added to its conflict with Japan prior to World War II?

—— 3. What assumptions can you make about a novel which is referred to as a classic?

—— 4. Name the major organs of the digestive system.

—— 5. What may have caused Achilles to choose youth and fame over long life?

—— 6. What are the two elements found in salt?

—— 7. Put into your own words what effect the philosophies of Aristotle and Plato had upon the generations which followed them.

—— 8. What would be the implications of an average world rate of 5.1 births per woman?

—— 9. Giving all points discussed in the readings equal weight what was the main argument favouring separatism?

—— 10. You want to get from Jacksonville to Miami, which is 360 miles. The speed limit is 55 mph. If you stay within the speed limit and drive at a steady speed, what is the minimum amount of time the trip will take?

—— 11. Can anyone give us an example of *iambic pentameter?*

—— 12. What fallacies appeared in the theory that the earth was the center of the universe?

—— 13. List the steps involved in operating a lathe.

—— 14. What do you think JFK meant by the "new frontier"?

—— 15. In Orwell's *Animal Farm* what techniques are used to persuade the animals to devote their all to the farm?

QUESTIONING TECHNIQUES

Redirection

The first step toward developing effective questioning techniques is to increase the amount of student participation. Typically, interaction patterns involve a teacher asking a question and a student volunteering a response to the question. As the activity proceeds those desiring to respond continue to be involved and those not desiring to participate drift away from the activity. The patterns can be well-established with those volunteering being the primary participators and the others rarely responding and often not even attending to the activity. As a result, a teacher often only has a portion of the class paying attention which, in turn, means only that portion is learning.

In general, teachers do not direct questions to particular students. Further, when questions are asked of individuals, the perceived high achievers are called on much more often than the perceived low achievers (Brophy & Good, 1970). An interesting and somewhat ironic aspect of both these phenomena is that teachers are quite unaware of the patterns and will, sometimes, deny their existence, even to an observer who has pointed them out to the teachers immediately after a lesson.

It is very important that teachers break these patterns. When different patterns are established, powerful results can occur. Kerman (1979) describes a project, one component of which involved training teachers to call on *all* students in a class approximately equally. The results of the project were very impressive. Not only did student achievement increase but both discipline referrals and absenteeism decreased.

Redirection can be a useful questioning technique to help establish positive patterns and high levels of interaction in a classroom. This technique involves the framing of a single question for which there are many possible responses and the receiving of responses from several students. The following is an example of how you might accomplish this task:

> "Having completed our overview of the presidents, who do you think was the greatest American chief executive? Tom?"
>
> "Abraham Lincoln."
>
> "Sally?"
>
> "Woodrow Wilson."
>
> "Joe, another one?"
>
> "George Washington."

You will notice the teacher does not respond to or discuss the students' replies. She simply redirects the original question and, in doing so, increases student participation while eliminating any possible domination of the discussion. Student participation by different members of the class has been shown to be a variable affecting both attention and achievement (McKenzil 6= Mixon, 1979).

In the next sequence, pay close attention to the ways in which the teacher redirects the question.

> "Some of you mentioned the presidents you believe to have been great. Why do you think they were great men? Yes, Betty."
>
> "I think Lincoln was great because he was able to hold the country together, and Washington was great because he got the country started."
>
> "Do you have something, David?"
>
> "I think Wilson was great because he was a man of peace and could see the problems beyond his time."
>
> "Mark, can you add anything else?"
>
> "They were all great men because they were strong and had the courage to fight for what they believed in."

It is important to note that, although the three students may not have been dealing with the same individual, they were all responding to a single question posed by the teacher.

Notice first in the example above that all the redirected questions were divergent. This, of course, is an obvious requirement. It is impossible to redirect a convergent question in any sensible way.

Second, you see that the questions were also high level. This further illustrates the value of redirecting. Not only is it a powerful technique in promoting interaction but it is also a convenient means for helping the teacher ask high level questions.

Questions that are very easy to redirect are those that require description and comparison. For example, using the illustration of the concept *simile* provided earlier, the teacher could present the sentence, "She is quiet as a mouse," and direct different individuals to describe the sentence requesting that each say something different about it. The interaction pattern could appear as follows:

Teacher:	What do you notice about the sentence? . . . Tim?
Tim:	It has six words in it.
Teacher:	What else, Sue?
Sue:	*She* is the subject.
Teacher:	And what else, Steve?
Steve:	It's about a girl.

This process can go on as long as the teacher desires or until it looks as if the class is ready to move on.

A sensible following step would be for the teacher to present a second example and ask for comparisons. For instance, the students may now have displayed before them the sentences: "She is quiet as a mouse" and "He was a rock of strength." The teacher could then ask, "What is the same or different about the two sentences?" The responses would vary and the question could be redirected to several students.

In summary, we have defined redirection as any question that is divergent and asked of several different individuals. It is a powerful technique in promoting involvement. Finally, teaching effectiveness research (Wright & Nuthall, 1970) found that redirection is significantly related to achievement. For these reasons, redirection is one of the most effective questioning techniques a teacher can employ.

EXERCISE 3.4

Read the following anecdote and identify the teacher's questions which are examples of redirection by marking them with an X. Then check your answers with the ones given in the feedback section at the end of the chapter.

—— 1. "We've been discussing immigration this week, and I want to see if we can tie things together at this point. Just for review, thousands of people came to America during the late 1800's. Name some of the countries they came from." (pause) "Bob?" "Ireland."

—— 2. "Paul, another one?" "Germany."

—— 3. "Do you have one, Pam?" "Italy?"

—— 4. "Fine. All good answers. Now let's use these countries as representative examples. What can we say about the people from these countries? Jim?" Jim doesn't respond.

—— 5. "Well, let's take a close look, Jim. Do you think they have the same religious structure?" "No."

—— 6. "Anything else, Jim?"

"Their languages are different."

—— 7. "Right. That's a good one. Anybody want to add another one? Pam?"

"Oh ... I can think of a lot of things like clothes, food, economic factors, political structure, and attitudes."

—— 8. "Fine, fine. What is the obvious point we can draw from this. Bob?" "That American immigrants, were different."

—— 9. "Different from what. Bob?" "From each other."

—— 10. "Good, now let's break off for just a second. How did the book define immigration?" (pause) "Nancy?"

"A person who leaves his country immigrates from his home."

—— 11. "O.K., let's look at the word closely. Does immigration make you think of *in* or *out?* Nancy?" "In."

—— 12. "So a person who is an immigrant .. .?" "Comes into a country," Nancy finishes.

—— 13. "And to emigrate ...?" "Is to leave a country."

—— 14. "Very good. Nancy!"

Prompting

What happens when we ask a student a question, and he either fails to reply or he responds incorrectly? Generally, teachers move on to another student in order to maintain interest and momentum. By doing so, the student who was unable to respond often becomes confused and psychologically removed from the discussion. We have stressed desirability of total involvement, but how can we deal with students who cannot answer questions or whose responses are wrong? The following sequence between a teacher and one student deals with this problem:

> "Regarding our discussion on international power patterns, which pattern does this equal arms scale demonstrate?" (pause) "Pat?"
>
> Pat seems to be confused and doesn't respond.
>
> "Any idea?"
>
> "I don't know."
>
> "O.K., left take another look at the scale. If this object is two ounces and the one on the other tray is two ounces, they are said to be. . .?"
>
> "Equal."
>
> "Right. Equal in what?"
>
> "Weight."
>
> The teacher nods. "Now, if we have these equal weights, one on each tray, what happens?"
>
> "They balance each other."
>
> "Fine. Left suppose each weight represents three countries and that the groups are basically opposed to each other. If they are equal in strength or power they would be . ...?"
>
> "Balanced."
>
> "Great! Then this demonstration represents what pattern of power?"

"The balance of power pattern."

"Now you've got it!!"

The above demonstrates the technique referred to as *prompting* and involves the use of hints or clues which are used to aid the student in responding successfully. This method can also be employed when a response is incorrect. Note the following example between a teacher and one student:

"To be specific, the pattern of power called *balance is* one in which two or more nation-states form a coalition in order to protect themselves from a specific enemy. Coalitions of equal power oppose each other; they are in balance and peace is preserved. However, once the balance is broken and one coalition tips the power scale in its favour, the likelihood of war is increased. As with our scale, if too much weight is added to one side, the other side will be overpowered. Now, let's apply the example. Does the United Nations represent a balance of power arrangement?" (pause) "Mary?"

"I think it does."

"Let's analyze it and find out. Mary, does the UN aid and support any group member attacked by an enemy?"

"It's supposed to."

"O.K. Is the UN a coalition of two or more nations?"

"Yes."

"Is the UN pledged against a specific enemy?"

"I'm not sure."

"Is there another organisation of equal size and power with which the UN is locked in mortal combat?"

"No."

"Then what do you conclude?"

"The United Nations is not an example of balance of power."

"Very good."

The effectiveness of prompting is supported by research. Anderson, Everston, and Brophy (1979) and Stallings, Needels, and Stayrook (1979) found that students benefited most, after giving an incorrect response, when the teacher asked a series of simple questions and gave clues to help them arrive at the correct answer. Merely giving the correct answer and moving to another student or asking another student to help immediately after the incorrect response were less effective than prompting.

Consider now one more example. In the previous section we used the sentences, "She is quiet as a mouse," and "He was a rock of strength." The teacher presumably wants the students to identify the first as a simile and the second as a metaphor. She probably has asked a series of divergent questions—descriptions and comparisons—which have been redirected to several individuals. However, let's assume that the students don't recognize the sentences as examples of the respective concepts. The effective teacher now prompts the students to arrive at the correct answer. The dialogue might appear as follows:

Teacher: What do you notice about *he* and *rock* in the second sentence?

Student: It says he is a rock.

Teacher: Does the sentence mean he really is a rock?

Student: No, not really.

Teacher: So we say the comparison is what?

Student: (Pause)

Teacher: Literal or nonliteral?

Student: Nonliteral.

Teacher: Okay. Good. We have a nonliteral comparison between two ideas. The same is true about the first sentence but there is a special word in it. What word?

Student: As.

Teacher: Yes. The word as is added. Otherwise, the two sentences are similar. What are they called?

Student: The first is a simile and the second is a metaphor.

Teacher: Excellent. We have identified the sentences.

As the research literature indicates, prompting *is* a very important technique employed by effective teachers. However, our experience in working with teachers suggests that it is difficult for them and isn't employed as often as would be desirable. The reason for the difficulty probably is that prompting requires *thinking on your feet.* While many other teaching procedures and skills can be planned and practiced in advance, prompting can only be practiced in the context of an actual lesson and a prompting question is formed and asked *on the spot,* following a student response. This can be difficult and requires practice. However, it can be enormously rewarding and frankly, it is enjoyable to help learners provide responses they previously could not provide. For these reasons we encourage you to persevere. With practice you will become skilled and will reap the intrinsic rewards of feeling that you have had a positive, direct, and tangible influence on student learning.

Careful preparation can be an aid that will help your prompting efforts. For instance, if a teacher knows in advance that he wants the students to identify, "nonliteral comparison without as or *like*" as the key characteristic of metaphor and "nonliteral comparison using as or *like*" for simile helps him to *think on his feet* because he knows what he wants from the students. He can then ask whatever questions it takes to get them to the idea.

As a reader you might ask, "How do you get them to supply the words and *metaphor* respectively?" The simple answer is, *you don't!* The teacher prompts the students to identify *characteristics* and if the students are unable to supply the label, the teacher supplies it for them. Remember, labels are items of fact learning and serve the purpose of communicating concepts, so telling the students the label is perfectly appropriate.

EXERCISE 3.5

Turn back to Exercise 3.4 and identify all of teacher's statements which are prompts by marking their numbers here with an X. Then compare your answers with the ones given in the feedback section at the end of the chapter.

___	1.	___	4.	___	7.	___	10.	___	13.
___	2.	___	5.	___	8.	___	11.	___	14.
___	3.	___	6.	___	9.	___	12.	___	15.

EXERCISE 3.6

Read the following anecdote and identify all of the teacher's statements which are either redirections (r) or prompts (p).

___ 1. "Today we're considering the properties of numbers. Here is a list of some numbers." The teacher points to a list on the board. "From the list show me a prime number. Bob?" "Three."

___ 2. "Another, Paul?" "Two."

___ 3. "Another one, Lynn?" "Five."

___ 4. "Now, give me a number that is not prime. Paul?" "Six."

—— 5. "Another one. Rudy?" "Eight."

—— 6. "O.K. Let's try something we haven't done yet. Six can be reduced to the product of two prime numbers. What are they. Bob?" Bob doesn't respond.

—— 7. "Let me help you, Bob. Now remember your times tables. What times what equal six?"

"Oh, three times two."

—— 8. "O.K., good. Now, from this list, select a number that is a perfect square." Bob adds, "Nine."

—— 9. "Good. Bob. Another one, Lynne?" "Sixteen."

—— 10. "O.K. Another one? Ralph?" "Twenty-four."

—— 11. "Let's check this one. First let's back up a step. A perfect square is some number that can be broken down into the product of another number times itself. What number did we say times itself equals nine?" "Three."

—— 12. "Good, Ralph. Let me continue to help you with this. What number times itself equals sixteen?" "Four."

—— 13. "Now, does any number times itself equal twenty-four?" "Hmmm. No, twenty-four isn't a perfect square."

—— 14. "O.K. Then can you name a perfect square from this list." "Twenty-five?"

—— 15. "That's the way!!"

Probing

At this point, you have identified the redirection and the prompting techniques. The former involves increased numbers of students, and the latter deals with incorrect responses. An additional situation arises when the student's reply is correct but insufficient because it lacks depth. In such a case, it is important for the teacher to have the student supply additional information in order to have better, more inclusive answers. This technique is called *probing*. Let's take a close look at this technique in action:

The teacher begins, "Do you think trees are important

to the land?" (pause) "Carmelina?"

"Yes."

"Why, Carmelina?"

"Because they help hold things together."

"What do you mean by that?"

"Well, the roots and all go down into the ground and help the ground stay in one place."

"That's very good, Carmelina, and as we learned yesterday, when the earth begins to move away to a different place, it's called *erosion.*"

It is important to note that no new ideas have been introduced. The purpose here is to get students to justify or further explain their responses thereby increasing the depth of the discussion. It also helps to move students away from surface responses. All too often, we don't take our students beyond the simple yes or no or correct answer response. We need to provide our students with increased opportunities to process information, to deal with the *why,* the *how,* and the *based upon what.* By doing so, the student not only gains experience in dealing with higher level tasks, but also experiences a greater feeling of success.

EXERCISE 3.7

Read the following anecdote and identify the teacher's questions that are redirections (r), prompts (pt), and probes (pb). Remember, not all questions will be one of these three types. After completing the exercise, check your answers with the ones found in the feedback section at the end of the chapter.

——— 1. "In front of each of you are two containers, each with a different substance. Look at the substances carefully and try to make some comparisons between them. What comparison would you make. Jim?"

"Well, they're both whitish colored."

——— 2. "O.K., good. Nancy?"

"They look sort of grainy. They both look sort of grainy."

——— 3. "Could you explain what you mean by *grainy*? "Well..."

——— 4. "Would you say they're chunky or powdery. Nancy?" "Chunky."

——— 5. "What do you call these chunks? Anyone?" Manny answers, "Crystals."

——— 6. "Good. They're both made of crystals. What else can we say about the two as a comparison? Tom."

Tom doesn't respond.

——— 7. "Tom, what could we do with the substances besides look at them?" "Well, we could rub them in our hands."

——— 8. "O.K., try that. Here." The teacher passes Tom the containers. "How do they feel?"

"This one is finer grained," Toms says as he holds one up.

——— 9. "Fine. How could you relate that to what we said about crystals?" "The crystals of this one are smaller."

——— 10. "O.K., good, Tom. Now. Jake, what else could we do with the substances to make comparisons?"

"I'm not sure."

——— 11. "Well, we've looked at them, and we've rubbed them in our hands to utilize the senses of touch and sight. What other senses could we use to extend our observations?"

Jake answers, "We could smell them."

——— 12. "O.K., try that." The teacher lets Jake smell the crystals. "What do you smell?" "I don't smell anything."

——— 13. "What do you suppose we should try next? Anyone?" "We could taste them." Murray replies.

——— 14. "Your idea is good, but remember I've said that for safety you should never put anything into your mouth until you're sure it's harmless. However, these are harmless sub stances, so, Jim, you taste this one, and Peter, you taste the other. How do they taste" Jim speaks first. "This one tastes like it would be isotonic with the body fluids." Peter follows quickly with, "This one tastes just the opposite."

——— 15. "Whoa! Could you clarify that statement Jim?" "O.K. It tastes like salt."

——— 16. "How about yours, Peter?" "It must be sugar."

——— 17. "O.K. What is the formula for salt, Jim?" Jim doesn't answer.

——— 18. "Let's try this, Jim. What is salt composed of?" "Sodium and chloride, I think."

——— 19. "That's right. What might the formula be then?" "NaCI?"

——— 20. "Right, good! Now, anyone, what is sugar composed of?" Murray says, "There's carbon in it."

——— 21. "Yes. What else? Nancy?" Nancy looks confused.

——— 22. "What is there a lot of in the atmosphere?" Nancy mumbles, "Oxygen?"

——— 23. "Right! Do you suppose there might be some oxygen in sugar, Nancy?" Hesitantly she says, "Yes."

——— 24. "You're right; there is. What else, Johnnie?" "Maybe hydrogen?"

——— 25. "Right. Now, would anyone guess at the formula for sugar?" A girl answers. "CHO?"

——— 26. "Good thought, Helene. It's consistent with what we said about salt. Suppose though that there are twice as many atoms of hydrogen as there are carbon or oxygen in sugar. What might the formula be then, Helene?" "CH_2O."

——— 27. "Right. That is an empirical formula for sugar. Now suppose that the molecular weight of sugar is 180. What would the formula be? Take a minute and figure it out." (pause) "Anyone?"

There is no response.

——— 28. "What is the weight of the empirical formula? Tom?"

"Hmmm ... 30?"

——— 29. "Right! Now what would the molecular formula be if CH_2O has a weight of 30 and the molecular weight is 180? Tom?"

Tom answers after a short pause, "$C_6H_{12}O_6$."

——— 30. "Good! How did you get that?"

"Well, 180 is 6 times greater than 30, so the formula should be 6 times CH_20."

——— 31. "Very good."

Summary

For review, let us simply mention the desirability of varying your questions. Good teaching involves the employment of different questioning techniques, levels, and directions.

First of all, try to redirect a question in order to involve as many students as possible. The point to remember here is to stay with the original question and "spread it around" the class. The prompting technique is very effective when students are unable to respond or a partial or incorrect response is offered. The major point here is to work with the student until he achieves some degree of success. Thirdly, use of the probe will increase the quality of your teacher-led discussions because the students will become accustomed to going beyond the surface.

The quality of your teaching will also be enhanced with the use of high level and divergent questions, both of which require increased amounts of data manipulation or intellectual processing on the part of the student. It is important to note, however, that low level and convergent types of questions play a critical role in facilitating certain learning objectives. We now want to see how these skills and techniques can be employed within overall teaching strategies.

EXERCISE FEED BACK

EXERCISE 3.8

---

1. (h) High. The teacher has asked an analysis level quesiton.
2. (h) High. This asks for clarification.
3. (h) High. This again involves clarification.
4. (h) High. This is a comprehensive question.
5. (I) Low. The teacher has probably led the students.

6. (I) Low. This is a memorisation recall task.
7. (I) Low. This is, once again, recall.
8. (I) Low. This, too, is recall.
9. (I) Low. This is a prompt leading to a right answer.
10. (h) High. Finding relationships is definitely not a recall situation.
11. (h) High. Again, making comparisons is not a recall situation.
12. (I) Low. This is a comparison of memorised definitions.
13. (I) Low. This, too, is a memorised comparison.
14. (h) High. Searching for similarities is not recall.
15. (h) High. Again, this is finding a relationship.
16. (I) Low. This is a recall task.

EXERCISE 3.9

1. (d) Divergent. There may be other things than likeness.
2. (d) Divergent. Self-expression would be, varied.
3. (d) Divergent. There is still a range of possibilities.
4. (d) Divergent. Examples would vary.
5. (c) Convergent. The teacher leads the students to only one conclusion.
6. (c) Convergent. The answer is a specific term.
7. (c) Convergent. This is a question with only one answer.
8. (c) Convergent. This is recall also.
9. (c) Convergent. The teacher is leading to a single answer.
10. (d) Divergent. There might be more than one relationship.
11. (d) Divergent. Again, there might be several relationships.
12. (c) Convergent. This is recall of definitions.
13. (c) Convergent. There is only one answer.
14. (d) Divergent. This is assuming there is more than one set. The question is convergent if there is only one.
15. (d) Divergent. There may be more than one possible relationship.
16. (c) Convergent. A single response is correct.

EXERCISE 3.10

1. (h/d) High level/Divergent.
2. (h/d) High level/Divergent.
3. (h/d) High level/Divergent.
4. (l/c) Low level/Convergent. There is only one correct list of major organs.
5. (h/d) High level/Divergent.
6. (l/c) Low level/Convergent.
7. (h/d) High level/Divergent.
8. (h/d) High level/Divergent.
9. (h/c) High level/Convergent.
10. (h/c) High level/Convergent.
11. (h/d) High level/Divergent.
12. (h/d) High level/Divergent.
13. (l/c) Low level/Convergent.
14. (h/d) High level/Divergent.
15. (h/c) High level/Convergent.

Note: that it is impossible to have a low level divergent question.

EXERCISE 3.11

1. No X.
2. X. After Bob had answered, "Ireland," the teacher posed the same question to Paul.
3. X. After Paul's response, the teacher once again posed the original question to Pam.
4. No X.
5. No X.
6. No X.
7. X. After Jim's response the teacher asked if anybody wanted to generate additional examples for the question posed.

8. No X.
9. No X.
10. No X.
11. No X.
12. No X.
13. No X
14. No X.

Note that in each case of redirection the teacher is getting more than one student to respond to a question. Once the teacher poses a new question, the redirection technique is no longer being used unless that new question is then redirected.

EXERCISE 3.12

---

1. No X.
2. No X. Redirection.
3. No X. Redirection.
4. No X.
5. X. After Jim could not respond, the teacher gave him a leading question for consideration.
6. X. In this same sequence, the teacher is urging Jim to think of other examples.
7. No X. Redirection.
8. No X
9. No X.
10. No X.
11. X. Although Nancy has already defined immigration, the teacher is beginning a sequence where she is given hints so she can use the two terms appropriately.
12. X. An unfinished question is considered prompting.
13. X. Nancy is prompted to define a term she may not already have known.
14. No X.

EXERCISE 3.13

1. Neither.
2. (r) Redirection.
3. (r) Redirection.
4. Neither.
5. (r) Redirection.
6. Neither.
7. (p) Prompt. The teacher is getting Bob to recall his times tables so that he can generate an appropriate answer.
8. Neither.
9. (r) Redirection.
10. (r) Redirection.
11. (p) Prompt. Statements 11 through 14 represent a prompt sequence. The teacher begins by providing additional information and helping the student to respond with appropriate examples.
12. (p) Prompt.
13. (p) Prompt.
14. (p) Prompt.
15. Neither.

EXERCISE 3.14

1. None.
2. (r) Redirection.
3. (pb) Probe.
4. (pt) Prompt.
5. None.
6. (r) Redirection.
7. (pt) Prompt.
8. (pt) Prompt.

9. (pt) Prompt.
10. (r) Redirection.
11. (pt) Prompt.
12. (pt) Prompt.
13. (r) Redirection.
14. None.
15. (pb) Probe.
16. (r) Redirection.
17. None.
18. (pt) Prompt.
19. (pt) Prompt.
20. None.
21. (r) Redirection.
22. (pt) Prompt.
23. (pt) Prompt.
24. (r) Redirection.
25. None.
26. (pt) Prompt.
27. None.
28. (pt) Prompt.
29. (pt) Prompt.
30. (pb) Probe.
31. None.

We are now to the implementation phase of the general teaching model where different strategies are used in helping students reach the objectives that teachers prepare in the planning phase of instruction. This chapter will incorporate the questioning skills described in preceding chapter and will show how the skills are directly applied within the strategies. The specific strategies discussed are *expository, discovery, discussion,* and *inquiry* techniques which are illustrated with examples from different disciplines. Similarities exist among the strategies, of course, and they aren't exclusive of each other. As a teacher you will probably incorporate features from more than one as you teach. This is desirable as you develop a personal style. However, we discuss them in separate and distinct presentations for the sake of clarity and the development of your initial understanding. As your thinking develops and your teaching evolves, you should make adjustments in the strategies to fit your personality, style, and students' needs.

Because expository and discovery are closely related in terms of goals, content, and procedures, we will initially present an overview of the two together in the first section before they are separately described in greater detail.

Objectives

Upon the completion of preceding chapter, you should be able to accomplish the following objectives:

1. For you as a pre/inservice teacher to understand the difference between expository and discovery teaching techniques so that, when provided with a description of a teaching episode, you will be able to identify it as discovery or expository and explain your choice.
2. For you as a pre/inservice teacher to understand the planning and implementing of expository lessons so that, when given a description of a teaching episode involving expository teaching, you will be able to identify all of the major steps.
3. For you as a pre/inservice teacher to understand the importance of examples in expository and discovery lessons so that, given a series of examples on different topics, you will write an analysis of their effectiveness for teaching the abstraction.

4. For you as a pre/inservice teacher to understand the planning and implementing of discovery lessons so that, when given a description of a discovery teaching episode, you will identify all of the steps.
5. For you as a pre/inservice teacher to understand the planning and implementing of inquiry lessons so that, when given a description of an inquiry teaching episode, you will identify all of the major steps.
6. For you as a pre/inservice teacher to understand the planning and implementing of discussions so when given a description of a discussion episode, you will identify the important features illustrated in it.

EXPOSITORY AND DISCOVERY TEACHING

An Overview

As an introduction to these two teaching strategies let's look at a math teacher working with her fifth-grade class.

Ms. Morton had been working with her class for the past few weeks on different geometric shapes. Today her lesson focused on circles. To begin the lesson, she gave the students rulers, string, and a handout containing a number of circles like the one shown in Figure 3.2.

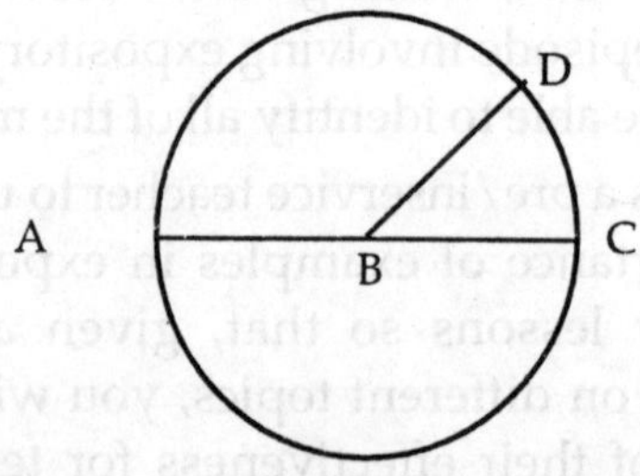

Fig. 3.2. Circles Handout

In addition to the handout containing the circles, she passed out a sheet that looked like Table 3.1.

TABLE 3.1

Chart Handout

Circle	*Radius*	*Diameter*	*Circumference*
A			
B			
C			
D			
E			
F			

She began her lesson by asking the class, "Who remembers what we call a line like BD? Susie?"

"I think it's called a radius."

"Good Susie. And who remembers how we defined the term *radius?*

Kevin?"

"It's the distance from the center of the circle to the outside."

"O.K., and now who can tell me what line ABC is called? Juan?"

"It's called the *diameter,* and that's a line from one end of a circle to the other that passes through the center of the circle."

"And what about the third column on your second handout? What does the word *circumference* mean, Jody?"

"Well, it's the distance around a circle."

"And how could we measure that? Could we use a ruler? Sarah?"

"We could, but it wouldn't be right because of all the curves. Instead we could put string around the outside and measure the string afterward with a ruler."

"Excellent, you remembered how we did that with other geometric shapes. Well, today we're going to see if we can find out some things about circles. To do this, I want you to measure the circles on the handout that I've given you and put these measurements in the chart. When you're finished, we'll talk about what you've done."

With that, the class went to work measuring the circles that Ms. Morton had handed out. When the teacher noticed that most of the class had completed the assignment, she drew the chart from the handout (shown in Figure 3.2) on the board and asked the students to tell her what measurements they had gotten. As the class did this, they realised that different people got different answers, which provided an opportunity to talk about the idea of measurement error. In discussing this concept, the class decided that one way of handling the problem would be to average measurements, which they did.

Once the chart on the board was completed (see Table 3.2), Ms. Morton continued the lesson by saying, "What do you notice about the numbers in the radius column and the numbers in the diameter column? Brad?"

"They're twice as big, almost. Well, usually the diameter is twice as big as the radius."

"And why do you think that is, Mary?"

"Because the diameter is like two radiuses put together."

"Fine. And now let's look at the diameter and the

circumference columns. What do you notice about these? Jamie?"

"When the diameter gets bigger, so does the circumference."

"O.K., anything else? No one? Well, let's see if we can figure out how the two change. Let's have this half of the class divide the circumferences of circles *A*, *C*, and *E* by their diameters while the other half of the class does the same for B, *D*, and F."

TABLE 3.2

Completed Chart

Circle	*Radius*	*Diameter*	*Circumference*
A	1	2	6.3
B	1.9	4	12.5
C	2.95	6	18.9
D	4.1	.8.1	24.9
E	5	10.1	32.5
F	6	11.8	38.0

TABLE 3.3

Chart with *CID* Added

Circle	*Radius*	*Diameter*	*Circumference*	*C/D*
A	1	2	6.3	3.15
B	1.9	4	12.5	3.120
C	2.95	6	18.9	3.15
D	4.1	8.1	24.9	3.07
E	5	10.1	32.5	3.25
F	6	11.8	38.0	3.22

When the class had done this, Ms. Morton added a new column with their results so the chart looked like Table 3.3.

> "What do you notice about the numbers in the column labeled C/D? Mary?"
>
> "They're all just over three."
>
> "Good. The reason all the numbers in this column vary is that our measurements weren't exact. If they were, the numbers in this column would all come out to be 3.14. This number is called pi and the symbol for it is π." She wrote the word and drew the symbol on the board. "Now, who can tell me a formula that we could use to find the circumference if we , know the diameter? Anyone?"
>
> "Oh, I know," responded Jill "Multiply the diameter times 3.14, and that will give you the circumference."
>
> "Hmm, does everyone agree? Let's try that idea and see if it works."
>
> With that, she drew a circle on the board using chalk and string. She measured the diameter for the class and gave this to them to work with. While they were multiplying, she had two members of the class come up to measure the circumference for comparison. After the class discussed the results of this problem, she passed out another worksheet which contained additional circles, and the class measured these to see if they too follow the πd equation.

Let's pause for a moment now to consider the preceding example. This anecdote was an example of a teacher using a discovery approach to teach abstractions, in this case, the formula $C = \pi d$. We call lessons like this *discovery* because students are provided with data and, through probing by the teacher, are helped to discover the particular abstraction described in the goals objective. An excellent discussion of the logic behind discovery lessons can be found in the article by Strike (1975).

Expository lessons are more teacher-centered than discovery lessons in that the teacher is the major provider of information, relating the examples to the abstraction being taught. The abstraction is stated by the teacher *before* examples are given, and then the examples are provided to help illustrate the abstraction. To show what we mean by expository teaching, read the following anecdote which describes a teacher using this method to teach the same content taught in the previous anecdote.

Mr. Hite wanted to teach his class the formula for computing the circumference of a circle. He began his lesson by saying, "Today we're going to learn the formula for computing the circumference of a circle. When we are done with the lesson you will be able to figure out the circumference when given the diameter. Now who remembers what the circumference is? Jan?"

> "It's the distance around a circle."
>
> "Good, and who remembers what the diameter is? Maria?"
>
> "It's a line from one end of the circle to the other that goes through the center."
>
> "Good. The formula that we're going to learn today is the circumference equals the diameter times pi."
>
> With this, he wrote the equation on the board and drew a circle. "Who knows what pi is? Anyone? Cal?"
>
> "It's a number that we use when we work with circles. I think it's about 3 or something like that."

"That's pretty close, Cal; it's actually 3.14. What if I told you that the diameter of this circle is 9 inches? What would the circumference be? Anyone?"

The class then computed the circumference and checked the results by measuring the circumference with a string and yardstick. Mr. Hite then gave the students a handout containing a number of circles, and the class measured the diameters of each and computed the circumferences. They checked their answers by measuring the circumferences of the circles with string and rulers.

These two anecdotes were presented as examples of two of the three teaching strategies that are discussed in this chapter. The first anecdote involved a teacher using a discovery method of teaching while the second involved an expository mode of teaching. The major differences between these two different teaching strategies are summarised in Table 3.4.

In expository teaching, the abstraction is stated first followed by examples to illustrate the abstraction. With the discovery strategy, the examples are presented first, and these provide the data that students use to form the abstraction. The teacher states and clarifies the abstraction at the beginning of the lesson in expository teaching, while in a discovery lesson, the students are responsible for defining and clarifying the abstraction.

TABLE 3.4

Comparison of Expository and Discovery Strategies

	Who States Abstraction	*Sequence*
Expository	Teacher	1. Abstraction 2. Examples
Discovery	Student	1. Examples 2. Abstractions

EXERCISE 3.15

Read the following teaching anecdoets and determine whether they involve expository (e) or discovery (d) teaching. Compare your answers with the ones given in the feedback section at the end of the chapter.

1. Mr. Hames was teaching a lesson on geometry. He began the lesson by passing out protractors and a sheet with a number of triangles on it. Then he said, "Today we're going to study some properties of triangles. Now, I'd like you to measure the angles of the triangles I've given you." After doing this, the class concluded that the sum of the interior angles of a triangle was equal to 180 degrees.

2. Mr. Jones, a language arts teacher, was trying to get his class to understand how rules govern the pronunciation of our language. He did this by putting the following words on the board.

cold	colt	cut	celebrate
can't	carry	cell	city
could	cud	celery	civil

   After a discussion, the class decided that when a *c* at the beginning of a word was followed by an *e* or an *i*, the *c* was pronounced like an *s*, but when it was followed by an *a*, an *o*, or a *u*, the *c* was pronounced like a *k*.

3. Mrs. Smith was teaching a lesson on the concept of set. She began the lesson by gathering her kindergarteners around on the rug and placing three clothespins in a yarn circle on the floor. Then she said, "This is a set. It's a group of objects that belong together." Then she put other objects in the yarn circle and described how they were also examples of set. At the end of the lesson, the students in the class were asked to make up their own set.

4. Miss Kirk was trying to teach her reading class to recognise inferences in written materials. She did this by going through a story and identifying a number of statements in it. Then she asked what all these had in common. After the class decided that inferences were ideas in the story that weren't actually stated, Miss Kirk gave them another story to read finding inferences.

A Comparison

Expository teaching is probity the most commonly used and abused teaching method used in the schools today. Ausubel (1968), is one of the strongest proponents of expository teaching, and you may wish to read his writings. The reasons expository teaching is widely used away from custom to convenience to efficiency. Typically, the role of the teacher in American schools has been one of information given. Teachers are thought to be persons who have knowledge and whose job it is to pass this knowledge directly on to students. No doubt this view of teaching is heavily reinforced when preservice teachers see college professors using this technique. In addition, the expository method is often thought to be the easiest type of teaching, with students believing that constructing and giving a lecture easier than using other types of more discovery- or inquiry-oriented activities. If expository teaching is equated with lecturing, this may well be the case, but expository teaching as we are defining it involves much more than just talking, as will become evident in the paragraphs that follow.

Another reason for the popularity of expository teaching is that it has the potential for being a very efficient means of teaching facts and abstractions. When the teacher defines an abstraction, he can be sure that the definition that the students learn is an accurate one, something that doesn't always happen in other forms of teaching. In addition, because the definition is provided from the beginning, the chance that students will develop misconceptions is minimised. Expository teaching is also very efficient in terms of time. Generally, it takes less time than discovery or inquiry teaching because the lesson focuses directly on the abstraction, and the students tend not to diverge to any significant extent.

Despite these advantages, expository teaching has probably suffered from more abuse than any other form. Teachers often mistakenly view it as being synonymous with lecturing, therefore presenting their lessons as monologues, often with devastating effects. When used properly, expository teaching should consist of an ongoing dialogue with students in which students are required to answer questions, relate points, and link pieces of information or data. An excellent discussion of these points can be found in Hyman (1974).

Given the fact that expository teaching is a proven, effective way of teaching content, one might ask why there is a need for alternative strategies. One answer to this question can be found in research done by Furst and Rosenshine (1971), who analysed characteristics of superior teachers. One of the characteristics they found in these teachers was that they tended to use a greater variety of teaching methods. The exact reason a greater variety of teaching techniques correlated with increased effectiveness is not known, but one reason may be increased motivation and attention. Students, like people in general, become bored with the same procedures used time after time. Further, different people learn in different ways, so when a teacher employs various techniques he will often increase the number of matches between teaching and learning styles.

Probably the single biggest advantage discovery teaching has over an expository procedure is that discovery teaching is inherently inclined to promote student involvement because it is strongly student-*centered*. Notice that we said student-*centered*. It is similar to expository teaching because it is strongly teacher-*directed*. Keep in mind that we are not defining discovery in a "pure" sense where the students, essentially on their own, "discover" concepts and relationships among concepts. Pure discovery is both student-*directed* and student-*centered*, and is a very desirable ideal. While we applaud any teacher's efforts to implement it effectively, we will retain the teacher-led features in our presentation of discovery as a strategy.

Because of its student-centeredness, discovery also has the advantage of being more motivational for the students. The opportunity for students to be involved without having to always provide the desired answer can be very motivating, particularly for those who aren't typically successful (Berlyne, 1960, 1965).

A third reason for the inclusion of discovery activities in the curriculum is that they give students opportunities to practice the processes of analysing data and forming abstractions from these data. One of the major goals of schools is to give students the intellectual tools to form their own abstractions later in life. School then becomes a preparation for life, and part of this preparation is training students how to form their own abstractions. The best way that we know of doing this is to provide them with data and give them the opportunity to practice forming abstractions.

The single biggest problem with discovery teaching is that because teachers don't typically use it and have had little exposure with discovery in their own learning experiences, they are initially uncomfortable with the strategy. As with questioning skills, discovery teaching takes practice and perseyerance but the results are worth the effort. A teacher with a variety of techniques at her disposal will be more effective than one capable of teaching only in one way.

In summary, expository teaching probably is more efficient in terms of time while discovery is more motivational and encourages greater development of thinking skills. Our position is that teachers should use both techniques, selecting the one most appropriate at a particular time and with particular content.

This completes our introductory discussion of expository and discovery teaching. Let's look now at a detailed description of the planning and implementing phases of each approach.

Expository Teaching

Planning. There are three essential steps involved in the planning process. (This assumes that philosophical factors such as the role of the school, the teachers' function, and student needs have already been considered. They are, of course, very important but a discussion of such philosophical issues is beyond the scope of this text.) The first step in planning is knowing exactly what you want the students to understand or be able to do. In other words, you identify a goal. You will know if the students have reached the goal by using a goals objective. This process marks the beginning of the planning sequence. For example, Mr. Hite's objective could have been stated as follows:

> For fifth grade students to understand the formula for computing circumference so that, given a ruler and four circles with the radius drawn in, they will calculate the circumferences of each without error.

The second step in the planning process is to identify the form of the content you want to teach. This determination is important because facts and abstractions are learned differently and should therefore be taught differently. Facts are memorised, so the students learn them by observation, reading, or listening to their teacher. For all practical purposes, there is little teaching strategy involved when facts are taught. The teacher employs certain procedures, such as drill and repetition in short, frequent episodes together with reinforcement for learning the fact or facts. Further, the teacher must be certain that the terms within the fact are familiar. For example, the fact "The Titanic struck an iceberg" would have no meaning for the students if they didn't know that the Titanic was a ship, or that an iceberg is a large mass of ice floating in the ocean. Finally, the memorising process can be aided by using devices such as mnemonics. A familiar example of a mnemonic device is "Thirty days hath September, April, June and November." Beyond these considerations, there is no strategy *per se* involved in teaching facts or planning for their teaching. We will discuss fact learning further in the next section.

Planning for teaching abstractions is quite different. If the content being taught is in the form of a concept or generalisation, examples need to be provided for the learner. Concepts and generalisations were discussed in detail in Chapter 2 and you may wish to review that chapter at this time.

The third step in the planning phase involves the selection or preparation of examples. The selection is quite simple conceptually but in practice can be difficult to accomplish. The simple part is recognising the traits of a good example. A good example will include the important characteristics, if you are teaching a concept, or include a relationship, if you are teaching a generalisation. *Include* means the learner can *see* the characteristics or the relationship in the example. The hard part involves finding examples that accomplish this task. For some unsophisticated concepts, the task is simple. For instance, the concept quadrilateral has the *characteristics four-sided, plane,* and *straight lines.* Examples abound.

Each of the above is composed of straight line segments, each is a plane figure and each is four-sided. These examples are simple to prepare.

On the other hand, finding examples for a concept such as *communism* can be quite difficult. In fact, this concept is rarely illustrated with examples. Instead, it is often only defined and how well students learn the concept depends upon the quality of the definition. As Klausmeier (1976) has stated, the problem with using only a definition is that a student may memorize the definition without understanding the concept. Feldman (1980) in a study involving sixth-graders and Tennyson (1978) in a study of college students found that using a combination of examples and non-examples together with a definition resulted in greater learning than using a definition only or examples only. Furthermore, Frayer (1970) found that students learned as much from four well-chosen examples as they did from eight examples.

In selecting these examples to teach concepts, the essential characteristics can be used as a checklist to compare the adequacy of the examples in conveying a complete and accurate concept. For example, suppose you were teaching the concept *adverb* and had determined that the key characteristics of the concept were that it was a word that modified a verb, an adjective, or another adverb. Examine the following list of positive examples to determine their adequacy:

1. The boy ran quickly across the lawn.
2. The boulder thundered loudly down the mountain.
3. She didn't know the answer to the vaguely phrased question.
4. The shark tugged relentlessly at the thin line.

As can be seen in these examples, there is no positive example showing an adverb modifying another adverb. Consequently the concept that students will form from this lesson will be inaccurate and incomplete. By checking examples such as these against a list of essential characteristics, a teacher can avoid potential pitfalls.

An additional aid in selecting examples is to analyze the concept in terms of coordinate and subordinate concepts. (Markle & Tiemom, 1970) The subordinate concepts can be used to generate positive examples, while the coordinate ones can provide negative examples which possibly could be confused with the positive ones. Presenting these as negative examples helps students to understand the difference between these closely connected ideas. Negative examples generated in this manner are much more helpful to the student than other types of negative examples. For example, if a teacher were trying to teach her class the concept of *reptile,* negative examples of amphibians, mammals, and birds would be much more helpful to the learner than negative examples like car, tree, ball, or boat. These latter examples are so far removed from the concept that they contain few characteristics in common with the concept and consequently provide little valuable information about what the concept is not.

In planning for the teaching of a generalisation, the teacher must also be sure that the examples used accurately illustrate the generalisation. This is a slightly more complex process because the examples must illustrate the *interaction* between concepts in the generalisation. For example, if you were a psychology teacher trying to teach the generalisation the amount of time between a behavior and its reinforcement is inversely related to the speed with which that behavior is learned, you would need to provide examples in which behavior was being reinforced with different time lapses and different related results. This could be done with either written anecdotes or live or videotaped examples.

In summary, the planning process, when teaching abstractions, amounts to identifying a goals objective and carefully selecting a few examples. It is a very reasonable task but it also requires thought and insight.

In Mr. Hite's lesson, the examples were developed as the students calculated the circumference and compared their results with a string and yardstick. The use of string and rulers was important in this case because it helped make concrete a relationship that would be quite abstract based on the calculation alone. Mr. Hite demonstrated very effective planning for the lesson.

EXERCISE 3.16

Answer the following questions involving the selection of examples. Then compare your respose to the ones found in the feedback section at the end of the chapter.

1. **A health instructor was trying to get her students to understand the generalisation that their strenuous the exercise, the more calories are used. To illustrate the generalisation, she select number of pictures of people playing sports of differing degrees of strenuousness. Analyze quality of her examples.**
2. **An English teacher was trying to teach that a verb is a word that denotes action or a state of being. To illustrate the concept, he selected the following sentences:**

____

____

A dog came along and chased the cat up the tree

The man hit the car when it wouldn't start.

The ship caught the breeze and wheeled to port.

She hadn't had a decent meal in ages.

Analyze the quality of the examples.

____

____

____

3. A teacher was trying to teach her class the concept *fruit*. What do the following two sequences suggest about the goals of the lesson or the ability level of students?

Sequence A	*Sequence B*
apple	tomato
cherry	avocado
orange	mango
mango	orange
avocado	cherry
tomato	apple

____

____

____

Implementing. The implementing of expositor lessons is a very logical process. The first step amounts to presenting to the students the abstraction identified in the objective. Mr. Hite did this when he said, "Today we're going to learn that circumference is diameter times pi." (Actually Mr. Hite clarified the terms first, which is normally the second step in implementing the lesson.) Presenting the abstraction to be learned on the board or the overhead provides a focus for the lesson and assures the students of the direction the lesson is to take. In this sense, then, the definition acts as an advanced organiser, Unking the new information to information in the learner's background and alerting students to the direction that the lesson will take (Ausubel, 1968; Ausubel & Robinson, 1969; Barnes & Clawson, 1975).

The next step in implementing an expository lesson depends upon the objectives of the lesson. If they involve learning factual relationships, then the primary role for the teacher is to make these facts meaningful and, therefore, resistant to forgetting. Both of these can be facilitated by making sure that the facts are embedded in some meaningful organisational structure. In addition, the key terms in the fact should be examined to make sure they are clear to the students.This helps not only initial learning but also retention (Underwood & Schulz, 1960; Shimmerlik, 1978). If at all possible, this examination should be done in an interactive manner, as is illustrated in the following dialogue involving a social studies lesson.

> "O.K., today we are going to talk about the Declaration of Independence. Who knows what the word *declaration* means? Kathy?"
>
> "Oh, it means kind of like to tell something, like a declarative sentence."
>
> "O.K., and what were we telling people. Jerry?"
>
> "We were telling people that we wanted to be independent or free."
>
> "And who were we primarily interested in telling this? Sue?"
>
> "England."
>
> "Good, what date did we do this? Mary?"
>
> "July 4, that's why it's called Independence Day."

> "And why did we want to be independent? How does this relate to what we talked about yesterday in terms of the taxes?"

A lesson like this, in which students are helped to see not only the meaning of a fact but also its significance in terms of a larger context, is quite different from one in which facts are mentioned in a lecture, to be memorised and repeated on a test.

When teaching concepts in an expository manner, the teacher must follow a number of sequential steps based upon the characteristics of the concepts. These steps are derived from suggestions by Clark (1971) and Klausmeier, Ghatala, & Prayer (1974). After defining the concept, the second step is to clarify the terms in the definition and relate the concept to a meaningful superordinate concept. This can be done by asking students to define the terms in their own words or by asking students to cite examples of the terms. The third and perhaps most critical step is to present positive examples that are linked to the definition. Negative examples should also be provided to help students understand what the concept is not. In presenting these examples, the teacher should try to get the students to relate these to the essential characteristics listed in the definition. This insures that the characteristics are meaningful to students and that they are linked to the examples in the students' minds.

After the teacher feels that the students understand the concept, he can provide additional examples for students to classify as either positive or negative. In doing this, he should encourage the students to explain the classification in terms of the characteristics listed. Having students classify examples and defend their answers serves several functions. It provides reinforcement for the concept being formed by the students. It encourages active participation by the students. It also provides an opportunity for both the teacher and the students to gauge how well they understand the concept. If their responses indicate that they do, then the teacher can ask the students for their own examples of the concept; if not, the teacher can provide additional examples to classify before calling for student-generated examples.

These steps are all summarised in Table 3.5 and are illustrated with an anecdote involving an elementary teacher teaching a lesson in language arts.

TABLE 3.5

Steps in the Expository Teaching of Concepts

Teacher:	1.	Define concept and clarify terms.
	2.	Link to superordinate concepts.
	3.	Present positive and negative examples.
Students:	4.	Classify and explain additional teacher examples as either positive or negative.
	5.	Provide additional examples.

> "The last few days we've been talking about different kinds of sentences. Yesterday we talked about interrogative sentences, and the day before, we talked about declarative sentences. Today we're going to talk about imperative sentences. When we're all through you should be able to pick out the imperative sentences from a list of mixed sentences."

Then she drew the following on the board:

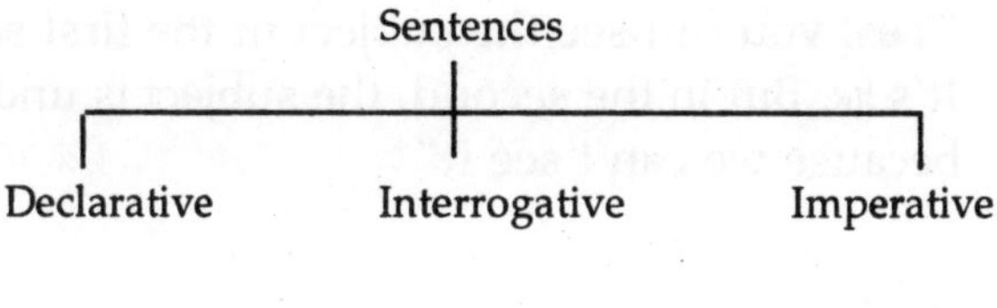

She continued, "Imperative sentences are a special kind of sentence that gives a command or an order, like these." She wrote the following on the board:

Don't do that!

Please pick up your clothes.

"Often the subject of the sentence, *you*, is understood. In the first example, the word *you* isn't in the sentence, but we understand that it means, 'Don't you do that.' You can see in both of these examples that someone is telling somebody else to do something. Also, almost always the verb in imperative sentences is in the present tense. Sometimes imperative sentences have exclamation marks in them to show that someone really wants something done. An example of this would be, 'Stop, or I'll shoot!' You would put an exclamation point at the end. Also, the verb is in the present tense, and *you is* understood."

Then she wrote the following on the board:

He didn't want to go.

Go or else I'll call the police!

"Now look at these two sentences and tell me if they are imperative sentences. Jenny?"

"I think the second one is, but the first one isn't because the second one gives a command, and the first doesn't."

"Also," added Tom, "the second one is in the present tense, and the first isn't."

"Anything else? Fran?"

"Yes, you can see the subject in the first sentence. It's *he*. But in the second, the subject is understood because we can't see it"

"Excellent."

She wrote one more sentence on the board.

Don't tell me any more lies!

"How about this sentence? Is it an example of an imperative sentence? Cal?"

"Yes, because it gives a command. Also, the subject is understood, and there's an exclamation point at the end."

"Good, now who can give me some additional examples of imperative sentences?"

•

Note how in this example the teacher follows all of the steps listed in Table 3.5 Note, too, that the teacher made her objective clear at the beginning of the and told students what they should be able to do when the lesson ended. In addition, she made the content organisation clear by illustrating the relation-between this new concept and the old ones with a diagram. All of these help to make the logic of the lesson more apparent to students, which should result in better initial learning and better retention.

Because generalisations are so similar to concepts in that they are both abstractions, the steps to follow in teaching them are quite similar to those involved in teaching concepts. The only added dimension involves making sure that the concepts contained in the generalisation are understood by students. This should be done at the beginning of the lesson as the generalisation is being presented. All of the steps involved in teaching an abstraction in the form of a generalisation are shown in Table 6 and illustrated in the following anecdote involving an elementary science lesson.

TABLE 3.6

Steps in the Expository Teaching of Generalisations

Teacher:	1.	State generalisation.
	2.	Clarify concepts within generalisation.
	3.	Present positive and negative examples.
Students.	4.	Classify and explain additional teacher examples as either positive or negative.
	5.	Provide additional examples.

Mrs. Swenson's class had been studying about sounds and how they are made. In this lesson, she wants her class to understand factors which influence the pitch of a sound. She prepared for the lesson by gathering together a number of sound-making objects like a bamboo flute, a guitar, and some rubberband instruments.

She began her lesson by saying, "We've been talking about how sound comes from vibrations. Now we're going to learn how to make different kinds of sounds that are high and low. Today we're going to learn that the longer the vibrating column, the lower the pitch; the shorter the vibrating column, the higher the pitch." She wrote this on the board and continued. "When we're through, you should be able to tell me how pitch is affected by the length of the vibrating column and show me how this works with an instrument. Who knows what pitch is? (pause) No one? It's how high or low something sounds."

She then illustrated the concept of pitch with a pitch pipe, having her students listen to different sounds and identifying these as being high or low in pitch. Once she felt that the students understood this concept, she continued.

"Look at this pitch pipe closely." She showed how it had different holes in it. "These are the openings for the different vibrating columns. The noise is made here and vibrates through these columns. That's what makes different kinds of pitch."

She then took the bamboo flute and showed the class how the different holes affected the length of the vibrating column. As her next illustration of the generalisation, she went to the piano and played the same key hard and softly, as well as fast and slowly, and asked the class if the pitch had changed. When they said no, she proceeded to lift up the top of the piano for the class to see. She explained how the hammer hitting the strings caused the sound and explained how strings could also form a vibrating column. Then she asked them to predict which of the strings would make high and low sounds.

As a test to determine whether the class understood the generalisation, she brought out a guitar and plucked the strings several times. Then she asked the class what would happen if she held down the strings part of the way down the neck. Some of the class could answer the question while others couldn't, so she thought another example might be helpful. She brought out empty soda bottles and had two students in the class blow into them to make sounds. After determining that the class understood what the vibrating column was, she asked them what would happen to the pitch if they put water in the bottles.

Let's pause a second and analyze this lesson in terms of the steps suggested in Table 3.6. The teacher began the lesson by stating the generalisatior and ascertaining that the students understood the concepts of *pitch* and *vibrating column*. She then proceeded to illustrate the generalisation with a number of positive examples and a negative one. The negative example in this case was hitting the same piano key in different ways so that the students could see that this was unrelated to pitch. (In teaching abstractions, positive examples are more useful than negative examples in helping students learn the abstraction, but negative examples still help them clarify what the abstraction doesn't include [Bruner, Goodnow, & Austin, 1956; Bourne, Ekstrand, & Dominawksi, 1971]. As a modification, some generalisations may be taught without negative examples.) The teacher followed the presentation of positive and negative examples with examples in which the student had to make predictions, which essentially involved classifying examples. The lesson ended, however, before the students had an opportunity to suggest additional examples of their own.

This concludes our discussion of expository teaching strategies. The next section discusses discovery teaching strategies.

EXERCISE 3.17

Read the anecdote below and then answer the questions which follow. Then compare your answer to the ones given in the feedback section at the end of the chapter.

> Mr. Hanes wanted to teach his English class about figures of speech so that they would be able to understand and appreciate literature better. He began his lesson by saying. "For last week we've been studying about different figures of speech. Who remembers what ensures of speech are? Kristin?"
>
> "They're devices in literature to make the writing more interesting."
>
> "O.K., and who remembers some of these that we've discussed?

Larry?"

"Simile and metaphor?"

"That's correct, and, Larry, do you remember the difference between the two?"

"Similes compare two things using *like* or *as*, and metaphors compare things but do use these terms."

"Fine. Well today we're going to learn about a third figure of speech called hyperbole. A hyperbole is a figure of speech which uses vivid, nonliteral exaggeration." With that he wrote the definition on the board and drew the following diagram.

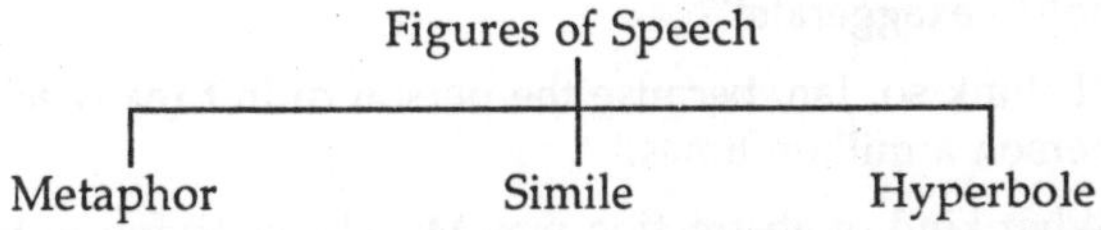

"When we're through with this lesson you should be able to tell the difference between hyperboles and other figures of speech. Now you all know what figures of speech are but you may not know what *nonliteral* means. Let me give you an example to help you."

He then placed the following sentence on an overhead:

I had a ton of homework to do last night.

"This would be an example of a hyperbole because the boy didn't really have a ton of homework to do. That's what we mean by nonliteral. It isn't actually or literally true. Let me give you another example. He added this sentence to the overhead:

When we broke up, I cried for weeks.

"This is another example of a hyperbole because it's an exaggeration that isn't literally true. The person didn't really cry for weeks, but the hyperbole is a colorful way of communicating how broken-hearted the person was. Let's try another one." He wrote on the overhead.

I could talk with her forever.

"This is another hyperbole. Can someone tell me why? Sandy?"

"Because it's a nonliteral exaggeration. The person couldn't really talk with her forever; he just said that for effect."

"Fine, now here's a sentence that isn't a hyperbole." He wrote.

Bill and Jim are going to see Mary.

"Can someone tell me why? Jake?"

"Oh that's easy—because the words mean exactly what they say."

"Good. Now it's your turn. Can anyone give me an example of a hyperbole? Jack?"

"Hmmm. How about, 'I was so embarrassed I felt like dying'?"

"What do the rest of you think? Is that a hyperbole, Jan?"

"I think so because the person didn't really want to die but just said that to make an effect. And I think I've got one too. Is this a hyperbole? 'If I've told you once, I've told you a million times not to exaggerate!'"

"I think so, Jan, because the person didn't really tell the other person a million times.'

1. What kind of abstraction was Mr. Hanes trying to teach?

   ____

2. How did he organize his content?

   ____

   ____

3. Mr. Hanes made one mistake in his lesson. What was it?

   ____

   ____

Discovery Teaching

Planning. Many teachers have the misconception that discovery lessons don't require planning and that the teacher only needs to turn his students loose to "discover" things about the world. While it is true that children are capable of discovering abstractions about the world on their own, this individual discovery process is often hit and miss and does not ensure that a student will learn a particular abstraction at a given time. A far more effective way of ensuring that students will learn a given abstraction is to make explicit plans for this to occur

A comparison of expository and discovery teaching

reveals that the planing phases for each are nearly identical. As with expository teaching, discovery strategies also begin with the preparation of an objective. Ms. Morton's objective could have been identical to Mr. Hite's. A consideration of background is also critical. Considering adjectives again, you can see that a student could not view the sentence, "He was a tall boy," and observe any relationship between *tall* and boy unless he had some idea of the terms *modification* or *description*. Having this background would allow the student, when prompted, to say, "*Tall* describes *boy*," or, "*Tall* modifies *boy*." The selection of examples is all the more important in discovery lessons because the students must rely solely on the data to form the abstraction being taught. In expository lessons, the teacher can perhaps make some allowances for the lack of adequate examples by explaining the abstraction more thoroughly (though the dangers of this have already been discussed). This option is not as available in discovery lessons since the students are totally de-pendent upon the examples provided by the teacher. If these are inadequate the abstraction being formed will be incomplete or inaccurate.

The first question to be asked in planning for a discovery lesson is what illustrations can I provide to help students attain the abstraction being taught? In the case of concepts, this amounts to selecting good examples, ones that have thè characteristics of the concept in them. For instance, a picture of a cow is much better than the word *cow* for teaching the concept *mammal* because the characteristics of the concept are much more observable in the pictures. The same criteria for selecting examples for expository lessons apply to selecting examples for discovery lessons.

The next step in the planning process is to order the examples you will use son. Placing obvious examples of an abstraction first will lead to quicker attainment of the abstraction while placing less obvious examples first will give students more practice in analysing data and forming hypotheses. The sequence examples can also be varied to match the difficulty level of the task with the of the students. A more difficult sequence might be used to challenge brighter students while an easier one might be used to help less academically talented students learn concepts with a minimum of difficulty and frustration.

One final consideration in planning for discovery lessons should be mentioned. Because the students don't have a definition or the generalisation written down to focus upon, their initial responses will tend to be more divergent than those in expository lessons. Therefore, the lesson may take longer than an expository lesson covering the same material. The extra time is probably well spent in terms of motivation and the possibilities for incidental learning, but time, nevertheless, is a factor the teacher should consider in planning discovery activities.

As a postscript to the planning phase, a comment needs to be made about facts. As we noted earlier, facts are either observed, heard, or read. As such, there is no discovery method for acquiring them (unless you call observing facts "discovering" them), so we will focus our discussion of the discovery method on abstraction.

Implementing. While the planning phase for expository and discovery lessons is virtually the same, the implementation phase is markedly different. In an expository lesson, *the abstraction is defined or described for the student while in discovery teaching it is not.* This doesn't mean, of course, that the teacher is less concerned with the students' acquiring the abstraction. It merely means they are to acquire it themselves using the teacher's guidance. The teacher facilitates this process by providing data for the students to analyze and by asking questions which encourage the students to move beyond the information provided to discover the abstraction contained therein. The specific steps involved in teaching a discovery lesson are listed in Table 3.7 and illustrated in the following anecdote. As you read, see if you can identify the steps as they're being taught.

TABLE 3.7

Steps in Discovery Teaching

Teacher:	1.	Present example.
Students:	2.	Describe example.
Teacher:	3.	Present additional examples.
Students:	4.	Describe second example and compare to first example.
Teacher:	5	Present additional examples and non-examples.
Students:	6.	Compare and contrast examples.
Teacher:	7.	Prompt students to identify characteristics or relationship.
Students:	8.	State definition or relationship.
Teacher:	9.	Ask for additional examples.

Miss Cane wanted to teach her students a generalisation about pronouncing words. To do this, she put the following words on the board:

beat   boat
meet   main
beak

She then said, "Class, look at the words on the board and tell me what you see. Henry?"

"They all have four letters."

"Good, anything else? Pam?"

"Some are verbs, and some are nouns, and some are adjectives, like *main*."

"They could all be nouns," interjected Jerry, "because *main* could be a noun like *water main,* and *meet* could be a noun like *track meet.*"

"Anything else? How about you, Jimmy?"

(Silence)

"Say the word b-e-a-t, Jimmy."

"Beat."

"And what did you notice about the sound, Jimmy?"

(Jimmy shrugs, indicating he doesn't know.)

"Say it to yourself again and tell me which letters you hear."

"The *b,* and *e,* and the *t.*"

"Excellent, Jimmy. And was the sound of *e* long or short, Pam?"

"Long."

"And what other letter is in the word, Bill?"

"a."

"What do you notice about the *a,* Stephanie?'"

"You don't hear it at all."

"Good, so we say it's ..." (Tentatively) "Silent".

"Yes! Super, everyone. Now look at the other words and compare them to *beat.* Mike?"

"They all have two vowels."

"And what about the sound of the vowels, Judy?"

"The first one is long in each case."

"Can anyone describe the pattern we see in all these words? Missy, you have your hand up."

"If you have two vowels together, the first one is long."

"What about the second vowel?"

"Oh, yeah, you don't say it."

"That's correct; it is silent. How about the rest of you? Does what Missy says agree with the words that we have on the board? Do all of you agree? Listen again, and I'll say it, 'When two vowels go together, the first is long and the second is silent.' Is that an accurate generalisation, Anne?" Anne nods. "Tell me why, using a word on the board."

"Well, *boat*. It has a long *o* and a silent a."

"Can you do the same with the last word on the list, Jason?"

"Yes, in that word the *a* is long and the i is silent."

"Excellent, now I'm going to give you some more words to see if they follow the rule." She wrote the following on the board:

pain
late
meat
man

"Some do, like *pain*, because the *a* is long and the *i* is silent," Janet said.

"Also *meat*, because the *e* is long and the *a* is silent," added Jess.

"Any others? Well then maybe our rule is correct. Let me write it on the board while you see if you can think of any other words that follow the rule."

Lets' stop now and analyze Miss Cane's lesson. First, look again at the steps outlined in Table 3.7. Second, consider the questioning skills discussed in Chapter 6. Miss Cane displayed four examples of the generalisation she was trying to teach. By doing so she actually departed slightly from the procedure as described but sometimes alternate procedures are equally effective. All the strategies discussed in this chapter are designed to be flexible and allow for teacher judgment and preference. Miss Cane exercised her judgment in deciding to display all the examples at once.

Miss Cane displayed an excellent command of questioning skills. She began by asking the students to describe the examples: a form of divergent question. She redirected the question to several students to promote involvement and asked for comparisons among the examples. She also did a very good job of prompting when the students didn't identify the pattern in the examples immediately.

Consider also the motivation in Miss Cane's lesson. Her questioning skills were designed to motivate the learners as much as possible. Typically, in most classrooms, teachers ask questions that have one right answer, and the same bright students are the quickest to answer these questions. This leaves a significant part of the class without the opportunity to participate, and consequently, their interest often wanes. This is a natural reaction. It's not much fun to sit back all the time and watch others get all the reinforcement for giving the right answers. Discovery lessons with opportunities for students to make observations with little fear of being right or wrong induce typical nonparticipants to join in the discussion. By asking the students to make observations, all of which are correct at that time in the lesson, the teacher allows everyone in the class to participate with minimum danger of failing.

A final comment should be made about Miss Cane's teaching. Note how, at the end of the lesson, she placed the abstraction on the board for the class to see. This is important for several reasons. Most importantly, it provides a semipermanent record for the class to view. This is crucial because most classes are composed of students of different interests and abilities, and even the best prepared lesson can leave some students behind. Placing the abstraction on the board or on an overhead allows all students to see it and provides them with the opportunity to relate it to the examples. Writing the abstraction somewhere for all the students to see also provides an alternate channel for learning by giving the teacher an opportunity to help the students phrase the abstraction well.

This concludes our formal discussion of the discovery mode of teaching abstractions. Readers desiring a more comprehensive coverage of this topic are referred to Shulman and Keislar (1966).

EXERCISE 3.18

Read the following anecdote, which describes a teacher using the discovery method to teach an a straction, and then answer the questions which follow. Compare your answers to the ones given the feedback section at the end of the chapter.

> Mrs. Steere, a kindergarten teacher, was trying to teach her students the concept *equality*. She prepared to do this by gathering together objects from around the room and asking a number of students to come work with her in a small group on the floor. The lesson began with her saying, "Today I've got some things for us to look at and talk about. I'm going show you some of them, and I want you to tell me what you see."
>
> With that, she brought out two books and two blocks and put them in two separate pil beside each other. Then she said, "Who can tell me what you see?"
>
> "There are two blocks over here."
>
> "One of them is blue."
>
> "The other is red."
>
> "There's the book we read the other day, Mrs. Steere."
>
> "Right, and what else do you see?"
>
> "The other book is about animals."
>
> "And it has a picture of an elephant on the cover."

"And how many books are there altogether? Jamie?"

"Two."

"Good. Now I want you to look at some more things."

She then moved the two groups of objects to the side, placing each group inside, and brought out three trucks and three spoons which she placed in two distinction groups. After she did that, she asked the class to tell what they saw.

"All the trucks are red."

"And there are three spoons over there."

"One of the trucks has a wheel missing."

"And how many trucks are there?" Mrs. Steere asked. "Let's count them together 2, 3. Are there more trucks or more spoons, Shelly?"

"They're the same."

Next the teacher brought out six beanbags and six pieces of chalk and asked the class make more observations. With prompting, the class decided that the numbers in each grid were the same. She repeated this procedure with several other equal sets of objects of student finally noticed that the numbers in the matched sets were always the same. With Mrs. Steere introduced the term *equal* to them. She wrote the symbol on the board and toothpicks for equal signs to show the students how the matched sets were always. Then she mixed up the objects, formed new sets, and asked the students to tell whether sets were equal or not. Some were, and some weren't. Then she had the students form own equal sets from the objects in front of them.

1. Identify the following steps in the anecdote:
   a. Initial presentation of examples.

      ___

   b. Presentation of additional examples.

      ___

   c. Students classify examples.

      ___

   d. Students provide additional examples.

      ___

2. Mrs. Steere told them that the term for "the same number" was *equal*. Is this all right in a discovery lesson? Explain your reasoning.

___

___

___

___

DISCUSSION STRATEGIES

We have now completed the sections on expository and discovery teaching. We have found that they are planned essentially the same way but are implemented in different sequences. As a reference point for our present discussion, however, the key common characteristics are that they are both strongly teacher-directed and that they are both designed to teach specific forms of content, such as a particular concept or generalisation.

Discussion strategies are quite different. They are less effective than an expository or discovery procedure for teaching specific content because they are typically less teacher-directed and more time-consuming. However, other important goals exist in a classroom that go beyond or are different from acquiring specific content. For example, consider the following goals:

1. To develop leadership skills.
2. To summarize group opinion.
3. To arrive at a consensus.
4. To become an active listener.
5. To appropriately handle controversy.
6. To develop paraphrasing skills.
7. To develop self-directed learning skills.
8. To develop analysis, synthesis, and evaluative skills.

There are others that could be added to the list but you can see from those above that an expository or discovery procedure would not be appropriate for reaching the goals. This marks the first major difference between these strategies and discussion techniques.

The second difference relates to the role of the teacher.

In a discussion activity the teacher becomes less a director of learning and more a facilitator. In many ways this role is more difficult because the teacher has less control of the lesson's direction and pace. Nevertheless, the role of the teacher remains critical for she must ensure the promotion of learning through student interaction and exchange of ideas. This can be accomplished through the teacher carefully initiating, regulating, informing, supporting, and evaluating the group activity. Let's now look at the planning and implementing phases of a discussion strategy.

Planning

While fewer actual materials are required to implement a discussion procedure than are required for an expository or discovery lesson, the thought and consideration needed are greater and will determine the success or failure of a group activity.

The bottom line in planning and implementing discussion lessons is *organisation.* It is absolutely critical that the activity be carefully organised or it will result in nonlearning at best or disintegrate into chaos at worst. The single biggest problem with discussion lessons is the tendency of students to drift away from the activity. Only careful organisation can help prevent this problem.

There are at least five decisions that must be made when planning and organising a discussion activity.

First, the teacher carefully considers goals. As noted above, the goal would likely be the acquisition of a cognitive or social skill, rather than the learning of a specific concept or generalisation.

Second, the teacher must decide if the activity would be best implemented in a large-group, teacher-led discussion or small-group, student-led activities which might be in such forms as buzz groups, mock trial, brainstorming, case studies, role-playing, or simulation. This decision relates to the goal. If the goal is to develop leadership skills, active listening skills, or another related skill, a small group activity would be appropriate. On the other hand, the development of analysis, synthesis, or evaluation skills should probably be teacher-directed.

Third, the teacher must consider the experience and development of the students. Young and/or inexperienced students need very explicit directions, a relatively simple task, and a short time period. As they acquire experience, they can take on more direction themselves. Discussion strategies are very developmental in this regard. A teacher hoping for success with the strategy needs a full grading period or more for the students to develop the skills for effective discussions.

Fourth, as already identified implicitly in the previous paragraph, the teacher must consider the time allotted for the activity. In general, the time given the students should be quite short. We have all had experiences where we were put into groups and we discussed the given task for a short time and then talked about everything from the weather to our clothes. This tendency to drift away from the task is one of the major problems with small groups. *A clear task that requires the students to produce something concrete and a short time period can help considerably with this problem.*

Finally, the discussion should result in a specific product such as a summary, list, series of conclusions, or something similar. The teacher in the planning stage must carefully consider the product so directions can be explicitly and thoughtfully provided.

EXERCISE 3.19

Examine the following goals and determine if they are most appropriately taught through discussion (d) or through some other technique (o) such as the expository or discovery techniques.

—— 1. An ecology teacher wants her students to know the major causes of air pollution in a typical large city.

—— 2. A middle school teacher would like input from her students in developing class rules for the year.

—— 3. A language arts teacher wants her students to be able to summarize briefly the opinions of other students.

—— 4. A literature teacher wants her students to understand the major characteristics in Steinbeck's *Tortilla Flat.*

—— 5. A social studies teacher wants her students to determine the feasibility of nuclear power as an energy source.

Implementing

Having determined that the goal is appropriate for discussion and having considered other factors in planning, the teacher is ready to begin. As an illustration of the implementation phase in a discussion activity, read the following scenario:

> Mr. Williams wanted his students to analyze and evaluate the president's constitutional right to impose a wage and price freeze without the Congressional approval.
>
> He began the activity by saying, "Today we are going to analyze the president's right to make executive orders without the approval of Congress. I'm going to show you a film and I want you to identify in the film the two positions taken and at least one item of information that supports each position. (Pause) Now tell me what you are going to do first, Tom?"

"We're going to identify the two positions on the issue."

"Exactly. Very good. Then, what will you do next, Mary?"

"We will identify one item of information that supports each position."

"Yes, that's right, Mary. Now let's look at the film."

Mr. Williams showed the film. After he stopped the projector, he asked, "All right. What are the two positions?"

Tony volunteered, "Well, they are really simple. One position was that he had the right to impose the controls and the other was that he didn't."

"Okay," Mr. Williams said with a smile. "Now, give me an item that supports each position."

Jill raised her hand.

"Jill?"

"Inflation was running at a 12 per cent annual rate and some people on fixed incomes were being squeesed terribly. That supports imposing the controls."

"Tom?"

"Technically, it's unconstitutional unless a national emergency exists. While the inflation is bad, it doesn't fit the standard definition of national emergency."

"Very good, everyone. Now listen carefully. This is what we are going to do. As you walked into class today you selected a number from one to six. You also see the numbers one through six hanging on the walls of the room. When I tell you to move, I want all the people with one's to group themselves under the one, those with two's under the two and so on. Now look at your numbers. In each group, all but one of you has the number in numeral form and one has the number written out. The one with the number spelled out will be the group leader. This was done at random and during the course of the year you'll each be a leader more than once. Leaders, it's your responsibility to appoint a recorder and lead the discussion. Recorders, you must summarize the information and report to the whole class. Each group's task is to take a position regarding the issues presented in the film, document the position in writing, and orally report your position to the whole class. Take either side of the issue. You must come to a group agreement. If one of you disagrees strongly, you may make a minority statement when reporting to the class."

Mr. Williams then reviewed the task with the class as he did before showing the film. Finally, he said, "You have 15 minutes starting now. Begin."

Mr. Williams then moved from group to group and announced the time at five minute intervals. At precisely the fifteen minute point, he called the class together.

"We didn't have time to finish," Sharon complained.

"We couldn't come to a consensus," Pam said from another group.

"Those are good points," Mr. Williams said sympathetically. "Let's discuss both of those problems."

With that he explained why he only gave them fifteen minutes and praised them for their diligence in the groups. He also explained that in time they would become more efficient. He then began a large group discussion on ways of reaching a consensus. Finally, he had each group report their results and said they would analyze the results in greater detail the following day.

Turn now to Exercise 3.20. We want to particularly emphasize this exercise and we want to strongly encourage you to be certain to read the feedback panel for this exercise.

EXERCISE 3.20

Consider the lesson illustrated in the scenario you just read and answer the questions that follow :

1. Mr. Williams had four goals that he wanted to develop in the lesson. Identify the four goals.

2. Mr. Williams used both large and small group techniques. Identify the portion of his lesson devoted to each.

3. Describe how Mr. Williams took the experience and development of his students into account.

4. What provisions did Mr. Williams make to ensure that the students stayed on the task to the greatest extent possible. There are at least four factors you should identify.

5. Consider our approach as authors. In presenting the description of implementing discuss, was our approach essentially expository or was it more inclined toward discover your answer making reference to the text description.

 ____

 ____

 ____

____

INQUIRY TEACHING

An Overview

In the first parts of this chapter we discussed the discovery and the expository approaches to teaching and showed how they could be used to teach various forms of content. This section of the chapter describes the *inquiry* approach to instruction and shows how inquiry strategies can be used to teach problem-solving skills as well as content.

Inquiry teaching involves providing students with content-related problems which serve as the focus for the class's research activities. In working with a problem, students formulate hypotheses or tentative solutions to the problem, gather data relevant to these hypotheses, and then evaluate this data and come to a conclusion. In working with this strategy, students learn not only content associated with the problem but also learn how to go about solving problems in the future. The application of this teaching strategy is illustrated in the anecdote which follows:

> Ms. Schmidt, a middle school teacher, was doing a unit on media and their effect on American life. During the course of the unit, her class had learned about the history of different media forms in America—the long life of the newspaper, the

invention of the radio and its growth, and finally the recent impact of television on our lives. As they investigated each of these topics, the role of advertising in each of these mediums was discussed. From students' comments about advertising, she realised that they didn't really understand how advertising functioned in the field of media. Therefore, she decided to let her students gather some information about this topic. She began the activity by saying, "We've mentioned advertising a number of times in our discussion of media. What are some of the things we've found out? Jack?"

"Well, advertising helps manufacturers tell people about their products."

"Also, it helps to pay for the cost of some media, like newspapers and magazines," Chad remarked. "We don't have to pay as much for them because they have advertising in them."

"And TV and radio are almost totally paid for by advertising," added Jim.

"Good, now I'd like for us to take a closer look at TV advertising and see if we can understand how it works. But first let's see how much we already know about TV commercials. Sharon?"

"Well, they're too long, and there are too many of them."

"O.K., anyone else? (pause) No one, hmmm. Well, let's see if we can ask some questions that would help us find out more about TV advertising. Pretend that there is a man here from the network to answer questions. What kinds of questions might you ask him? Let's break up into our small groups and see if we can make a list of questions."

After a period of time, the groups came back together again to share their ideas. As they did this, they found that me following two questions commonly occurred:

How often do TV commercials occur?

What kinds of products are advertised most?

When Ms. Schmidt asked the class to form hypotheses about the answers to these questi~ns, a heated debate arose. Some people thought that commercials came on every five minutes while others thought they came on every fifteen minutes. Also the members of the class disagreed about the major products advertised on TV. Some said they were toys, others said beer and cars, and still others claimed they were food and detergent. To settle these arguments, Ms. Schmidt said, "A lot of you have different ideas about the answers to these questions. Let's write them on the board and call them hypotheses, and then let's try to gather some information to see which of these are correct."

With that, she wrote the following on the board:

Hypotheses

1. Commercials occur every five minutes.
2. Commercials occur every fifteen minutes.
3. The most commonly advertised products are:
    a. toys
    b. beer
    c. cars
    d. food
    e. detergents

Then she added, "Well, at least we found that we

don't all agree about the answers to some of these questions. Now how can we go about finding which of these hypotheses are correct? Any ideas?"

Some members of the class suggested that someone write to the stations for the answers. Others suggested that perhaps the answers could be found in magazines or books, while others suggested finding the answers by actually watching TV. After some discussion, they decided to break into teams to gather data by watching TV. In organising for this, the class decided that each team would watch at a different time but that they all would watch the same station. They agreed to use clocks to time the commercials and to write down what they found in notebooks to share with the class. After a week, they brought their information back to class, and Ms. Schmidt helped them to organize the information into a chart, a part of which is shown in Table 3.8.

TABLE 3.8

TV-Viewing Chart

Time of Day	*Type of Program*	*Product Advertised*	*Length of Commercials*	*Intervals of Commercials*
early	cartoons	cereal	20 sec.	10 min.
morning		toys	30 sec.	10 min.
			45 sec.	
midday	serials	detergents	20 sec.	10 min.
	talk shows	food	30 sec.	8 min.
		household goods	45 sec.	
evening	sit-coms	snacks	25 sec.	15 min.
	specials	beer	35 sec.	12 min.
	movies	cars	45 sec.	
weekend	sports	beer	25 sec.	15 min.
afternoon		cars	35 sec.	12 min
			45 sec.	

Ms. Schmidt began the discussion by saying, "Look at the first three columns of the chart and tell me what you see. Tony?"

"Well, on the same channel there are different kinds of programs during the day."

"Anything else? Terry?"

"And there are different kinds of commercials during the day, too."

"Good, and why do you think there are different kinds of programs on at different times of the day? Josh?"

"Because different people like to watch different things."

"Anyone else? Cassie?"

"Also because people watch TV at different times. Like the only time my Dad gets to watch TV is at night and on weekends."

"And so what does the information we gathered tell us about our third hypothesis? What is the most commonly advertised product? Jim?"

"Well, it depends on when you watch. If it's during the day, the products are for kids and mothers, while at night they're for the whole family and for dads."

The class then continued to analyze the data they had collected, using the hypotheses they had formed to guide their discussion.

Let's pause for a second now and take a look at this lesson to see how it was an example of inquiry.

An inquiry lesson typically consists of four parts. In the first part, some problem is encountered by the class. Ms. Schmidt initiated this phase of the lesson by asking the class how much they knew about television commercials. In the second phase of an inquiry activity, hypotheses are formed. *Hypotheses* are tentative suggestions about how the world operates. They are, then, ideas about how the data that will be gathered might turn out. Ms. Schmidt wrote these hypotheses on the board for the whole class to see. The third part of an inquiry lesson involves data gathering. The class did this by watching TV and noting the length and kind of commercials that occurred. The final phase of an inquiry lesson involves data analysis in which the data gathered are compared to the hypotheses formulated. These steps are summarised in Table 3.9.

The inquiry strategy can be a valuable tool in a beginning teacher's repertoire for several reasons. One is that it provides the teacher with a means of teaching students problem-solving skills. By seeing how problems are solved in the classroom, they are provided with a model to follow in solving problems in other areas of their lives. In addition, the stages in the inquiry model provide students with practice in information gathering and analysis, skills with wide application in other facets of life. A third reason for using inquiry strategies is that they provide alternate means of teaching content to students who may already be saturated with more teacher-oriented, expository techniques. Because students are actively involved in each of the phases, inquiry activities can be a motivating alternative to other approaches.

TABLE 3.9

Steps in Inquiry Lessons

Students:	1.	Identify problem
(with teacher	2.	Form hypotheses
guidance)	3.	Gather data
	4.	Analyse data and form conclusion

EXERCISE 3.21

Read the anecdote below which describes a college instructor using the inquiry approach and then answer the questions which follow. Compare your answers with the ones given in the feedback section at the end of the chapter.

> Mr. Hayes's methods class had been talking about factors which influence the effectiveness of different types of media. He began this new lesson by saying, "Now I'd like to have us take a look at factors which influence the readability of different texts. Let's take a second to think about factors that might influence how easy something is to read. Any ideas? Cal?"
>
> "How about the number of pictures?"
>
> "O.K., that's an idea. Anyone else?"
>
> "Also the kinds of words. Longer words are usually harder to understand than shorter ones," added Leeann.
>
> "And the length of sentences, too. The longer the sentence, the harder it is to conderstand," Mike contributed.
>
> "Another thing is the number of graphs and charts," said Christine "These make at hard to understand."
>
> "Fine," answered Mr. Hayes. "Now does anyone have any suggestions of how we find whether or not these ideas are correct?"
>
> The class discussed the matter for a while and decided to look at textbooks at different levels in terms of the variables they had mentioned. They selected texts at the first-four and eighth-grade levels and compared them to high school and college texts. In company them,· they counted the average numbers of the following: syllables per word, words persistence, illustrations per ten pages, and graphs or charts per ten pages. The results of this investigation were then compiled into the chart shown in Table 3.10.

TABLE 3.10

Information Texts

Level	*Syllables*	*Words*	*Illustrations*	*Charts or Graphs*
First-Grade	1.2	6.2	6.0	0.0
Fourth-Grade	1.3	8.4	5.1	0.0
Eighth-Grade	1.4	12.8	4.4	2.1
High School	1.6	15.0	3.1	24
College	1.7	17.0	2.0	2.5

The lesson then continued with Mr. Hayes asking, "What does the data tell us about our hypothesis linking grade level and number of syllables per word, Don?"

"It was correct because we can see that the number of syllables per word increases with each grade level."

"O.K., and how about the number of words per sentence? Kerry?"

The lesson continued with the class analysing each of the columns in terms of the hypotheses they had formed.

Identify where the following phases occurred in the anecdote.

1. Problem identification

___

___

___

2. Formulation of hypotheses

___

___

___

3. Data gathering

___

___

___

4. Analysis of data

___

___

___

___

Planning Inquiry Lessons

In planning for inquiry activities, the first step is identifying a problem in a particular content area. Essentially, this involves examining the areas of content being taught and determining if any of these can be taught using a problem-solving approach. This isn't always possible, but when it is, it allows the teacher to teach both content and inquiry skills at the same time.

Often these problem situations arise spontaneously in the course of other lessons. When this happens, the teacher has to be able to recognize situations like this in order to capitalize on them. For example, one of the authors witnessed an elementary science lesson in which the class was discussing some seeds they had planted weeks earlier. Some of the seeds had sprouted while others hadn't. The class was trying to figure out why. The teacher seized upon this situation to initiate an inquiry lesson focusing on what factors cause seeds to germinate. The class then proceeded to generate hypotheses about these factors and to investigate them by germinating seeds under various growing conditions.

In this case, the inquiry lesson followed naturally from a question or a problem that arose in a previous lesson. This is an especially effective way to initiate inquiry lessons for several reasons. One is that students can view the lesson as a functional response to a need rather than a perhaps nonfunctional topic imposed by the teacher. In addition, students are able to see the utility of the process of inquiry in solving problems that they encounter in their environment.

Often however, it isn't very likely that inquiry lessons will arise naturally from problems encountered in class. Or, a teacher may have a particular topic that needs to be covered. In situations like these, the teacher must be able to recognize times when inquiry activities are beneficial and structure the content appropriately. Typically, inquiry strategies are most appropriate when there is some type of causal relationship involved in the content area. For example, in the science lesson mentioned, the inquiry lesson focused on factors that caused or influenced germination. In a similar manner, the lesson on readability focused on factors that influenced or affected readability. When areas of content are addressed in this manner, the first phase of the inquiry lesson, identifying a problem, is already satisfied.

The second and final task in planning for an inquiry lesson is to make some type of arrangement for the data-gathering process. This doesn't pose any major problem if the materials needed are readily available, as was the case in the lesson on TV commercials. At other times, the teacher must plan ahead to make sure that the necessary materials will be available when needed. For example, the instructor in the methods class had to make arrangements for the availability of textbooks at different levels, and the science teacher had to bring pots, seeds, and potting soil to class to allow her students to gather data about germinating seeds. Anticipating these needs ahead of time allows the process of inquiry to proceed with a minimum of wasted time and effort. Others would argue that this efficiency in terms of time and effort imposes an artificial smoothness on the inquiry process. These same people contend that a major part of the value of inquiry lessons is to provide students with realistic experiences with problem solving. In other words, students should be given the opportunity to devise their own data-gathering procedures. Providing them with this freedom takes longer but allows them to see how inquiry works in the real world. To make the problem serving too efficient artificially distorts the picture that students get of the inquiry process. The critics who say this are more interested in the process of inquiry than in the content taught. Other more content-oriented teachers would contend that time constraints limit the amount of time that can be spent in any particular lesson, and that teachers should go ahead and help students by arranging for the data-gathering procedures. This is another educational decision that you as a professional will have to make if you decide to use inquiry strategies.

EXERCISE 3.22

Examine the following topics and determine whether they could be taught using an inquiry approach (i) or whether a discovery or expository approach (d/e) would be more appropriate. Then compare your answers with the ones given in the feedback section at the end of the chapter.

—— 1. An elementary teacher wants students to know things that affect plant growth.

—— 2. A language arts teacher wants students to understand the term *gerund*.

—— 3. A health teacher wants students to know the relationship between exercising and put rate.

—— 4. A home economics teacher wants students to know the effect volume buying has on cost per unit.

—— 5. A social studies teacher wants students to know the difference between capitalism a socialism.

Implementing Inquiry Lessons

As previously described, the first phase of an inquiry lesson involves presenting a problem. The problem provides the focus for the remainder of the lesson as well as giving direction to the next phase of implementation—the formulation of hypotheses. The problem can occur as the result of a situation encountered in a previous lesson or can be initiated by the teacher. When the latter is done, it is sometimes helpful to provide a focusing event which captures the students' attention. For example, a teacher who wanted to teach a lesson on the factors affecting the preservation of food might bring out two apples that had been cut open at the same time, one refrigerated and one not. The teacher would then ask the class to observe the condition of the two and try to explain why this occurred. The focusing event in this lesson provides a natural and tangible starting point for the inquiry lesson.

Similar events could be constructed for other types of inquiry lessons. For example, the teacher in the lesson on television advertising might have turned on a television prior to the lesson and asked the students to observe the commercials. In a similar manner, the methods instructor might have read two different passages on the same topic, one written at the fourth-grade and the other at the college level. His beginning question might be, "How and why are they the same? How are they different?" In all of the examples, the focusing event provides a concrete experience to which the students can relate. Focusing events can be motivating if they're eye catching and helpful in getting students to see the relevance of the problem to the world around them. However the problem is introduced to the students, though, the formal statement of it should be written on the board or overhead for all to see and consider.

After the students have had time to think about the problem, the teacher should encourage them to offer ideas about solutions. Often these hypotheses are produced spontaneously; at other times it is necessary for the teacher to prompt the students to offer them. For example, the teacher wanting her students to focus on factors affecting food spoilage and preservation might ask, "What kinds of things do we do in our kitchens to keep food from spoiling?" or, "If you were going on a week-long hike, what kinds of foods would you take?" Answers to these questions would help students to identify factors that might be included in hypotheses.

Once the hypotheses have been formed, the next task for the class is to gather data to test these hypotheses. The data-gathering process can take place in several ways. It can occur as an in-class group activity or as an individual activity outside of class time. Probably the major factors to be considered here are time and equipment. If classroom time is scarce or the equipment needed is unavailable in class, then the data-gathering process can be assigned as an out-of-class activity. Having students gather data in their homes can have several advantages. One is that it reinforces the idea that inquiry is not just something that's done in the classroom. Also, having students gather data at home provides an opportunity for parents to become involved in the activity.

The final phase of the inquiry process is data analysis. The major goal of this phase of the activity is to examine the hypotheses, while analysing the information gathered, to determine if they agree. If they don't, the hypotheses need to be revised and alternative conclusions offered. In essence, this part of the lesson involves a summing up of the activities of the lesson into some types of conclu-sions that students can take with them. These conclusions would form the major content outcomes of the lesson. Because of this, these conclusions should be written on the board for all the class.

As mentioned previously, organising the data in some way facilitates the process of analysis. This can be done by placing the information in charts or by graphing it. The experience of wrestling with data and attempting to come up with an optimal organisational pattern is an educational experience in itself, in addition to its help in facilitating the data analysis. Often students wall have had no previous experience with this process and will experience difficulty. The teacher who first tries to involve students in the analysis of data should not get discouraged. This is a skill that can be taught and the best way of doing it is through the experience itself.

SUMMARY

The purpose of this chapter has been to present four basic teaching strategies for your consideration. The majority of the chapter involved the presentation of examples and anecdotes designed to clearly establish the differences between the planning and implementing of expository and discovery lessons. In addition, the planning and implementing of discussion and inquiry approaches to instruction were also presented. These discussions included overviews, comparisons, and exercises which allowed you to become familiar with these strategies.

In addition to the appropriate selection, planning, and implementation of the strategies themselves, their success is often dependent upon verbal interactions during activities such as teacher-led discussions, presentations of examples, and observable exercises. For instance, you may have noticed the frequent use of the term *prompt* or the many times the teachers asked the students to generate examples or provide observations. These ideas drew from the material developed in preceding chapter.

EXERCISE FEEDBACK

EXERCISE 3.23

1. (d) Discovery. The lesson began with the students gathering and analysing data and forming the abstraction that the sum of the interior angles of a triangle is 180 degrees.
2. (d) Discovery. The sequence of the lesson was from examples to abstractions, and the class formed the abstraction themselves rather than having the teacher state it.
3. (e) Expository. The lesson began with the teacher defining the concept set and illustrating the concept with examples.
4. (d) Discovery. Students were provided with examples of inferences and then formed their own definition. Miss Kirk then reinforced the concept by having the class locate additional examples.

EXERCISE 3.24

1. The problem with the examples is that they don't show the interaction of the concepts in the generalisation. The generalisation links the concepts of strenuousness and calories. To illustrate this, the instructor would need to supplement the pictures with information about the calories burned in a given time period in each of the sports.
2. The examples used to illustrate this concept are inadequate because they only relate to one of the two kinds of verbs, action verbs. In addition, all of these verbs were in the past tense, thus giving students the impression that all verbs have to be in the past tense. These would need to be supplemented with additional examples like the following to give students a complete picture of the concept.

   The team was first on the floor.

   I am not going to be late again.
3. These two sequences of examples differ in terms of the order of difficulty or familiarity of examples. Because the initial examples used in sequence A are more familiar than the initial examples of sequence B. the goal would be attained more quickly using sequence A. Therefore, a teacher who wanted to teach this concept as quickly as possible or who wanted a more easily understood sequence for a given group of students would use sequence A.

EXERCISE 3.25

1. Mr. Hanes was attempting to teach the concept *hyperbole.* He did this in an expository manner by first defining the concept and then illustrating it with examples.
2. He organised the content by linking the new concept to the superordinate concept of *figures of speech.* This told the class how hyperboles were similar to metaphors and similes.
3. In the lesson, Mr. Hanes failed to let the students classify his examples. This wasn't a major mistake because he still had students explain his own classifications and also had students provide their own examples of the concept. However, by not having them classify his examples, he missed an additional opportunity to gather data about the students' knowledge of the concept.

EXERCISE 3.26

1. a. The teacher began the lesson by presenting the matched sets of blocks and books and asking the group to make observations.
   b. Additional examples were provided when she brought out the trucks and the spoons and then the other objects.
   c. The students classified the examples when they told the teacher whether the sets were equal or not.
   d. The students provided their own examples when they constructed equal sets of their own.

2. In discovery lessons, the responsibility for forming the abstraction is placed on the students. Mrs. Steere did this in her lesson when she had them come up with the idea that all the matched groups were the same in terms of number. This is really the concept of *equal*. Mrs. Steere was correct in providing the symbol and name for the concept since the students had already acquired the idea. No amount of prompting would have gotten them to arrive at the symbol or concept name if they hadn't already have known it. It should be emphasised that what students discover in a discovery lesson is the *meaning* of the abstraction, not the *symbol* or *word* for it.

EXERCISE 3.27

1. This topic involves the transmission of information and would be best taught by a discovery or expository procedure. A next step for this topic could be to have students develop a plan to solve these problems.
2. Here is an example of discussion groups being used to elicit student input on classroom management rules, a topic to be discussed further in Chapter 9.
3. This is a goal that could be implemented in a large group discussion activity. Large group discussion would be preferable because it would allow the teacher to give immediate feedback to each student and other students could learn from the feedback as well. In a small group activity the teacher would have difficulty determining to what extent the summary was accurate.
4. This goal involves acquiring knowledge and would not be an appropriate topic for a discussion.
5. This would be an excellent discussion topic.

EXERCISE 3.28

1. Mr. Williams's goals were for his students:
   a. to take and support a position with evidence
   b. to develop leadership skills
   c. to develop summarising and speaking skills
   d. to develop techniques for arriving at a group concensus

   His first goal was stated explicitly and the other three were more implicit.
2. Mr. Williams used a large group activity initally when he first showed the film and asked for one item of information that supported each position. He also used a large group procedure in discussing procedures for moving to a concensus. He planned further large group discussion for the following day after the groups reported their respective positions. He used a small group procedure in having the groups take and document a position. The small groups were also used in developing leadership, recording data, and summarising information.
3. Mr. Smith understood that his students wouldn't be efficient in this activity. This was an attempt at using a discussion strategy when the students were inexperienced. He planned for their leadership development when he noted that each would have more than one chance to be a leader. Also, he discussed ways of increasing efficiency and techniques for reaching a consensus. Presumably, he would review all this prior to the next discussion lesson and gradually, the students' skill would increase with each discussion lesson.
4. Mr. Williams's organisation and lesson development were excellent.

   First, he helped the students to have the necessary background by showing the film which provided them with all the information needed to carry on the discussion.

   Second, he gave very explicit directions prior to watching the film and reinforced the directions by asking students to repeat them before he turned on the projector. He also gave very precise directions for getting into the groups and in identifying the task for each group.

   Third, Mr. Williams gave the class only 15 minutes to complete the activity. It purposely was short, perhaps too short. However, considering the students' developmental level, more time probably would have become inefficient. He knew that the students were inexperienced and planned to help them develop their skills through a series of discussion activities over the course of the year.

Finally, Mr. Williams required a product. The students had to take their position and support it in writing. These results were then reported to the whole class.

5. We used a form of ,discovery approach in describing implementation of discussions. We presented an example in scenario form and the conclusions are essentially described in this feedback. This is the reason we emphasised Exercise 3.28 and particularly its feedback.

EXERCISE 3.29

---

1. Problem identification occurred at the beginning of the lesson when the teacher asked the class to identify factors which affected the readability of a text.
2. Hypotheses were formulated when the class listed variables that would affect readability.
3. The class gathered data when they analysed the different texts in terms of the variables listed in the hypotheses.
4. Mr. Hayes helped the class analyze the data by asking questions which required the students to compare the data in the chart to the hypotheses they had formed.

Several additional comments should be made about this lesson. First, note that the teacher identified the problem to be studied rather than having the class do it. This method of identifying the problem occurs when the teacher has a specific topic to be covered. Alternate ways of initiating the inquiry process will be discussed in the planning section which follows. Also, note that the teacher in this lesson organised the information that the class collected into a chart, as we have also seen earlier. Organising data in this manner is not essential in an inquiry lesson but can be helpful when there are large amounts of data to consider. Organisation makes the data easier to interpret and analyze in terms of the hypotheses formed earlier.

EXERCISE 3.30

1. (i) Inquiry. The teacher might begin the lesson by asking, "What kinds of things influence how fast a plant grows?" After hypotheses were formed, these could be investigated by growing plants and comparing their growth rates under different conditions.
2. (d/e) Discovery or Expository. Since a gerund is a concept, it would be more effectively taught using a discovery or an expository approach.
3. (i) Inquiry. This topic involves a cause and effect relationship. Such a lesson might begin with the teacher asking, "What things affect how fast your heart beats?" The class might then investigate this topic by surveying its members in terms of how much they exercise and then compare their respective pulse rates.
4. (i) Inquiry. The teacher could begin the lesson by asking. "What factors affect the price of a product?" The students could gather data relating to this question by checking the prices of different kinds and quantities of products.
5. (d/e) Discovery or Expository. Since these two terms are concepts, they would be better taught with a discovery or an expository lesson.

4

Strategies of Learning

INTRODUCTION

Mastery Learning is rapidly being introduced in our nation's schools. School systems and individual schools throughout the nation are implementing Mastery units of instruction and entire courses of study. An outstanding example of systemwide implementation is found in Johnson City, New York while thousands of schools in Chicago, New York, Denver, New Orleans, Jacksonville, San Jose, and other cities are using Mastery Learning.

A growing trend is also evidenced by the numbers of workshops, institutes, and presentations at local, state and national conferences which involve Mastery Learning. One of the reasons for this widespread implementation is the amount of research which continues to support its effectiveness. Block's works in 1971 and 1974, reviewing literature, were highly supportive. Okay's research, published in the *Journal of Teacher Education*, involved more than 300 students in 26 classes and, in every instance, the pupils in the Mastery classes outperformed the nonmastery pupils when the teacher followed the Mastery plan.

More recently, Hyman and Cohen, in *Educational Leadership*, presented ten conclusions after studying 3,000 schools' experiences with a learning for mastery curriculum for 15 years. They concluded that the learning for mastery curriculum is consistently more effective than traditional curriculums and that students in mastery learning environments master more objectives during a given period of time compared to students in non-mastery environments.

In their recently published book, *Effective Instruction,* Levin and Long reviewed Mastery Learning and presented current studies which support their position that mean performance level of mastery groups is significantly higher than the levels of nonmastery groups.

These books are only two examples of the large amount of research which supports the authors' position that Mastery Learning is more effective than traditional methods.

An additional and equally important reason for the widespread implementation of Mastery Learning is that it can be easily and efficiently installed in the traditional classroom setting. Before viewing this implementation, however, let's briefly focus our attention on the basic Mastery concept.

In 1963, John B. Carroll presented a conceptual model which, in its least complex form, stated that if a student is given sufficient time to attain an acceptable level (regarding a specific skill or competency) and he uses that time efficiently, he can succeed at the task at hand.

In 1968 Benjamin Bloom developed a practical model, based upon Car-roll's work, which emphasised variations in learning time and learning materials. These variables, as pointed out by Jeter, can be easily adapted in ordinary classroom instruction and can be used at all grade levels and in all subject areas.

OBJECTIVES

After completing the last Chapter 8, you should be able to accomplish the following objective:

For you as a pre/inservice teacher to increase your awareness of Mastery Learning so that, when given a list of statements discussing the characteristics of Mastery Learning, you will be able to correctly identify appropriate characteristics with 80 per cent accuracy.

THE TRADITIONAL MODEL

When a teacher uses the traditional setting, or model, she begins with an objective and presents primary instruction to the entire group. Primary instruction is most often presented in the form of lectures, textbook readings, teacher-led discussions, mediated presentations, drills, seatwork, or possible combinations of any of these procedures. The critical point to be made is that all the students are involved in the same activity at the same time.

After the primary instruction, the teacher issues formal examinations, referred to in Mastery Learning as summative evaluations, in order to measure and evaluate student achievement. The teacher then moves on to the next objective regardless of the results of the examination on the first objective. This cycle of objective-primary instruction-examination is repeated until the course content or curriculum has been taught.

Obj. # 1 ———> Primary ————————> Examination ————>Obj # 2
Instruction

Fig. 4.1. The Traditional Model

Before we focus on how Mastery Learning can be incorporated into the traditional model, it is critical to note at the onset that in using the term "traditional", we are not implying that all teachers utilize such an approach. However, it would be difficult to deny that a sizeable number of teachers dp employ such a model.

TRADITIONAL AND MASTERY MODELS

Mastery Learning is an individualised approach which readily lends itself to implementation in a traditional environment. As with traditional teaching, the instructor using the Mastery model begins with an objective but quickly inserts a step prior to the primary instruction. This step is a preassessment. The purposes of a preassessment are to determine if the students have the prerequisite skills to enable them to begin the unit of study and to establish whether or not the students have already mastered the unit's objectives. The pretest, due to the information it provides, is critical to the effectiveness of the unit of study because, according to Bloom, there is a direct relationship between student involvement in learning and prerequisite skills and knowledge.

MEASUREMENT

Measurement is a process which is common to all sciences, including the social sciences and education. It involves the collection of information or data; therefore, it depends on our five senses. In the process of measurement, the senses are used to collect information from the environment.

Measurement can take many forms, differing in type and precision. First, let us consider the different forms which measurement can take. Using a ruler on a piece of paper, lowering a weighted rope into a lake, watching an odometer on a trip, and observing the relative heights of two buildings are all methods of measuring length. Stepping on a scale, lifting two rocks, and picking up a child are all methods of measuring weight. And placing milk in a cup before use in a recipe, trying on a new dress, and appraising the size of a meal before eating it are all methods of measuring volume. What all of these measurements have in common is that perceptual processes (sight, hearing, or touch) were used to gather some type of data.

As mentioned previously, measurements differ in terms of their preciseness. For instance, lifting two rocks by hand is less accurate than placing them on a scale. Estimating the size of two buildings is less precise than taking ropes to the tops of the buildings, lowering them to the bottom, and then using a tape measure to calculate the lengths. In general, the accuracy of measurements is related to what is being measured by what instrument.

How the nature of what is being measured affects the accuracy of the measurement may not readily be apparent. For example, it is much easier to measure the weight of a rock than its chemical components. Also, it is easier to measure the height and weight of a child than it is to measure his intelligence. Both of these illustrations show how differences in what is being measured affect the precision of the measurement.

The availability of instruments also affects the precision of measurements. For instance, when following a very complex recipe for French pastries, a set of measuring cups and spoons is much preferred over regular ones. The measuring cups and spoons are finely calibrated to make precise measurements. In measuring a person's intelligence, the availability of instruments also affects the precision of the measurements. Some crude indicators of a person's intelligence might be the answers to such questions as "What is 11 times 11?" or "What is the capital of Maine?"

or "What is a proper noun?" As rough as these measurements are, they are better than nothing at all for predicting a person's intelligence. However, a more precise indication would be his performance on a standardised intelligence test which had been constructed and administered by testing experts.

The topic of measurements is an especially important one for educators because of the hundreds, if not thousands, of measurements which teachers make daily (Jackson, 1968). Like all measurements, these differ as to type. A teacher takes measurements when she walks around the room and observes the behavior of her students. She also takes measurements when she asks questions or gives a quiz or a test.

Measurements differ as to whether the teacher consciously planned to take the measurement and consequently altered the environment or whether he took the measurement as part of the ongoing flow in the classroom. The most obvious type of measurement is the former. Quizzes, tests, and questions asked in class are all types of intentional measurements in which the teacher alters the classroom environment to gather the information. However, the most important types of measurements may be those taken during the usual activities of the day. Noticing the reactions of students to a movie shown in class, listening to students' comments while they are doing homework, or noticing a student's appearance as he enters class are all forms of this second type of measurement.

The measurements that a teacher makes do not have to be used immediately but can be stored for later use. This can be done either by writing the measurement down or by remembering it. Putting attendance figures in a book would be of the former method. Probably the most common form of measurement storage takes place in the teacher's head.

As with all measurements, the measurements a teacher makes differ in terms of their accuracy. This difference in precision is due to the two factors mentioned previously—what is being measured by what instrument. For instance, a teacher can obtain much more precise measurements of Johnny's knowledge of multiplication tables than he can of Johnny's creative ability. The difference in accuracy here relates to what is being measured. Creativity is harder to measure because it is more nebulous. Whether a child knows the alphabet can be measured more precisely than can her reading comprehension. Again the difference in the accuracy of the measurement is related to what is being measured.

Additionally, measurement accuracy is determined by the instruments used to make the measurements. For instance, standardised reading tests, when administered and interpreted correctly can give a more accurate measurement of a child's reading level than informal methods. Also, IQ tests give more accurate measurements of intelligence than do other types of measurements such as grades in history or behavior in math class.

A primary goal of the teacher should be to increase the accuracy of measurements. The teacher should be constantly alert to factors which influence this accuracy and should try to control factors which influence it. The purpose of this chapter is to help you learn to measure student understanding as accurately as possible.

PREPARING ACCURATE MEASUREMENT ITEMS

Basic Considerations

The previous section was written to help you understand

the difference between measurement and evaluation. We want you to understand evaluation so that the evaluations you make as a teacher will be rational rather than whimsical or emotional, and we want you to understand measurement so that you will be aware of the basis for your evaluations and measure as accurately as possible.

This section of the Chapter will be devoted to a discussion of measurement and ways of preparing items to make your measuring as accurate as possible. Keep in mind as you read that no measurement is infallible. For example, in a multiple choice item, you are actually measuring three things. First, you are measuring the students' understanding of the material; second, you're measuring their ability to take a multiple choice test; and third, you are measuring their reading ability. Any of these factors can affect the accuracy of the measurement. Keep this in mind as you prepare items. One way of dealing with the problem is to frequently measure each student in different ways. For example, observing a student in class and talking with him are both excellent ways of measuring. If a conversation with a student reveals that he understands the material better than his performance on a written test would suggest, that may mean the written measurement was inaccurate. The main point is that an alert teacher will not only give written measures but will supplement these with observation, discussion, and other appropriate means of information gathering.

Paper and pencil tests are widely used, not because they are more accurate than other forms but because they are more efficient. It's very time-consuming to discuss a topic with each student in a large class, but giving a single paper and pencil test can be accomplished quickly. We neither praise nor condemn paper and pencil tests; rather, we describe ways of making written items as accurate as possible. If you want a more complete discussion of the strengths and weaknesses of any of the forms of measurement, refer to Ebel (1970) or Mager (1973).

Let's turn now to a more specific discussion of measurement. As noted earlier, measurement is considered in the planning phase of the activity because the form of the measurement is specified in the goals objective. In considering the goal and the measurement of it, the teacher asks herself several questions and makes several decisions in answering these questions. To illustrate this, let's look at the goal statement about nouns described at the beginning of the chapter:

> For third graders to understand nouns.

Before even writing the goal statement, the teacher asks herself "What do I want the child to know, understand, do, or feel?" The answer in this case is "I want them to understand nouns." The next and very critical question is "How will I know if they understand nouns?" The answer to this specifies the remainder of the goals objective—the evaluation statement. This is not always easy; for an excellent discussion of the problems involved in measuring student understanding, see Anderson (1972). Before the teacher can answer this second question, two subordinate questions must be asked—"At what level do I expect them to understand?" and "Will I determine their understanding through having them recognize correct statements or by having them produce statements of their own?"

Recognition involves providing the students with a series of choices and having them select the correct or most appropriate one(s). Multiple choice items involve recognition, as do true/false and matching items. In a true/false format you merely recognize the statement as either true or false, while matching involves recognising the relationship between two words or statements. Don't be confused, however! Recognition items do not mean merely knowledge level tasks. Very high levels of thinking can be measured with recognition items. This point is illustrated later in the chapter.

By comparison, production items require that the students generate their own responses rather than recognize correct ones. Short answer and essay questions are examples of this. We will compare recognition and production items after we've seen some examples, but first let's look at Figure 4.2, a diagrammatic representation of the decision-making process we've just described.

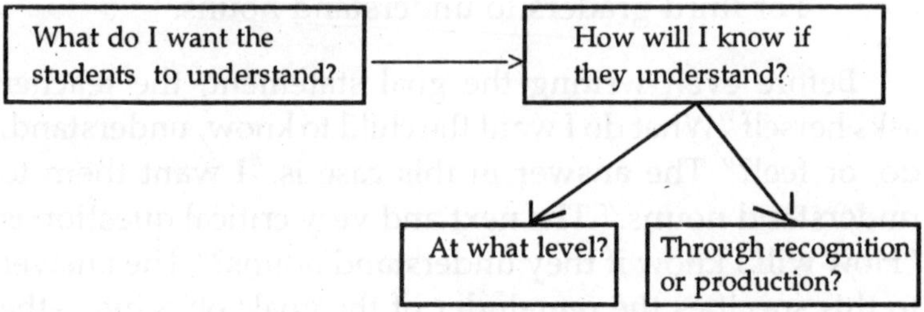

Fig. 4.2. Decision-Making Model for the Planning and Evaluation Phases

Teachers must answer each of these questions for themselves in order to state the complete goals objective. The evaluation statement in the objective specifies the answer to these last three questions regarding the level and the method of measuring student understanding. Again, this illustrates how powerful the goals objective is as a tool to help teachers become systematic when developing instructional units.

In a sense, this chapter should be coupled with the planning phase of teaching in that measurement *decisions* are made prior to implementing the learning activity. We are placing it here, however, because the actual measurement process occurs after the students have completed the learning activity.

Let's look now at some actual measurement items.

Measuring the Learning of Facts

As noted in Chapter 2, facts are forms of information learned through drill, and measurement of their attainment exists only at the knowledge or low level. For example, a feet level objective might be:

> For students to know American presidents so that, when provided with a major event in American history, they will provide the name of the person who held the presidency during that period.

An appropriate item to measure this objective could be

The president during the Civil War was:

a. Alexander Hamilton
b. Robert E. Lee
c. Abraham-Lincoln
d. William Jennings Bryan

The preceding example is a recognition item. A question in the form of a production item for the same objective could be:

Who was president during the Civil War?

Alternate formats for measuring fact learning include true/false, matching, and short answer completion. A discussion of these formats can be found in texts by Ebel (1970), Gronlund (1968), Mager (1973), and Schoer (1970). Let's move on to a discussion of the measurement of concepts.

Measuring the Understanding of Concepts

To this point we've covered the idea of measurement, the difference between production and recognition items, and measuring the attainment of facts. We now want to move to a discussion of the process of measuring students' understanding of abstractions. However, in addition to discussing ways of measuring the learning of abstractions, well use examples to discuss the strengths and weaknesses of production versus recognition items. In addition, well discuss multiple choice items more thoroughly than other recognition formats because it is the most widely used and perhaps the most efficient way of measuring. So, keep in mind both themes—measuring for abstraction, and in this section, concept learning and analysis of item formats.

First, while concepts can be measured at the knowledge level (as you will see in later paragraphs), they are most commonly measured at the comprehension level. This is accomplished quite easily and efficiently by asking students to identify unique examples of the concept. (To refresh your understanding of comprehension refer to Chapter 4.) For example, suppose you want preschool students to comprehend the concept *between*. Their comprehension could be measured with the following item.

Place an X on the picture where the dog is between the two boys.

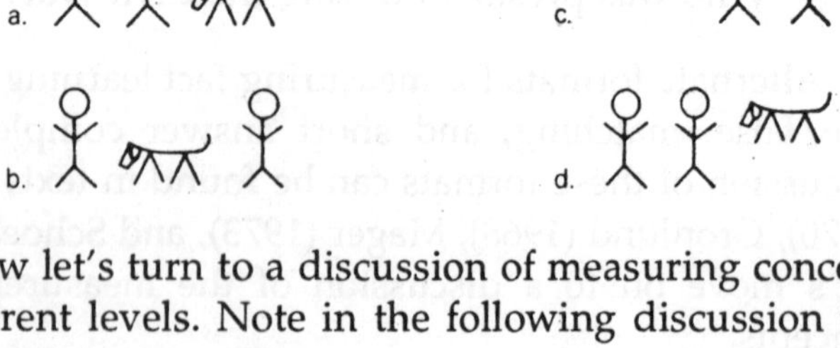

Now let's turn to a discussion of measuring concepts at different levels. Note in the following discussion that some of the objectives go beyond the understanding of a concept *per se* and into the analysis of relationships. As we noted in the preceding discussion, understanding of concepts themselves is primarily a comprehension level task.

Let's look again at the example with nouns. There are a number of evaluation statements that can facilitate the goal statement. As noted earlier, the form of file evaluation statement reflects the answers to the questions in the model (Figure 4.1). The goal and some sample evaluation statements follow:

For third-grade students to understand nouns so that

1. without aids, they will write the definition of nouns.
2. given a list of definitions, they will identify the one for nouns.
3. given a list of words, they will circle all those that are nouns.
4. given nouns they will correctly use them in sentences.
5. given a list of sentences, they will underline all the nouns.
6. given a sentence, they will describe the author's intent by interpreting the meaning of the nouns in the context of the sentence.
7. given a sentence and a list of meanings of a noun as determined by context, they will select the best interpretation.

So, you can see that decision making is not so simple! The one goal statement about a straightforward concept such as *nouns* allows for at least the seven possible evaluation statements we've listed here.

Let's look now at how the wording of the evaluation statement in the objective determines the form of the item that is designed to measure the students' attainment of the goal. Each evaluation statement and a corresponding item follow:

---

1. Evaluation Statement:

   Without aids, they will write the definition of nouns.

   Item:

   On the line below write the definition of nouns.

2. Evaluation Statement:

   Given a list of definitions, they will identify the one for nouns.

   Item:

   Circle the best definition of nouns.

   a. A noun is a word that modifies verbs, adjectives, or adverbs,
   b. A noun is a word that shows action.
   c. A noun is a word that represents a person, place, or thing.
   d. A noun is a word that describes other words.

3. Evaluation Statement:

   Given a list of words, they will circle all those that are nouns. Item:

   Look at the words below. Circle all those that are nouns.

a. hat	e. if	i. St. Louis
b. is	f. and	j. Michigan
c. door	g. to	k. pencil
d. small	h. girl	1. under

4. Evaluation Statement:

   Given nouns, they will correctly use them in sentences.

   Item:

   Look at the following nouns and, on the line, write one sentence using each properly.

   a. sun ______________________________

   b. table ______________________________

   c. rock ______________________________

5. Evaluation Statement:

   Given a list of sentences, they will underline all the nouns.

   Item:

   Read the following sentences and underline *all* the nouns in each.

   a. Jim, a large boy, rode his bike to the store.
   b. The noise in this town is murder!
   c. How fast were you going when the police officer stopped you?
   d. This is the last time I'll run through those woods.

6. Evaluation Statement:

   Given a sentence, they will describe the author's intent by interpreting the meaning of the nouns in the context of the sentence.

   Item:

   Consider the use of the noun *man* in the sentence below. Describe the meaning of the noun in each case according to the context of the sentence.

   Man! That man is a *real man*.

   Man! ______________________________

   man ______________________________

   man ______________________________

7. Evaluation Statement:

   Given a sentence and a list of meanings of a noun as determined by context, they will select the best interpretation.

   Item:

   Look at the first use of the word *man* in the sentence below.

   Man! That man is a *real man.*

   Choose the best interpretation of the meaning of *Man!*

   a. It is a noun used as a subject in a sentence.
   b. It is a noun used to describe an element of masculinity or toughness.
   c. It is a noun used as a direct object in the sentence.
   d. It is a noun used as slang to express amazement or impressiveness.

Let's look now at the seven illustrations and discuss them in view of the material we've presented so far. We can say several things about them.

First, each of the seven items is a formal measurement designed to provide data to help the teacher evaluate his students' understanding of nouns. This is contrasted with informal measures such as observing the students at work or hearing a variety of responses from them.

Second, the items are written at different levels. Items 1 and 2 are knowledge level, 3 and 5 are comprehension level, 4 is application level, and 6 and 7 are probably at the analysis level. As we noted in Chapter 4, exact determinations of level are sometimes very difficult, so you shouldn't be overly concerned with uncertainty between levels such as application and analysis, or analysis and evaluation. Our primary goal is for you to be aware of and sensitive to the higher levels of the taxonomy so you can encourage your students to improve their thinking skills. Consequently, you will want to measure at the higher levels as well.

Third, some of the items are production and some are recognition. Items 1, 4, and 6 are production items; the students were asked to produce, respectively, a definition, a sentence, and an analysis. Items 2, 3, 5, and 7 are recognition items; the students had to recognize, respectively, a definition, nouns in a list, nouns in a sentence, and a correct interpretation of a noun's usage.

Let's look now at recognition and production in a bit more detail. First, production items are generally more difficult than recognition items at the same taxonomic level. For a psychological explanation of this difference, see Brown (1976) and Wickelgren (1977). Items 1 and 2 are both knowledge level, but it-calling and stating the definition is more difficult than merely recognising it. Another example of the simpler nature of recognition as compared to production is found in our vocabulary. It is *generally* believed that our comprehension vocabulary is several times larger than our speaking vocabulary. This means that we recognize the meaning of many more words than we are able to use in conversation.

A second observation about these two types of items is that recognition items are much easier for the teacher to evaluate. A production item results in each student giving a slightly different response, leaving you in a position of having to decide whether the produced statement represents an adequate understanding of the concept. We are not suggesting that production items shouldn't be used but are merely pointing out that they are more difficult to evaluate. For example, compare Item 6 to Item 7. Item 6 puts much more demand on the learner; he must interpret what is being asked, organize his thoughts, and put them down on paper. In Item 7, he must merely select the choice he believes is best. Also, in Item 6, students will give a variety of responses since this is a divergent question as opposed to a convergent one such as Item 7. Therefore the teacher needs to make more evaluation decisions with Item 6 than with 7 where it would be much easier to be consistent in scoring.

One other factor to consider in deciding upon the item format is the amount of work involved. Production items are easier to prepare while recognition items are easier to score. The decision of which to use depends on your concerns with the item. If you want to have students learn to express themselves in writing, you may choose to use a production item. You must keep in mind, of course, that you would be measuring writing ability in addition to the understanding of the concept. Let's look at what the student must be able to do or must know in order to correctly respond to Item 6:

Be able to read.
Be able to organize thoughts.
Be able to write in a clear and precise way.
Know how nouns are used in sentences in order to describe the way each is used in context.

By comparison, let's look at what the student must be able to do or must know in order to correctly respond to Item 7:

Be able to read.
Know the concept *subject*.
Know the concept *direct object*

Know the meaning *of slang.*

Know the meaning of *amazement* and *impressiveness.*

Being able to organize thoughts and express them in writing is very demanding for many students; consequently, this together with consistency, is the reason we see recognition items on standardised tests.

These factors are not mentioned to suggest that accurate measurement is extremely difficult or even impossible. On the contrary, measuring can be an enjoyable task because it gives you information about your students and your own teaching. Instead, these factors are a reminder of considerations that must be undertaken in measuring—again, all in an effort to increase rational decision making.

Let's look now at other items and consider these factors further. (You will notice that to complete this discussion we're using as an example $C = \pi d$, which is actually a generalisation. Well discuss measuring generalisations more fully in the next section.)

Think back to Mr. Hite's lesson on circles in Chapter 7, page 174. His objective was

For fifth-grade students to understand the formula for computing circumference so that, given a ruler and four circles with the radius drawn in, they will calculate the circumference of each without error.

An item to measure Mr. Hite's objective would be:

A. Calculate the circumference of each of the following circles.

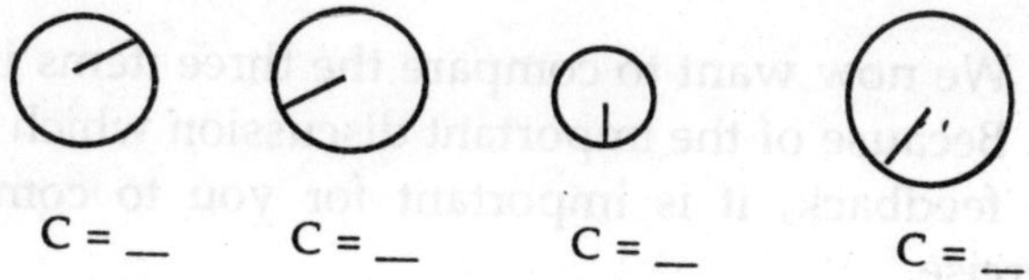

C = __ C = __ C = __ C = __

Suppose now that Mr. Hite's evaluation statement was a bit different and his objective was stated as follows:

For fifth-grade students to understand the formula for computing circumference so that, given, four diameters of circles, they will calculate the circumference of each without error.

An item to measure his objective in this case could be:

B. Calculate the circumference of each of the four circles from the diameters given below:

Diameter = 2 cm. C = ____________

Diameter = 4.5 cm. C = ____________

Diameter = 13.22 cm. C = ____________

Diameter = 6 cm. C = ____________

There are still other possibilities. For instance, suppose Mr. Hite's objective was stated:For fifth-grade students to understand the formula for computing circumference so that, given the formula and four diameters of circles, they will calculate the circumference of each without error.

An item to measure his objective in this case could be:

C. Use the equation $C = \pi d$ to calculate the circumference of each of the four circles whose diameters are given below.

Diameter = 2 cm. C = ____________

Diameter = 4.5 cm. C = ____________

Diameter = 13.22 cm. C = ____________

Diameter = 6 cm. C = ____________

We now want to compare the three items in Exercise 4.1. Because of the important discussion which follows in the feedback, it is important for you to complete this exercise.

EXERCISE 4.1

Consider Items A, B, and C from the previous section and answer the following questions. Then compare your answers to the ones given in the feedback section at the end of the chapter.

1. **List what the student must be able to do or must know in order to respond correctly to each item.**

   A.

   1) ______________________

   2) ______________________

   3) ______________________

   4) ______________________

   5) ______________________

   6) ______________________

   7) ______________________

   8) ______________________

   B.

   1) ______________________

   2) ______________________

   3) ______________________

   4) ______________________

   5) ______________________

   6) ______________________

   C.

   1) ______________________

   2) ______________________

   3) ______________________

   4) ______________________

2. **At what taxonomic level is each item written?**

   A. ______________________

B. ______________________________

C. ______________________________

3. Identify each item as either production or recognition.

   A. ______________________________

   B. ______________________________

   C. ______________________________

While the next section deals with the selection of possible answers, one final factor should be mentioned here about these examples. In terms of the demands on the learner, computing the circumference for *d* = 13.22 cm. is more demanding than computing it for *d* = 2 cm. Again, the choice of a difficult or easy problem depends on the judgment of the teacher and what she wants the students to be able to demonstrate. Level of difficulty is, however, a factor to be considered.

Let's look now at a common recognition item, the multiple choice format. Our purpose here is to discuss distracters in some detail. *Distracters* are the incorrect or inappropriate choices listed in a multiple choice item. Multiple choice items are an efficient method of measuring all forms of knowledge. We saw in the example with nouns how recall of a definition can be measured. Let's look now at an analysis of distracters through an example of measuring comprehension of concepts.

Consider Mr. Hanes's lesson from Chapter on *hyperbole. Hyperbole is* a concept, and, as noted earlier, an efficient method of measuring students' understanding of a concept is to have them identify examples of it. (Of course, *noun* is also a concept, and we saw that it can be measured at a variety of levels.)

Let's look at two items designed to measure students' comprehension of *hyperbole:*

1. Which of the following is a statement of hyperbole?
   a. He is like an old shoe.
   b. He was a rock of a man.
   c. The night's bright eyes shone through the inky blackness.
   d. I was so sad I could have cried a river.
2. Which of the following is a statement of hyperbole?
   a. He went to town.
   b. Three large boys rode by on their bikes.
   c. Susan looks like her mother.
   d. I was so sad I could have cried a river.

In both items the correct choice is *d*, but the distracters are much better in Item 1 than those in Item 2. Looking at Item 1 in detail, we see that choice *a* is a simile, choice *b* is a metaphor, choice *c* is personification, and choice *d* is hyperbole. All four choices are figures of speech and the learner must know hyperbole from other figures of speech in order to answer the item correctly. In Item 2, no other figures of speech are used as distracters; therefore, the learner might not know hyperbole from other figures of speech and might still answer the item correctly. This would then be an inaccurate measurement leading the teacher to conclude that students understand hyperbole when they actually don't. The purpose in choosing good distracters is not to trick students but to measure their learning as accurately as possible.

Let's consider recognition versus production in this case. A critical factor in using the identification of examples to measure comprehension of concepts is that they are novel, having never been encountered by the students before. If they had previously encountered the example, "I was so sad I could have cried a river," as an example the teacher used to teach the concept, the measurement would merely be at the knowledge level because it had been memorised. If students are asked to produce an example, they may merely recall one rather than produce an original. In this case, a recognition item may be preferable because the teacher can be as sure as possible that the examples are unique. Again, the whole purpose is to measure as accurately as possible.

Let's look now at the recognition item distracters in the feedback for Exercise 4.1. The item was written as follows:

Look at the following circle:

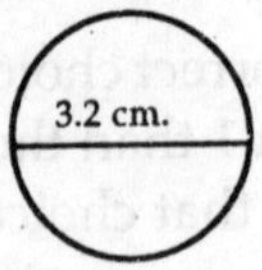

The circumference of the circle is:

a. 1.6 cm.
b. 8.04 cm.
c. 10.05 cm.
d. 5.02 cm.

These numbers were not selected arbitrarily. For example:

a. 1.6 cm. = the radius (half the diameter)
b. 8.04 cm. = the area πr^2)
c. 10.05 cm. = the correct answer (πd)
d. 5.02 = πr

If the learner is confused between area and circumference he might choose *b*. If he doesn't remember that circumference relates to diameter and not radius, he might choose *d*. In either case the measurement is more accurate of the students' understanding of circumference and, therefore, more likely to help the teacher identify students' misconceptions than if the numbers were chosen arbitrarily. Again, the purpose is to measure accurately and not to trick the students. Let's now consider another example as an exercise.

EXERCISE 4.2

Look at the following two items designed to measure a preschool child's concept of rectangle. A suming the directions are given orally, choose the better item and explain your choice. Then compare your answers to those given in the feedback section at the end of the chapter.

1. Look at the three shapes on your paper and mark the one that is a rectangle.

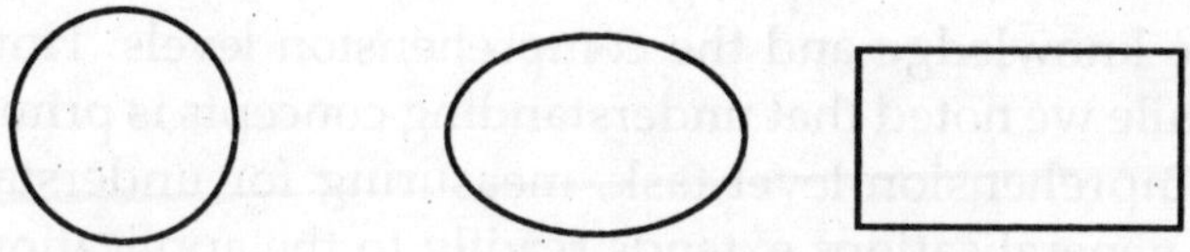

2. Look at the four shapes on your paper and mark the one that is a rectangle.

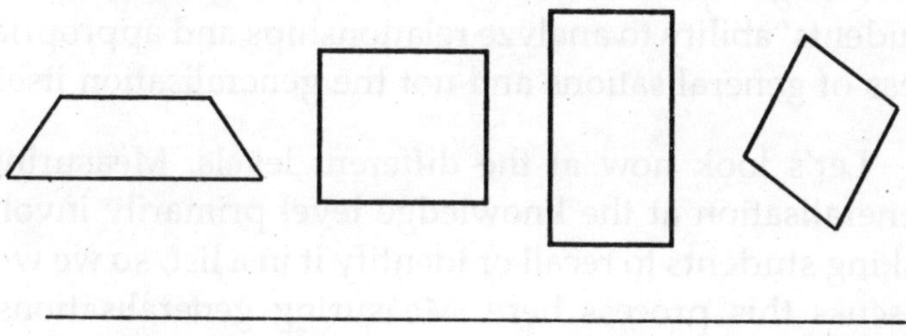

EXERCISE 4.3

As a production exercise, develop a recognition item to measure a preschool child's concept of *mammal.* Assuming the item and the distracters would be presented in pictorial form, write a multiple choice question with one correct answer and three distracters. Then compare your item to the one given in the feedback section at the end of the chapter.

Measuring the Understanding of Generalisations

As with concepts, generalisations can be measured at the knowledge and the comprehension levels. However, while we noted that understanding concepts is primarily a comprehension level task, measuring for understanding of generalisations extends readily to the application level of the taxonomy. As with concepts, levels beyond application exist for generalisations, but they are designed to measure students' ability to analyze relationships and appropriateness of generalisations and not the generalisation itself.

Let's look now at the different levels. Measuring a generalisation at the knowledge level primarily involves asking students to recall or identify it in a list, so we won't discuss this process here. Measuring generalisations at higher levels is quite another task. Let's look at the following objective:

For psychology students to understand the

generalisation, intermittent reinforcement produces persistent behavior and slow extinction, so that, given a series of illustrations, they will identify the cases in which the generalisation applies.

The item appears as follows:

Which of the following illustrate the generalisation, intermittent reinforcement produces persistent behavior and slow extinction? Circle the letter of all choices which apply.

a. Mrs. Williams was trying to encourage Johnny's seatwork. For a week she gave him a reward every five minutes whenever he was working quietly at his desk.
b. Mr. Smith assigns homework nightly but checks it only periodically.
c. Johnny, a spirited third-grader, acts up often. Generally his teacher is firm but strict. Sometimes, though, Johnny's behavior is so funny, she has to laugh.
d. When encountering a locked door, people generally wiggle it several rimes and then leave or hunt for a key.
e. Mr. Jones put 500 into the washing machine at the laundromat. It didn't come on, so he tried another machine.
f. People who go to Las Vegas usually lose, but they win every once in a while.
g. Mr. Anderson caught a fish in a particular spot in the St. Johns River. Now he fishes in that spot whenever he can and does fairly well.

In this item, the students have to identify cases where the generalisation is illustrated; in other words, they are identifying examples of the generalisation. In this sense, the measurement is similar to having the students identify examples of a concept, which is also a comprehension level task.

Note the format of the item. The student, in responding, makes a decision abort each choice individually. The item then essentially operates in a true/false format. The directions could just as easily have read:

> Mark as true the following cases that illustrate the generalisation, intermittent reinforcement results in persistent behavior and slow extinction.

To make the item simply multiple choice, the instructor would merely have to reduce the number of choices to four or five with only one correct. We will not discuss the relative advantages and disadvantages of the true/false format and the multiple choice format beyond a description designed to make you aware of and sensitive to the difference.

Let's look now at another example:

> People in an institution were being paid 50¢ a day for doing maintenance work around the grounds. After the work was done, the trustee, who inspected the work, would come and then pay the money to the workers. After a while, in that the work was always satisfactory and the workers always got paid, the administrators decided that they would just pay all the inmates in the morning at roll call and save the management the problem of paying people when the trustee came around.

Which of the following best describes the consequence of the change in routine.?

a. There would be no change and the operation would proceed more smoothly.
b. The inmates would like it better because they knew they would get paid, and, consequently, they would work harder,
c. The inmates would work less hard because they got paid whether they did the work or not.
d. The inmates would work less hard because they would be insulted by the small amount they were being paid.

The preceding is another example from psychology. Notice the difference between the two examples. In the first, the students were asked to identify illustrations of the generalisation, which is a comprehension level task. In the second, they were asked to use the generalisation, reinforcement is most effective following desired behavior, to predict consequences, which is an application level task.

EXERCISE 4.4

Read the following item and then answer the questions at the end. Compare your answers to the ones found in the feedback section at the end of the chapter.

Which of the following cases relate to the generalisation, people who smoke tend to have a higher incidence of heart disease than those who don't?

a. Mr. Smith is a robust man in his late thirties. He runs two miles a day and lives a generally healthy life. He eats two eggs and has bacon for breakfast in order to get enough protein, and loves beef because "it keeps my energy level up." His only problem is that he has a heart murmur.
b. Mr. Jones has a generally healthy living style. He has only

two vices. He smokes a half a pack of cigarettes a day and has one strong drink before dinner. Otherwise he watches his diet by keeping fatty foods to a minimum and plays tennis four days a week. He is in his late thirties and is in excellent health.

c. Mr. Anderson lives a generally comfortable life style. He smokes a few cigarettes each day but lays off the beer. He plays tennis and everyone tells him how good he looks. However, he has two arteries partially clogged that his doctor says will eventually require surgery.

d. Mr. Holt is a generally healthy man in his early thirties. His only problem is he sometimes has heart fibrillation. This is hard to imagine because he has a clean life style. He is a vegetarian and his weight is what it was in high school. He doesn't smoke and doesn't drink at all.

1. At what level is this item?

____

2. Analyze the four choices in terms of the appropriateness of the distracters.

   a. ___________________________________
   b. ___________________________________
   c. ___________________________________
   d. ___________________________________

____

Note in each of the previous examples that measuring understanding of a generalisation required a short scenario either in the stem of the item or in the distracters. When measuring generalisations, this will often be the case since a generalisation is broader and more inclusive than a concept. With practice, you will learn how to write scenarios which can be used in questions used to measure your students' understanding of generalisations.

Let's look now at an example that doesn't require a scenario. Refer to Chapter 7 in which a teacher wanted her students to understand the generalisation, when two vowels are together in a word, the first is long and the second is silent.

An item to measure this generalisation could be as follows:

(Teacher reads) Look at the list of words in front of you. I'm going to pronounce each word and you mark the ones in which the rule, when two vowels are together in a word, the first is long and the second is silent, is illustrated.

bought	sleigh	receive
either	protein	great
read	eight	load

Notice in this item that both the words and their pronunciations were required because the rule linked the sound of the word to its spelling. Merely showing the students the words and asking them to state in which cases the rule applied wouldn't be appropriate. In order to respond correctly, a student would have to know how the word was pronounced; that being the case, the example couldn't be unique, which would mean the item was only at the knowledge level. This example is an excellent illustration of the teacher's need to think carefully about the measurement process.

EXERCISE 4.5

Using a scenario, write a multiple choice item to measure the following objective:

For students to understand the generalisation, climate affects culture, so that give a description of a culture, they will identify a statement that illustrates the generalisation.

Then read the item given in the feedback section at the end of the chapter.

Measuring Inquiry Skills

Now we will briefly consider the measurement of inquiry skills. This represents a departure from the themes of the text up to this point because measuring inquiry learning amounts to measuring an intellectual skill. The skill involved is the ability to relate data to an hypothesis or the ability to decide which of two or more hypotheses is most supported in light of the data. As an example, consider the following situation involving the relationship of data to hypotheses.

The following is a partial map of a coastline:

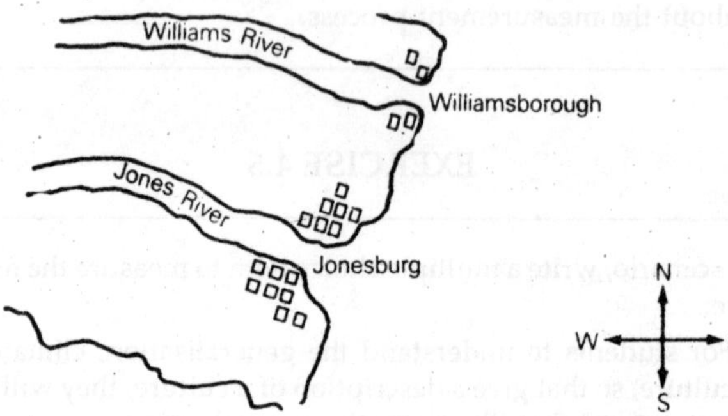

Both cities are on the coast and exist at the mouths of rivers. However. Jonesburg is a large and busy transportation center while Williamsborough is small and insignificant. The following were proposed hypotheses which explained the reason for this difference:

a. While both Williamsborough and Jonesburg are on the coast and are at the mouths of rivers, Williamborough's harbor is smaller than Jonesburg's, and the winds and tricky local currents made entrance dangerous in the early years when sailing ships were used.

b. The coastal range of mountains isolated Williamsborough but dwindled to foothills by the time they reached Jonesburg, which left it accessible to overland shipping.

The following data were gathered in reference to the hypotheses. Based on the data, decide which hypothesis is more logical and explain your choice briefly.

1. The current along the coast runs from north to south.
2. Jonesburg's harbor is larger than Williamsborough's.
3. About the same number of ships ran aground near Jonesburg as ran aground near Williamsborough in the sailing days.
4. Jonesburg and Williamsborough are over 100 miles apart.
5. The mountains around Williamsborough are more rugged than the mountains around Jonesburg.
6. The local winds around Jonesburg are more variable than they are around Williamsborough.

Keep in mind here that you're measuring the student's ability to relate data to hypotheses which means the particular content of the item is not important. An inquiry lesson could present a topic in science while the item could involve social studies content. This is not inappropriate because you're measuring an ability or an intellectual skill on the part of the students rather than information about an area of content. This is often a unique experience for a student and initially can be disconcerting. However, once this ability is developed, the students have acquired a powerful thinking skill.

EXERCISE 4.6

Read the following example of an inquiry situation and then respond to the data which follows Check your responses with the ones given in the feedback section at the end of the chapter.

A study reported an investigation of longevity in various groups of people around the world. The investigators found two particular groups with a wide disparity in the average life expectancy between them. Furthermore. Group A (the long-lived group) had a much lower overall standard of living than Group B (the shorter-lived group). The average expectancies were Group A—85 years, and Group B—70 years. The investigators proposed the following explanation for this startling phenomenon:

While the standard of living for Group A is lower, they live in a manner conducive to good health. They are basically agrarian people, leading active and hard-working lives tending livestock and farms. Hence, they stay slim and avoid becoming overweight. They live in the mountains away from the psychological stresses of urban living. Their intake of potentially harmful items such as alcohol, tobacco, and high cholesterol foods is kept at a minimum. On the other hand. Group B was sampled from an urban environment where psychological stress causing blood pressure problems is high, the air is dirty from factories, and the people lead sedentary lives.

The following is data that was found relative to the two groups. In each case, decide if the data supports the explanation (s) or does not (ns).

—— 1. Group A people averaged about 5'10" and about 190 Ib., while Group B people averaged about 6'0" and approximately 180 Ib.

—— 2. The average protein intake per capita per day was:
Group A: All sources—60 g.
Animal sources—1 g.
Group B: All sources—100 g.
Animal sources—95 g.

—— 3. Group A people average 6 oz. per person per day of an alcohol resembling a cross between gin and vodka.

—— 4. Group A people spent an average of twelve working hours per day walking in the mountains as sheepherders.

—— 5. The city from which the Group B sample was drawn was noted for its "soft" industry such as insurance companies and clearing houses for photocopying companies rather than heavy industries such as steel making.

—— 6. The companies noted in number 5 employed many supervisors and salespeople with each company priding itself in its success competing with rival companies.

—— 7. The companies noted in numbers 5 and 6 also prided themselves in their comprehensive recreational programmes including a variety of team and individual sports. They noted that each supervisor and salespeople averaged a minimum of five hours per week of vigorous physical activity.

—— 8. Group A people enjoyed smoking a ground-up root resembling pipe tobacco in their leisure time. The investigators tried it and found it made them lightheaded when they inhaled, but the natives said it was easy to get used to.

—— 9. In interviewing Group A people, a typical remark heard was, "It is good here where we can sit in the evening, watch the sun settle over our land, talk quietly, and watch our children grow."

—— 10. In interviewing Group B people, typical remarks were. "I love my work. The only problem is that it's a bit of a hassle on the go all the time. It's really nice to get home and away from the grind. The traffic in this town is murder."

You've now seen what is perhaps a unique form of measurement for teachers and students, measurement of the inquiry process. Of course, the teacher could still measure the students' understanding of the content that came from the lesson in one of the conventional ways already discussed. Our purpose here is to give you a brief introduction to the idea of measuring inquiry skills. This introduction is sketchy because complete discussion of measuring for inquiry skills is beyond the scope of this text, but we hope this initial exposure will help you get started toward developing an important thinking skill in your own students.

5

Activity Method of Teaching

The particular intention behind this first group of activities is to strengthen understanding by linking it to active response. For example, it is usually important when organising listening activities to make sure that the children have something to do as a result of what they hear. This means that they are having to process the language they hear, and are not just letting the noise of it into their ears.

1. Write Down the Number of the One Your Hear

In this activity the children have to identify which promptcard you are talking about. This is a very simple activity and as the four stars show, is one you might consider making part of your core. It is useful as a way of introducing something new. It is a way of providing plenty of meaningful listening practice before the children are asked to produce the sounds themselves. There was an example of this in the five word lesson on other page. There, it was being used to introduce colours. In this example, it is being used for a different purpose but the process is the same.

Language Focus in this Example

Understanding directions, e.g. turn left, turn right, go straight on, cross the bridge, take the second right, take the third left.

Material Required

— A set of drawings to prompt the language you want to practise, e.g.:

Note 1:

You can simply draw the symbols on the board or make a quick set of promptcards. Promptcards take time to make initially but have the advantage that you can move them around. You can hold them, arrange them in various combinations on the board, or hand them out to pupils. They do not have to be complicated. Some of the commercial flashcards are very attractive but too detailed, big and heavy. If you make your own cards, you do not have to go to the expense of buying actual card. You can use paper. One sheet of ordinary A4 paper will make four 'cards' of about the right size. Use a strong coloured and thickish felt tip pen and just draw the essential elements or a symbol rather than a detailed picture Children are quite happy with this. It is also easier for you.

Note 2:

You don't have to have promptcards to do this activity. In fact, in most of the activities suggesting cards, you can write or draw on the board instead, though it is slower and more restricting.

— Blutack or something similar which can be used to stick the cards temporarily to the board.

— The children need something to write on. Rough paper will do.

Preliminary Work

Briefly introduce the new phrases in the following way.

— Stick each prompt on the board, saying each one once or twice again as you do so:

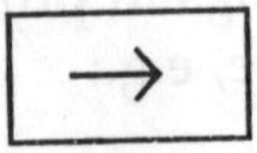

Teacher: Turn right… turn right… turn right…

— Stick each prompt on the board, saying each one once or twice again as you do so:

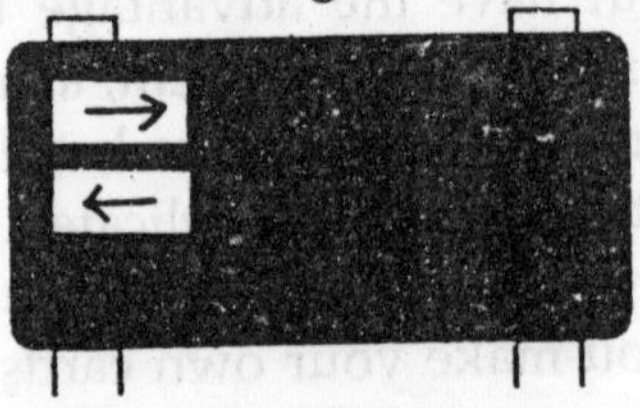

Teacher:Turn right… turn right…
Turn left… turn left…

— Go through the whole set of promptcards once more fairly quickly.

— Get a child to come to the front and point to whichever one you say. Do this several times with different children.

Now move on to 'write down the number of the one you hear'.

Suggested Procedures

— Number the prompts on the board.

– Number the prompts on the board.

— Say one of the phrases and, on another part of the board, write its number. Do this for all the phrases but in any order you like.

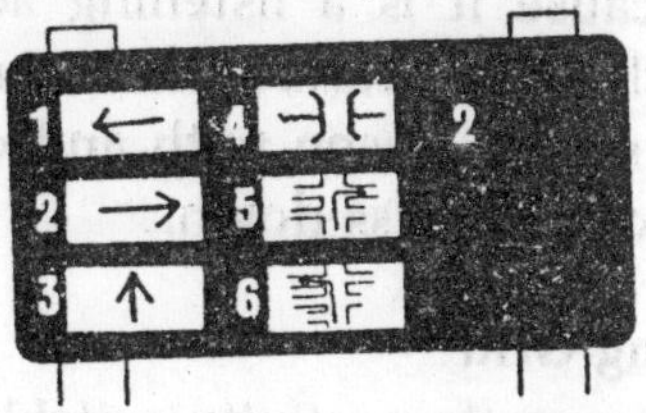

— Do the same again but get one of the children to write on the board the numbers of the phrases you say.

— Now get the whole class to write down on their paper the numbers of the phrases you say. (Remember to keep a record for yourself of the order you say them in!)

— Check quickly by simply writing up the numbers of the sequence of phrases you said. The children check their own.

— Repeat the exercise several times with increasing speed and with a different order each time.

Variation

To practise parts of the body you can get the children to draw a pin man and to write the numbers on the appropriate parts.

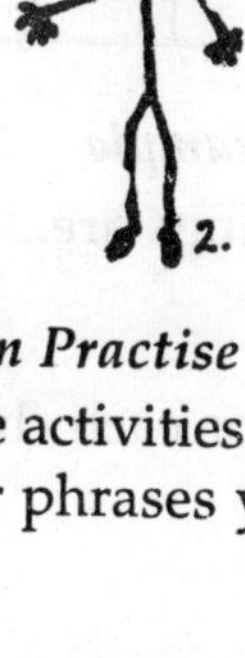

Other Language You can Practise with this Activity

This is one of those activities you can use to introduce any group of words or phrases you want to teach.

Final Comments

This is an example of an exercise which provides 'written' work without expecting the children to be able to write. Because it is a listening activity and because it occupies the whole class at the same time, it makes a good settler to start a lesson with and can also be used mid-lesson to calm a class down.

2. Listening Grid

Here is another activity suitable for your 'core'. It too is intended to provide active response to new language. For this activity, the children have to mark on a matrix or grid the information read out by the teacher. The example below is practising prepositions. The teacher has so far read out:

'The cup is on the table.'
'The cat is under the chair.'
'The girl is in front of the tree.'

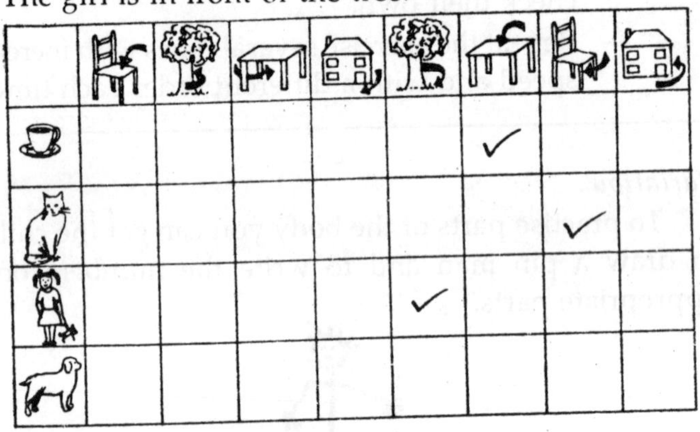

Language Focus in this Example

Describing where things are.

Material Required

— A small grid for each child.

Note: If it makes life easier for you, there is no reason why they should not draw their own grids, but it takes time so if you are fortunate enough to have access to a photocopier, it is much simpler to draw the grids and duplicate them yourself. They do not have to be big. Dividing an A4-sized piece of paper into four is perfectly satisfactory. It also cuts down on costs!

— Promptcards which are the same as the pictures on the grid.
— Blutack or something similar which will allow you to stick your pictures temporarily on the board.

Preliminary Work

The previous 'write down the number' activity makes a very good lead-in to this.

Suggested Procedures

— First pre-check the various elements of the grid quickly and build up an example grid on the board. You can do this by saying each phrase two or three times and putting the matching promptcard up as you say it, in the same position as it appears in the grid:

TEACHER: On the chair ... on the chair.

Behind the tree ... behind the tree.

Under the table ... under the table.

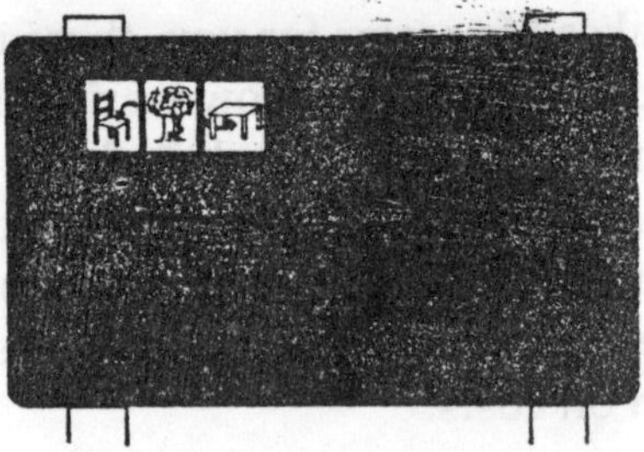

In this way, build up the complete grid pattern of cards on the board.

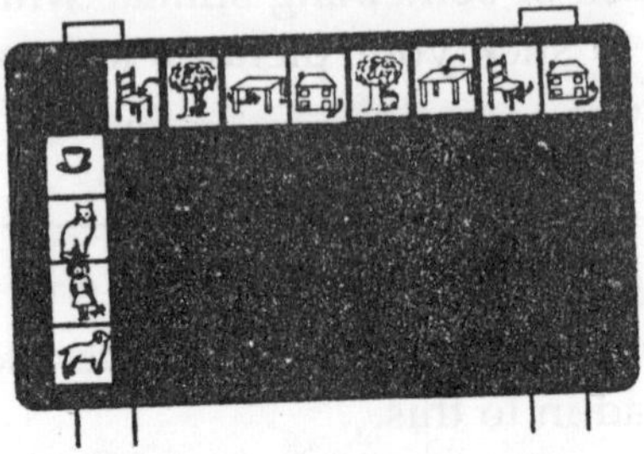

(If the class look as if they are falling asleep, you can slip in the occasional chorus repetition, but at this stage you are still just asking them to listen.)

— Now draw in the lines round your cards so you have a board grid.

— Make a statement and mark in the appropriate box:

TEACHER: The cat is on the table.

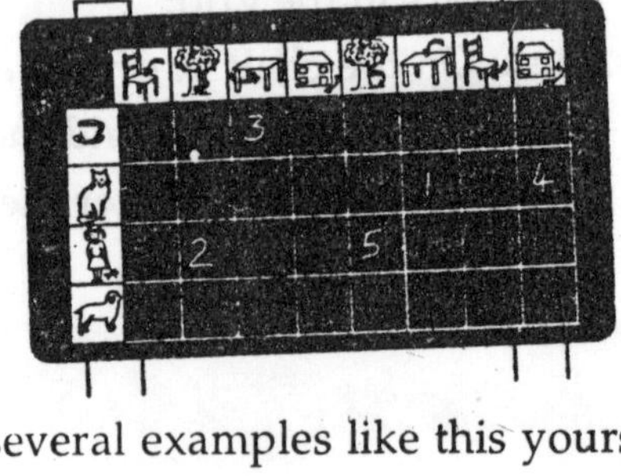

— Do several examples like this yourself then get

a child to come to the board to write the numbers in the appropriate squares. (With some classes you may want to do this several times to check their understanding before you start them working on their own.)

— Hand out the class grids.
— Rub out the numbers from the grid on the board and start again. This time, the children fill in their own grids. If some of the class are looking a little unsure, you can always do the first one or two on your board grid with them so they can see that they have got the right idea.
— When you have finished, check by reading through the statements again and getting a child or children to write up the numbers on the board grid. Each of the class checks their own grid against the board version as you go through it.

Possible Follow Up

As Chapter 3 pointed out, you do not want to spend a long time preparing something like these grids and then throw them away after five minutes. So, once the grids have been completed as a listening exercise, you can use them again in several different ways, either immediately or in a later lesson. For example:

a) Further Listening: True/False

— Make a statement like '2 ... The cat is on the chair.'
— The class look at the grid and tell you 'Yes, it is.' or 'No, it isn't.'
— When you have done this several times, you can rub off the answers from the board grid, get the children to turn their grids over, and challenge

them to say from memory whether your statement is true or false.

b) Later Oral Work with the Teacher

At a later stage, after the children have done some repetition work of the phrases and can now say them well, you can go back to the grids and the class can challenge you and each other to a game of true/false along the lines described above.

c) Later Oral Work in Pairs

Once they can say the phrases and are used to playing true/false with you as a class, they can do the activity in pairs. Child A looks at the grid to 'memorise' it, then turns it over so she can't see it. Child B then makes a statement from his grid, e.g. The dog is behind the tree.' Child A has to say 'Yes, it is./No, it isn't'

d) Later Written Work

After they have done some reading work on the phrases, you can get them to make up and write out several sentences of their own from the grid.

Variation

These grids are simplest if you have only one piece of information per line and if you give the information in the order it appears on the grid, so that the children do not have to search too frantically. On the other hand, more able or older children will enjoy having to search all over the grid for what you have just said. By altering the order in which you give the information you can adjust the level of the activity to suit your class.

Other Language You can Practise with this Activity

The possibilities are almost limitless but, for example, you could combine:

Colours and clothes.	Places and directions for getting to them.
Times and activities.	People and activities.
People and places.	Days of the week and the weather.
Rooms and furniture.	Shops and things bought in them. etc.

Final Comments

This kind of listening grid has a great deal to commend it. It involves all the children in the class at the same time. It makes them think hard about what they are hearing and is therefore mentally engaging as well as actually occupying. It can provide worthwhile sustained listening work so we don't rush too soon into oral work with new language. It is a 'writing' activity they can do long before they can write the words. It is also possible for all children in a mixed ability class to work with the same grid quite happily. That is why it is recommended as a core activity.

3. Listen and Find

This is a rather more lively activity. This time the children have to pick out the real object which the teacher is talking about. In the example here it is a team game. In fact it is quite a 'stirrer'. It is designed to provide physically active listening practice *before* the children have moved on to speaking. (It can of course also be used later as a fun revision activity too.) The version described here is called 'The washing line game'.

Language Focus in this Example

Clothes and colours.

Material Required

— At the front of the room, have two boxes or bags, each containing identical sets of the items you want to practise.

— Some clothes pegs if you have them, but they are not essential.

Preliminary Work

Pre-check the vocabulary in some way, even if they seemed to know it yesterday! You can do this by just telling them quickly,

---

Suggested Procedures

— At the front of the class, get two children to hold a short length of rope between them like a washing line.

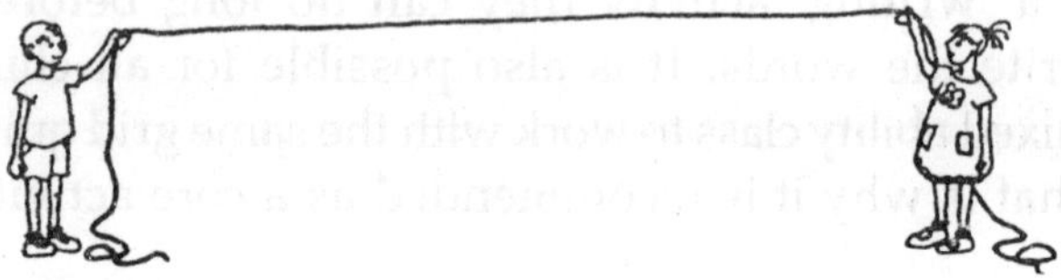

— Dmivide the class into two teams and get a representative of each team to come to the front.
— Ask for an item from one of the boxes:
TEACHER: Please bring me a blue sock.
— The two representatives search their boxes to identify and take out the object concerned. The first one to hang it on the line is the winner and that team scores a point.

Variation

If your classes come to school reasonably well provided

with felt tip pens or crayons and if they like drawing, you could practise the same items in the form of a kind of drawn lotto. It would look like this:

Suggested Procedures

— Each child draws their own small washing line with four items of clothing on it. They then put a dot of colour on it to show what colour it is. (If we let them colour them in properly, it will be next week before some of them have finished!)

— You read out a list of items:

'I have a blue sock.'

'I also have a green shirt.'

'I have a red shirt ...

and a blue skirt ...'

and so on until one child has been able to cross off all the items on their line and has won that round. Remember to keep a list of what you say or you will have a rebellion on your hands!

Other Language You can Practise with this Activity

This activity is more suited to practising separate vocabulary items rather than whole phrases. It is most fun if you can use real objects but it is perfectly possible to do it with two sets of picture cards or word cards.

Final Coment

Any competition like this tends to stir a class up so you will probably want to follow it with something settling.

4. Listen and Arrange

This time the children are being asked to arrange a picture or diagram according to the information they hear.

This is another activity which aims to strengthen understanding by linking it to response. It again asks the children to respond physically to what they hear, although not in the energetic way that the washing line game demands. It is not such obvious fun as the washing line game but is still mentally engaging because the children have to work out the significance of what they hear. At the same time, it is much more involving than the washing line game because every child is doing something at each moment. That makes it a good settler.

Language Focus in this Example

Rooms in the house.

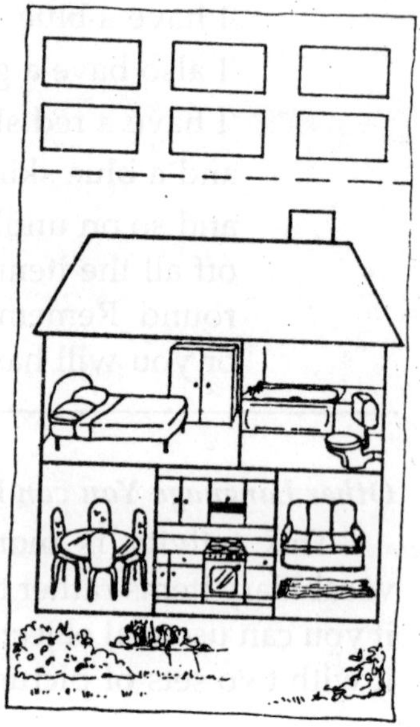

Material Required

— For this activity you need, for each child or pair of children, a base sheet like this one of the house and some name slips. If the children in your class are used to using scissors, they can cut out the name slips for you and put them in an envelope at the end of the activity. You can then reuse the materials with another class or on another occasion.

— Blutack if you have it.

Preliminary Work

To show the class what to do, you need five names on slips of paper and an outline of the house on the board.

— Make a statement like: 'Lizzie is in the bedroom. and stick the name slip in the appropriate place.

NOTE: It is better to stick the name slip in the right place if you can, because that is what the children are going to have to do. Otherwise, you can simply write in the names on the board.

— Do a couple more examples with them, glancing round to see if most of the children are following.

— Remove the name slips.

The children should now be ready to work on their own.

Suggested Procedures

- — Hand out the base sheets to the class. If you have not already done so, the children write the five names on the name slips and cut them out.
- — Make the first statement, e.g. 'Kevin is in the bedroom.'
- — The children put the name slip in the right room. (You can check supportively for the first one or two by putting the names in the right place on the board after they have all had the chance to put theirs on their sheets. In this way, you and the class will know that all is well.)
- — Continue until all the name slips are placed.
- — Use your board version to check back.
- — Repeat the exercise as often as you like, changing the combinations of people and rooms.

Possible Follow Up

You can follow up with the same activities as were suggested for following up the listening grid

Variation

This activity can also be changed to an interactive activity for pairs like the arrange and describe activity on previous pages.

Other Language You can Practise with this Activity

This activity lends itself best to any work involving locations, for example: Shops in a street.

Furniture in a room.

Or, by using speech bubbles, you could also use it for phrases and expressions:

Final Comment

The advantage of this paper arranging activity is that you can reuse your base sheet because the children are not writing on it. You can also reuse the same base sheet on another occasion but with different items to arrange.

5. Listen and Work Out the Order

In this activity, the children are given a set of pictures which are in the wrong order. The teacher describes the pictures in the correct order and the children have to identify them in sequence. They may not understand everything they hear. That is quite deliberate. We are encouraging them to use their ability to work on partial information and to take risks. It is easier for them to do both these things with listening than speaking, because they are being asked to respond not to produce the language themselves.

Language Focus in this Example

Food.

Materials Required

— For each child or pair of children you need a sheet of pictures like the example below. (Remember they are in the wrong order!)

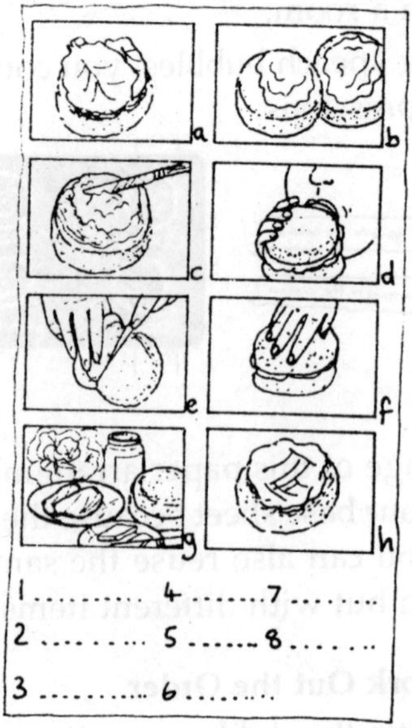

— For yourself you need a list of sentences which describe the pictures. These are in the *right* order:

To Make a Ham and Lettuce Sandwich

1. You need a slice of ham. a roll, some lettuce, some butter and some , mayonnaise.
2. First cut the roll in half.
3. Butter the two pieces of roll.
4. Put the ham onto the bottom half of the roll.
5. Spread a little mayonnaise onto the ham. Be carefull Not too much!
6. Now put some lettuce on top of the ham.
7. Put the top of the roll on top and press it down.
8. Eat it!

Preliminary Work

This activity would fit well into the general topic of food. It is best if the children already know the words for some of the food which comes into the activity, but it is not necessary for them to know everything. For example, they may not yet know the words 'hair and 'mayonnaise'. The whole idea is that they should be encouraged to guess the meaning on the basis of the clues in the pictures, their existing knowledge of the topic, or possibly the sound of the word.

Suggested Procedures

— Hand out the picture sheets, keeping one for yourself.

— Give the children a couple of seconds to look at the pictures so that they know what is there.

— Hold your picture sheet so that it is facing them and ask them to look at you.

— Read out the first sentence and show that you are looking for the picture which matches:

TEACHER: You need a slice of ham, a roll, some lettuce, some butter and some mayonnaise. ... Is it this picture? *(pointing to the wrong picture)* ... or this one? *(pointing to another picture)* ... or this one?

— When the children agree which picture it is, show them that you are going to write the letter alongside 1...... on the sheet.

— Read out the next instruction, start searching for it as before, and let them tell you what number picture it is.

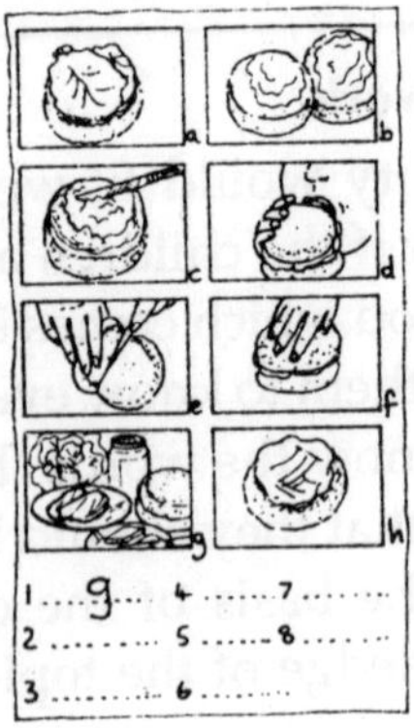

— Read out the third instruction, but this time make them decide for themselves which number picture you are talking about. They write down the number without telling you. (A quick glance at the papers of one or two children near you will tell you if they are getting the idea.)

— Carry on with the rest of the instructions, giving them time to find the right picture and write down the number each time.

Possible Follow Up

If the children can write, they might like to devise their own surprise sandwich. They can take the basic pattern of instructions from the board but choose their own ingredients. Let them use their imaginations, even if you would not like to eat the sandwiches they describe!

Other Language You can Practise with this Activity

You can use this basic format of jumbled pictures for any sequence of sentences you like. For example, they could be simply a list of shops the children are asked to 'go to' and the things they are asked to buy:

Shopping List

1. First please go to the bakers ...
2. ... to buy some rolls.
3. Next, please *go* to the post office ...
4. ... to buy some stamps ...
5. and post two letters to England.
   etc.

Or the pictures could tell a story.

6. Let's Tell a Story Together

You tell the story. They do the actions! It is an actively fun and simultaneously involving form of responding by doing.

Language Focus in this Example

The story actually practises prepositions but that is a very dull way to think of it!

Materials Required

You can use any short story which has plenty of repetition and which contains plenty the children can mime. Here is one which all the children can mime at the same time, sitting in their seats. It is a version of a story called 'The Lion Hunt'. It is set out in two columns so you can see what prompts and actions might be useful.

Suggested Procedures

First tell the story with pictures or symbols on the board.

TEACHER'S WORDS	SYMBOLS
We are going on a lion hunt.	
Off we go!	
First we walk along the path.	

Then we go over the bridge.

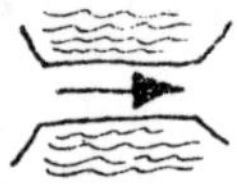

Next we go up the hill.

Then we run down the hill.

Next we walk across the swamp.

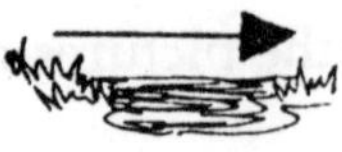

Now we walk through the long grass....

... Wait a minute, whatever's this? ... It's got four legs... . It's got a long tail... . It's got a big head... . Help! It's the lion! Quick... !

(Now go back the way you came - but fast! Point to each drawing as you go.)

Through the long grass.

Across the swamp.

Up the hill. *(Remember you are going the other way!)*

Down the hill.

Over the bridge.

Along the path.

Home! Hooray!

Now sit down yourself and tell the story again, this time with the actions as follows. Get the children to copy the actions and do each one with you before you move on to the next stage.

TEACHER'S WORDS	TEACHER'S ACTIONS
We are going on a lion hunt.	
Off we go!	
First we walk along the path.	*Make walking noises on your* knees with your hands, left, right, left, right.
Then we go over the bridge.	*'Walk' on the desk to make the hollow sound of the bridge.*

Next we go up the hill.	*Slow down, it's a steep hill!*
Then we run down the hill.	*Speed up.*
Next we walk across the swamp	*Make squelchy noises and lift your hands as if lifting them from something sticky.*
Now we walk through the long grass....	*Part the long grass with your arms, making swishing noises.*
... Wait a minute, whatever's	
this? ... It's got four legs....	*'Feel' each leg.*
It's got a long tail... . It's	*Feel the tail.*
got a big head... . Help! It's	*Feel the head.*
the lion! Quick... !	

(Now go back the way you came - repeating the actions in reverse order - but fast!)

Through the long grass.

Across the swamp.

Up the hill. *(Remember you are going the other way!)*

Down the hill.

Over the bridge.

Along the path.

Home! Hooray!	*Slump in your chair and wave your hand in victory.*

Possible Follow Up

The children could draw the story in their books using very simple symbols like those above. The drawings can then be used for later repeat tellings of the story as in the variations below. If the class can write, they could write the story out too to go with the pictures.

Variations

(a) In this form, the story has been kept very simple so you may find one of the class would like to tell it instead of you. Leave the symbols on the board and practise them with the whole class first. Then choose a volunteer to come to the front and be the storyteller.

(b) You can also turn this into pairwork with all the children taking turns to tell their partner the story while they both do the actions.

(c) Best of all, get the children to make up their own simple story in pairs and teach it to the rest of the class.

You can make up your own story to practise almost any language you want.

Final Comment

This activity is very definitely a stirrer so think of something quiet to follow, like drawing the pictures as suggested above.

MANAGING YOURSELF—2

What are Your Strengths and Weaknesses?

Each of us has strengths and weaknesses. Identifying them as accurately as possible helps us to determine the base line from which we begin and plan for our future development. We have listed opposite a number of qualities and skills which managers in schools require. Think about each one carefully and try to assess your own competency. If you feel yourself to be excellent score yourself six; if you feel yourself to be quite poor score yourself one. As you consider each in turn, try and bring to mind recent examples which support your judgement.

What Can You Develop?

Some people believe that there is always the opportunity for self-development; others that self-development is unlikely, that their personalities and abilities are more or less static. We very much take the former view. Of course, some aspects of our lives will remain the same but we are conscious of changes which have occurred in our own lives and of friends and colleagues we have known. Change, or more accurately, development is possible.

Some Qualities and Skills of Management

Thinking creatively	1	2	3	4	5	6
Thinking logically	1	2	3	4	5	6
Keeping abreast of developments	1	2	3	4	5	6
Translating theory into practice	1	2	3	4	5	6
Setting targets	1	2	3	4	5	6
Creating plans of action	1	2	3	4	5	6
Evaluation	1	2	3	4	5	6
Budgetary control	1	2	3	4	5	6
Managing time	1	2	3	4	5	6
Coping with stress	1	2	3	4	5	6
Adjusting to change	1	2	3	4	5	6
Selecting staff	1	2	3	4	5	6
Motivating people	1	2	3	4	5	6
Leading	1	2	3	4	5	6
Negotiating	1	2	3	4	5	6
Controlling	1	2	3	4	5	6
Handling conflict	1	2	3	4	5	6
Making presentations	1	2	3	4	5	6
Appraising	1	2	3	4	5	6
Developing people	1	2	3	4	5	6
Conducting meetings	1	2	3	4	5	6
Record keeping	1	2	3	4	5	6

We need to identify those areas in our own lives where development is important to us. Look at the range of weaknesses you identified elsewhere on these pages and fill them in on the chart below. Mark on the chart those in which you feel development to be urgent and those in which you feel it to be non-urgent.

Then mark those in which development seems more immediately possible and those in which it seems possible only in the longer term. (Why not start with success?) If you can identify a weakness where development is both urgent and possible you have found a starting point.

Possible areas of development	*Urgent*	*Non-urgent*	*Possible*	*More difficult*

Because development is possible this doesn't always make it easy. Some aspects of change and development can be very threatening. We are, after all, likely to be disturbing a reasonably comfortable notion of 'who we are'. Sometimes, too, the threat of development causes us to entrench ourselves in even more inflexibility.

At other times, though, development is enhancing in itself. The feeling that comes from being able to do something better can be very exciting, spurring us on to further development and sparking otherwise dormant aspects of our selves.

It has been suggested that there are three stages to self-development. They are:

- a picture in our minds of what it will be like when we have changed

- acting out the 'role' of a person like that (without quite believing it to be 'me')
- after a period of time, the assimilation of that acted behaviour into our everyday 'selves'.

This idea certainly makes sense when we think of aspects of adolescent behaviour. How does it match with your own experiences? Can you think of parallels in your own personal and professional lives which prove this to be the case? Looking at one of the possibilities you identified for development earlier, try and use this strategy as a way of planning your own self-development.

What do You Need Compensating For?

Few of us will achieve a state of competency in everything. We will always have our own strengths and weaknesses. Having weaknesses is not a failure but simply a description of the situation. As a manager (and as a person) our task is to find ways of coming to terms with these weaknesses and, where possible, of compensating for them.

The concept of teamwork is important. The task is to identify those aspects of our own selves for which compensation is important. Such identification may come from the list we compiled earlier; the list of abilities which it is urgent for us to develop but which present greater immediate difficulties. Having such a list helps us to define who to turn to for help, what qualities to look for in others and what it is possible or less possible to do. Try and answer the following questions.

- How easy do you find it to accept and admit areas within your 'self which need development?
- How easy is it to admit those to other people?
- What areas have you identified which might be compensated for?

- Who is there around you who might be of help?
- Which areas remain?
- What can be done about them?

What Do Others Think of You?

We mentioned above that our self-knowledge comes in part from the messages we pick up from others about our abilities and performance. What happens in practice is a continual interaction between your 'self, the interpretations your 'self makes of the responses of others and the actual views of those others.

The research that is available suggests that we are less aware of others' perceptions than we think. Sometimes our interpretations of what we *think* they are thinking are inappropriate; at other times our natural reserve precludes open discussion amongst even close friends or colleagues.

Yet the views of others are important; they represent an important part of our 'selves' in action. Self-knowledge is concerned with how we feel about our 'selves' but also about how our 'selves' are perceived by others.

Although there are formal situations in which others' awareness of our 'selves' can be explored, they are not easy to arrange on a day-by-day basis. Finding out the views of others is difficult. As a beginning, try the following.

- Identify any obvious mis-match between your perception of your 'self in a situation and someone else's perception. Does it reveal a mis-understanding or a different viewpoint?
- Consider the different viewpoint carefully
- Find someone sympathetic to what you are doing and begin to explore perceptions of each other. Allow the opportunity for either of you to stop at any time.

INDIVIDUAL PERSPECTIVES

'Starting from where people are' is in danger of becoming one *of the* hypocritical management statements; we all seem to say it a lot and do it very little. The truth is we often feel frustrated by the very existence of individual differences.

Starting from where people are is fine until where people are is the very thing which slows us down, gets in the way, causes frustration. Suddenly, we don't want to start from where people are; we want them to be where we are.

In spite of the frustration we need to accept that the speed of change is governed as much by the individual perspectives of others as it is by our own. The fact that we are generally less than satisfactory at starting from where people are doesn't make it less important to do so.

The simple fact that people are different seems very hard to take on board sometimes and even harder to remember. It is, however, self-evident.

Think of your own views about

- footballers hugging each other after a goal has been scored
- Heavy Metal rock music
- eating meat
- being called by your first name as a teacher
- eating in class
- the balance between skills and knowledge in science
- whether teachers should strike.

The chances are high that you will have a view about

most of these. The chances are high, too, that it won't take you long to find a colleague who thinks differently from you.

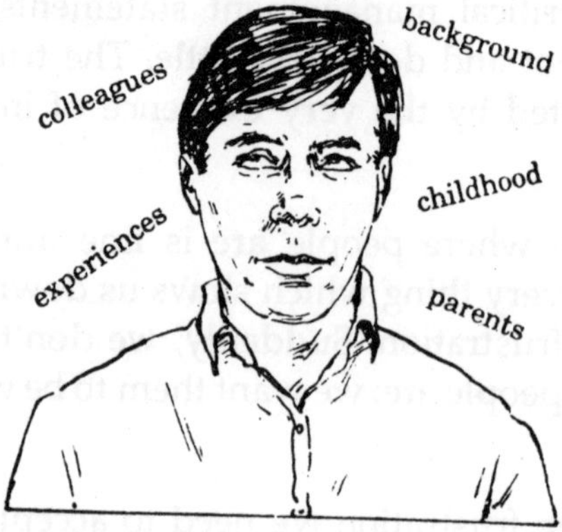

The kinds of views we have are based on a number of factors and the inter-relationship of those factors:

- our own interests and commitment the amount of knowledge and understanding we have of a subject
- our background
- our personality
- our influences.

The problem, and the excitement, of education is that most of the really important decisions cannot be made definitively. Consider the following questions:

- Is science a good thing for primary children?
- Should we abandon our reading schemes?
- How much calculator work should we do in mathematics?
- Should children be allowed into school before the official starting time?
- How much money should be allocated to each curriculum area this year?

- Does the way we do playground duty contribute to a good atmosphere in the school?

Opinions and views about such questions are too diverse for simple decisions to be made, precisely because the issues are so very important. The only decisions in a school which can be taken quickly and with more or less full agreement are those which are important for the moment but not for the longer term. For example, "Is it a wet playtime?", "Is the lavatory seat broken?" or "Were you in the playground ten minutes before school began?"

Many of the real issues which affect children's learning are more complex than that and are open — quite rightly and naturally—to different points of view.

> One of the tasks of management is to know when individual viewpoints can be held without damage to the school and when individual viewpoints need to be merged into generally acceptable policies.

To make these management decisions we have to be concerned with

- knowing what people think
- how strongly they feel things
- the likelihood of change within them.

Near Zones and Far Zones

Two Americans, Glaser and Strauss, have suggested that our ideas and beliefs fall into 'near zones' and Tar zones'. Those which fall into our near zones mean much more to us than those which fall into our far zones.

However, our feelings, ideas and commitments don't always fit consistently into the same category. Different factors can cause them to change.

> "Towards the end of a hot sunny day when we are all tired I just don't want to make them work as hard as I otherwise would."

Here 'hard work' has moved from a near zone to a far zone.

> "I suppose the National Curriculum has made me take more interest in science. I mean, if we have to do it I'd better get clued up."

Here, science has moved from a far zone towards a near(er) zone.

'Near zones' and Tar zones' are good tools for trying to assess the strength and importance of the ideas, feelings and understandings of colleagues and of ourselves.

Whether we choose to admit it or not the group of people with whom we work will have a different range of ideas, viewpoints, commitments and abilities.

It is hardly surprising that things should go awry if we begin to manage ourselves and our colleagues as if we were all the same. We can only hope to manage situations involving people competently by starting from the basis of our differences — and finding out as much about them as possible. As Robert Zend said, "People have one thing in common: they are all different."

GROUP PERSPECTIVE

The previous pages quite rightly concentrated on the importance of understanding how we each think, what our interests are, what we know and what we want to do as individuals.

Schools, though, are more than a collection of individuals. Whether it is in the classroom or staffroom, people group together for all sorts of reasons. For example

- being in a group often helps people feel better, feel more secure
- group members can 'help each other by using strengths and supporting weaknesses
- groups can unite in opposition to ideas which are unpopular.

Groups will form in different ways, too. They may

- unite around a single common idea
- form around a strong leader
- form for self-protection.

Near zones and far zones (see page 24) are as important for groups as they are for individuals.

One of us spent some time a few years ago in a particular primary school which everyone who visited, it described as very good', 'marvellous' and so on. The children and staff worked hard, the relationships between staff and children were good, the quality of the school's policies was very high and the buildings were well-cared for. On any normal judgement of a 'good school' this one was respected by the majority of teachers who knew it and the majority of parents whose children attended there.

One of the noticeable things about the school was how everyone, staff and children, used the word 'we' rather than T. The staff, in particular, had a very strong group feeling; they always talked of 'we'.

Interestingly, when each of the staff were spoken to on their own their independence from each other was revealed quite clearly. They all had different individual views from each other, liked each other more or less and had all sorts of differing hopes for their future.

The distinctions and divisions between them could have pulled them apart. In some schools they most certainly would have.

What held that staff together - what was in their near zones - was the collective view that they could best help the children there by having common policies which really worked. They were prepared to fight for what they thought was right, but once a decision was made they all accepted that their own personal views had to be held in suspension.

Although they understood that they were different from each other they were able to use the group feeling to immense benefit both for them and the children in the school.

Positive and Negative Power

The power of group feelings can be both positive and negative. In the case of the school described in the box the power the staff group gave to the school was both strong and positive; in another instance the group could have power. Later in the book, we will examine this a little more.

Group Membership

We can often belong to a range of groups simultaneously. In Richard's school he is a member of different groups. They include

- the group of staff members interested in sport. Sport takes up much of the social discussion in the staffroom and many of the teachers in this group often support a school team together
- the group who visit the pub on a Friday evening. These are people who like a drink and use the pub as a safe place to vent their feelings. Sometimes Richard agrees with all the grumbles but sometimes he doesn't agree with any — but he still enjoys being in the group
- the group interested in teaching science. Richard holds a post of responsibility for science, is very keen and has a number of colleagues who continually come to him for advice. This group attend INSET together.

There may be other groups of which Richard is a member too. At different times each group will have a different degree of importance to him because of his own individual perspectives. The groups, too, will have different levels of importance at different times. The first hint of the National Curriculum probably increased the strength of the 'pub group'. The realisation that science had to be taught as a third component of the core curriculum and is the first subject to be assessed probably increased the importance of the science group.

As with individual perspectives, those of us managing classrooms or schools ignore group perspectives at our peril. Groups can react both positively or negatively. They can act in public or they can act anonymously.

> "We had made all the decisions about our maths teaching and we all agreed that problem-solving was important. It was only about six months later that I realised that two or three of the staff hadn't really wanted it and just hadn't done anything about it. They said they had, but it only became clear when the children changed classes and their new teachers said that they didn't seem to have any idea about problem-solving at all."

We will look in more detail at working with groups later in the book when we discuss consensus, collegiality and analysing our own organisations.

TEACHER PERSPECTIVES

We began this book by stressing the importance of knowing our 'selves' as much as possible and managing our 'selves' on the basis of that knowledge. Such an understanding helps us to work more effectively and to understand that those with whom we work have different, but similar, 'selves', too.

One of the ways in which those 'selves' are revealed is through the perspectives we hold. Teachers in schools hold both individual perspectives and group perspectives; it is important to understand what they are and that there will always be a range of them with which we have to be concerned.

On these pages we are going to explore briefly some of the views which teachers hold. We are indebted for the basic classification to Units 9 and 10 of an Open University Course 'Educational Studies' E202. If you can get hold of this course book it will repay much re-reading.

The Dimensions of Teachers' Views

The dimensions come directly from the Open University course book. The comments which illuminate each are from teachers with whom we have spoken.

1. Definition of the Teacher's Role

a) authoritative role... no distinct role

"I rue the day when most of these parents were allowed into schools. They don't know what they are talking about when it comes to education."

"Well, I see my job as... more or less the parent in the classroom. I don't think there's much that I do which couldn't be done by anyone else."

b) curriculum... method

"I don't care how, but by the end of this term I'm going to make sure these children know everything they have to know."

"The skills of history are just so important. We've spent years teaching children facts. How they do it is so important."

c) narrow... wide

This 'caring' thing is all a bit of nonsense, really. We can't be expected to do that. Let's just teach them what we have to."

"Caring's not nonsense at all. Education is about the whole child. How can we ignore that?"

d) high teacher control ... low teacher control

To find two classes like that in the same school was amazing. In Mrs L's class no one could move without her permission. She literally moved her eyelids to let them go out to lunch. In Mrs M's class they just seemed to know when it was time, packed their things away and went out."

e) universalism... particularism

"I know some people make excuses, but I don't. They've all got to achieve the same things as far as I am concerned."

"It's not surprising that William underachieves. Just look at the background he has had."

f) product... process

"They got twenty out of twenty in the maths test I've just given them. I'm really pleased."

"Yes, that's good. But how were they working things out? Was there anything interesting or unusual?"

2. *Conceptualising Pupil Action*

a) childhood continuous... childhood unique

"It seems to me that we have to prepare children as soon as possible for the world of work. There's no getting away from it."

"Young children just aren't ready to be treated like miniature adults. They need things arranging especially for them."

b) pessimistic... optimistic theories of human nature

"Look, if we let children stay in at lunchtime, you know what will happen. They'll wreck the place."

"If we give them the responsibility they won't. They enjoy taking responsibility and being trusted. You know that."

3. Conceptualising Knowledge

a) objective knowledge... personal knowledge tied to particular purpose or culture

There are certain facts about the first World War. That's what we ought to teach."

"I disagree. Children ought to be thinking about their own responses and why different people behaved as they did."

b) hierarchical structure... little hierarchy

"At least with maths schemes what they have to learn is ordered for you. It's all there, done for you."

"That's why so many children have difficulties. Who says you have to learn this before that, anyway? Lots of children come to school with all sorts of understandings we just ignore. They're not in any order at all."

c) discipline-bound... general

"All this topic work is just flimflam. Why can't we get back to history and geography as separate lessons?"

"All through my secondary school I never realised that so much of the geography we were doing had an effect upon our history, too. Look at the Norman Invasion, for example. Why weren't history and geography brought together? It would have made much more sense."

4. Conceptualising Learning

a) collective... individual

"One of the advantages of working in groups is that the children can share what they are doing. They learn from and stimulate each other."

"Well, I don't think they should talk. It might not be their work and it has got to be all their own work, hasn't it?"

b) extrinsic... intrinsic motivation

"The only way I can get my class to learn anything is to promise them a test on Friday. It's the only thing which works."

"The trouble is, children only learn when the interest really comes from inside them. That's when learning really takes place."

c) learning by hearing about... learning by doing

"What's the point of all this doing? If I want them to know something I tell them. Simple."

"Doing things is so important for young children. They can't abstract very well and doing it makes it mean so much more to them."

5. Preferred Techniques

a) imperative mode of control... reliance based on personal appeals

"If you are not ready by the time I count to ten then we'll all stay in at playtime."

"Look, how often do you see me do that? What happened last week when Susan did it to you? You were upset, weren't you?"

b) class tests... assessment compared to past performance

"It's not good enough. Only six out often is below the pass mark. See me later."

> "Well done, Billy. Really good this week. A big improvement on your last piece of work. Keep it up!"

The range of views we have highlighted is not comprehensive and you will certainly be able to think of others we might have included. This doesn't matter at the moment. Neither does your own agreement or disagreement with the views expressed.

What does matter is to illuminate and acknowledge the range of views which does exist and within which and from which children's learning and schools have to be organised and managed.

Teachers are not a uniform group of people who all think the same, although many management 'techniques' seem to assume that they are. The differences are not only between individual teachers, either; often they are within individual teachers. It might seem easy to create groupings of views which seem to hold together. Resist the temptation. There is little evidence that our views are logically coherent.

What is important is that we understand the views of those with whom we work. This understanding is another important component in effective management.

OTHER PERSPECTIVES

The previous section gave a flavour of the range of teacher perspectives and underlined the importance of understanding the perspectives of those with whom you work.

The working group of those who manage classrooms or schools is not restricted to teachers, however, and it is equally important that you work towards understanding as much as possible the perspectives held by all the others who are likely to influence the working of the school.

This is a large group. It comprises at least:

- children
- supply teachers
- ancillary helpers
- midday supervisors
- support staff (psychologists, doctors, etc.)
- administrative staff
- parents
- governors
- visitors
- LEA officers
- councillors
- neighbours
- community officials
- PTA committee members.

Each group, and each individual within each group,

shares the same breadth of perspectives we saw teachers sharing. (Not the same perspectives, of course, but the same breadth.)

So, midday supervisors are no more an homogenous group than are teachers. You will probably be aware of that through talking and listening to those with whom you work; it is the extent of that breadth of points of view which needs exploring and understanding.

Teaching involves as much human interaction as any other job you care to name. Each action you take or decision you make in your classroom and school will ultimately be filtered through, interpreted by and acted upon by others. Understanding the perspectives of others enables us to:

- make decisions about which actions are likely to be successful or unsuccessful
- reveal the "backstage' work which needs to be undertaken with groups or individuals before action takes place
- present what we have to say or what we want to do appropriately to different audiences
- respect as honestly held the views of those with whom we work (even though we might not be in agreement)
- reduce the level of tension inspired by surprise opposition
- challenge the views we hold by presenting opposing attitudes
- help develop teamwork and collegiality by accepting the validity of others' viewpoints.

Each of the groups, and each member of the groups, will have their own super-ordinate and sub-ordinate constructs, near zones and far zones, too. So, of all the points of view we come to understand, some of them will matter far more than others to their holders.

In other words, if you ask a midday supervisor for a view about history teaching in the primary school you will probably receive one. This doesn't mean that the particular view expressed ranks in importance in the mind of the midday supervisor with the level of disciplinary back-up available at lunchtime. You need to be able to assess the weighting of the perspectives you gather.

Look back to the groups listed above. Ask yourself what you think is of importance to them. How do you know? Does this apply to the particular group with whom you work, since this is the group of greatest importance to you?

Listen carefully to members of each of those groups over the next month. If you have time, jot down views which agree and views which are contradictory within each group. Continue to gather as much evidence as you can.

One final reminder. You will undoubtedly disagree with many of the points of view you hear expressed; you may even get irritated or annoyed by some of them. As a manager of a classroom or school, try and put your agreements, disagreements, irritations and annoyances to one side. They are not the issue.

What is important is that you both understand and accept these points of view as being important in defining the context within which you have to work and, therefore, manage.

DEALING WITH DIFFERENCES

Differences of opinion and attitude are inevitable in schools.

Children
Supply teachers
Governors
Ancillary staff
Visitors
Midday supervisors
Support staff
Admin
Councillors
LEA officers
Parents
Neighbours
Community officials
PTA Committee members

All organisations have them. Organisations such as schools are particularly open to differences since so much of what they do is, at the very least, problematic. The first sections of this book have considered some of the perspectives teachers and others hold toward schools and education. The variety is enormous. So you are going to have differences within and between colleagues, parents, governors and children.

Dealing with differences, sorting them out, co-ordinating them is one of management's main tasks. We can carry out this task in two ways, by creating situations in which the number of differences is reduced and by dealing with those which remain.

Reducing the Differences

1. Treat Differences as Inevitable

The only way that differences won't occur in your school is if you pretend that they don't exist. Some differences will certainly be solved if you turn a blind eye, but others will simply grow worse and worse.

Becoming irritated about differences is equally unrewarding however. Anyone who tries to sort out a quarrel by displaying their own irritation at it is likely to either make the original quarrel worse or transfer its focus onto themselves.

Treating differences as inevitable should enable us to stay calmer about them, to be more able to think carefully about the situation which has caused them and what action we can take to help solve them.

It will also provide a good model from which children in your school can learn. There is little point conducting five assemblies each week on the theme of The world is full of differences' and then becoming obviously irritated each time they occur in your own school. Actions speak louder than words.

2. Treat Differences Differently

Not all differences have the same importance as each other. Their importance is often connected to the situation in which they occur and the perspectives of those involved.

December in primary schools often seems to bring out a rash of differences which are forgotten by January, but two teachers of conflicting styles and personalities working next to each other in an open-plan school may require more significant handling than the after-school sherry provided following the infant carol service.

We need to be sensitive to the level of importance differences have for the participants and for the school.

3. Reduce the Likelihood of Differences Happening

Though differences are inevitable, some can certainly be avoided. School policies and job descriptions (well-negotiated) are good tools for allowing people to know what is expected of them and where they stand. They can't neutralise every difference but they can forestall the development of many common differences in schools.

Good interviewing can prevent differences occurring for years ahead. Allowing candidates to find out whether they really want to work in your school, and assessing their character and abilities to make sure they will contribute to team building rather than team disintegration, are both positive steps towards reducing differences.

4. Create an Atmosphere in Which Differences are Accepted

One of the key things leaders appear to do is to create atmospheres. If, as a leader, you want to work in a classroom or school where differences are both tolerated and dealt with properly then you have to take some of the responsibility for creating the situation within which that can happen.

Ways of doing this include:

- always discussing differences with children and colleagues
- showing delight in the appreciation of different arguments
- genuinely valuing the different contributions colleagues and children make
- revealing strengths and weaknesses in your own personality
- setting up structures and meetings in the school where differences can be revealed formally.

Whichever route you take, schools are about more than telling people things. At a quite profound level differences are fundamental to the educational process. Schools should reflect this.

Dealing With Those Which Remain

1. Identify the Problem

Don't try and solve differences unless you are sure of the problem. As with analysing your school, analysing differences requires sufficient evidence for a decision to be made. Insufficient evidence will exacerbate the problem. Gather as much evidence as you can before you step in to help.

Differences may be due to

- personal problems
- staleness
- significant disagreements
- lack of understanding

- disappointments
- insecurity

2. Negotiate between the Parties

Negotiation is a very difficult skill and there are no hard and fast rules despite the large amount of research which has taken place in the last few years. Nevertheless, there is reasonable agreement that all negotiators need

- to be as neutral as possible. Differences are unlikely to be resolved if one party feels out of favour with the negotiator to understand and present the case relating to each of the different arguments as fully as possible. Nothing should be omitted to present solutions which are viable. Solutions which clearly won't work increase rather than decrease differences and reduce the status of the negotiator who suggested them
- to know that those who hold the differences are willing for agreement to be reached. Agreements which are rejected as soon as the meeting is over are useless
- to have a strategy which enables a logical, understandable and fair sequence of events to take place during the negotiation.

A Negotiating Strategy

There is no perfect negotiating strategy and, because those involved in the negotiations may behave less than calmly occasionally, negotiators may have to temporarily abandon any strategy they have. Nevertheless, certain factors seem to be useful.

1. Try and create as little other tension as possible. The room setting, introductory remarks, tone of voice are all important.

2. Allow each party to state its case uninterrupted. Repeat and confirm each case when both parties have finished speaking.
3. Iron out different interpretations of the facts.
4. Identify those areas where agreement is most likely and try to achieve this early on.
5. Introduce the notion of compromise for the remaining, and most difficult, issues. Like differences themselves, compromise is almost inevitable. Use real examples of compromise in action.
6. Try to ensure that one party's compromise is met by another from the other side. Don't allow one party to do all the work.
7. Agree on what has been agreed. Both parties must be clear about what has been agreed and what hasn't. If they aren't, the agreement is unlikely to last.

SCHOOLS AS ORGANISATIONS

INTRODUCING SOME BASIC CONCEPTS OF ORGANISATION

Schools are organisations. As such many of the ideas developed by organisational theorists can be usefully applied to schools to help us understand them. However, there are two cautionary notes to sound: first, there is a bewildering array of concepts so we need to be selective; second, most organisational concepts are derived from institutions other than primary schools so we need to think about applicability. The following concepts, therefore, have been selected because they are applicable. The concepts are first outlined in a general sense, though we have chosen to raise them as questions in order to provoke the reader into applying them. Second, we have also tried to apply the concepts to primary schools specifically.

Basic Organisational Concepts

1. Objectives

What are the aims of the organisation? Why is it there? What is the organisation planning to do?

Any organisation has aims, intentions, expectations and, perhaps, a mission.

2. Structure

What are the roles, responsibilities, tasks and duties of the members? How are communications organised? How are tasks coordinated? How are decisions taken? Who works with whom?

3. Leadership

Who provides leadership? Who 'gets things going? Who has responsibility and offers direction?

4. Power

Who has authority to do things? Who uses power positively or negatively?

Who has overt and/or covert influence? Is the informal power network matched/mismatched with the formal power network?

5. Culture

Each organisation has its own culture. Culture is determined by the organisation's underlying beliefs and values. What are the core values of your organisation? What are the ways of doing things which are taken for granted?

Some organisations have a single culture, others have

several subcultures; organisations can be mono-cultural or multi-cultural.

6. Environmental Relationships

Any organisation exists in an environment. To what extent does the environment affect the organisation? What links does the organisation have with the environment?

Applying These Concepts to Primary Schools

1. Objectives

What is the school trying to achieve? Curriculum aims and statements of interest to parents in brochures, prospectuses, etc. often provide insight into a school's objectives. However, another concern arises in respect of the extent to which these aims are shared, both within the school and between the school and groups 'outside' it (for example parents, governors, the community).

2. Structures

Primary schools are full of structures: class groupings of children, teams/ departments of teachers, staffing quotas, responsibility posts (for example incentive allowances, curriculum posts), timetables, meetings, roles of ancillary and secretarial staff. The list could go on and on. However, one important feature of primary school structure is to consider those structures which are determined externally (for example salary scales, admission and leaving ages) and those decided internally (for example allocation of allowance posts, use of time, meetings).

3. Leadership

Usually leadership is visible in respect of the roles of the headteacher, deputy head, coordinators and/or allowance postholders. But recent studies (Nias et al. 1989) suggest that leadership is also exercised by secretaries, ancillaries, individual teachers. The chairperson of governors may also exercise leadership.

4. Power

Power in primary schools might be located in many persons. Formal and informal power might underpin any of the aforementioned leaders. Similarly, authority (which is legitimate power) might stem from an individual's expertise (in art, music, science or with reception infants) or experience (through long acquaintance with the school, age group, or profession). Even from this brief outline power can be seen to be, potentially, widely and differentially distributed. Of course, the principal source of power in a primary school is usually the headteacher.

5. Culture

A primary school's culture is an amalgamation of social, moral and academic values. How do staff and children relate to one another? What are the values which define these relationships (for example courtesy, care, consideration, competition, individuality, mutual dependence)? What is considered right and proper (for example helpfulness, winning, cooperation, respect for others, single-mindedness)? What are the beliefs upon which the academic curriculum is based (group work, individualised programmes, subjects, cross-curricular projects)?

The answers to these questions begin to map out a school's culture.

6. Environmental Relationships

All primary schools are affected by their contexts. The context relates to:

- school type: infant, junior, JMI, first, lower, Church of England, County, Roman Catholic, Community
- catchment area:– eg. the area from which the children are drawn rural, suburban, urban; housing conditions; socio-economic factors

- the LEA: eg. policies and procedures of the Local Education Authority in respect, for example, of LMS and its formulae; curriculum policies; school inspections and reviews; teacher appraisal; support agencies and groups; admissions; suspensions; special needs
- school governors: eg. their expectations, involvement, ambitions and general views and means of working with the school
- central government (and its agencies): statutory policies in respect of National Curriculum Council, Schools Examination and Assessment Council, Employment Law, rules of School Governors.

We have expanded on some of these concepts elsewhere in the book: leadership; culture; environmental contexts.

If you would like to follow-up any of the ideas introduced here we suggest the following texts as useful starting points:

T Bush *Theories of Educational Management* (Harper & Row, London, 1986)

C Handy *Understanding Organisations* Second edition (Penguin Books, London, 1981)

D J Pugh, D J Hickson & C R Hinings *Writers on Organisations* Third edition (Penguin Books, London, 1983)

TYPES OF ORGANISATION

Organisational theorists have promoted many ideas for examining and understanding organisations. However, we felt it might be best to look at some of the factors which most directly affect the nature of any particular primary school. We have chosen to look at the following factors.

1. Hierarchy

All primary schools are hierarchical. There is always a headteacher and staff either teaching or non-teaching—usually both. In all but the smallest schools there are deputy heads and in medium sized and larger schools there are staff with specified responsibilities and incentive allowances. Some schools will be very hierarchical, others will be more collegial.

2. Size

A factor relating to hierarchy is school size. Hierarchies tend to be more pronounced the larger the school. Moreover, with larger schools the presence of structure also tends to increase. Large schools have departments, teams, coordinators, etc.

School size is a big factor and, in common parlance, there are really only three types of school - small, medium and large.

3. Design

School design plays a major role in affecting the type of organisation. Two obvious school types are cellular (for example, enclosed classrooms) and open-plan (for example, open teaching spaces or bays). However, the effects of having or not having any of the following appears to influence the school as an organisation:

- split site
- corridors
- dining hall
- assembly hall
- gymnasium
- sinks
- headteacher's office

- staffroom
- temporary classrooms
- community use
- specialist areas

4. Designation

The title of the school is very important; nursery, infant, junior, JMI, primary, middle (deemed primary) denominational (either controlled or aided), community. One or more of these will have a considerable impact on the school as an organisation.

5. Culture

The ways of doing things in a school which are taken for granted affect how the school 'works'. Culture is often a product of history, the building and patterns of interaction. Culture also reminds us that what matters most in a school is how *people* relate to one another. Schools have a subjective, interpersonal dimension.

6. Cohesion

This refers to the extent to which people and policies work together. Any primary school, even a small one, is really an amalgam of many parts. The extent to which these parts cohere or fragment indicates the extent to which the school is a whole or not (see Southworth, 1987).

As a result of these factors a school might be described as:

ST. ELSEWHERE C. of E. (Aided) Community Primary School. A large, open-plan school with collegial relationships which occupies a single site. The building is modern and purpose-built. The staff work together in a collaborative culture and ensure that all programmes of work are congruent with the whole school's policies.

Sounds too good to be true! In effect what St. Elsewhere really shows is that a primary school is a mix and blend of a number of factors and concepts. Consequently, when we describe a school we are already classifying it as some type of organisation, but the *type* rests on the precise placement of the school along a series of continua:

hierarchical	<—	—	—	—>	collegial
large	<—	—	—	—>	small
cellular	<—	—	—	—>	open-plan
cohesive	<—	—	—	—>	fragmented

Thus to recognise a school's type we illustrate this we have done this for need first to plot it on each continuum two schools: and then look at the profile. To

Downside County Primary

hierarchical	✓				collegial
large			✓		small
cellular	✓				open plan
cohesive				✓	fragmented

St. Elsewhere School

hierarchical				✓	collegial
large	✓				small
cellular				✓	open plan
cohesive	✓				fragmented

Thinking about Primary Schools as Organisations

Before looking at basic concepts of organisation and school types we need to ask, "What is an organisation?"

Rather than answer this ourselves we have drawn on Reid, Bullock & Howarth (1988) who have also attempted to answer the question. They show that primary schools are organisations, that we need to treat with care some of the concepts organisationalists use, and that primary schools have some specific differences from other kinds of organisation. These ideas will be taken up on some of the following pages.

6

Working with a Coursebook

This chapter looks at three aspects of working with a class coursebook:

— choosing a book;
— supplementing the book if necessary;
— planning your progress through the book.

There are two common but extreme attitudes to coursebooks. The first is that it is wrong to deviate to any appreciable extent from what you have been given. The second is that it is wrong not to! Not only are both of these views unhelpful, they have also missed the point. The question is not 'Is it a good idea or a bad idea to use a coursebook extensively?' The important questions are 'What does the coursebook do well?' and 'What does the teacher do better?' When we have answered these questions we can each decide to what extent using a coursebook will suit our particular circumstances, what kind of coursebook will be appropriate for us and our classes, and how best to use it.

What a Coursebook Does Well and What a Teacher can Often do Better

The coursebook helps the teacher by providing:

- — a clearly thought out programme which is appropriately sequenced and structured to include progressive revision;
- — a wider range of material than an individual teacher may be able to collect;
- — security;
- — economy of preparation time;
- — a source of practical teaching ideas;
- — work that the learners can do on their own so that the teacher does not have to be centre stage all the time;
- — a basis for homework if that is required;
- — a basis for discussion and comparison with other teachers.

The coursebook helps the learners by providing a teacher who is more secure because of all the above. It also offers the learners:

- — a sense of purpose, progression and progress;
- — a sense of security;
- — scope for independent and autonomous learning;
- — a reference for checking and revising.

Together these make quite an impressive list of advantages. No doubt you could add others. However, there are several things that the teacher can often do better than a book, which are vital to successful language teaching and which tie in very closely with the priorities identified in Chapter 2. For example, the teacher is usually much better than the coursebook at:

- — providing the spoken word in spoken exchanges;
- — adjusting work in response to the reactions of the children;

— using communication other than words and pictures to back up language elements;
— setting up learning activities which encourage learners to talk and profit from interaction.

We need to keep these points in mind when choosing a coursebook.

Choosing a Coursebook

Choosing a book for whole class use is always something of a leap in the dark. It may well be that you will not have a really good picture of its suitability until you have been working through it for some time. However, identifying the potential strengths of coursebooks generally, as above, can give us a starting point for looking at the strengths or weaknesses of any specific book. On this basis, we can make ourselves a list of questions about a book we are considering. If you set the questions out as a chart which you complete by blocking in a score from 1-5 (1 is poor, 5 is very good) you can get a clearer picture of the potential of any book. By dealing with several books in this way, you then have a comparative basis for making a decision.

The point about making and blocking in a chart like this is that it allows us to see where the strengths and weaknesses of any one coursebook lie far more clearly than we can do by just answering the questions in our heads. We can then match the results on our chart up to our individual circumstances and needs. In the above case, for example, the book is clearly strong in a majority of key areas. The weakness in question F might not matter very much if you and your learners have good contact with native speakers and culture through other channels such as tourism, television and pop culture. Similarly, the setting of tests (question J) may not be relevant in your particular case. On the other hand, if you did choose this particular

What does this book offer? FROM THE POINT OF VIEW OF THE TEACHER	1	2	3	4	5
A Do the book's priorities match with your priorities? e.g: If you take learning through communicating as your priority, does the book aim to set up genuine interaction? Real language use?				▨	
B Does the book seem to do what it claims to do? e.g: If it claims to set up real language use does it provide pairwork which really involves communication and not just learnt dialogues?					▨
C Is it clear how to use the book?				▨	
D Is the book clearly structured and sequenced?				▨	
E Does it provide integrated revision of key items?					▨
F Are there additional materials provided which you personally can't otherwise obtain? e.g: Authentic materials? Native speaker tapes?	▨				
G Does it offer lots of practical ideas?		▨			
H Does the book develop a balance of the language skills of listening, speaking, reading, writing which suits your needs?				▨	
I Does it provide plenty of varied practice of any one set of language items?			▨		
J Does it help you to set tests if they are required by your school?	▨				
K Does it manage to avoid sexual, racial and cultural stereotypes?	▨				
FROM THE POINT OF VIEW OF THE CHILDREN:					
L Does the book look interesting and fun?			▨		
M Can the children easily see what they have to do?				▨	

	1	2	3	4	5
N Does the book provide much for them to do independently?		///			
0 Does it give them activities and tasks which are interesting and worthwhile in themselves and which are not just language exercises?				///	
P Does it provide plenty for those children who cannot yet read and write with confidence?			///		
OTHER QUESTIONS OF YOUR OWN: Does it Does it Does it					

coursebook, you would now be aware that you would have to counter the stereotyping it presents (question K). In any case, you would want to apply this system to more than one book before you finally decided on a coursebook.

Clearly, when it comes to working out the significance of results shown in the chart, you will need to ask yourself some questions both about yourself and the learners you will be working with. For example:

— *Are you working within a system which requires you to cover certain topics?* If so, the first and most obvious concern is to look at the coverage of these provided by the book. The next question then follows.

— *Are you sufficiently confident about your own use of the language to be able to provide any missing elements?* If so, the question of coverage is less significant.

— *Do you have lots of teaching ideas yourself or will you rely on the coursebook for ideas?* If you are going to be relying on the coursebook, then a poor score in question G is significant no matter how attractive the book is in other ways. Some books provide excellent basic material but leave you to sort out how to teach it. If you are not getting help from elsewhere, such a book may not suit you.

— *Does your school expect you to provide homework?* If so, you might want to make sure the book has things in it which you could use for this purpose and preferably has suggestions to make about what the homework should be.

— *Do your children have to buy their own books?* If so, price becomes a major consideration and would be one of the questions you would add to the chart.

— *How much time have you got for preparation of supplementary materials?* Good language teaching will often demand some extra preparation by the teacher, but there is no point in committing yourself to more than you *know* is realistic. If you have very little time to spare, you will give priority to a book which already provides plenty of practice of each topic.

— *Are you yourself confident with the grammar but not the sound of the language?* If that is the case, you may want to give priority to a coursebook which is accompanied by cassettes.

— *Are the children well intentioned but very* stow? In that case, again, you will be looking particularly for something that provides varied practice of the same things.

— *Are you going to use the book with one of the more difficult classes you have encountered?* Your priorities here would probably be attractively presented materials and ones which were simple and clear. Already restless children do not wait long to be persuaded that the work is worthwhile, and if they cannot immediately get into an activity, they are more likely to become silly.

— *Are there many children in the class who are weak at reading and writing?* If so you must consider choosing a book which does not rely too heavily on words or on your explanations of them to show what is to be done. The answer to question P becomes particularly significant however much the book appeals to you in other ways.

If you ask yourself these kinds of questions and complete a chart like the one above, you are unlikely to make a bad choice of coursebook. However, it would be even better if you could discuss the matter with another teacher or a group of teachers. First you should agree on the questions for your chart. Then, ideally, each of you would fill in the chart independently for two or three books agreed on in advance. After that, you could discuss points where your judgements are the same or differ. You could follow this by discussing which elements you consider essential and which of them you are willing to , compensate for. Finally, you could exchange ideas on how to compensate for the books' shortcomings. Even if there is only one book easily available, or if you have had the choice made for you, it is worth filling in a chart because it can give you a clear overview of the book you will be using and the demands it is going to make on you.

However, even if we have been fortunate enough to be able to choose our own books, most of us find ourselves at some stage working with a coursebook which is not totally suitable. This is particularly true when it comes to setting up real language use. As we have seen, this is something the teacher can usually do better than the book. Coursebook writers have a real problem here. The printed page is a very difficult medium for setting up genuine interactive work. The majority of books in schools still have not found a way round the problem. The teacher, on the other hand, is in a position to set up real communication much more easily than the average coursebook can. The book can provide the material but it is usually the teacher who can best organise the events which turn that material into a real language exchange.

Increasing the Real Interaction and Communication Offered by a Coursebook

Here are two brief examples to show why it may be a good idea to adapt some coursebooks slightly and to remind you of how it can be done fairly simply by using activities like those in the preceding section.

Coursebooks often use a series of pictures like this to introduce the new words or phrases they are practising.

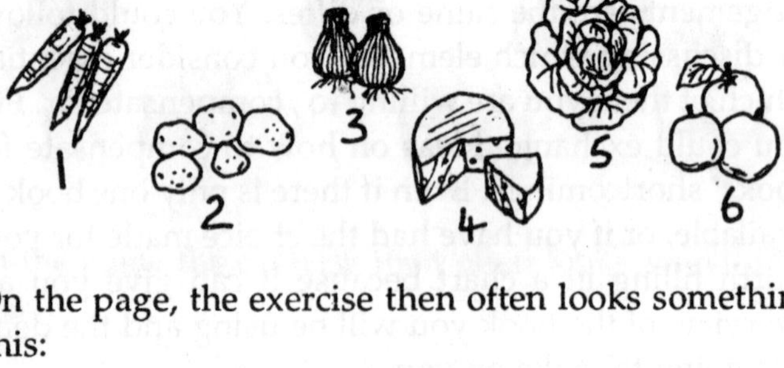

On the page, the exercise then often looks something like this:

Exercise A

Make up questions for each picture. e.g.
Do you like carrots?

The children go through the exercises making up a question for each picture in turn. (So far so good.) The problems, though, are firstly that the children only say each question once. Secondly, the element of true interaction is slight. Most importantly of all, the language is just a response to the pictures, it is not part of a genuine act of communication. However, it is possible for the teacher to use the same exercise from the book but to give it a little communicative 'twist'. If you have just read *Practical Activities I*, you will know that it would be easy to use these same pictures to practise question formation as real language use by turning the exercise into one of the 'guess' activities. For example:

Guess Which Picture I'm Thinking of

— Get a child to choose a picture without telling you or the class which it is. They can write down the number.

— Start guessing to show the class what to do.

Teacher: Do you like onions?
    Child: No, I don't.
Teacher: Do you like cheese?
    Child: No, I don't.

— Now get the class to help by asking their own questions. When they have guessed what the first child has chosen, let someone else choose a picture. After a while, this adapts very easily to pairwork with the children taking it in turns to guess what the other child has chosen.

You will be surprised how long the children will happily go on doing this. Compare it with the exercise provided by the coursebook where, once done, any repetition becomes empty and boring.

Although the exercise in its altered form sets up a genuine act of communication between the children, it is still an exercise not a genuine exchange of information.

Your book probably sets up pairwork. For example:

Exercise B
Work with a partner. Find out what they like.
e.g. *Do you like carrots?*
Yes. I do./No. I don't.

This is better because each child is genuinely finding something out about a friend, but the activity is still rather limited, in its impact if you stay tied to the book, because again the exchange, if it is to remain genuine, can only be done once. However, it does not take much to turn this exercise into a class survey of the kind set out in the previous section, where the children get up, move around and interview each other. In this form, they practise both the questions and the answers over and over again and are still genuinely finding out something about their classmates.

You will find that most of the activities suggested in the previous section are designed to be based on or grow out of coursebook work in this way. However, you may well be fortunate in your coursebook and may, in fact, not need to alter or add very much. Indeed, unless you are working from a book which is overwhelmingly unsuitable, it is probably a good idea first time through to use a book very much as the author suggests. After all, a great deal of thought has gone into the writing of it. By doing what the author suggests, you can also discover what the book really does or does not do.

However, whether you do adapt the book or just basically teach it 'straight', you will in any case have to work out how to pace your progress through it.

Pacing Your Progress Through the Book

Some coursebooks will tell you roughly, how fast to move through them, i.e. how many lessons they expect you to spend on a unit with the mythical average class.

Often, however, you will have to make your own decisions. Some teachers like to play it by ear and to see how the learners get on. They tend not to move on until the children have fully mastered a section or they move on quickly because the children seem bored. This is an attractive idea because it appears to have the merit that it puts the child's needs first. In fact, you could just as well be creating difficulties for the children. If they have to continue their programme with someone else next year, particularly if this involves transfer to secondary school, it will not help them (or your successor) if you have either done lots of topics sketchily, because the children quickly got bored, or so methodically and exhaustively that you have not completed the course.

It is probably a good idea to work out the overall distribution of the work for the year, much as you probably have to for your other work schemes. Working out a schedule like this is not a matter of being too teacher centred or rigid. You are not saying that you will stop unit 6 on December 6th whatever has happened. You may decide that the children need longer. The point is that if you do decide to take longer than originally anticipated, you now know that you will have to look for another perhaps easier area which you will be able to do more quickly than anticipated. Similarly, if you find that you are covering ground very much faster than you expected, you can ask yourself whether you are giving the children enough opportunity to *use* the language as opposed to just 'covering' it. If the answer is still 'yes', then you have a chance to do something independently of the coursebook. You could, for example, explore the possibilities of integrating language work and other subjects along the lines suggested in Chapter 6. In this way, a rough schedule prevents us from getting into difficulties without noticing it, and helps us to take advantage of opportunities that arise. Contrary to the view you will sometimes hear expressed, predicting your timing is a sign of effective flexibility not rigidity. You can do the initial time allocation as follows.

— Check first how long the book suggests you take over each unit. It may talk in terms of weeks or lessons, but either way it will give you some idea of what kinds of adjustments you are going to have to make for your circumstances.

— Divide the book into the number of school terms you have. You can perhaps allocate slightly more time to units at the beginning and the end of the book on the grounds that you and the class will need to get warmed up and that you will also need time for revision. (Don't forget, too, those elements of the school year which temporarily but effectively suspend serious study, e.g. religious festivals, school events, exams, special summer activities.)

The rough allocation over a three-term year for a book of twenty units could look something like this:

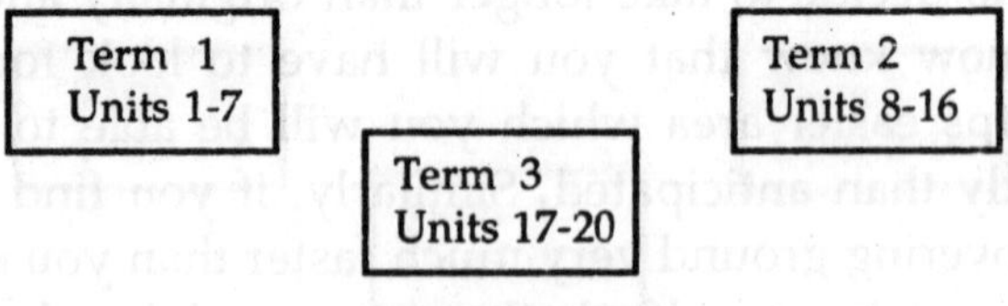

— Next do the same rough allocation for each half of the term. The outline scheme now looks like this:

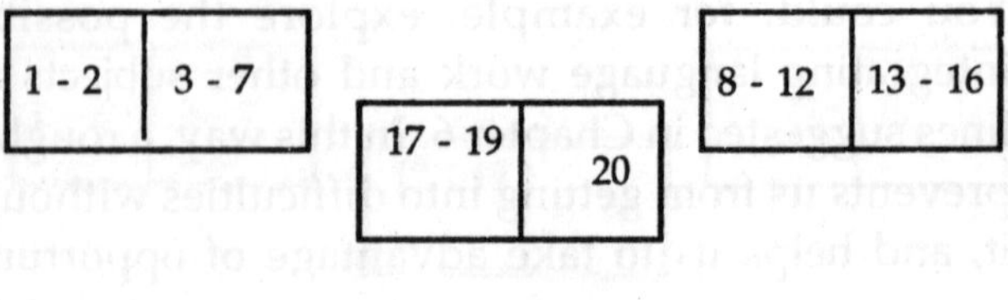

By now, it will be fairly clear that if you are to finish the book efficiently, you will have to do approximately *x* units in *y* weeks.

The consequences are clear. If you have little time each week for language work then you will have to put some of your preparation time and energy into identifying the essential items within the book and working out how to concentrate on those. If, on the other hand, you have plenty of time, your ingenuity will have to be directed towards working out how to provide plenty of additional and varied practice of the same topic. If the amount of time you take rests with you, you have a different set of decisions to make.

> This chapter has looked at ways of shaping a coherent and effective programme around a coursebook. The need for coherence and structure becomes even more critical if you have to create the whole programme by yourself. Working without a coursebook is the focus of the next chapter.

7

Think for Yourself!'

In languages, just as in other subjects, we need to leave the children as much mental space as we can to do their own generating and organising of ideas. This is the particular focus and intention of the activities in this section, and it ties in very closely with the need to engage the children mentally in a combination of language use and thinking. It is a vital part of the process of helping them to make the language their own, which is one of the priorities identified earlier.

1. Listing

The children are being asked to group words according to categories.

The activity combines the mental engagement of thinking for yourself with actual occupation. It provides a good way of learning vocabulary and phrases in their written form, because it provides meaningful repetition and demands that the children handle the concepts, not just the words. It appeared earlier, in the form of an activity for practising shops and shopping. Here it is again with a different topic.

Language Focus in This Example

Clothes and seasons.

This particular example asks the children to group various items of clothing under the time of year when they are likely to wear them:

Materials Required

No special materials are required.

Preliminary Work

This kind of writing activity follows on from plenty of practice in hearing, saying and reading the words.

Suggested Procedures

— Ask the children to work in pairs to make a rough list of any words they know for clothes. Give them a couple of minutes to do this.

— On one side of the board collect together the words they have thought of. (This is your chance to spell their rough versions correctly. Simply write them correctly yourself, however peculiar their version has sounded and don't ask them to spell the words at this stage.)

Child: Pulver.

Teacher: Good idea ... pullover *(writes it up).*

— When you have a reasonable list, read the words through quickly with the class so that they are reminded of the sounds before they write them. This will also give you a chance to check the meanings.

— Next, write the four seasons on the board as four headings:

— Read one of the items of clothing from the list and ask the children when they wear it:

Teacher: A pullover .... Do you usually wear a pullover in winter?

Child: Yes. *(Teacher writes it on the board under the right heading.)*

Teacher: *(Continues)* And do you wear a pullover in spring?

(Make it clear that things will come in more than one category.)

— Do a couple of examples like this and then set the children to write the column headings in their books and to copy the items into the column that *they* think is appropriate.

Possible Follow Up

The children could make their own little dictionaries in little booklets like those suggested at the end of this section on page 104. One column from the above exercise could become a page entry and the children could draw a little picture alongside some of the items.

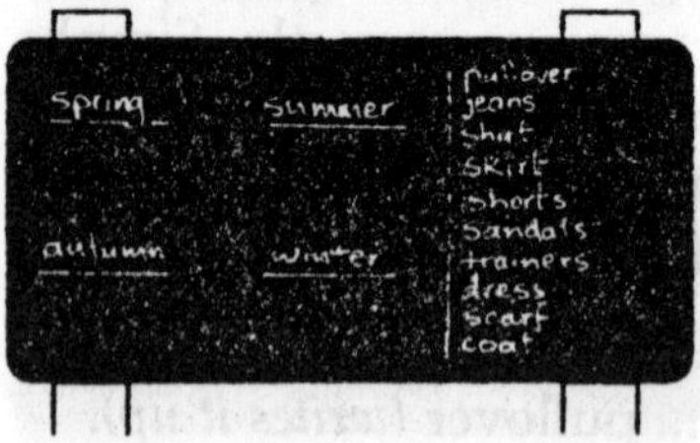

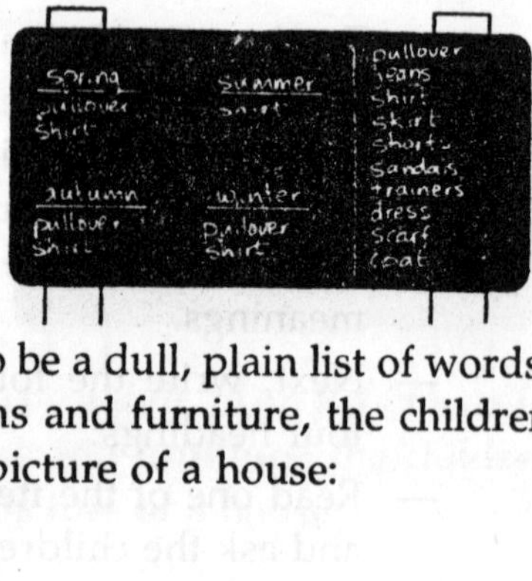

Variations

The list does not have to be a dull, plain list of words. If you were practising rooms and furniture, the children could write their lists on a picture of a house:

Or a list of sports could be written inside big weather symbols:

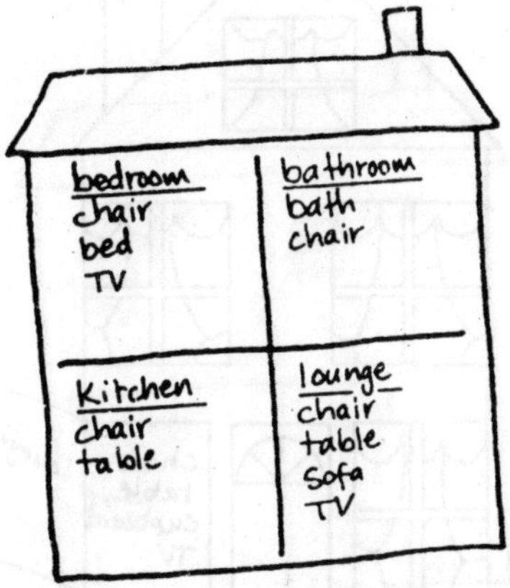

Or if they were making a list of what animals eat, they could write the words inside the animals:

Let the children use their imaginations. Remember, we want them to make the language event their own. For example, here is a house made like an advent calendar by an eight-year-old French girl. The lists of furniture are behind the doors and windows.

Other Language You Can Practise with this Activity

It is quite fun working out combinations of categories and objects. Look through your textbook or syllabus to see what possibilities it offers, for example:

Rooms and furniture	Weather and hobbies
Weather and seasons or months	Days of the week and school subjects
Sports and clothes	Colours and food, etc.

Final Comment

The children do not have to be able to write the words already to do this activity. In fact, it is intended to help them learn *how* to write them. So, when they make their rough lists, they can write the half-remembered words down as they like. This allows the children to take risks and draw on their partial knowledge in the way we are trying to encourage. They can, however, do it safely, because you are going to write the words correctly on the board a few minutes later.

2. Imagine

Instead of asking children to describe what you and they can both see, the idea of this activity is to stimulate them to find the words for what they imagine. We saw this on previous pages, where the children were given a picture of an animal's lair and asked to describe the monster they imagined lived down the hole.

Language Focus in this Example

In this present example, the children are going to make up a character and life this example for the child in the picture. In the process, they will practise the words and phrases they need to describe their own lives. This can be a purely oral activity or it can lead to imaginative written work.

Materials Required

— You need one interesting, largish picture of a child for all the class to see.

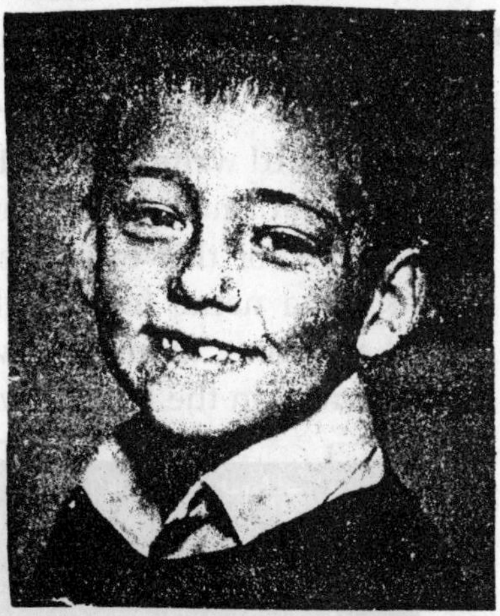

(The picture should be big enough for the children at the back of your classroom to see but they do not have to see all the detail because, remember, they are not going to describe the picture.)

— A collection of several small pictures of children. You can cut these from magazines and stick them on paper so that the edges don't get too worn and you can use them again.

Preliminary Work

You will want this activity to be preceded by plenty of other work on describing families/hobbies/likes and dislikes, so it is a useful way of drawing together several topics.

Suggested Procedures

Stage 1: It helps if you structure what the class are doing. You are going to leave the content and the end product to the children, but their imagination needs something to start it off. Total freedom is rather inhibiting! So ...

— On the board write up question prompts for the kind of information the children are going to make up. For this example, they are going to think up a name for the child in the picture. They are going to imagine where he lives, who else there is in the family, what his hobbies are,

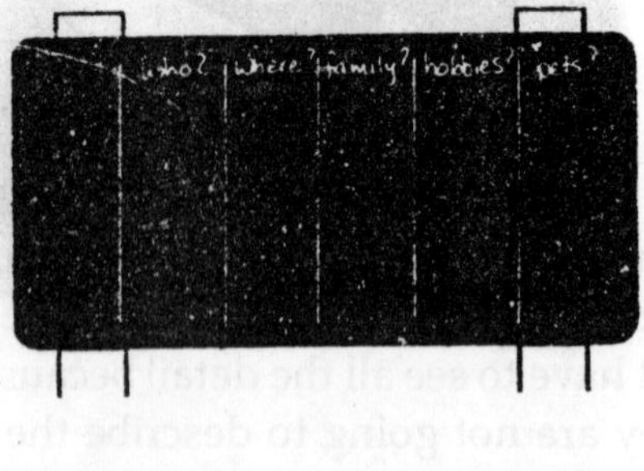

and whether he has any pets. So the headings are: *Who? Where? Family? Hobbies? Pets?* (Once the children get the idea, they might like to suggest the topics themselves.)

— Discuss the picture with the class, taking suggestions for the subject's name, where they live, etc. Take your time talking round the picture, reacting to and extending the children's suggestions if you can. The importance in the activity comes from exploring the possibilities:

Teacher: What is his name? What shall we say? Nick? Brian?
(Suggests several to show there is no right answer.)
Child:Max.

Teacher: Um... Max ... that's a good, name. OK. Has he only got one name? Perhaps he has two names ... perhaps he has three names. Imagine ...

Another Child: Stefan.

Teacher: *(Writes up both names.)* OK. Max ... Stefan.

Later:

Teacher: Where does he live? ... What shall we say?

Child: England.
(Teacher writes up 'England'.)

Teacher: Is it a house or a flat? Imagine ...

Child: House.

Teacher: Oh, he lives in a house, not a flat, does he? Is it large or small? *(Writes up a child's suggestion.)* How many bedrooms has it got? Ten? That *is* big!

— As the children offer their ideas, write them on the board in note form so that the children can see what to do later when they are working on their own.

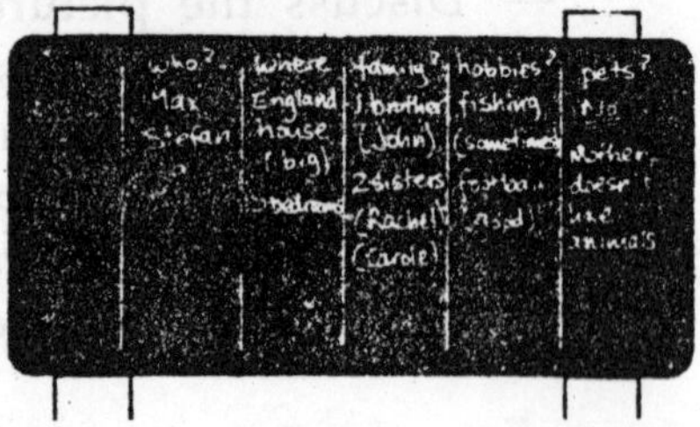

— In this way you build up a story on the board.

— When your notes are complete you can tell the story from them:

'This is Max Stefan. He is nine years old. He has one brother and two sisters. His brother is called John.' etc.

— Then get someone in the class to tell you the story too.

Stage 2: Having shown the children what to do, you now want them to work on their own in simultaneous pairs or small groups.

— In their books or preferably (because this is rough work) on scrap paper, the children draw the starter grid and copy in the headings.

— Give the small pictures out to the pairs.

— The children talk in pairs and agree on a story for their picture. You can go round and help them.

— When they have finished, choose one or two pairs to tell their story to the others in the class. You can make more of this by noting their versions on the chart on the board as they offer them.

Possible Follow Up/Variation

a) You can make more of the opportunities for oral work which this activity provides if you get the children to pass the pictures to another pair when they have finished their own story. In this way, each pair creates a life for more than one picture. If you do this, number the pictures for easy reference. The class can then compare ideas:

Pair 1: This girl is called Anna.
Pair 2: No, she isn't. She is called Jane. etc.

b) You can extend the activity in another way by getting the pairs to write up their story. They could write it in their exercise books or they could turn it into a little story book as the next activity suggests.

c) Another variation would be to get the children to imagine a conversation. You could find a picture of two people talking. For example, you might find something fun like these drawings of two imaginary beings. The children invent a conversation, perhaps on the topic you are practising at the moment. You can make this a regular feature of classwork by using it as a way to round off a topic or unit in a textbook if you are using one. If you have a classroom of your own with wall space where you can put up the children's work, this could make an interesting display.

Other Language You Can Practise with this Activity

This kind of activity lends itself to descriptions (as the monster in its hole, pages 7-8) and personal details (as in the example above). You can also use it to encourage the children to tell a story about an imaginary day excursion. For example, start with a picture of a place like the seaside or a big town, perhaps on a travel poster.

The prompt questions on the grid could then be:

When?	Day, month, time.
Who?	Remember that this is an exercise in imagination. There does not have to be anyone in the actual picture. The children can write themselves into the story if they want to.
Why?	A reason for going, e.g.: 'It is my birthday.'
What is going to happen?	'I am going to swim.'

Final Comments

(i) By asking the children to make up their own story instead of just getting them to describe what they can already see, you are creating real language use, which is one of our priorities.

(ii) Do not worry if they use a mixture of foreign

language and mother tongue in the notes and discussion. This doesn't matter. They are only preliminary rough notes to act as a prompt for oral feedback which will be in English.

(iii) If you have some children in your class who are not very confident or able, *you* can tell the story in English from their rough notes, so that they feel they have played a full part in the lesson.

3. Writing Booklets

The idea of this activity is to get the children to make their own little booklets for their class..

Language Focus in this Example

Describing their home town or village.

Materials Required

You can make each booklet out of two sheets of A4 paper. Fold the sheets into four, staple them down one of the long folded edges, and cut them to provide a quick, attractively-sized, sixteen-page booklet. You could, of course, get the children to make them for you at some point in a handicraft lesson. This is all part of making sure that language work is not isolated from the children's other work. The first time you do this activity with them, it may help to have a finished model to show what they are going to do.

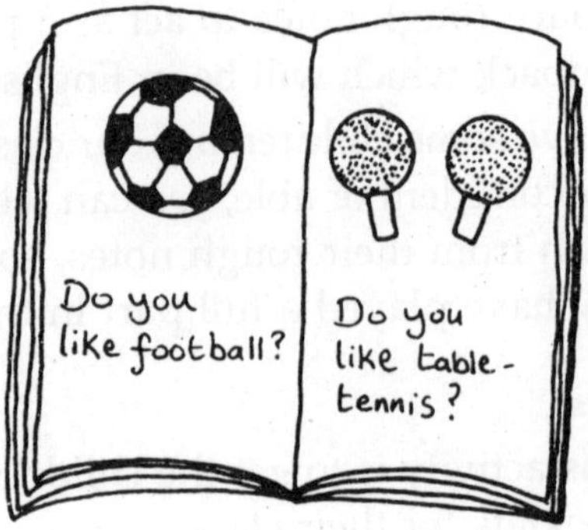

Preliminary Work

This activity would come at the end of a topic when the class has already had plenty of practice on the topic.

Suggested Procedures

- When the children are thoroughly familiar with the phrases in spoken and written form, write the key phrase on the board. In the example illustrated above the key phrase would be:

  'In my village there is ..."

- On *rough* paper, they make their lists of twelve things they will include in their booklets. Choosing twelve leaves enough room in the booklet for the much decorated title page and a 'hard words' list at the end.
- You could help them by discussing as a class what they might like to include and writing it up on the board for reference.

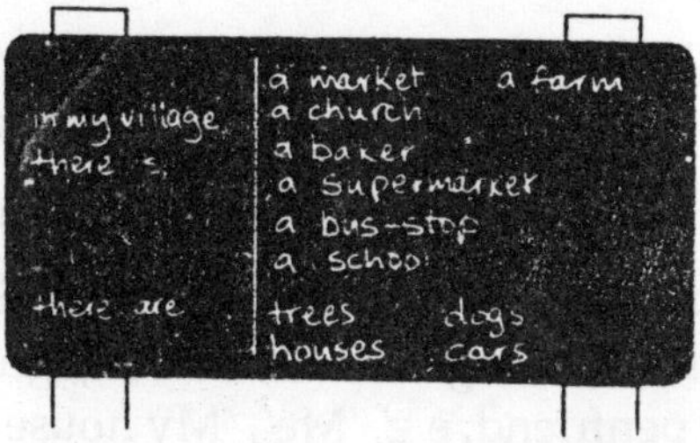

— When they have made their choice of items, the children have their spelling checked by you.
— They copy up the checked sentences into their booklets.
— They can then do the illustrations. (If you let them start with the illustrations, some of them will never reach the writing!)

Possible Follow Up

When completed, these booklets can be hung on the wall or put in a class library box to provide material for early finishers or quieter moments.

Variations

(a) The children could make little workbooks to practise a particular structure, e.g. 'How many...?' or 'Do you like ...?' They write the answers at the back of the book.

(b) The children could also write up a small story based on a picture as in the previous activity.

Other Language You Can Practise with This Activity

You can use this activity to practise writing the kinds of personal things the children might want to write to a future penfriend, e.g. 'Me', 'My house', 'My family'. (Some children might like to use photographs instead of drawings to illustrate them.)

Final Comment

You may prefer some classes to do the neat version of their writing on bits of paper which they then stick onto the pages of the booklet they have made. The advantage of this is that it allows for things going wrong without spoiling the whole booklet. The disadvantage is that it means you have to deal with the glue!

4. Design Your Own Sticker

Most children seem to love badges and stickers. Why not get them to design their own? In doing this, they are expressing a genuine personal opinion or enthusiasm and in the process they are producing their own individual phrase in the foreign language. What they write is theirs. It is not an answer to a teacher's question. It is not an exercise where everyone in the class is trying to produce the right answer. The children can make up something that no one else in the class has thought of.

Language Focus in this Example

The example below is intended to encourage the children to use colours and to combine them with any other words which they choose.

Materials Required

— Circles of plain paper. (You can get the children to make these if you like.)

— Coloured pens or pencils.

Preliminary Work

This would make a good final activity in a sequence on colours.

Suggested Procedures

— Tell the children what they are going to do. (If you have a sticker to show them it will help.)

— Draw a big circle on the board so you can design a sticker as an example.

— Remind the children of the colours and write them up on one side of the board.

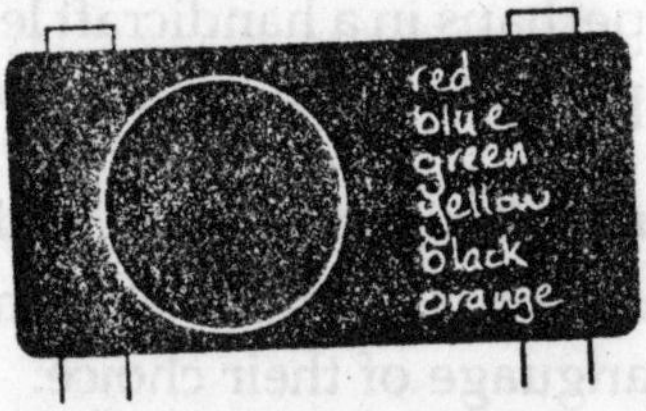

— Write your starter phrase in the circle:

— Think aloud about what you are going to put in the space:

Teacher: I like ... red. I like red ... apples. Yes. I like red apples.

(Writes it in the circle and draws the picture.)

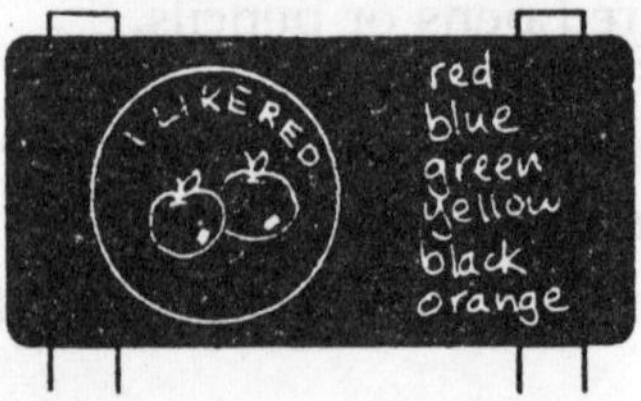

— Give out the paper and let the class make their own stickers.

Possible Follow Up

These would make a very attractive display to put on the classroom window (facing outwards) or on the wall.

Variation

The children could make badges out of cardboard and safety pins (perhaps in a handicraft lesson) and stick small circles of paper onto them to make personal badges.

Other Language You can Practise with This Activity

Any short phrase which the children can combine with other language of their choice:

'I like' + sport
+ pop stars
+ food
+ animals

Or: 'I am' + adjective
+ age

Or. 'I can' + verbs

Final Comment

The children may ask for words they don't yet know or perhaps words you don't know. It doesn't matter. In fact, it can provide a useful introduction to dictionaries and their peculiarities. Any new words which come up can be written on the board and later shared with the whole class.

5. Logical Puzzles

The last example in this section is the most difficult and is really only suitable for the top of the primary range. In this activity, the children have to solve a logical problem. To do this they have to do more than just understand the words. They have to work out the implications of what they read.

Language Focus in This Example

Shops and shopping.

Materials Required

A problem sheet for each pair of children.

Derek, Ann, Rob and Richard all go into a big shop. They each go to a different floor of the shop. One buys some sweets, one buys some pencils, one buys a book and one buys a tee shirt. Can you work out: What does Derek buy? Where does he buy it? What does Ann buy? Where does she buy it? What does Richard buy? Where does he buy it? What does Rob buy? Where does he buy it?

We know some things already.

1. Derek goes to the first floor.
2. You can buy pencils on the fourth floor.
3. Rob goes to the second floor.
4. Ann buys a tee shirt
5. Derek does not buy sweets.

Use the grid to help you find your answers.

floor	*who?*	*what?*
1		
2		
3		
4		

Suggested Procedures

— Give out the problem sheets and let the children try to read them for themselves first.

— Quickly draw the grid on the board.

— Read the text to them slowly.

— Enter the first piece of information (Derek goes to the first floor) on the grid on the board so that the children can see what they have to do.

floor	*who?*	*what?*
1	*D*	
2		
3		
4		

— Let the children work it out in pairs.

Other Language You Can Practise with This Activity

You can combine any three elements of information you choose and make a different puzzle for another occasion. You can reuse exactly the same format if you like. In the following example, the activity has been changed to practise people and possessions. (The names have been kept the same so that you can see how the formula has simply been transferred.)

The Animals have Escaped!

Here are four children called Derek, Ann, Rob and Richard. They live in these four houses. They each have a pet. One has a dog. One has a rabbit. One has a white mouse. One has a cat. The animals have got out. Can you work out: Whose cat is it? Which house does it come from? Whose dog is it? Which house does it come from? Whose rabbit is it? Which house does it come from? Whose white mouse is it? Which house does it come from?

We know some things already.

1. Derek lives at No. 1.
2. The rabbit comes from No. 4.
3. Rob lives at No. 2.
4. Ann has a cat.
5. Derek does not have a dog.

Final Comment

Not everyone finds this kind of logical puzzle easy. That is why this variation uses exactly the same format as the original activity! If you need to use a different pattern, you can find puzzles like this in children's puzzle books. You will also find other ideas in them which you can adapt to the language classroom.

This first selection of practical activities has shown how we can give our priorities real form in the materials we choose and the kinds of learning experiences they offer. However, in order to be effective, any activity needs to be set within a coherent overall framework. The second half of the book looks at the kinds of decisions and choices teachers have to make when creating a language programme or when implementing a programme they have been given.

8

Teaching of Social Studies

In America the term "social studies" has for over eighty years raised considerable debate among academic scholars and professional educators, as well as among questioning laymen. Despite some variations in definitions and conceived purposes, most conceptions of the nature of the social studies have seemed to crystallize around two extremes.

At one extreme are those who equate the content of the social studies with that of the parent social science disciplines. Advocates of this view hold that the social studies are essentially microcosmic versions of history, geography, political science, economics, and, the other social sciences. They believe that teachers in the schools should ask similar questions and follow similar procedures of inquiry as do practicing scholars in these disciplines. They warn that unless such a procedure is followed, the students will not have a clear and adequate understanding of the social world, let alone of the nature of the social science disciplines. The prime purpose here is to develop young, objective, social analysts.

Those who disagree with this position hold that the social studies, instead of being minor replications of the parent subjects, are, rather, carefully selected aspects. These advocates argue that the task of social studies curriculum planners and teachers is to select from the disciplines that data necessary to accomplish the objectives of the school and society. they emphasize the use of those portions of the parent subjects which will help attain their purposes, arguing that the function of the social studies is not to produce miniature social scientists but moral and intelligent citizens who are able to use their knowledge to make their world more meaningful and to work for worthy human ideals.

Both the social sciences and the social studies are in "flux. Indeed, the social studies with their focus upon contemporary affairs and attention to youth needs, as well as their applied nature, should probably be changing even more than their parent disciplines. But generally they are not. Traditionalists in the schools maintain a spirited rear-guard action against innovations; some continue to question even the concept of the social studies. Among the social sciences, however, new directions are the order of the day although it must be admitted that there are academicians who resist new emphases and approaches.

Disciplinarians from each of the social sciences are actively redefining their subjects. They are attempting to identify key generalisations accruing from research and are delineating the processes and relevant skills whereby their subjects become meaningful and purposeful to students of society. Some academicians see progress resulting from the extension of their subjects down into the elementary grades and want the high schools to offer electives or even to require courses in their particular specialties. Others prefer topical or problem-type courses or curricula in which the content and methods of a number of the relevant social sciences are brought to bear on a given issue.

Today almost no one calls for amalgamated offerings entitled "social studies." Many social scientists believe that a broadfield social studies course, often with a single social study title, is preferable to a narrowly conceived or "pure" course in history, geography, government, or any other social science. Multidisciplinary explorations and interdisciplinary approaches to the resolution of social problems are increasingly common. It is also true that the geographer, the anthropologist, the economist, and the historian, for example, can each claim his subject as the ideal base for social education. In the years immediately ahead, one great challenge in the lower schools will be the bringing of the social studies into line with the new departures and discoveries of the social sciences. Much more research, however, is needed before we can be certain as to the best base and the most appropriate scope and sequence of social learnings. Until then, every specialist is obliged to be a generalist. Academic borders seldom exist in the world of interaction outside the school. It was Lancelot Hogben who explained so fittingly that the boundaries of his province are the last thing the scientist discovers, and that when he has discovered them, he has set the limit to further progress!

The articles which follow discuss in varying but related degree the nature of the social studies and the social sciences. Can you differentiate between the two? In what ways are they related?

JOHN DEWEY

John Dewey wrote this late in his career, after he had become Emeritus Professor at Teachers College, Columbia University.

What is Social Study?*

In the new proper emphasis upon social studies, the primary problem, it seems to me, is to determine the scope

---

* Progressive Education, XV: 367 69. May 1938. Used by permission.

and range of the subject-matter designated by "social." More definitely, the question is: how far that which is social can be separated and treated by itself, and how far the social is a limiting function of the subject-matter of all studies what philosophers might call a category by which all materials of learning are to be interpreted. This is of course a restricted sense in which it is correct enough to isolate social materials. Questions of family life, of politics and economics, of war and peace, are obviously social questions. The problem I am raising is how far such materials can be understood and be educative in the full sense without a background of study of matters which lie outside of the social as thus limited.

No one would deny. I suppose, that many political questions at the present lime have economic roots. Issues of the relation of capital and labour, of concentration and distribution of wealth, of economic security and unemployment, occupy the attention of our legislative bodies. They are primarily economic questions but they find their way into political action because their impact upon human relations and their public consequences are intense and widespread. Can the student stop when he has traced these political themes to their economic sources? Or does understanding of the economic situation demand going further?

It would probably be admitted on all hands that the present economic situation is a historical development, and that while present facts may be amassed in quantities, the information thus gained needs to be placed in an historic setting if it is to be intelligently grasped and used. Many, perhaps all, of the economic questions have also definitely geographical aspects. I he problem of the farmer comes to mind, for example, and that of the railways as means of distribution of products. So does that of soil conservation and reforestation. The question of the distribution of population, of congestion in industrial and commercial centers, is an other aspect of the same general question. Careful studies show that in recent years there have been a number of great regional migrations which have left certain large regions in a slate of relative desolation while the burdens of relief, hospitalisation, etc., have been greatly increased in the areas to which they have gone. That miners live and work where there are mines and lumbermen work where there are still forests, as well as that farmers live on farms, and that certain centers are what they are because of facilities of transportation and need for reshipment of products, are obvious facts. But they raise the question how far are social studies to be conducted in the light of fundamental geographic and physiographic knowledge?

The reference that was made in an earlier paragraph to the historic context of economic questions suggests in turn the scientific background. The industrial and commercial change which has taken place in the world in the last century, in the past forty years, is the product of the great change which has taken place in physical, chemical and, more recently, biological science. The prime factor in the economic and political history of this period is what is known as the industrial revolution. The story of that revolution is the story of new technologies in the production and distribution of goods, which are themselves the result of a scientific revolution. Any vital comprehension of existing economic and political issues demands insight into processes and operations that can be grasped only through understanding of fundamental physical and chemical operations and laws. I will not press the paint further, though it might be extended into the subjects of literature, the fine arts and mathematics. The obvious objection that may be made to what has been said is that if it is accepted it swells the social studies beyond all limits; that they have so many ramifications and absorb so much of other studies that teacher and student alike are confronted with an unwieldy, unmanageable mass. The objection, when it is analysed, brings us to the other aspect of the educational question.

When I asked how far the social is from an educational point of view the limiting function of all the studies, the question I had in mind was whether such subjects as, for example, the history, geography and natural science already mentioned can be isolated, so as to be treated as independent subjects; or whether from the beginning and constantly they should be treated in their social bearings and consequences—consequences in the way, on one side, of problems and on the other side of opportunities. The human and cultural is after all the embracing limit to which all other things tend. In the higher reaches of school education there must, of course, be provision for training of experts and specialists. In them, a certain amount of relative separation of subjects from their social context and function is legitimate. But it is a fair question whether society is not suffering even here because the expert specialists have not the educational background which would enable them to view their special skills and knowledge in connection with social conditions, movements and problems.

But the particular point I would make is that in any case we have carried the isolation of subjects from their social effects and possibilities too far down the educational scale. From the psychological and moral stand-point it may be urged that for most boys and girls the material of studies loses vitality, becomes relatively dead, because it is separated from situations, and that much of the need which is felt at the present time for resorting to extraneous devices to make subjects interesting or else to coerce attention is a necessary effect of this isolation. Natural docility leads to acceptance. But underneath, there is the subconscious questioning, "What does all this mean? What is it for? What do the studies signify outside of the schoolroom or do they only belong there?"

The problem of congestion of studies and this version of aims with resulting superficiality is a pressing one today. The progressive and the reactionary agree in this one thing on the negative side. Both insist that there is kick of unity of aim, that there is dispersion and confusion. As far as I can see, the one hope of obtaining the desired unification is that which has been suggested. The natural focus, the assembling point, of the various studies is their social origin and function. Any other scheme of unification and correlation seems to me artificial and doomed to only transitory success. Progressive education has reached a point where it is looking for a lead which will give coherence and direction to its efforts. I believe it will find it here and that in the end emphasis upon social studies as a separate line of study may only add to the confusion and dispersion that now exist! Not because they are not important, but precisely because they are so important that they should give direction and organisation to all branches of study.

In conclusion, I want to say that in my judgment what has been said has a definite bearing upon what is called indoctrination, or, if one prefer, teaching, with respect to preparation for a different social order. Social studies as an isolated affair are likely to become either accumulations of bodies of special factual information or, in the hands of zealous teachers, to be organs of indoctrination in the sense of propaganda for a special social end, accepted enthusiastically, perhaps, but still dogmatically. Young people who have been trained in all subjects to look for social bearings will also be educated to see the causes of present evils. They will he equipped from the sheer force of what they have learned to see new possibilities and the means of actualising them. They will be indoctrinated in its deeper sense without having had doctrines forced upon them.

9

Magnets and Their Properties

Primary Emphasis

At the Primary Level Magnets are Probably studied more widely than any other topic. Growing numbers of young children have their own magnets and magnetic toys. Many learn something about magnets even before enrolling in school. For these reasons, we shall go into the subject more deeply than has been customary at this level.

The properties of magnetism are the theme. Among other things, children will learn how magnetism attracts through different materials;[1] how it can be studied although invisible; and how it is preserved or destroyed. If only several magnets are available for this unit, encourage pupils to bring theirs from home. Also, the third section of this unit includes some directions for "making" magnets. Many forthcoming activities are suitable for either groups or individuals.

GENERALISATIONS

I. Magnets commonly attract objects made of iron and steel.

---

* Wristwatcbes should be removed before working with magnets.

Credit for chapter opening photograph. Bernice Abbett-Photo Researchers, Inc.

II. A magnet attracts objects without touching them because there is a field of force around it; the field is most powerful at the ends, or poles.

III. Magnetism can pass through many materials.

IV. Iron or steel are the commonest materials magnetised by a magnet; steel holds its magnetism longer than iron.

V. The field of force around a wire carrying electricity can be used to magnetize iron or steel objects.

VI. Compasses are magnets that show directions because of the earth's magnetism; unlike poles of magnets attract, like poles repel each other.

VII. Dropping, heating, or storing a magnet improperly will weaken its force.

Magnets and What They Attract. There is no scarcity of magnets about us for examples in teaching. In kitchens, cloth pot holders containing magnets are placed conveniently on the sides of stoves. Automatic can openers contain magnets to hold opened can lids. Cabinet doors remain closed because of magnets. Some women wear magnetic earrings. Beauty operators use magnets to pick up dropped hairpins. Physicians sometimes employ them to extract pieces of metal from wounds. Toy stores contain a variety of toys that in some way use magnetism.

In nearly all these cases, the metals attracted tó a magnet are iron and steel. Less well-known magnetic metals are cobalt and nickel. Among the commoner metals not attracted by magnets are brass (an alloy of copper and zinc), aluminum, tin, silver, stainless steel (an alloy of several metals), copper, bronze (an alloy of copper and tin), and gold.

It will be helpful to know several facts about situations that may cause some confusion in this unit unless they are understood. For example, a question may arise about the attractable property of so-called "tin" cans. These are made of thin sheet steel and coated lightly with tin. Although tin is not attractable, steel is. Confusion also result if some straight pins are attracted by a magnet and other identical-appearing pins are not. Scraping off some silver coating on the nonattractable pins will usually reveal that they are made of brass. Also, whereas pure nickel is ordinarily magnetic, the United States five-cent piece is largely composed of copper and so should not be used as an example.

Natural magnets are sometimes called "lodestones," or "leading stones," perhaps because ancient mariners used them as crude compasses. Lodestones are composed of magnetite, an iron ore found in different locations on the earth's crust. Since only some of these deposits are magnetised, theories have been developed to explain this phenomenon. One such theory holds that lightning may have been responsible. It is thought that electricity discharged into the ore may have arranged many atoms within the ore in a manner similar to that found in magnets. Traces of magnetite are common in soils. A magnet dragged along the ground or in a playground sandbox may attract many particles. These particles can be an effective substitute in experiments where iron "filings" are used.

Man-made or artificial magnets are often composed of steel and magnetised by electricity. Named for their shape, there are *bar, V, U, horseshoe,* and *cylindrical* magnets, to give the more familiar varieties. (Figure 9.1.) Each of these magnets attracts substances most strongly at the ends, or poles. The U, V, and horseshoe magnets are more powerful than the others, when all factors are equal; they are bent so two poles attract instead of one.

Powerful *alnico* magnets are now available to teachers at scientific supply houses and in commercial kits. These are made from aluminum, cobalt, nickel, and iron. Alnico magnets are used for such home and commercial purposes mentioned at the beginning of this section, as well as for a variety of others.

So far, we have described permanent magnets. Though useful, they do not compare with the enormous importance of temporary magnets, or more accurately, *electromagnets.* These will be discussed more fully later.

The strategy of the first sequence is to build an understanding in the children of the materials that magnets will attract. This understanding can then be used to figure out why, given a number of apparently identical objects, only some are attractable. An extending activity will require thinking about how to control variables, and how to interpret data.

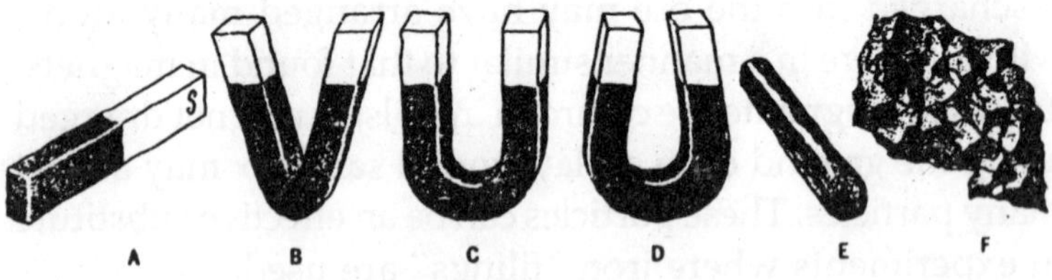

Fig. 9.1 Magnets, (a) bar, (b) V, (c) U, (d) horseshoe, (e) cylindrical and (f) lodestone.

Generalisation I: Magnets Commonly Attract Objects Made of Iron and Steel

1. *Materials:* several magnets (have one attached to a 2-foot string); iron roller-skate key; shoe box of numerous attractable and nonattractable objects, metals and nonmetals, including the following chart materials or substitutes. (Be sure to have examples of the six metals listed. Children can bring these objects from home, although the exact

purpose should not be revealed; all can be returned.) If the children can read, have this material written on the chalkboard and concealed by a pull-down map:

Name:	*Made of:*	*We Think:*	*We Found Out:*
nails	iron	—	—
wire	copper	—	—
pins	steel	—	—
hair curler	aluminum	—	—
penny	bronze	—	—
scissors	steel	—	—
screws	brass	—	—

You might begin with this bridge: "Let's say one day you are walking over some very large rocks. You have a roller-skate key in your hand. While jumping from one rock to another the key slips out of your hand and falls in between two very big rocks. The space is too small to get your arm into, even though you can see the key is just an arm's length below. How can you get the key back?"

Be prepared for a variety of approaches, some ingenious. (One trial class child said, "I'd use a stick with chewing gum on the end.") Finally, if no one suggests it, ask how a magnet and string can be used. Does it make any difference what the key is made of? What metals *will* a magnet pull?

Reveal the chalkboard material. Hold up one listed item at a time. Will a magnet pull this kind of metal? Ask pupils to make a guess about each of six to eight different objects of varying metals. Before and after each one is tried, write "yes" or "no" in the appropriate columns. (You need not be concerned about children learning the names of most of the metals. The important thing is for them to realize gradually that only a few metals are attractable.)

How about other objects and materials? What will a magnet attract? Distribute all of the materials to small groups and invite the children to follow a similar guess-test procedure. They can separate the materials into two piles, one "yes" pile for attractable objects, one "no" pile for unattractable objects. After a short work period, the several smaller piles can be added together to make two large "yes" and "no" piles on a table in front of the class.

Have a class discussion. What do the "yes" materials look like? What do the "no" materials look like? Let someone make a subset of "no" metals. What do "no" metals look like? Help pupils infer that it is more likely that materials in the "yes" pile were made of iron or steel than the other materials. Now hold up a skate key. What metals does it most look like? (Iron or steel.) Will a magnet attract it? Let someone try it.

2. *Materials:* nail file, or small coarse rock; magnifying glass; magnet; several identical-appearing straight pins of brass and steel on a table. (Test with a magnet to determine which are steel.)

Ask someone to put the straight pins in a box. Have him use a magnet to make the task "easier." When failure is experienced with some (brass) pins, let the children first define the problem, then raise hypotheses as to why failure occurred.

Their previous input with nonattractable objects including metals should prompt some children to guess that some of the pins are made of one or more nonattractable metals. If not, review their initial experience. If this guess is made, ask for a test.

Pupils may decide that attracted and un-attracted pins may be nibbed against a nail file or rough stone. As the thin coating is worn away, steel pins will appear dull gray, and brass pins yellowish. Let the test continue until a pattern develops. All attracted pins will be one color, all unattracted pins another. This will help verify the hypothesis. Have them compare the ma-terials with the half-dozen metals identified in activity 1. Can they identify the two different pin metals?

Bring out that some pins were made of steel, and some of *brass*—a metal that is attracted by magnetism.

EXTENDING ACTIVITIES

1. Have a magnet power test. You will six or more magnets, a box of *small* paper clips, a box of carpet tacks or brads (small nails), masking tape and crayon for marking the magnets. (You might mark the magnets with a masking tape strip of a different color to help the class learn colors, or letters of the alphabet to aid this learning.)

Line up all the magnets on a table. Which magnet is most powerful? Ask for reasons why some are picked. (Most children will cite larger size.) Suggest that they test the magnets and order them from strongest to weakest. But there will need ' to be some "rules" (controls) to make sure everything is fair. Work these out with the children, but keep the list small:

Only one end (pole) is used.
The same size paper clips are used.
Clips are completely picked up, end to end in a chain (not bunched).

Record the data on the chalkboard:

Magnet	*Clips*	*Rank*
A	3	
B	2	
C	4	

D	5
E	2
F	3

Probably there will be a few ties, since the paper clips are a crude measure. How to break the ties? See if the children suggest a more sensitive test, such as using carpet tacks or brads. After ties are broken, get pupils to rank the magnets in order of power (first, second, etc.) by interpreting the numerical data. This can be done on individual worksheets while you circulate around the room checking the work and helping where needed.

Why weren't the magnets equally powerful? Develop that not all magnets are made of the same materials or made in the same way. Another reason is that some are not properly cared for.

2. Acquaint the class with some standards for the care and keeping of magnets. It is suggested that no attempts be made at this time to reason through these standards, as this requires input that will be acquired in the unit. However, tell the children that these standards will help keep their magnets in good condition. See Figure 9.2 A-B for some model charts. Chart A uses soft iron "keepers" in two instances. If regular keepers are not available, nails or other soft iron objects will do. Two strips cut from a tinned can work well with bar magnets. (Caution: File down jagged or sharp edges to make them safe for handling.)

3. If possible, provide several different kinds of magnets for exploration. Teach their proper names. Some magnets might be brought by class members.

Magnetic Field of Force. As children explore with magnets, they will observe that a magnet will attract from a distance. For example, a small nail or paper clip will "jump" to the magnet. They will also see that the attractive force is strongest at the poles. This offers an opportunity to illustrate the field of force surrounding a magnet.

Although it is impossible to see the field directly, its presence may be inferred. Sprinkle iron filings on a sheet of stiff white paper placed over a magnet. Observe that their distribution is orderly, with the greatest concentration of filings at the poles. (Figure 9.3.) Theoretically, a magnetic field extends outward to an infinite distance. But for practical purposes the field ends where its presence is no longer detectable.

Fig. 9.2 A—B

Generalisation II: A magnet Attracts Objects without Touching them Because there is a Field of Force Around it; the Field is Most Powerful at the Ends, or Poles

Materials: for each small group, container of iron filings (a salt shaker is useful); a sheet of stiff, white paper; carpet tacks or small paper clips; two powerful magnets.

Place the foregoing materials on a table. You might want to begin with a demonstration-discussion. Hold up a magnet and ask, "How close must this magnet be to attract iron or steel objects?" Allow several children to try different distances with a magnet and carpet tacks or small paper clips. Have them find which part of the magnet appears most powerful. If several magnets of differing strengths are available, let the children demonstrate that some will attract over a greater distance than others. "How is it possible for these magnets to pick up things without touching them?" Most children will realize that "something" is causing interaction between the two objects, but will not be able to identify what the "something" is. After the class reacts, you might remark, "Here is a way we can find out."

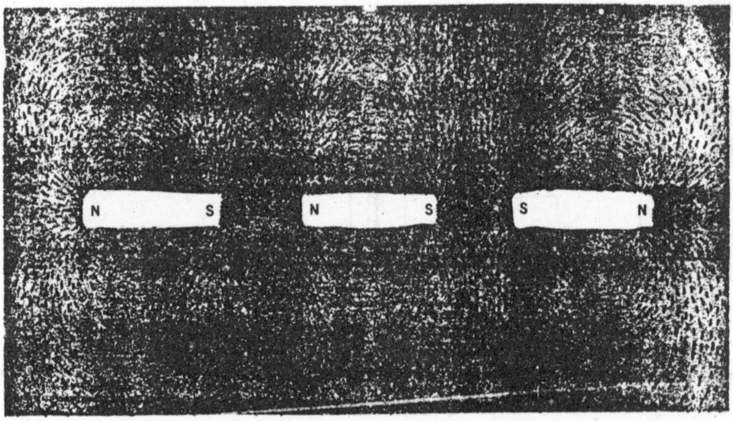

Fig. 9.3 Besides revealing fields of force, iron filings in this picture indicate that like poles of magnets and unlike poles attract each other.

Lay the magnet on a table and place a sheet of stiff white paper over it. Explain that the container holds small bits of iron, called "filings." Sprinkle some filings on the paper above the magnet. Tap the paper gently to assist in the distribution of filings. Have the children observe that the filings are arranged in an orderly pattern some distance around the magnet. Tell them that this area is the magnet's *field of force.* The idea of field (area) and force (push or pull) might be explained simply here, if needed.

Note that concentrations of "lines" of force shown by the filings seem greatest at poles. Bring out that this is probably the reason the ends of the magnet seemed more powerful than its other parts. Observe that this force is invisible, but that we can see what it does through this demonstration. Help the class to realize that an iron or steel object can be attracted without being touched as long as it is within the magnet's field of force. Point out that the magnet's strength and weight of the attracted object determine whether this attraction becomes noticeable.

Encourage groups to explore various patterns they can make by arranging one or two magnets in different positions and sprinkling iron filings on white paper placed over the magnets. Who can tell how the magnets are arranged underneath just by looking at the iron filing patterns? inferences

EXTENDING ACTIVITY

Prepare several simple-to-harder "magnet inference sheets" from permanent records of lines of force made with one or several magnets. The object is for the child to observe the magnetic field record, then try to duplicate it. He should be given the permanent record sheet, the original magnet or magnets used, a stiff sheet of white paper, and a shakerful of iron filings. A sketch of the original magnet positions on the back of the magnet inference sheet may help to verify these positions for some pupils, but is not needed if the patterns are reasonably clear. Some ambiguity is desirable to require careful observing and interpreting of possible matching patterns. It is also good for pupils to learn self-reliance in getting answers.

Permanent records can be made in several ways, including blueprint paper or plastic spray. Arrange one or two magnets in various positions on a cardboard tray. Put blueprint paper on top and sprinkle with iron filings. Place this carefully in a windless, sunny area, without disturbing the pattern or magnets. Expose for 5 to 10 minutes, then remove the filings. A blue-and-white record of the lines of force will remain. (Look on the blueprint paper package for possible extra steps to insure a permanent record, such as running cold water over it.)

For a more realistic-appearing record, use plastic spray to fix the filings on a stiff sheet of white paper. Hold the aerosol can at sufficient distance so filings are not blown away. For best results, be sure to use fine, powder-like filings and to sprinkle lightly. *Let the spray dry before removing the sheet* from the magnets.

Magnetic Transparency. An intriguing phenomenon of a magnetic field is that it can pass through many substances without apparent loss of effect. It seems as though these materials are "transparent" to the passage of the lines of force. This makes it possible for magnetic earrings to be worn, and for wristwatches to be affected unless precautions are taken. Plumbers may use magnets in locating pipes (iron or steel) behind walls or under floors. In fact, the field of force will penetrate any nonmagnetic materials the class may test.

Materials of iron and steel are considered "opaque" to this force. When touched by a magnet, the force passes inside them and back into the magnet.

Generalisation III: Magnetism Can Pass Through Many Materials

Materials: for you, a brimful glass of water with a paper clip inside; a magnet; for each small group, flat, thin pieces of glass, steel (can tops), plastic, aluminum or aluminum foil, wood, and so on; magnet; thread; small paper clip; ruler; books. (Place the objects on a table and set up the magnet as in Figure 9.4. However, leave the attached paper clip lying on the table until after your bridge.)

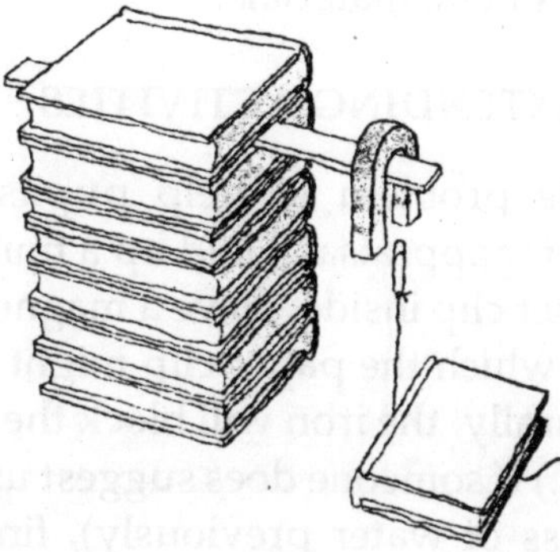

Fig. 9.4.

Hold up the brimful glass of water with a small paper clip inside. Who can get this paper clip out of the glass with a magnet without putting the magnet into the water? Probably someone will show that a strong magnet can be touched to the glass adjacent to the paper clip to attract the clip. If the magnet is moved carefully up the side of a glass, the paper clip will follow. Bring out the apparent reason. Probably the magnetism went through the water and glass.

Now, suspend the paper clip, as in the model of Figure 9.4. Pull the thread end gently to lower the clip to just above the point of falling. Elicit that the magnetic field is attracting it through air. "How can we use this setup and materials on the table to see if magnetism will go through objects?"

Have some children try slipping various flat objects in

the space between the magnet and paper clip. Relate their findings to the initial problem.

When a tinned can top and other attractable objects are placed in the space, they will note that the paper clip falls. Guide them to understand that magnetism will penetrate nonmagnetic materials, but does not seem to pass through magnetic materials.

EXTENDING ACTIVITIES

1. Try this little problem to help pupils apply their knowledge, and for appraisal. Hold up a tinned can full of water with a paper clip inside. Have a magnet in full view. Ask for ways in which the paper clip might be gotten out of the can. (Naturally, the iron will block the magnetism if a magnet is used.) If someone does suggest using a magnet (as with the glass of water previously), find how many agree and disagree, hold an evaluative discussion, and then test the idea.

2. Prepare some "hidden object" boxes. These can give children a chance to make inferences from indirect evidence, and to improve in communication skills. The activity can take three or more forms, each progressively harder.

In the first form the child receives a shoe box and a magnet. On the box is a card that identifies several hidden objects which have been taped by you anywhere inside except on the bottom. (Figure 9.5.) The box is not to be opened, picked up, or shaken, although it can be turned around for convenience. The child tries to find the exact locations of the objects by sliding his magnet around the box's outside surface. He also tries to identify the proper objects in these locations and to infer whether they are in a parallel or perpendicular position relative to the box base. (The last task can be skipped to make it easier.) For a second version of the game, the searcher tells someone else what he thinks the objects might be, exactly where to find them, and their positions relative to the box base. The "catch" is that he must verbally give the directions once, and without gestures.

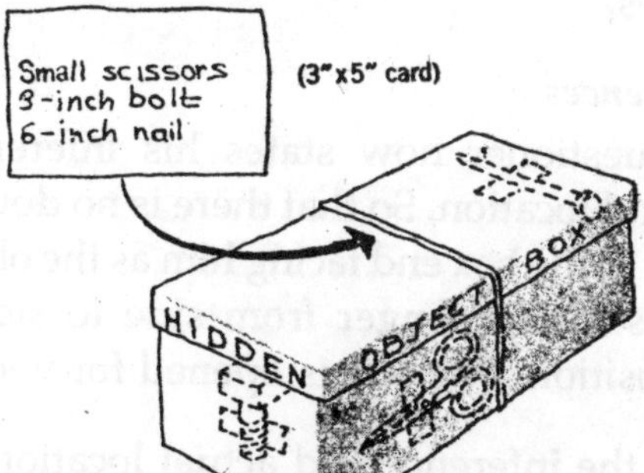

Fig. 9.5.

In the third version the searcher is the data source for someone else. Tape only one object, or two at the most, inside the box. If two objects are used, one need only be identified as the "big object," and the other the "small object". After the searcher has used his magnet to explore all over the box surface for possible box contents, a partner (who has not observed the exploration) tries to extract the data from him by asking questions that can only be answered by a "yes" or "no" response. The measure of success is to ask the fewest questions possible to locate and describe the object. (This can be discussed in an evaluative session.) Here is an example of how the third version might go, using one taped object:

"Is the object in the half of the box nearest me?"

"Yes."

"Is it on one of the long sides?"

"No."

"Is it on the top?"

"No."

"Is it parallel to the box bottom?"

"Yes."

Make Inferences

The questioner now states his inference about the contents and location. So that there is no doubt about it, he also points to the box end facing him as the object's location, and moves his forefinger from side to side to show its parallel position. The box is opened for verification.

When the inference and actual location are different, the partners discuss possible reasons for the discrepancy. Perhaps the searcher has made some faulty inferences from his search data. Perhaps the questioner has made a faulty inference from the information he received from the searcher.

When two objects are used (each should be taped in a different location), the game is played in the same way. The effect is simply to introduce another set of variables that must be discovered by the searcher and questioner.

All taped objects in these games must be both attractable and sizable for successful inferences. Probably none should be smaller than a 3-inch iron nail. If more than one object is used, each should vary at least 50 per cent in size from other objects.

Making Magnets. A magnet can be made from a piece of iron or steel by stroking it in one direction with one pole of a permanent magnet. Its power increases with the number of strokes applied. If a piece of over six or eight inches is used, stroke with one pole from the object's center outward for at least twenty strokes. Repeat the procedure on the remaining half, but this time with the magnet's opposite pole. This should produce good results. Be sure to lift the magnet clear at the end of each stroke before bringing it back to start another. Merely rubbing it back and forth will produce unsatisfactory results.

Although it takes longer to induce magnetism in steel than in iron, steel retains its magnetism longer. Common materials made of steel include scissors, some knitting needles, sewing needles, screwdrivers, hacksaw blades, and knife blades. Perhaps the commonest useful examples of soft iron are nails and wire coat hangers.

A more efficient way to induce magnetism is by using electricity. This is developed in another basic generalisation of the unit.

Generalisation IV: Iron or Steel are the Commonest Materials Magnetised by a Magnet; Steel Holds its Magnetism Longer than Iron

This activity leads to four controlled experiments with magnets. The beginning phase provides some of the input necessary to perform these experiments intelligently.

Materials: several large (4-inch) nails; box of carpet tacks; magnets; steel straight pins; paper clips; large steel sewing needles; needles; screwdriver; or similar objects.

Place your materials on a table. Invite a child to pick up a carpet tack and try to attract another tack with it. Then have him use a magnet to attract a tack. Guide him to build a "chain" of tacks, using each magnetised tack to attract another. Permit him to continue until the chain is broken. Probably by this part of the unit the children will have made many "chains" in magnet play.

If a powerful magnet is available, hold a pole of the magnet just above the head of a tack without touching it.

It should be possible to make a small chain of tacks dangle from the first tack. (If the tacks you use are too small to be held conveniently in your fingers, just use a small nail in place of the first tack.) Magnetism is induced in the tacks by the magnet's field of force. Ask a few questions. "What could we call each tack that attracted another tack? Was each tack a magnet to begin with? What caused each tack to become a magnet?" Bring out that magnets can be made out of steel and iron objects.

Now demonstrate how to induce magnetism in several objects. Use a large nail, a large steel sewing needle, or similar materials. Show first that these are not magnetised by touching them to a tack. With either pole of a magnet, stroke the object its entire length *in one direction only.* Call this to the children's attention. Lift the magnet at the end of each stroke for about twenty to thirty strokes. Demonstrate that the object is now a magnet.

For follow-up activities, say, "Here are some questions that need experiments to find the answers. Let's see if you can think of ways we can find these answers." (Each experiment will need controls the children can construct, if they are guided to see the necessity for them. After each question, briefly discuss how the experiment should be done. Substitute appropriate materials where necessary.)

a. "Will this nail's magnetism get more powerful the more it is stroked?" (First, test the nail for magnetism by seeing if it attracts paper clips. It should not. Test again after each ten strokes with a magnet.)
b. "Which can be magnetised more easily—a soft iron nail or a sewing needle made of hard steel?" (Each object is first tested for magnetism, stroked once before each test, tested again with tacks, and soon.)

c. "Which will keep its strength longer— the magnetised, soft iron nail, or the magnetised needle made of hard steel?" (Same procedure as above is followed, except that objects are initially stroked more times and tested after a 10-minute or longer interval. The difference will be greater if the objects are used normally rather than left undisturbed during the waiting period.)

d. "Will a magnet you make be more powerful if stroked in one direction or back forth in two directions?" (Use two nails. Test to see if magnetised. Stroke each thirty times—one in a single direction and one fifteen times each way. with tacks.)

If you have a capable primary class, the problems to various small groups so procedures can be thought through. Allow enough time for thinking to take place and for the experiments to be tried several times.

Discussion afterward can begin by asking first for the problem, then for specific procedures followed in individual groups. With your aid, procedures can be constructively analysed by the children. After discussion of specific findings, summarize by asking, "How can a magnet be made?" and "How can a long-lasting magnet be made?"

EXTENDING ACTIVITIES

1. What objects can be magnetised? Have children try to magnetize any object they wish. (First, each should be tested for magnetism.) If the same "yes" and "no" materials are used as in the first activity of Generalisation 1, pupils will discover that all the objects that were attractable in that activity also can be magnetised. Those that were nonattractable cannot be magnetised.

2. Here is a difficult but interesting problem for children: Give two large sewing needles to each child or group. One needle is magnetised, but one is not. Which one is the magnet? The only permissible way to find out is to touch the needles, rather than to use a compass, suspend a needle from a thread, etc. The key to finding out is to know that a magnet is weakest in its center part. The children should have found this out in the previous activities in order to do well in this one. For example, if you try to place small nails or tacks along the entire length of a bar magnet, they will fall from, or adhere very weakly to, the center portion. Studying iron filings in a field of force also confirms this area of weakness. (Later, when your pupils find out more about positive and negative poles, you might ask them why the center part of a magnet is weaker. When one third-grade teacher did, the reply was, "Since it is right in between the poles, the magnet is undecided.")

Notice in Figure 9.6 A-B how the magnetised needle is discovered. In A there is no noticeable attraction when the non-magnet is held against the middle part of the magnet. When the needle positions are inferences reversed (B), the nonmagnet leaps to the pole of the magnet.

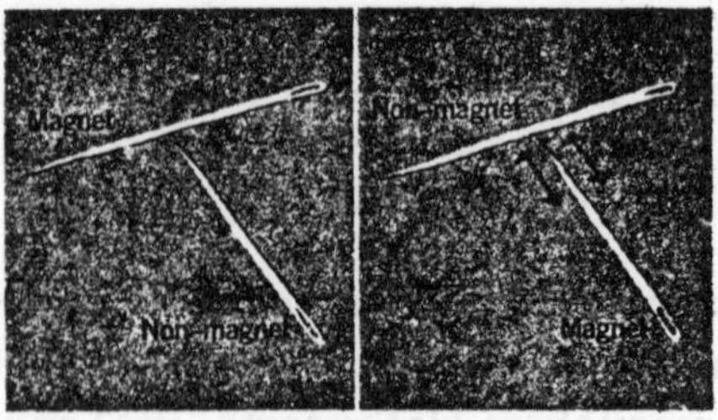

Fig. 9.6. A-B

The Electromagnet. Connect a wire to a flashlight battery or dry cell, and the wire will attract iron filings. It is an *electromagnet.* If the wire is fashioned into a coil, this concentrates the effect, making it a more powerful magnet. Other ways of boosting magnetic force are to use an iron or steel core in the coil, and to increase the flow of electricity going through the wire.

Variations and applications of electromagnets are virtually endless—motors, doorbells, generators, telephones, and so on. (We shall examine a few of these in the next unit.) One of the easier and more interesting applications for children is the electromagnetic crane. (See Figure 9.7.)

Basically the same things are present in the crane as are needed in a related, upcoming lesson: a source of electricity, wire to carry the current, and a soft iron core around which the wire is wrapped. (See Figure 9.8.)

Children need to be made aware that a soft iron core is used in electromagnets rather than hard steel, since steel tends to become permanently magnetised. If they have studied the previous generalisation, most should have no trouble understanding this fact. They will also realize the advantage of having a magnet that can be shut off or turned on whenever needed.

Fig. 9.7. An electromagnetic crane at work. (1) shows the metal cover, (2) where the wire is coiled around an iron core and how the wire leads to the cab, (3) where the storage batteries or generator are housed.

A question may be raised if certain lightweight materials such as tacks or pins continue to be attracted to the electromagnet after electricity is shut off. This is due to "residual" magnetism, or the small amount that remains for a while in the soft iron nail or core. These materials will usually fall off when shaken slightly. Stove bolts typically have less residual magnetism than nails of comparable size.

Generalisation V: The Field of Force Around a Wire Carrying Electricity Can be Used to Magnetize Iron and Steel Objects

1. *Materials:* for each pair of pupils or group, a 6-foot length of plastic insulated Number 20 copper wire (remove an inch of insulation from each end so proper contact can be made when it is connected to a battery); a large iron bolt or nail; a steel rod (a screwdriver will do); several tacks or steel straight pins; a "D" flashlight battery; a projection of an electromagnetic crane, as in Figure 9.7.

Show your class the crane sketch and ask, "What is happening in this picture?" If necessary, draw attention to the manner of lifting. Scrap metal objects appear to be sticking to the device suspended from the crane. Bring out that probably some kind of large magnet is attached to the crane and its apparent purpose is to move scrap iron and steel from one place to another.

"If this is a big magnet, how can the crane operator remove materials from his magnet?" Observation of the electric wire may help the children in guessing. Guide toward a hypothesis that permits the crane operator to turn the magnetism on and off. Ask *how* this is possible. If no one knows, tell the class the crane has a magnet attached to it that operates through electricity. It is called an *electromagnet*.

Using the sketch, point out three features: (1) a metal core; (2) wire wrapped around the core inside the cover; and, tracing the wire from the core to the crane's cab, point out (3) a place where batteries or generators are kept to provide electricity. Indicate the materials and ask, "How could these objects be used to make an electromagnet?"

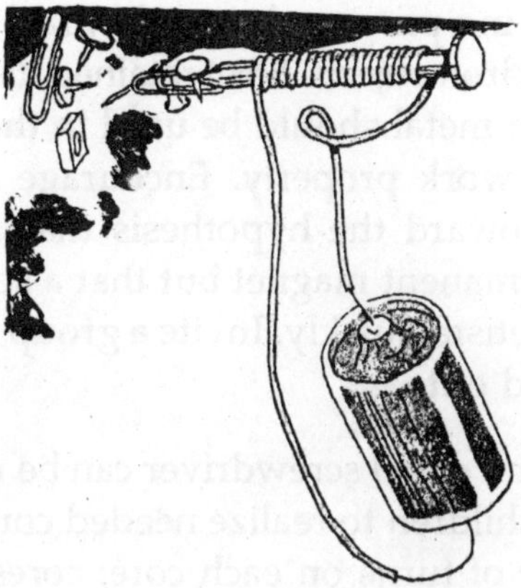

Fig. 9.8 A wire carrying electricity makes an effective electromagnet when wrapped 20 or more times a large nail.

Pupils may need assistance in touching the wire ends properly to the terminals of the battery (Figure 9.8). Although the wire ends can be taped to the terminals, a direct connection of this kind will completely drain the battery's power if left for a length of time. Both wire ends can be touched to the terminals when power is desired, and pulled away when power is to be shut off. Or a single wire end can be taped and the other end touched and pulled away to control the electricity.

Give the children time to play with the electromagnets. They will try touching and removing the wires alternately from the terminals. They will note that nails or other attracted objects fall off after the wire is disconnected.

(Remember, if lightweight objects are used, residual magnetism in the electromagnet may continue to attract them for a time even after the wire is disconnected.) If needed, suggest that they experiment with the number of turns of wire. They will observe that increasing the number of turns increases power.

2. Review that in a previous lesson they had magnetised hard steel and soft iron objects. Steel retained its magnetism longer. Ask which metal should be used in the core of an electromagnet to work properly. Encourage reasons for answers. Guide toward the hypothesis that a steel core will become a permanent magnet but that a soft iron core will lose its magnetism quickly. Invite a group to set up an experiment to find out.

A large nail and small screwdriver can be used for the cores. Guide the children to realize needed controls: same wire and number of turns on each core; cores should be about the same size; the same battery should be used, and same objects attracted. Both iron and steel cores must be tested for magnetism before the experiment.

Children should find that a steel core will become a permanent magnet, and is therefore unsatisfactory for this purpose.

Magnetic Poles. Suspend a bar magnet from a string in North America and a curious thing happens; it points toward the north magnetic pole. Do the same in South America and it points toward the south magnetic pole. (This assumes no interference from nearby metal deposits or objects.) A magnetised needle placed horizontally on a floating wood chip or slice of cork also points toward a magnetic pole.

To see why this is so, consider the poles of a magnet.

When another magnet or magnetised object is held near a suspended or floating magnet, the like poles (north-north or south-south) repel each other. The opposite poles (south-north or north-south) attract each other.

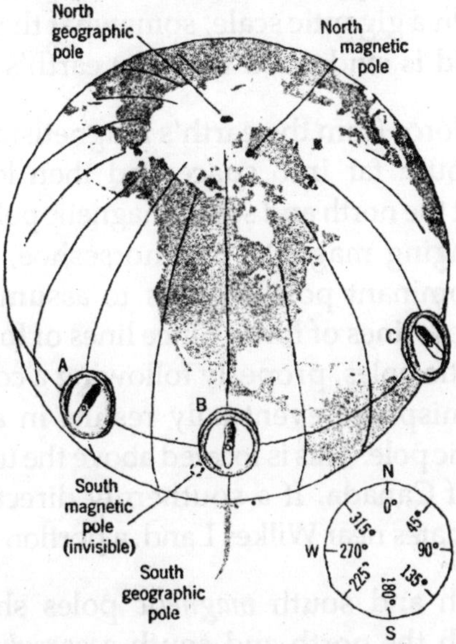

Fig. 9.9. Note in A, B, and C an angle between the meridian on which the compass is located and the direction toward which the needle points. These are variations that must be added or subtracted from a compass heading to determine true north. For example, true heading for A, B, and C should be 0°, or north. Actual readings are 35°, 5°, and 315°. A chart would indicate the need to subtract 35° from A, 5° from B, and to add 45° to C.

The earth itself acts like a giant magnet. No one knows why, but there are some theories. One explanation holds that several parts of the earth's interior rotate at different speeds. The resulting friction strips electric particles from atoms. This causes an electric current to be generated which creates a magnetic field. Since the earth's core is supposedly made of nickel-iron, the effect is that of a huge electromagnet buried within the earth.

Recall the activities before that dealt with magnetic fields of force. When iron filings were sprinkled on paper placed over a bar magnet, they revealed lines of force looping from one pole to another, and concentrating at both poles. On a gigantic scale, somewhat the same type of magnetic field is evidenced with the earth's magnetism.

Lines of force from the earth's magnetism run roughly north and south far into space and then loop down to concentrate at the north and south magnetic poles. Therefore, a freely swinging magnet—bar, horseshoe, or any other type with dominant poles—tends to assume a direction parallel to these lines of force. Since lines of force terminate at the magnetic poles, properly following a compass in the northern hemisphere eventually results in arrival at the north magnetic pole. This is located above the upper Hudson Bay region of Canada. If a southernly direction is taken, the trip terminates near Wilkes Land, a portion of Antarctica.

The north and south *magnetic* poles should not be confused with the north and south *geographic* poles. The geographic and magnetic poles are about 1000 miles apart in the north and 1500 miles apart in the south. In other words, when a compass points north, it does *not* point true north, or toward the north star. Charts must be made for navigators which show the angular variation between true north and the direction toward which a compass points. These charts must be periodically changed, as the magnetic poles are slowly but continually shifting. (See Figure 9.9.)

Many persons are surprised to discover that a bar magnet or compass points with its "N" or *north* pole toward the earth's *north* magnetic pole. Yet it is known that *like* poles *repel* and unlike poles attract. How is this apparent paradox explained? The answer lies in antiquity. Compasses were used long before reasons for their operation were understood. So it became customary to speak of the end of a magnet that points northward as the north pole. It is more accurately called the *north-seeking* pole, and its counterpart the *south-seeking* pole.

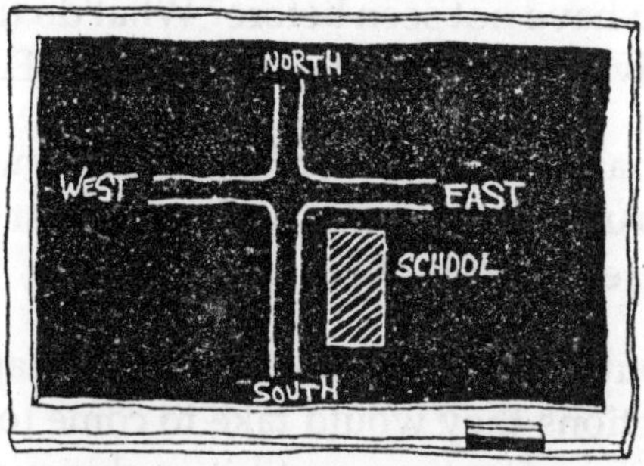

Fig. 9.10.

Of course, these explanations of magnetic variation and misnaming of the magnet's poles are intended more for your background than for presentation to most pupils at the primary level. Compasses and earth magnetism are not easy for primary pupils to understand. Unless you have a very able group, you may want to consider skipping this generalisation or using it only with older pupils.

Generalisation VI: Compasses are Magnets that Show Directions Because of the Earth's Magnetism; Unlike Poles Attract, and Like Poles Repel Each Other

This sequence is designed to gradually introduce the functions of magnetic compasses and what makes them work.

1. *Materials:* two bar magnets (or two magnetised steel knitting needles, or rods, or hacksaw blades); 18-inch thread; four cards marked *north, south, east* and *west* respectively; cork; needle; brimful glass of water; masking tape; compass; 6-inch piece of copper wire.

Place directional cards prominently on the walls. If the walls are not aligned with reference to a cardinal direction, cards can be affixed to chairs or taped down on the floor.

You might ask, "What do you notice today in our room that you have not seen before? What do these words tell us? Who lives north of our school? South? East? West?"

Draw a chalkboard sketch of the school and two main streets that run north-south and east-west. If this is impossible, use a sketch of Figure 9.10.

Picking out various locations on this "map," ask the children directions they would take to come to school, go home, and so on. Continue until it is obvious that most everyone knows the four cardinal directions.

2. Suspend by a thin thread a bar magnet or substitute. (A 6-inch copper wire bent into a J-shaped "cradle" will save fumbling around in attaching the string and balancing the magnet. First, make an oval of the wire; twist the ends together. Turn the oval sideways and bend it into a J shape. Attach a thread to the top of the cradle. For a stand, use an overturned wooden chair, or pile of books with a ruler tucked part way into the top book. Cover the magnet's poles with masking or adhesive tape, so that pupils will need to identify poles for control purposes. To save time, it will be helpful to set up these materials before working with the class.)

Develop Procedures

Ask a child to spin the magnet around *lightly*. (Otherwise the spinning takes too long to stop.) After the magnet stops, ask the class toward what main direction the magnet is pointing. Repeat this procedure. When the children again say the magnet points north, ask how they can be sure, since both taped ends are alike. They should then see the need to mark one end for control purposes.

Use the same procedure with another suspended magnet (at least 10 feet away). Are similar results obtained? (Make certain no iron or steel objects are close enough to affect the magnets.) Elicit that these magnets seem to point reliably in one direction. Develop that if one direction is known, then other directions are also known.

3. Continue this sequence with a floating needle demonstration. (Figure 9.11.) Have ready a needle, a magnet to magnetize the needle, a brimful glass of water, and a thin cross section of a cork top. (Make a shallow groove across the top to cradle the needle, otherwise it may roll off.)

Hold up the needle, and ask someone to magnetize it. To avoid confusion, the needle should be stroked from its blunt end to its point with the magnet's "S" pole. This will insure that the sharp end points north. Develop speculation as to what direction it will point if placed horizontally on a cork and floated in water.

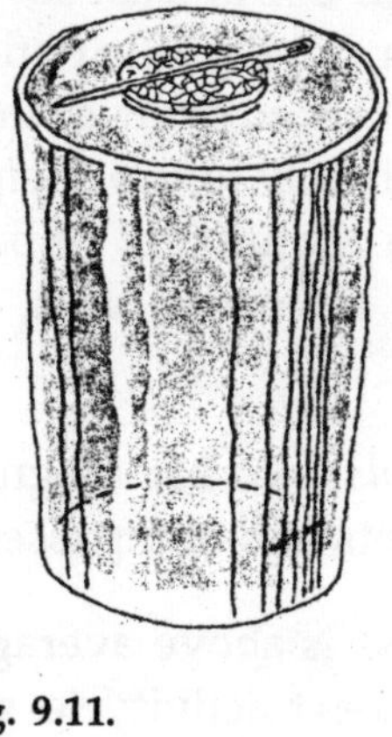

Fig. 9.11.

Again an approximate north-south alignment should be indicated. Elicit that a magnetised needle, too, can point out directions.

(Sometimes this demonstration is interfered with by the cork's tendency to drift against a container's sides. This is caused by the attraction of the water molecules to the sides, which creates a slight rise around the rim of the water line. Since a floating object floats to the highest possible point, it naturally drifts toward a container's sides. By using a *brimful* glass of water it stays centered, since this tends to be the highest area.)

4. Keep the bar magnets in activity 2 and needle in activity 3 set up and pointing northward. Produce a compass, or several, for close inspection by everyone. Establish that it is pointing in the same direction as the other materials. Elicit that it, too, is probably a magnet.

Set up some hypothetical situations in which the children can use a compass. For example, they are at sea; no landmarks exist. They know, however, land is northward. In what direction shall they sail? Continue with south, east, and west. Use at least several compasses, if possible, for maximum pupil participation and understanding. For further clarification, draw a simple chalkboard sketch of a compass, with only four principal directions and a needle. Bring out the advantages of being able to use a compass when tost in a wooded area, sailing at sea, or flying at night.

5. *Materials:* two bar magnets, one suspended from a string; magnets and compasses for the children.

If the class is above average, it will be worthwhile in this and the next activity to go into *why* magnets point north. With one magnet suspended and the other in his hand, have a child demonstrate what happens when the like poles are brought together. Have him try opposite poles. Use often and together the words "pull" and "attract," "push" and "repel" until the children are reasonably aware of their meaning. Have pupils try a similar procedure with compasses and magnets. A similar effect will be observed with the compass needles. After sufficient trial, bring out as clearly as possible the fundamental law of magnets: unlike poles attract and like poles repel each other.

6. Ask someone to explain why magnets point north-south, rather than in other directions. A satisfactory explanation will probably not be given. Now draw a chalkboard sketch of Figure 9.12.

Explain that deep inside the earth are huge amounts of magnetised metals. Although these metals do *not* look like the big bar magnet drawn in the picture, they do attract and repel magnets in much the same way. Have the children recall how they previously discovered that magnetism could penetrate many substances. Bring out that the earth's magnetic field of force exists everywhere on earth. Its effect can be seen with magnets or compasses, whether underwater, in the air, or on land.

EXTENCING ACTIVITIES

1. Try several additional activities to clinch the important idea of like and unlike poles. You will need two strong bar magnets, one with the poles clearly marked and the second with concealed pole markings; several small nails.

Suspend three or four small nails in a chain" from a pole of the marked magnet. Elicit from the class that each nail is now a tiny magnet, each with a pole. Speculate where the N and S poles are on the first nail, second nail, and so on. Have various children draw on the chalkboard their versions and describe their supporting reasons.

Now have someone bring a pole of the *unmarked* magnet near the end of the last nail in the chain, as in Figure 9.13. Let him reverse the poles. The nail will be either repelled or attracted in turn. Can we predict pole is next to the nail? Discuss reasons for the predictions, then reveal the poles' identity. Like poles repel, unlike poles attract.

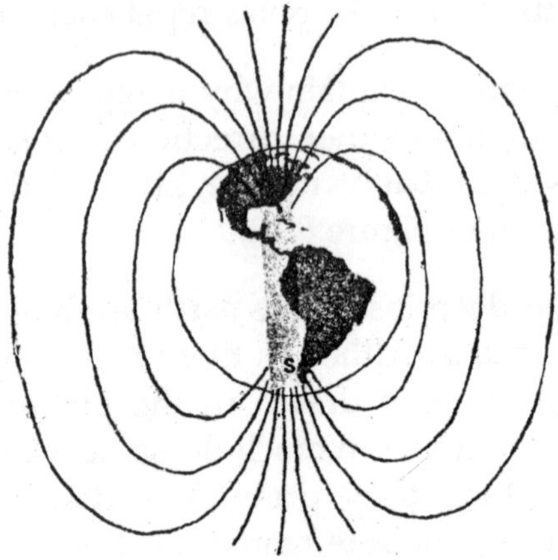

Fig. 9.12.

2. Suspend several "mystery objects" around the room. Are they magnets or not? Children can use a magnet to find out. (The objects may be prepared by wrapping a bar magnet in construction paper and suspending it from a string; a wrapped nail of similar length can serve as a nonmagnetic object. When a magnet is brought close to the concealed magnet one pole will be repelled. Children may also notice a more powerful attraction between the unlike poles of the two magnets than between a nail end and a magnet's pole.)

3. Discuss the difficulty of finding one's way without landmarks. Inform pupils they can help several classmates

find their way out of an imaginary, unfamiliar forest. Provide one compass and two large cardboard boxes with open tops. Take the class to the playground. Let two volunteers place the boxes over their heads. Give the compass to one child. Each child should walk straight ahead for 300 steps, then retrace his steps. (You might need to do the counting.) The child with the compass should follow its needle due north, then due south after he makes a turnabout. The object, of course, is to see which child will come closest to the starting point.

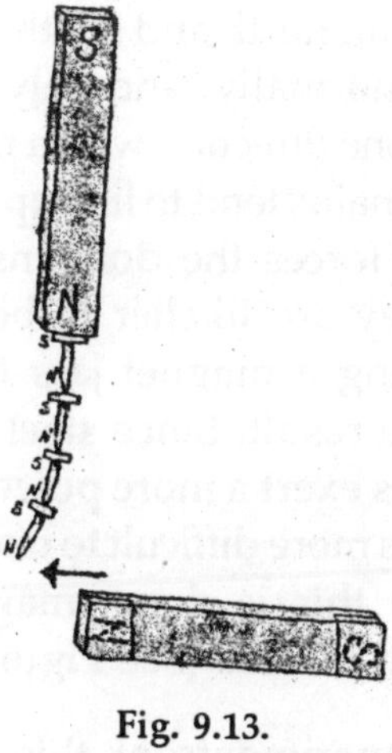

Fig. 9.13.

Take caution to insure that ground markings, noises, and so on do not give directional clues to the participants. A discussion in the room before the demonstration, about procedures and needed controls, will be worthwhile.

4. For an agreed time period, have all those with compasses try to discover a location where their compass needle will *not* point north. Caution them about nearby interference from iron or steel objects, or let them discover such faulty procedure for themselves.

Magnetic Theory and Magnet Care. Important as magnetism is, science has yet to provide a satisfactory explanation of its cause. One theory, capable of being understood by young children, is based on observations they can make for themselves. It has been known for many years that heating or repeatedly dropping a magnet will cause it to lose its magnetic properties. And, although a magnet may be broken into smaller and smaller pieces, each fragment continues to have a north and south pole.

It is believed that small clusters of atoms within these materials each contain north and south poles. Such clusters, called *domains,* are normally randomly arranged. When an object is stroked in one direction with a magnet, or otherwise magnetised, the domains tend to line up in a single direction. Heating a magnet forces the domains into more violent motion, and so they are likelier to become disarranged. Repeatedly dropping a magnet jars the domains out of line, with the same result. Since steel is harder than soft iron—the molecules exert a more powerful attractive force on one another—it is more difficult to rearrange the domains' makeup. But once this is done, magnetism is retained longer for the same reason. (See Figure 9.14.)

The closing experiments of this unit are based on standards for magnet care. They can be performed at an earlier time, but placing them at the end permits more pupil planning and thinking than would be possible without these experiences. It is recommended that only the effects of heating and dropping magnets be tested. Experiments on improper storage and use of a keeper are too subtle and time consuming for most primary classes.

Generalisation VII: Dropping, Heating, or Storing a Magnet Improperly Causes it to Lose its Magnetism

1. *Materials:* propane burner or alcohol burner; two

large, identical nails; magnet; pliers; carpet tacks; can of water.

Try this bridge: "You have learned that to take good care of magnets they must be stored properly, and never dropped or heated. What do you think would happen to a magnet that is dropped a few times?" (Pause for comments, then hold up the nails.) "Rather than perhaps ruin our regular magnets, what could we do with these materials?"

To avoid confusion, treat the magnetising of the nails and "dropping" test as two distinct activities. Make sure both are stroked the same number of times, and tested with tacks. The same number of tacks should be attracted in both cases. If not, apply additional strokes as needed.

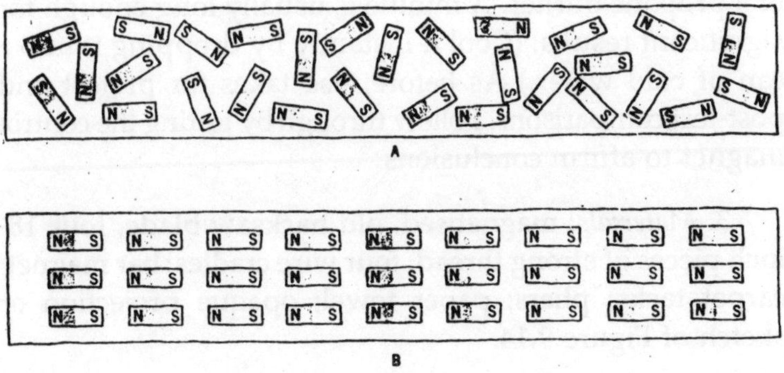

Fig. 9.14. A-B An unmagnetised (A) and Magnetised (B) steel Bar.

With the "dropping" test, drop only one magnetised nail, about thirty times. This should produce a noticeable difference in its attractive force. Help pupils to record their pretest and post-test results in this or a similar way:

	Dropped Magnet	*Other Magnet*
Before:	5 tacks	5 tacks
After:	2 tacks	2 tacks

(Since iron nails do not retain their initial magnetised strength very long, it is possible that the control magnet will also be weaker on the post-test. The change should be slight, however.)

Help them reason that dropping one magnet probably causes the difference in tacks attracted. To gain additional assurance of this conclusion, guide them in testing the second (control) magnet in the same way.

2. Remagnetize the nails. Develop a procedure with heat as the critical. Pliers or tongs should be used to grasp the magnetised nail while it is held vertically in the flame of a propane burner. A minute is usually long enough for significant results. (Cool it instantly by dropping it into a can of cold water.) As before, use takes for pretest and post-test comparisons. Follow through by testing the control magnet to affirm conclusions.

3. *Materials:* magnetised, old hacksaw blade, four 18-inch pieces of strong thread; four wire cradles; bar magnet; carpet tacks; pliers; paper towel; opaque projection or sketch of Figure 9.14.

Present the projection or sketch of Figure 9.14. Explain it shows an unmagnetised and magnetised steel bar. Develop the following ideas:

a. Magnets seem to have inside them tiny bits called *domains*. Domains in the sketch do not look like real domains. They are drawn that way to help pupils learn what happens when something is magnetised.

b. When domains are lined up, they act like tiny magnets which are pointed in one direction. Stroking a needle or nail with a magnet is one way to arrange them in a line.
c. When heated or jarred, the domains get out of line and repel each other. Storing like poles together pushes the domains out of alignment, too. This causes a magnet to lose some of its force.

Call attention to the way the poles are aligned in Figure 9.14B. Elicit that the left end is the N pole and right end the S pole. What would happen to the poles if the bar is broken into two pieces? (Remain the same.) Broken into four pieces? (Remain the same.) Produce the magnetised hacksaw blade. Show that it is magnetised by picking up some tacks with both poles. If desired, suspend the blade from a string and show with a bar magnet that one end is repelled and the other attracted. Will it still act like a magnet with opposite poles if it is broken into two pieces? Four pieces? Invite predictions on the basis of how they interpret Figure 9.14B.

After marking the poles, break the blade in half with pliers, with the blade wrapped inside a paper towel. This will prevent any pieces from flying should the blade be brittle. Let pupils use the same, previous test on each half to show no change in the magnetic poles. Also, carpet tacks will continue to be attracted. Break the parts into smaller parts and test. Pupils should infer that when a magnet is broken into smaller and smaller pieces, each retains its magnetic properties, and continues to have two poles.

EXTENDING ACTIVITIES

1. Invite the class to draw their versions of a *partially* magnetised steel bar. In this case, some "domains" should appear aligned and some unaligned.

2. Have a display of many magnetic toys gathered by the children. Each should be explained before exhibited. Where possible, bring out ideas learned during the entire unit as such explanations are made.

10

The Energy of Electricity

Upper Emphasis

One way to appreciate the advantages of a ready source of electricity is to count the number of electrical devices in a modern home and then try to devise none-electrical substitutes for them. Yet appliances alone do not represent the full importance of electricity in our lives. The atom itself is composed of electrical particles and forces. Thus it seems that anything that exists cannot escape the influence of electricity. In the study of this unit, children should begin to appreciate some of the instruments that make electrical energy available, and, more importantly, the principles that make them work.

GENERALISATIONS

I. Current electricity flows when there is a complete circuit; circuits may be opened and closed through the use of switches.

II. Circuits may be designed in series and parallel.

III. The kind, size, and length of materials used affect the flow of electricity.

IV. Short circuits and overloaded circuits may create dangerously hot wires; fuses or circuit breakers are used to eliminate this danger.

V. Electromagnets can be made because a magnetic field is generated around a wire carrying electricity; electromagnets may be used in many ways.

VI. Matter contains electrons which may be accumulated through friction into electric charges; unlike charges attract, and like charges repel one another.

Circuits and Switches. Each time we push a button or flip a switch that "turns on" electricity, there is a flow of electrical energy in wires continuously connected from the generating plant to our appliance and back again to the plant. On a smaller scale, much the same thing happens when a battery is connected to a miniature lamp. If there is a continuous connection between the source of electricity and the appliance or device using it, lights go on, bells ring, or motors spin. This continuous connection is called a *closed circuit.* Anytime there is a break or gap in the circuit, the electric flow stops. This condition is called an *open circuit.*

Regardless of their shape, size, or method of operation, electric switches serve only to open or close a circuit. They offer a safe and convenient method of supplying the flow of electricity when we want it by merely providing a linkage through which the energy can flow to the connecting wires. In studying the first generalisation, pupils can discover how to make circuits and switches.

Much of the work in this unit calls for the use of dry cells, copper-wire, and flashlight bulbs. Number 6 dry cells or "D" flashlight cells should be used because they are safe, fairly long lasting, and relatively inexpensive. When fresh, they deliver one and one-half volts of electricity, as contrasted with 110 to 120 volts or so supplied in the home. In other words, it would take as many as 80 of these cells connected together to have a force usually supplied by the current found in the home. *Caution the* children *that house current is dangerous for electrical investigations and should never be used by them for this purpose.* For an experiment needing a relatively large supply of current, twelve D or Number 6 cells connected together are a very safe maximum. However, in this unit and most other units at the elementary level, three or four connected cells are all that will ever be needed. D-size flashlight "batteries" can be substituted for Number 6 dry cells, though being smaller they become weaker and wear out faster than the larger dry cells. Incidentally, although individual flashlight cells are often called "batteries," it is correct to use the term "battery" only when a combination of two or more cells is used.

Since the unit calls for experiments with miniature bulbs (flashlight-type bulbs), it will be helpful to understand how to use them properly. Miniature bulbs are designed to be used with a loosely specified number of one and one-half volt dry cells. Thus there are 1-cell, 2-cell, 3-cell, etc. bulbs. One-cell bulbs are sometimes marked "1.2v," 2-cell bulbs "2.5v," and so on. If three dry cells are connected to a 1-cell bulb, it is likely that the thin tungsten filament in the lamp will burn out quickly. So it is best to use the proper bulb for the number of cells employed. Too many cells will cause the bulb to burn out quickly; too few will cause it to glow feebly, if at all. A good compromise for this unit is the Number 13 (3.7 volt) bulb.

Many unit activities call for the use of commercial-type miniature bulbs and sockets. While several substitutes are possible, these are usually cumbersome and less useful. For maximum ease in using miniature sockets, large 3/4 by 3/8 of an inch) Fahnestock clips should be fastened to each side of the socket with the screws found there. See

Figure 10.1 for an example. Notice that the large Number 6 cell is also supplied with clips, rather than the usual binding posts with screw caps. The suggestion to use Fahnestock clips may seem to be a minor one, but they can make a big difference in your time and overall accomplishment.

The wire you use should also be selected with an eye to convenience. Number 20 wire is excellent for almost every activity. You will need a spool of about one hundred feet. Get plastic-covered solid copper wire, rather than cotton-covered wire consisting of many small twisted strands. These become unraveled at the ends, and cotton insulation is harder to strip off than a plastic covering. Insulation can be quickly removed with a *wirestripper* (Figure 10.2); this device also cuts wires efficiently. However, with the wire suggested here, scissors may serve both purposes almost as well.

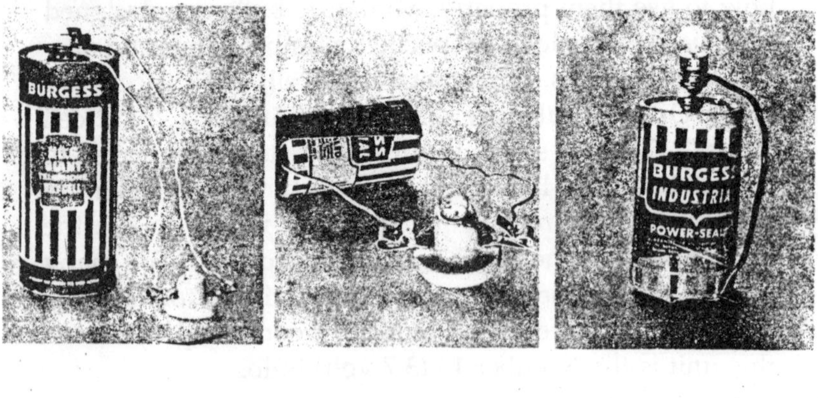

Fig. 10.1. A number 6 dry cell and two D cells connected in complete circuits.

There are several easy ways to connect cells and bulbs, depending on the kinds of materials you have. Figure 10.1 shows how a D cell can be substituted for a Number 6 cell.

(Since the smaller cell is much cheaper and easy to get, more pupils will be able to participate directly.) A small, wide rubber band will hold the stripped wire ends snugly against the D-cell terminals. The center terminal (positive), recognizable by the bump, corresponds to the center terminal on the large cell. The opposite terminal (negative) is equivalent to the rim-mounted terminal on the large cell. The third arrangement needs only a single wire touching the terminals and bulb base to complete the circuit. One end is wrapped around the bulb base to serve as a bulb holder.

The investigations in this unit have been carefully worked out to help insure teaching success. However, occasionally an investigation may not go as planned. If this happens, use the occasion as an opportunity for learning. Most difficulties with materials in this unit can probably be handled by posing one or more of the following questions. Through knowing about them in advance, you should experience little difficulty in tracing the source of the "trouble."

Bulb—Is, it screwed in tightly? Burned out? Is there correct voltage?

Wire—Is it in good condition? Is the insulation stripped from the ends where contact is made? Is a complete circuit made? Short circuit?

Dry Cell—Is it in good condition? Is it powerful enough for the circuit?

Connections — Are they secure? Is enough contract being made for the current to flow easily?

Other Materials — Are the devices used in good operating condition?

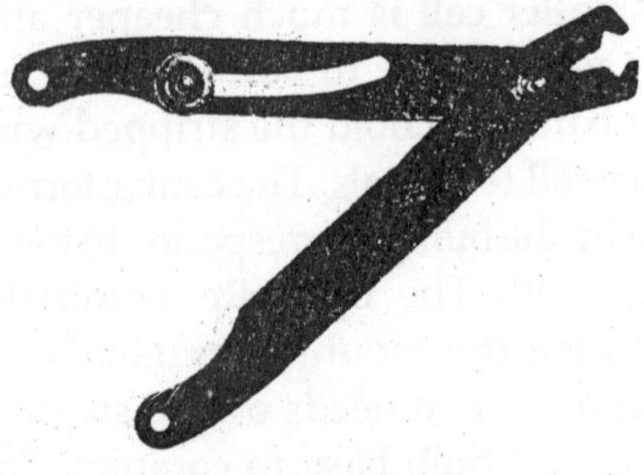

Fig. 10.2. A wirestripper.

Generalisation I: Current Electricity Flows When There is a Complete Circuit; Circuits May be opened and Closed Through the Use of Switches

Contributing Idea A. Current electricity flows only when there is a complete circuit; there are several ways to make a bulb light.

1. *Materials:* for each pair of children or small group, D cell; two bulbs; two 8-inch wires. (Either bare or insulated wires may be used in all the activities except where otherwise indicated. If insulated wire is used, be sure about 1½ inches on each end are stripped for effective contact with cells or bulbs.)

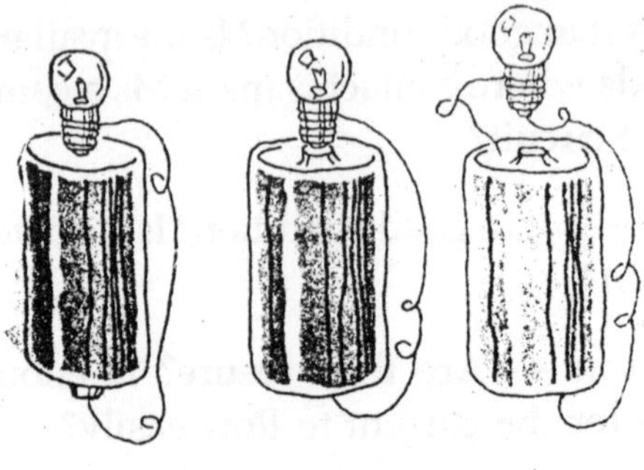

Fig. 10.3. Three ways to light a bulb. Since the terminals on most D cells are Joined to a metal plate at each end touching the plates anywhere may complete a circuit.

Invite the children to make *one* bulb light up by using the cells and wires they have been given. Suggest that they find as many ways as possible to do so, and sketch on the board any method that is successful. Some will use one wire, some two, in a variety of ways. In all cases, however, a connection must be made with both terminals (or ends) of the cell, and the side and bottom of the bulb's base. (Figure 10.3.) Notice that in the center connection of Figure 10.3, one wire could be eliminated without affecting the light. Observe in the right side example that the top wire does not need to touch the cell's top terminal. This is because the entire top is metal. When the cell top is not metal, the wire must touch the terminal for the bulb to light.

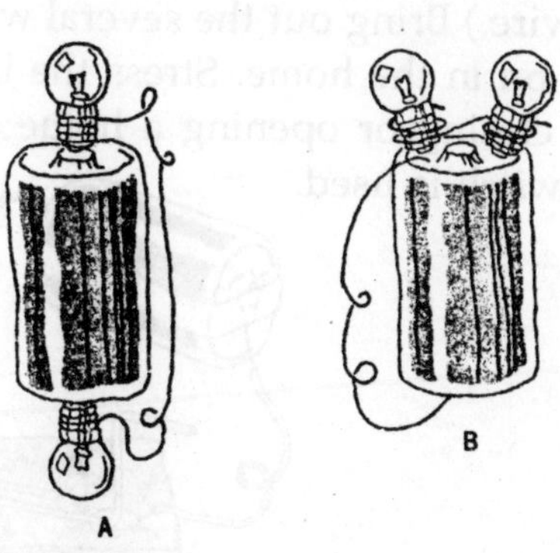

Fig. 10.4 A-B.

2. Now challenge them to make *two* bulbs light up at the same time with one battery. Again methods may be sketched on the chalkboard. Some typical results to anticipate are shown in Figure 10.4 A-B.

Most of the children will notice that bulbs connected as in A are much dimmer than they are in B. Reserve for later extended discussion as to why this occurred. (These are examples of series (A) and parallel (B) connections, which we shall take up in the next generalisation.)

3. *Materials:* for each small group, three 8-inch wires; miniature bulb and socket; D cel! and rubber band; two brass paper fasteners; 5- by 8-inch piece of cardboard; paper clip.

This activity will reveal how to connect a complete circuit with a bulb and socket, and how to make a paper clip switch for the circuit. (Figure 10.5.)

Ask the class to connect two wires to the battery and socket so that the bulb lights. Most pupils will realise quickly how to slip the wires under the rubber band to connect the D cell. Ask for several ways in which the light might be turned off. (Unscrewing the bulb, disconnecting or cutting the wire.) Bring out the several ways lights are turned off and on in the home. Stress the inconvenience and hazard of closing or opening a home circuit unless some kind of switch is used.

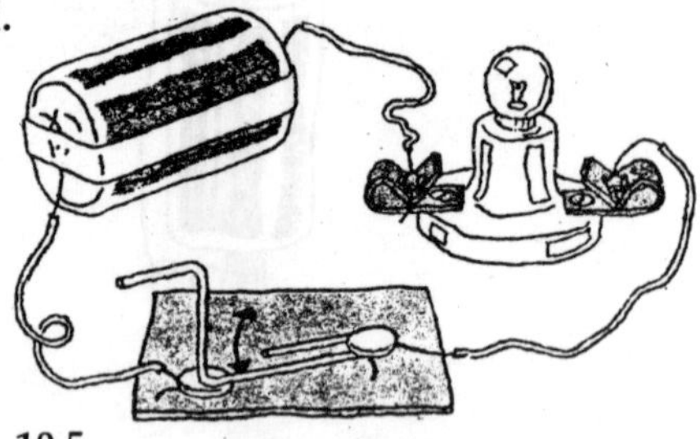

Fig. 10.5.

Invite the children to make a paper clip switch for their circuits, so that they may be closed and opened conveniently. Let them try to work this out independently for the most part. Many finished switches may look like the one in Figure 10.5.

4. *Materials:* as in activity 3; one extra brass paper fastener; 4-inch wire.

Here, small groups can pair off and pool some of their materials to arrange *two* switches to control a single light.

A good real-life example for discussion is a hall light controlled by an upstairs and downstairs switch. Notice in Figure 10.6 that the "hall" light may be switched on "upstairs," then turned off "downstairs," or the reverse. A few hints may be needed to get the children on the right track, but don't be surprised if several see almost instantly how the connections might be made to accomplish the purpose. A good way to spark such insight is to get various children to draw their suggested models on the chalkboard for discussion. After try cuts, let pupils relate their constructions to such switches in their homes.

Review the work accomplished so far. Develop that in each case a continuous connection was necessary between two parts of the bulb and the cell's two terminals for the bulb to light. If needed, introduce the term *circuit*, and that switches are used to *open* and *close* circuits.

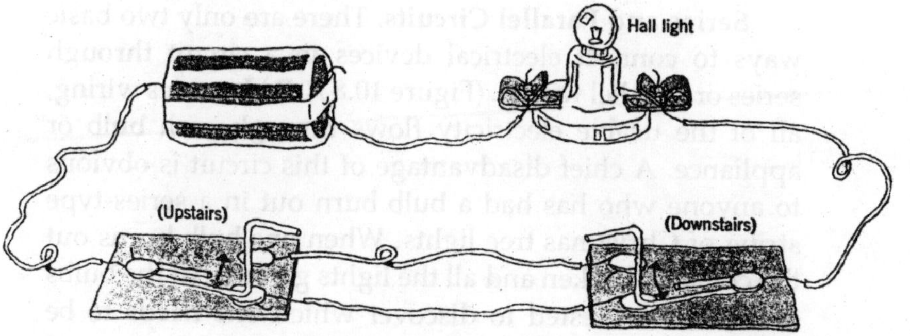

Fig. 10.6.

EXTENDING ACTIVITIES

1. For extra appraisal of how well pupils grasp the circuit concept, draw on the chalkboard or a ditto worksheet the sketch of a two-cell flashlight shown in Figure 10.7. See if they can trace the circuit by drawing in a dotted line with colored

chalk or crayon.

2. Ask the class to make a list of all the places in the home where switches are used and tell how they are turned on and off.
3. Encourage the children to bring in switches of all kinds to examine how they work. (Electric appliance repair stores are often willing to donate worn materials.)
4. Have the group examine different kinds of flashlights and make diagrams of how they work.

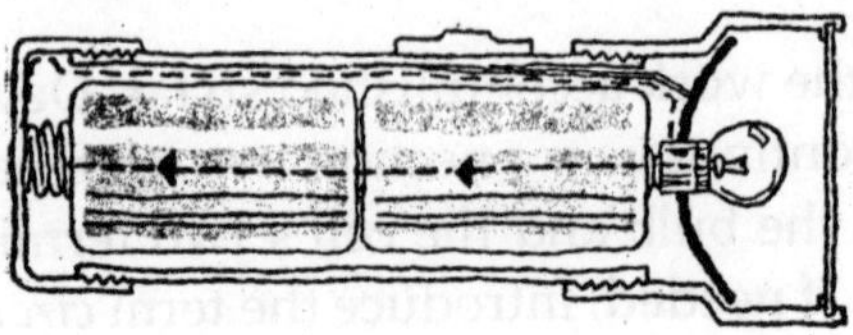

Fig. 10.7.

Series and Parallel Circuits. There are only two basic ways to connect electrical devices in a circuit through series or parallel wiring. (Figure 10.8 A-B.) In series wiring, all of the usable electricity flows through each bulb or appliance. A chief disadvantage of this circuit is obvious to anyone who has had a bulb burn out in a series-type string of Christmas tree lights. When one bulb burns out the circuit is broken and all the lights go out. All the bulbs must then be tested to discover which one needs to be replaced. When flashlight cells are the source of power, adding extra bulbs to the series circuit steadily decreases bulb brightness.

To avoid the difficulties of series circuits, most wiring for home and commercial use is parallel wiring. In this kind, electricity flows through a main wire and through branching wires connected to it as well, as shown in Figure 10.8 A-B. (In this Figure, the Fahnestock clips represent the branching wires.) If a light or other fixture should burn out, no other light or fixture is affected. They receive electricity whether or not the others are in use. In their parallel circuits, children will notice no change in bulb brightness as bulbs are added.

Cells also can be arranged in series and parallel, as shown in Figure 10.9 A-B. In the series examples the top drawing shows the easier way to connect D cells. A wide rubber band can serve to affix wires, but the cells will buckle where they join unless they are enclosed. A sheet of rolled, stiff paper or a cardboard cylinder from a roll of bathroom tissue can be used for this purpose. If children work in pairs, these holders will not be required, as four hands should be able to hold everything together. To keep the cells from rolling, they can be placed between two books. Note that in all the series examples, negative terminals (—) are joined to positive (+) terminals. In the parallel examples, positives are joined to positives and negatives to negatives.

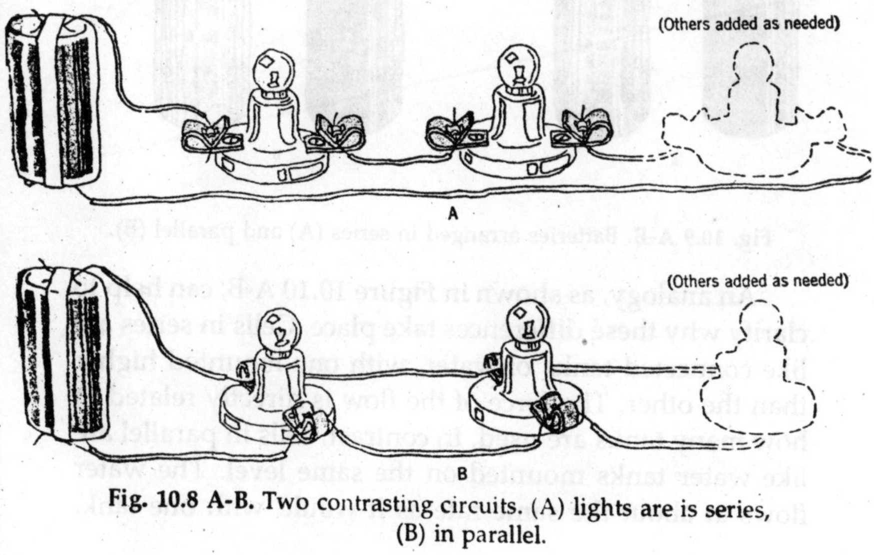

Fig. 10.8 A-B. Two contrasting circuits. (A) lights are is series, (B) in parallel.

Hooking up cells in series increases the *voltage,* or pressure, behind the flow of electricity. In contrast, arranging several or more cells in parallel makes available a longer lasting supply of current without increasing the voltage. For example, a bulb connected to two cells in series will burn about twice as brightly as if the cells are connected in parallel. However, the bulb will burn about two times longer with the parallel arrangement.

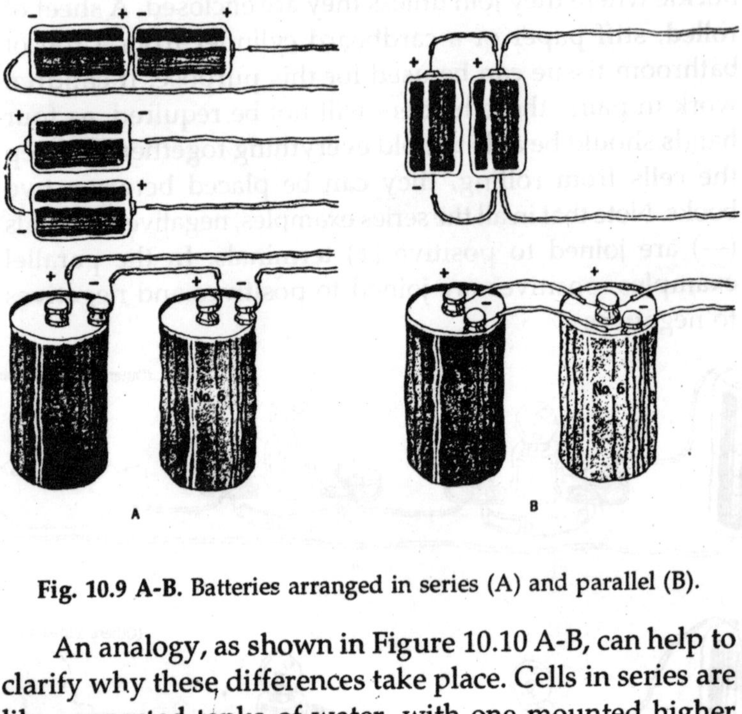

Fig. 10.9 A-B. Batteries arranged in series (A) and parallel (B).

An analogy, as shown in Figure 10.10 A-B, can help to clarify why these differences take place. Cells in series are like connected tanks of water, with one mounted higher than the other. The force of the flow is directly related to how many tanks are used. In contrast, cells in parallel are like water tanks mounted on the same level. The water flows at about the same rate as it would with one tank.

Therefore, the water supply lasts longer than in the other setup, up to twice as long.

In studying circuits, children can have many interesting opportunities to make predictions about which bulbs will light, and to make inferences about hidden wires. Such activities are included in this section after introductory experiences with the two kinds of circuits.

Generalisation II: Circuits May be Designed in Series and Parallel

Contributing Idea A. Batteries may be connected in series or parallel.

Materials: for each small group, two D cells; miniature bulb and socket; four 8-inch wires.

Ask the children to make the bulb light with *two* cells as the power source. Hint that there is more than one way. Have successful and unsuccessful arrangements sketched on the chalkboard. The successful setups will resemble those in Figure 10.9 A-B. Label the connections *series* and *parallel* as needed.

Most of the pupils will notice that the parallel connection is not as bright as the series connection. Get them to describe how much brighter the light shines when the cells are in series. Descriptions probably will be vague. How can we *measure* brightness? (Through how many pieces of paper will the bulb be visible in each setup?) Children can use small, torn pieces of notebook paper in "sandwiches" of varying layers to place on the lit bulb. Have them all use the same kind of paper and record the number of paper layers needed to obscure the light in each case. Compile the data on the chalkboard:

Group	*Series Battery*	*Parallel Battery*
Bill	14	8
Dana	18	7
Alice	15	8
John	13	7
Ann	10	6
Peter	16	9
Darlene	12	5
Totals:	98	50
Average:	14	7-1/7

Can they describe the difference in brightness more accurately now? (The bulb was about twice as bright when the cells were in series.) Have them examine the data closely. Why are there so many differences among the groups? Bring out the variables that might have affected the measurements.

Contributing Idea B. Bulbs may be set up in series or parallel circuits.

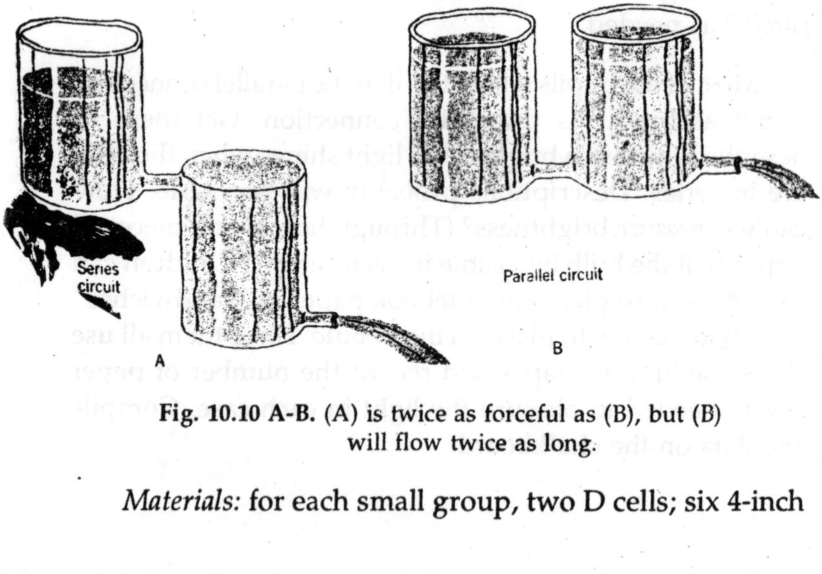

Fig. 10.10 A-B. (A) is twice as forceful as (B), but (B) will flow twice as long.

Materials: for each small group, two D cells; six 4-inch

and two 8-inch wires; three miniature bulbs and sockets; extra Fahnestock clip.

To begin with, suggest that the children try to set up a circuit with three bulbs and *one* D cell. Probably most will arrange the bulbs in series and the bulbs will barely glow. If no one has discovered how to arrange the bulbs in parallel, hint that there is another way. When it is discovered, contrast the two circuits and discuss why the brightness varied. How can the series bulbs be made brighter? (Use two cells in series.)

See if children can make predictions about which lights will go out when a series and parallel circuit are disconnected in several places. Sketch Figure 10.11 on the chalkboard. What will happen if the wire is disconnected at 1 or 2 or 3? Pupils can test their predictions with their materials. All the bulbs will go out in each case. What will happen to the other lights if any bulb is removed? (The remaining bulbs will go out.)

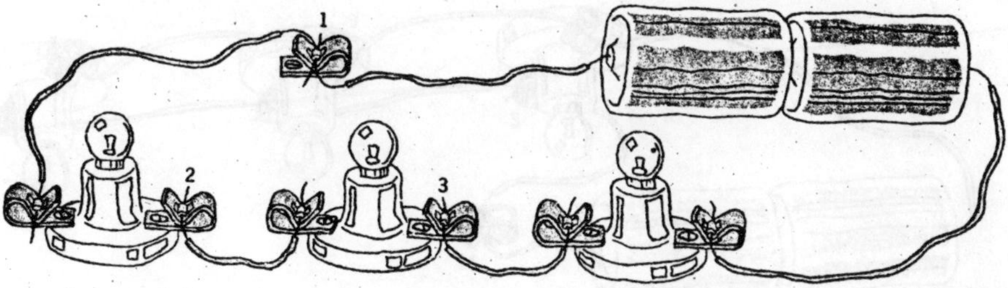

Fig. 10.11.

Sketch Figure 10.12 on the chalkboard for more predictions. Mention for clarity that a Fahnestock clip connects two wires at place 1. What will happen to the lit bulbs if the wires are separated at place 1 ? (All will go out.) Separated at place 2? (All will go out.) Separated at place 3? (Only the bulb opposite place 2 will stay lit)

Separated at place 4? (The two inside bulbs will stay lit.) Let them test their predictions with the materials.

Sketch a variation of the last circuit as in Figure 10.13, for a more challenging test of pupil's predictive ability. In this circuit one bulb is wired in series and two in parallel. Ask questions like these:

What will be the brightness of bulbs 1, 2, and 3? (Bulb 1 will be bright, 2 and 3 dim.)

If bulb 1 is removed, will any other lights go out? (Both 2 and 3 will go out.)

If bulb 2 is removed, will any other lights go out? (No.) If not, what will be the relative brightness of 1 and 3? (About the same.)

If bulb 3 is removed, will any lights go out? (No.) If not, what will be the relative brightness of 1 and 2? (About the same.)

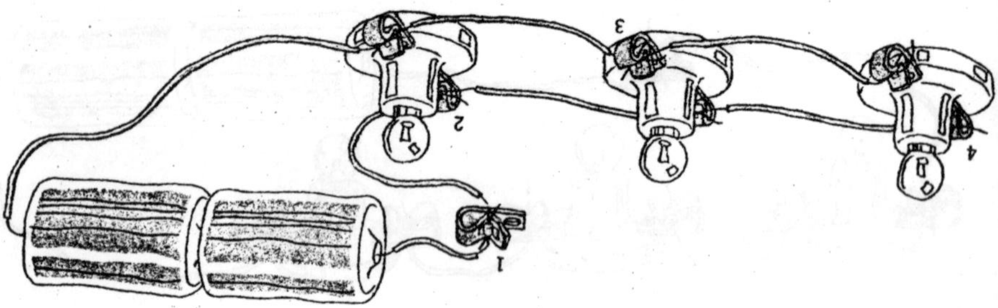

Fig. 10.12.

After predictions are made and recorded, children can test them with their materials.

Contributing Idea C. Circuits may be inferred from tests if the wires are hidden from view.

1. *Materials:* three regular-size (9 by 11-3/4 inches) manila folders or substitutes; D cell with rubber band holder; seven 8-inch wires; bulb and socket, with Fahnestock clips; paper clip.

Your class will be interested in learning that it is possible to detect how a circuit may be connected even though the wires are out of sight. In the process, they will discover that several inferred patterns may explain a circuit equally well. To introduce some simple hidden circuits, you will need to prepare circuit "boards" from the materials, as in Figure 10.14 A-C. Punch three holes in one cover of the first folder (A), and number them as shown. Insert three paper fasteners into the holes. Open the folder and attach inside the ends of one wire to fasteners 2 and 3. Spread out the fastener ends as needed to keep the paper fasteners secure and to hold the wire. A paper clip will keep the folder closed and the wire location hidden. Boards B and C can be prepared in the same way except that the wiring patterns are different as shown, and C has an additional paper fastener terminal.

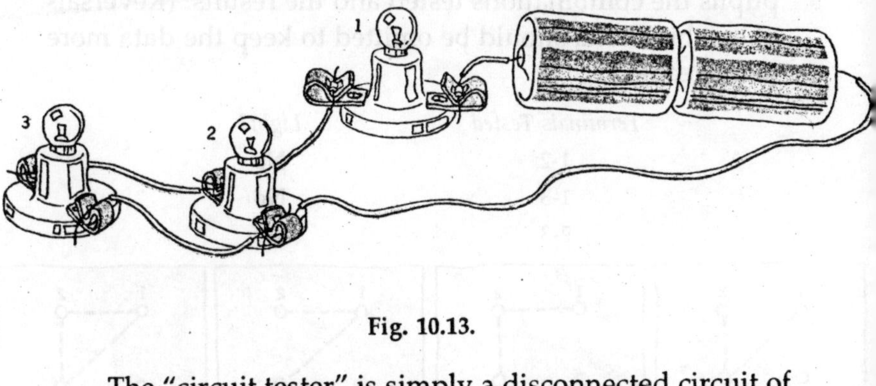

Fig. 10.13.

The "circuit tester" is simply a disconnected circuit of two wires, D cell, and bulb with socket. To make the bulb light in pattern A, just touch one end of the wire to terminal

3 on the folder, and the outside Fahnestock clip to terminal 2. If your bulb socket does not have clips attach a wire at the appropriate place on the socket; touch the bared end of the wire to terminal 2 to light the bulb.

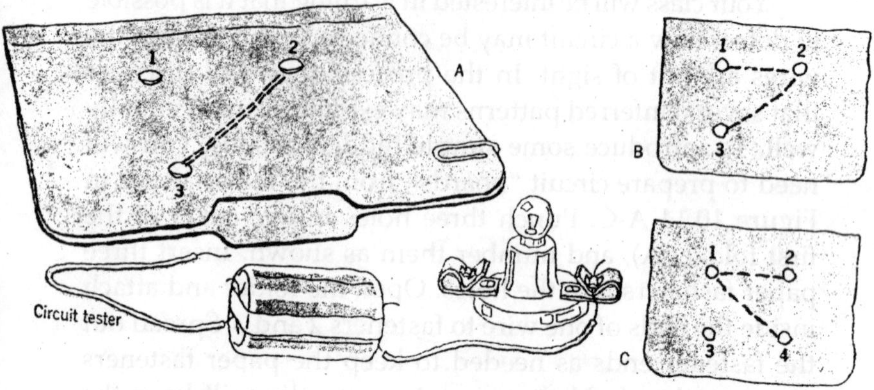

Fig. 10.14 A-C.

Pin circuit board A to a suitable place in front of the class. Mention that it has a concealed circuit. Show how to check the possible circuit by using the tester. Elicit from pupils the combinations tested and the results. (Reversals of combinations should be omitted to keep the data more manageable.)

Terminals Tested	*Light?*
1-2	No
1-3	No
2-3	Yes

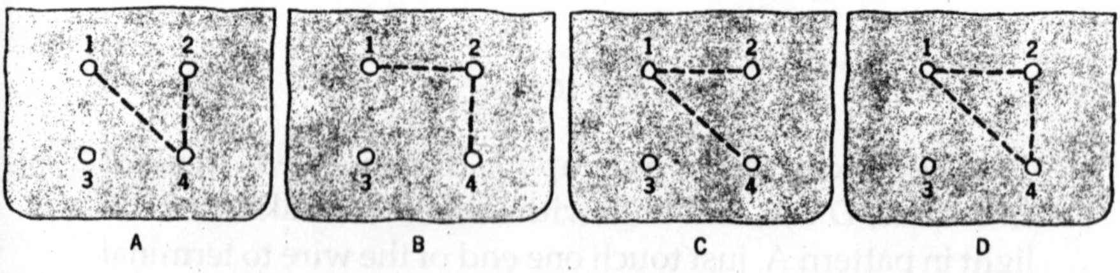

Fig. 10.15 A-D.

Can the circuit be inferred from these data? Most pupils will realise that a wire is attached to terminals 2-3. Open the folder cover and verify that this is so. Now try board B.

1-2	Yes
1-3	Yes
2-3	Yes

Suggest pupils draw the possible wiring pattern or patterns on a sheet of paper. While they are doing this, circulate around the room and check the results. Some patterns will resemble Figure 10.14 B, *but some may have an additional wire drawn between land 3.*

Does this additional wire do anything that cannot be performed or explained with just two wires? (No.) Bring out that when several possible ideas or models explain something equally well, it is usually more efficient to choose the simplest one. (In science, this is called the "law of parsimony").

With this input, the children should be prepared for circuit C. With four terminals, there are more data to consider:

1-2	Yes
1-3	No
1-4	Yes
2-3	No
2-4	Yes
3-4	No

Pupils can again sketch all the possible patterns on a sheet of paper. The four possibilities are shown in Figure 10.15 A-D. Is any pattern less preferable? (Yes, D.) Draw out that A, B, and C account equally well for the data. Reveal the actual wiring pattern, but emphasise that it should not be considered more "correct" than the two others.

2. *Materials:* chalkboard sketch of Figure 10.16.

Given some data, the children should now be able to predict which combinations would light up a bulb tester. Elicit the fifteen possible combinations (excluding duplicates) in the six-terminal chalkboard model:

1-2	2-3	3-4	4-5	5-6
1-3	2-4	3-5	4-6	
1-4	2-5	3-6		
1-5	2-6			
1-6				

Pose some problems; allow plenty of time for pupils to think through and record responses:

If the tester bulb lights when 1-4 and 3-4 are touched, what other combination or combinations should work? (1-3.)

If the light goes on when 1-2, 2-6, and 3-6 are touched, what else should work? (1-3, 1-6, 2-3, 3-6.)

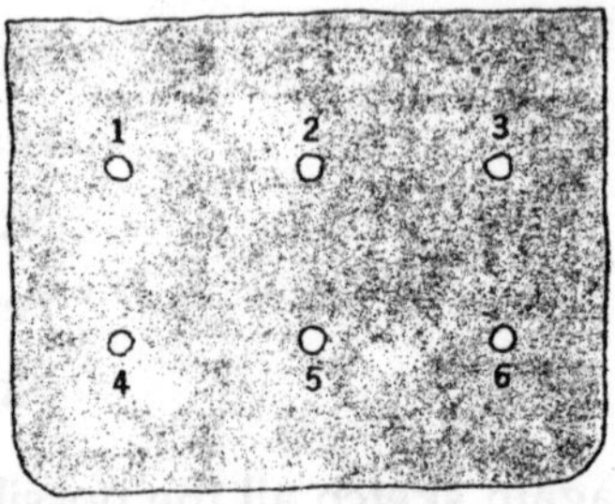

Fig. 10.16.

If 1-2, 2-5, 5-6 work, what else should work? (1-3, 1-5, 1-6, 2-3, 2-6, 3-6.)

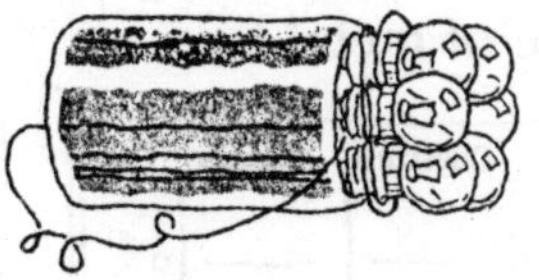

Fig. 10.17.

Should enough materials be available, let small groups construct boards to test their predictions. Or, the possible circuit patterns may be drawn on paper or chalkboard for checking.

EXTENDING ACTIVITIES

1. Invite the children to pair off and make their own circuit boards, either on paper or with real materials. If materials are used, each pair will need a bulb-and-socket tester, D cell, six paper fasteners, six wires, and a manila folder or substitute (chipboard folded in two, 5- by 8-inch cards, cardboard, etc.). Each child should try to challenge his partner's ability to make inferences by creating an original pattern. Can the partner discover it or the equivalent through testing and reasoning?

2. Have a contest to see which team can figure out how to light the most miniature bulbs at one time. Mention a few restrictions: it must be done without socket holders, using only one D cell and two bare wires. (Up to about six bulbs can be lit at one time by the method in Figure 10.17. One wire serves as a bulb holder. Make six single loops along the wire by bending the wire once around a pencil

for each loop; then screw in the bulbs. The second wire touches the negative cell terminal and a bulb base.) If the supply of bulbs is limited, proposed models can be drawn on the chalkboard. An evaluative discussion can serve to select likely prospects for testing. (For this to work the cell's ends must be of metal.)

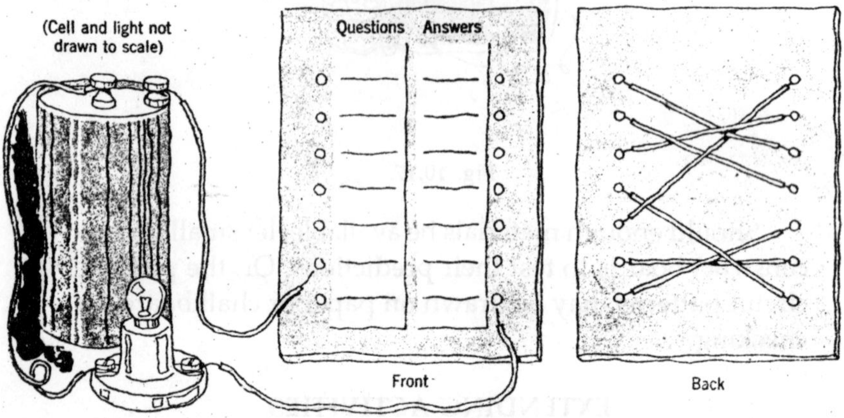

Fig. 10.18.

3. Let the children construct an electrical questioning board, as in Figure 10.18. Use chipboard, masonite, or plywood for the base, bell wire for the circuits. Paper fasteners are useful for terminals, but stove bolts and nuts are more durable. To permit easy interchange of the wire pieces, Fahnestock clips are more satisfactory to use than nuts. Otherwise, nuts must be loosened and tightened each time if the wiring setup is changed to avoid the possibility of children memorising the correct positions of the connectors, in place of knowing the correct answers. Fahnestock clips may be purchased at radio-TV repair stores.

An easy way to prepare questions and answers is merely to type them on two long sheets of paper. Have spaces between questions and answers corresponding to the spaces between the connectors on the board. Sheets may be fastened with a tack at each end. Be sure that the answers are "scrambled" out of order with regard to the questions.

When children prepare questions and answers, it is convenient to have them written on 3- by 5-inch cards. These can be tacked next to the terminals or placed in shallow pockets made from paper folded at intervals to correspond with the terminals.

Conductors and Their Properties. The term "conductor" is usually given to any substance that permits an easy flow of electricity. Metals are by far the best conductors of electricity and so are commonly used for wires. Although several of the precious metals are better conductors, copper is most often used as it is comparable in efficiency and yet cheap enough to produce in quantity.

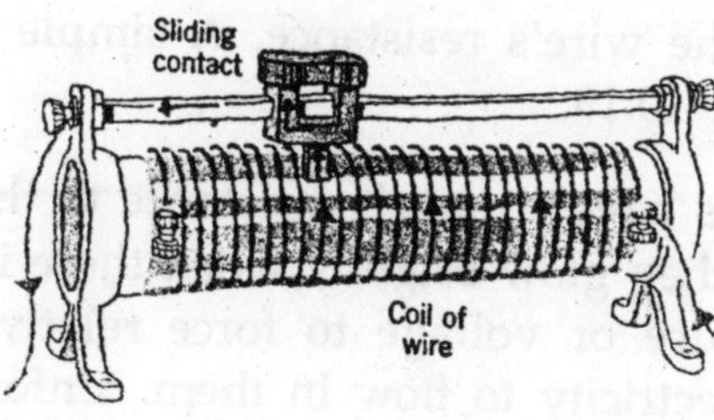

Fig. 10.19. A simple rheostat.

We often hear the term "nonconductor" applied to such materials as rubber, glass, plastic, cloth, and other nonmetallic substances. This is a misnomer, as virtually anything will conduct electricity if given sufficient voltage. These materials may be more properly considered as poor conductors, or *insulators*. This is why electricians may wear rubber gloves, and electric wires are covered with cloth, plastic, or rubber. It also explains why appliance plugs are covered with rubber or plastic and glass separators used on power line poles to keep apart high voltage lines.

Some poor conductors become good conductors when wet. Pure or distilled water is a poor conductor, but with the addition of dissolved minerals it becomes a fairly good one. Wet human skin is a far better conductor than dry skin. For this reason it is safer to turn appliances on and off with dry hands.

Although metals conduct electricity much better than nonmetals, there is still some resistance in metal wire to the flow of electrons. Of course, the longer the wire the greater will be the resistance. You may have experienced the gradual dimming of lights in a theater or adjusted the brightness of dashboard lights in an automobile. The change in both cases was probably achieved by a *rheostat*. A rheostat is a device that increases or decreases the length of wire through which electric current flows, thereby increasing or decreasing the wire's resistance. A simple model is shown in Figure 10.19.

Some metals have so much resistance to the flow of electricity that they glow brightly when there is enough electrical pressure or voltage to force relatively large quantities of electricity to flow in them. Unfortunately, most metals melt or evaporate within a short period of time when hot enough to give off light. This caused an agonisingly long search by Thomas Edison for materials to be used as bulb filaments before he was able to achieve reasonable success. Some of the materials he tried indicate the exhaustive character of search: bamboo slivers, sewing thread, even human hair, were carbonised and tested!

Tungsten, sometimes called wolfram, is the metal used in *incandescent* bulbs today. (Any bulb that gives light from a very hot filament is called an incandescent bulb.)

With a melting point of almost 6200 degrees Fahrenheit, tungsten is well able to withstand the temperature caused by the movement of electricity through its highly resistant composition. An inactive gas, such as argon, is pumped into the bulbs to help prevent burning away of the filament. However, some of the tungsten evaporates eventually and the filament is separated, breaking the circuit. The ever-darkening appearance of the portion of the bulb next to the filament indicates the deposition of the evaporating tungsten.

Electric heaters also have wires of highly resistant metal. Most heaters today use nichrome wire, a combination of nickel and chromium.

So far, length and composition of wire have been mentioned as important factors in resistance to the flow of electricity. Another factor is the diameter of the wire. Perhaps the use of an analogy here will be helpful in explaining why size of wire affects resistance. Imagine part of a large crowd in a sports stadium converging into a narrow passageway. As some of the people begin to enter the passageway the forward speed of the crowd slackens. At the end of the passageway the forward pace again picks up.

A thick wire presents a broad pathway for the flow of electricity. A narrow wire constricts the flow. In the "effort" to crowd through the narrow pathway much friction is created and the wire grows hot. If thin enough, and when made of material such tungsten, it can also produce much light as it glows.

Most devices that produce heat, such as heaters, toasters, and electric irons, have relatively thin, long, highly resistant wires. The wires cannot be as narrow in diameter as a light filament—one reason is that they are exposed to the open air and would rapidly evaporate away—but they are relatively thin compared to other wires designed to carry a similar voltage.

It would be helpful when teaching this section of the unit to acquire some real examples of toasters and heaters for observation. Discarded electric irons, toasters, and heaters can often be obtained free of charge from electrical repair shops. These can be taken apart and closely examined—something that perhaps better not be tried with someone's new appliance!

Generalisation III: The Kind, Size, and Length of Materials Used Affect the Flow of Electricity

Contributing Idea A. Conductors are materials through which electricity passes freely; materials that tend to block the flow of electricity are called insulators or nonconductors.

Materials: poor or fair conductors, such as plastic, wool, cotton, glass, pencil lead, chalk, paper, rubber, etc.; good conductors-objects made of various metals; miniature bulbs and sockets; wire.

In this activity, pupils can distinguish between conductors and insulators. Set up a simple circuit with two wires, bulb and socket, and D cell. Disconnect one from a Fahnestock clip. Now this becomes a circuit tester like the one used in the preceding activities (Figure 10.14 A-C). Remind the children that the circuit tester bulb lights when a wire bridges the gap between the two ends of the tester. Are there any materials on the table that could also make the tester bulb light? If needed, touch the tester ends to some metal object to demonstrate that a circuit results and the bulb lights.

Point to a table on which many materials are displayed and raise conjecture as to which will or will not let the bulb light when the tester is used. Materials can be tentatively divided into two piles before testing. With some objects (pencil lead, for example) pupils may discover that adding more cells in series to their tester will enable the bulb to glow at least feebly.

Mention that materials that permit the easy passage of electricity are called *conductors;* those that block or retard the passage of electrical current are called *nonconductors* or *insulators.* Discuss the kinds of materials they have observed covering plugs, commercial switches, or other devices that must be touched by the hand or foot to be operated. These are insulators, for safety reasons. Bring out that, by adding more cell power, some so-called "nonconductors" conducted enough electricity to make the tester bulb light. Help them understand that almost any material will conduct electricity if the electrical source is very powerful.

To avoid confusion in their own discussions, perhaps the children can develop their own operational definition of a "good conductor." One class decided that an object was a good conductor if, when touched by a tester using one new D cell, the bulb glow was visible through eight or more thicknesses of arithmetic paper held against a 2.5 volt bulb.

Contributing Idea D. Thinner wire has more resistance than thicker wire.

Materials: several worn-out house bulbs; house bulb with transparent glass (if possible); paper bag; hammer; short strand of iron picture wire, number 6 cell; two pliers.

Let the class examine a transparent light bulb to observe the filament. If no transparent bulb is available, get a worn-out bulb and place it in a bag. Holding it downward and against a wall or other solid structure, tap it lightly with a hammer until it breaks. The filament may now be observed. Ask the class why it is so thin. When someone hypothesises that a thin wire will "light up" faster than a thicker wire, point to the strand of picture wire and cry-cell. Ask how an appropriate experiment can be performed with these materials.

A thin strand may be unraveled form the picture wire for the smaller diameter wire. The remainder of the strand can serve for the larger diameter. Place the thin strand across the posts of the dry cell to observe how long it takes for the strand to glow. Record the amount of time needed to glow for the thin wire first; abandon attempts to make the thicker wire glow after it becomes obvious that it is taking longer. *Caution:* Use two pliers or clothespins to hold the wires, as the wires will heat up fast. Hold the wires on the posts as short a time as possible, since this quickly dissipates the cell's energy.

Let some pupils read to confirm their tentative conclusion that thinner wires offer more *resistance* than thicker wires.

Contributing Idea C. Longer wires offer more resistance to electricity than shorter wires made of the same material.

Materials: 3-foot Number 32 bare nichrome wire (sold in radio stores); piece of sticky tape; D cell; miniature bulb in socket; two wires.

Use the analogy of a garden hose to help the children think through the next experiment. Inquire whether a very long hose would have as much pressure at the nozzle as a short one. Point out that the friction taking place inside the hose as the water slides along gradually reduces the force of the water. Now, raise conjęcture about whether longer wires have more resistance to electricity.

Connect the materials as shown in" Figure 10.20; slide an end of the connecting wire up and down the nichrome wire. Encourage the pupils to observe keenly the brightness of the light. Explain that this is a *rheostat*—a device that decreases or increases current by decreasing or increasing the resistance to the flow of electricity. Mention that the thin wire used is nichrome wire, made of nickel and chromium rather than copper.

Have the children read to confirm their conclusion that the length of the wire affects the resistance.

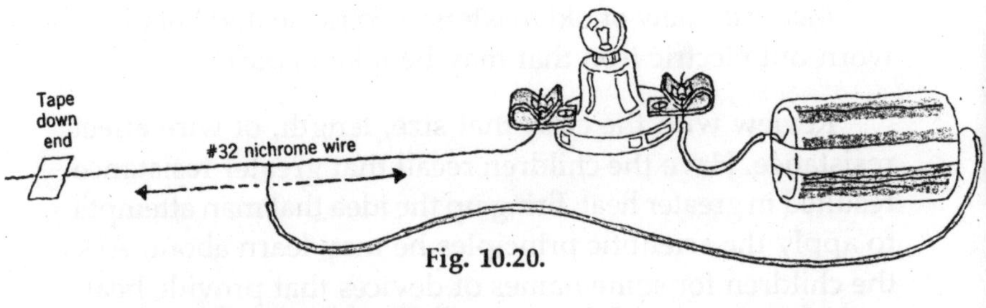

Fig. 10.20.

Contributing Idea D. Some metals have more resistance to electricity than others.

Materials: two bare 3-foot wires, one nichrome and one copper; D cell; sticky tape; miniature bulb and socket; two wires.

Set up this demonstration just like the previous one, except now substitute for the nichrome wire a piece of copper wire of equal length. Have the children observe the brightness of the bulb as the connecting wire is slid up and down the substitute wire. The bulb should burn brightly with the copper wire with no detectable change in brightness.

Ask the children what can be concluded from their observation. They may forget that the *diameter* of the wire might also be a factor. If so, you might ask them to recall what they previously learned about wire and resistance. How could the control be set up? Ideally, now is the time to have pieces of iron picture wire and copper wire of equal diameter and length for testing. If not, the class might read to confirm that the composition of the metal does affect its resistance to electricity.

Contributing Idea E. Devices that produce heat, such as heaters, toasters, and electric irons commonly have relatively thin, long, and highly resistant metal wires or ribbons.

Materials: new or old toasters; electric heater; hot plate; worn-out electric iron that may be taken apart.

Review with the class that size, length, of wire affect resistance. Have the children recall that greater resistance resulted in greater heat. Bring up the idea that man attempts to apply the scientific principles he may learn about. Ask the children for some names of devices that provide heat. Invite them to predict what the heating elements would look like.

Let them observe the above devices for confirmation or rejection of their predictions.

It will be helpful to use several questions to stimulate their thinking during the observations of these devices. For example:

Why aren't the wires as thin as those in the bulb? (They would otherwise burn out soon in the open air.)

Why are the wires a different color from ordinary wire? (They may be made of a different material, such as nichrome.)

Why are the wires partly coiled or zigzagged? (This

enables more wire, and thus heat, to be provided in the available space.)

EXTENDING ACTIVITIES

1. Invite someone to report on Thomas Edison's invention of the first practical incandescent lamp. Emphasis might be on the long and frustrating search for materials that would not quickly burn away, with illustrations of these materials where possible.

2. Have an interested child read and report why bulbs appear to explode when dropped. (They are filled with nitrogen gas to retard the burning of the filament. If the filament were not enclosed and surrounded by this gas, it would quickly burn out—oxygen supports burning.)

Circuit Hazards and Fuses. We have seen that when bulbs or appliances are wired into a circuit they show resistance to the flow of electrical energy. At the place where the energy enters these resistors, however, a transformation of energy takes place—some of the electrical energy becomes converted into heat (if it enters a heater) or light (bulb) or sound (radio) or motion (motor). In other words, a significant amount of electrical energy is "used up," or changed. Suppose, however, there is no resistor connected in the circuit. Since the copper wire has relatively low resistance, a great surge of electricity flows through the wire. The wire now heats up rapidly, even though it normally offers little resistance to a current.

In house and commercial circuits intense heating of the wires may come from a "short" circuit. This may happen when two bare wires touch each other, thus preventing the main supply of current from flowing through the resistor. Since the resistor is largely bypassed, a huge amount of electricity flows. A common cause of short circuits occurs when an appliance cord is placed under a heavily traveled rug. If the insulation between the two internal wires wears away they may touch and a "short" develop. Notice in Figure 10.23 that a circuit is not necessarily shortened in length for a "short" circuit to occur. The essential thing is that the resistor—in this case, the bulb—is bypassed. Since children are sometimes confused by the term "short circuit," an activity in this section is designed to clarify it.

Overloading a circuit is perhaps an even more frequent cause of wires overheating. Many older houses, for example, were wired when only a few of today's common appliances were in widespread use. Small-diameter, lightly insulated wires were formerly adequate. However, as more and more of today's appliances continue to be plugged in, intense heating occurs that is a potential source of fire.

Fuses and circuit breakers protect us from the fire hazard. A screw-in type fuse contains a narrow metal strip that melts at a fairly low temperature. When a fuse is placed in a circuit, the electricity must travel through the strip. Should the wire heat up dangerously, the strip melts and the circuit opens, thereby shutting off the current.

Occasionally, someone will replace a burned-out fuse with a penny to avoid the "inconvenience" of another fuse burning out. Unfortunately, if the initial source of the difficulty is not corrected the wires may grow so hot the house may catch fire. An acceptable fuse has two requirements: it must be a good conductor, and have a low melting point. A penny meets only the first requirement!

A bimetallic strip circuit breaker may be used instead of a fuse. This consists of two thin, metal ribbons fused together. The ribbons are made of two different metals. When placed in a circuit and heated, the bimetallic strip bends away from one of the contact points, opening the circuit. The bending, as mentioned in Unit 1, is due to different expansion rates of the metals.

Another modern type of circuit breaker works from the fact that any wire containing current electricity generates some magnetism. Increasing the supply of current has the effect of increasing the magnetism. When a movable steel rod is enclosed in a coil of wire placed in a circuit, it may be pulled upward as the current (and so magnetism) increases. If the rod is connected to a contact point, its upward movement will result in the circuit being opened. A spring catch that can be reset by hand is used to prevent the rod from dropping down again. An electromagnetic device that operates this way is called a solenoid. (Another section will present more on electromagnetism.)

Children can be taught to calculate the number of resistors that can be safely placed in a circuit. In order to do this they will need a bit of general knowledge about the meaning of the terms *ampere, volt,* and *watt.* An *ampere* is the rate of flow of electricity. Technically, it is defined as the flow of 6.3 billion billion electrons per second past a given point. This figure can be presented to the class (a six, followed by eighteen zeroes), but, of course, will be meaningless. The idea to stress is that ampere means the rate of flow. If a fuse is rated at 30 amperes, then only those appliances can be operated whose total rate of current used is under 30 amperes.

We have indicated before that the term *volt* is a unit of pressure. A dry cell has an electrical pressure of one and one-half volts, house current 110 to 120 volts. Sometimes a special line which carries 220 volts is attached to a house circuit for such heavy users of current as electric clothes dryers and ovens.

The term *watt* is used to measure power, or the rate at which electricity is used to do work. It is found by multiplying amperes by volts. A watt-hour is the amount of energy needed to keep a one-watt device functioning for one hour. Since a houseful of appliances may use hundreds or thousands of watts per hour, wattage usually is expressed in kilowatt-hour units (1000 watts for one hour).

Activities are included in this section to help children understand how electric power company bills are calculated for consumers.

Generalisation IV: Short Circuits and Overloaded Circuits may Create Dangerously hot Wires; Fuses or Circuit Breakers are Used to Eliminate this Danger

Contributing Idea A. A short circuit results when a resistor is largely bypassed; the increased flow of electricity increases the heat of the wire.

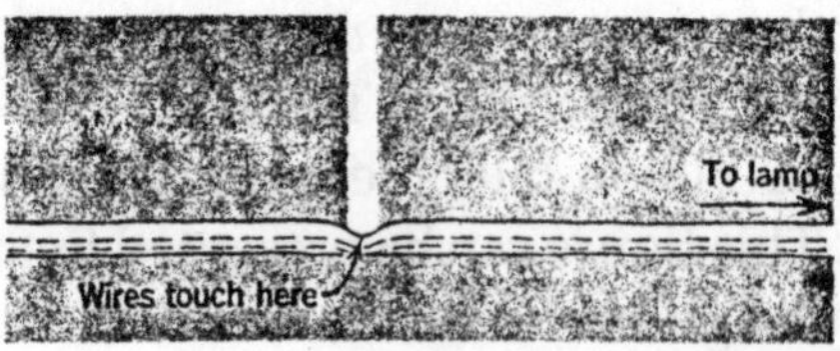

Fig. 10.21.

Materials: miniature bulb and socket; insulated wire; D cell; wire stripper.

Have on the chalkboard the sketch shown in Figure 10.21.

Use this bridge: "We are often warned not to place electric wires under a rug, particularly where they are liable to be stepped on or pushed down. Why is this so?" Discuss this for a moment. Now turn to the sketch and inform the class that it shows a table leg pressing on a wire whose insulation at one point has gradually worn away. Explain that the lines to represent the wires are drawn as broken lines; this shows that the wires are invisible because of the insulation. Point out that electricity is streaming into the top wire. Encourage the pupils to hypothesise as to the probable path of the electricity at the point where contact is made. Also, seek a prediction as to whether the lamp will light at this time.

Indicate the materials and ask how they can be set up to test the hypotheses. The insulation must be scraped away on the two wires where contact will be made. The assembly may look like Figure 10.22. *Caution:* Do not permit anyone to hold the bare wires at the contact point, as the wires will quickly grow hot. It will also be best to do this demonstration fairly quickly, to avoid greatly draining the cell's energy.

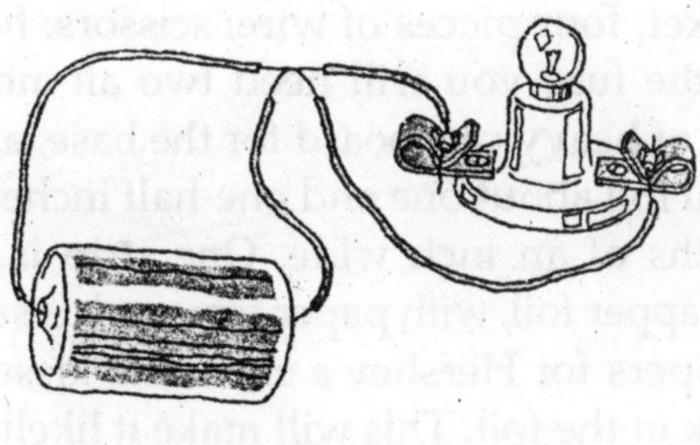

Fig. 10.22.

After it is observed that the light goes out, have several children feel the insulated part of the wire in front and in back of the bare contact point. Have someone notice that the short-circuited part is hot while the wires beyond the contact point are cool. Draw out from pupils that this helps confirm the hypothesis of electricity not flowing beyond the contact point. It should be pointed out, however, that there is a very small current still flowing through the other part.

Bring out that this experience is an example of a *short circuit.* Try to elicit a reasonable explanation as to what happened. The children should understand that when a resistor such as a lamp is bypassed, a huge amount of current will surge through a wire when contact is made; there is very little resistance to check its flow. Again call attention to the great heat produced as a result of this short circuit.

Contributing Idea B. Fuses are designed to open a circuit that is heating up before it becomes dangerous.

In the following sequence pupils observe how several kinds of short circuits may melt their improvised fuses, and find out why lack of a fuse might be dangerous.

1. *Materials:* 2 D cells connected in series; miniature bulb and socket; four pieces of wire; scissors; fuse device. (To prepare the fuse you will need two all-metal thumb tacks, a piece of heavy cardboard for the base, and several strips of metal foil about one and one-half inches long and three-sixteenths of an inch wide. One strip is used at a time. Gum wrapper foil, with paper removed, is satisfactory; also the wrappers for Hershey's chocolate kisses. Make a V-shaped nick in the foil. This will make it likelier that the foil will burn out instantly.) Set up the materials as in Figure 10.23, but for the present keep out of view the extra wire used in method 2.

Get your pupils to speculate about the fire hazard when a short circuit takes place. Bring out that, because of the hazard, measures are taken to avoid it. Ask the children if any heat would occur if the circuit were opened. Ask for a logical way a circuit might be broken with heat. Help them reason that a device introduced into the circuit which would conduct electricity well and yet have a low melting point would be applicable.

Show the improvised fuse and other materials. How can these objects be used to see that will happen if the circuit is "shorted"? Several children might set up and "short" the circuit, as in method 1. Bring out that the circuit size was decreased when the bulb was largely bypassed.

Now hold a piece of wire by the bulb socket terminals as in method 2. Point out that if the wire ends are touched to the terminals *you will be increasing the size* of the circuit. Will a "short" circuit result here, also? Why or why not?

After the demonstration, suggest that pupils develop an operational definition for a "short" circuit. The essential ingredient in the definition should be the bypassing of the resistor rather than change in circuit length.

2. *Materials:* same as above; substitute a penny for the foil.

Review reasons the fuse worked: (1) it conducted electricity satisfactorily while the circuit was normal; and (2) having a lower melting point than the copper wire, it melted when the increased current created increased heat. Now repeat the previous demonstration, but this time use a penny instead of a foil strip between the two tack heads. The tacks, of course, will need to touch the penny. The penny and wires should begin heating up.

Bring out that while the penny is a good conductor, it has a high melting point. Ask the class if it would be sensible to substitute a penny in place of a fuse when it burns out. Bring out the foolishness of ignoring a warning sign or symptom by "correcting" the symptom and not the cause.

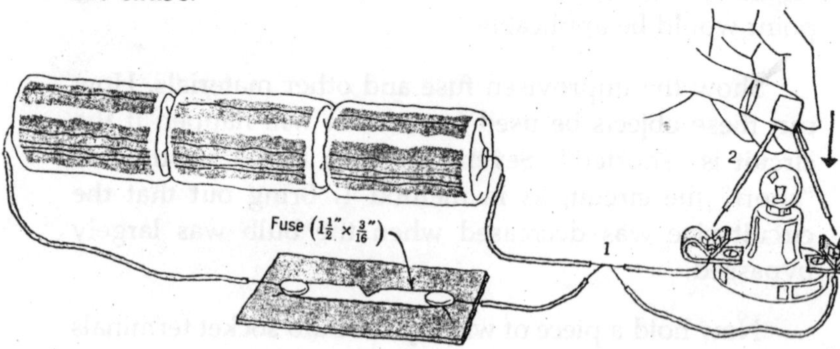

Fig. 10.23. Two ways to make a "short" circuit and burn out a foil fuse. In 1, the circuit length is decreased, in 2, it is increased.

Help pupils understand that overloading a parallel circuit may also overheat the wires. Remind them that a house usually has parallel wiring. The power station supplies a steady voltage regardless of the number of resistors used in the circuit. If too many resistors are used, excessive current will pass through the wires and make them very hot unless a fuse or other device opens the circuit.

3. *Materials:* various commercial fuses including automobile electric fuses.

If several commercial fuses are available, it would be especially helpful to show them at this time. Electrical shops may be good sources for worn-out fuses.

Contributing Idea C. Arithmetic may be used to find out the number of resistors that can be safely placed in a circuit.

1. Develop the idea that we do not need to leave to chance whether a fuse or circuit will open a circuit. If a 30-ampere is available, mention that the label "30 A." Otherwise,

mention that are 30 A fuses. Such fuses melt when 30 amperes flow through the circuit. Explain that the safety margin can be calculated through the use of arithmetic. To understand how to do this, first the term *ampere* must be learned.

Begin with the analogy of two water hoses. Both are the same length. But one is a narrow garden hose and the other a wide fireman's hose. Both are hooked to the same fire hydrant. Ask which has the larger amount of water flowing out of the nozzle and why. (The larger hose, because it can carry more water.) Apply the idea to electricity now, and acquaint pupils with the word ampere, used to mean the rate of flow. Tell them that one ampere is a flowing of more than six billion billion tiny particles of electricity a second. Have them recall their previous experiment with thick and thin wires. Will a thick copper wire have more flow (amperes) of electricity than a thin copper wire of the same length? (Yes.) Mention some typical house appliances, and the amount of electricity each might need to operate. For example:

	Amperes
Coffee maker	5
Toaster	5
Waffle iron	8
Sun lamp	5
	23

Point out that by adding the amperages of these appliances one knows whether they are totally within the capacity of a 30-ampere fuse.

Have the pupils add an 11 -ampere iron and five 1-ampere bulbs to the list. Inquire if the new total will exceed the rated capacity of a 30-ampere fuse.

2. Continue with the analogy of the water hose. Many children have noticed the water pressure varying to some noticeable degree while playing with or using a hose. This happens when someone else in the house or a neighbor is also using outlets. Point out that sometimes the water will shoot out powerfully for a great distance from the nozzle, but sometimes only a short distance. Mention that the push or force behind the water is greater in one case than the other. Would more water flow into a bucket within 10 seconds with a forceful stream or with a weaker one? (Forceful stream.)

Help the children to summarise the two ways they could increase the amount of water flowing at any time: by using a bigger hose, to provide a wider pathway; and by increasing the push or pressure behind the water. Continue by making the application to electricity. Point out that the unit of pressure is the *volt*. Have someone read the voltage rating of a D cell and a No. 6 dry cell (one and one-half volts). Inform them that the pressure of house current is about 120 volts. If class members can work with decimal divisors, request them to calculate how many new dry cells it would take to equal this voltage by dividing 120 by 1.5. (80 cells.)

Remind the children that in the lessons on series and parallel wiring they have already learned how to increase the voltage of dry cells by attaching them in a series. Have them recall that the light got brighter as the second cell was added in series, but that the brightness did not change as the cell was added in parallel. Repeat this demonstration, if needed.

3. *Materials:* five D cells; miniature bulb and socket; wire.

If a bulb can be sacrificed in the interest of science education, let the children connect the bulb to a dry cell, and then gradually add more cells in series until it burns out. Allow a half-minute or so of bulb burning time for each additional cell. Five cells will probably have more than enough voltage to burn out the bulb, unless it has a fairly high voltage rating.

4. Mention that household appliances may not have the amperage rating stamped on them, but have instead the number of *watts* used. Explain that the wattage is merely the flow of electricity times the pressure, that is, amperes times volts. Thus, 5 amperes x 10 volts = 50 watts. In other words, a watt tells how fast electricity is being used. Show the class that it is possible to figure out amperes if the voltage and wattage of the appliance is known. Write on the board the formula:

$$\text{Amperes} = \frac{\text{Watts}}{\text{Volts}}$$

Pose some problems such as the following:

An electric drill uses 240 watts on regular 120-volt house current. How many amperes does it use?

$$\frac{240\ W}{120\ V} = 2\ A$$

An electric iron uses 1200 watts on regular house current. How many amperes does it use?

$$\frac{1200\ W}{120\ V} \quad 10\ A$$

5. Ask the class to calculate the following problem to determine if all the appliances could be used without

overloading a house circuit. (Assume a 120-volt supply.) The circuit breaker is rated at 30 amperes.

	Watts
Coffee maker	360
Waffle iron	960
Toaster	600
Iron	1200

The class should total the wattages (3120W) and divide by 120 *V*. The answer is 26 amperes. It would not actuate the circuit breaker.

EXTENDING ACTIVITIES

1. Invite the pupils to find out the rated capacity of the fuse or circuit breaker used in their home or apartment. Have them find the wattages or amperes used by the lights and appliances and total them. The total may then be compared with the circuit capacity. If a few children are unable to find the wattage rating of some appliances, perhaps the following list of typical appliances may be convenient to use:

	Watts
Electric blanket	600
Electric frypan	1100
Dishwasher	1200
Oven	3000
Washing machine	1600
Electric dryer	5000
Vacuum cleaner	700
Waffle iron	1100
Iron	800

2. Pupils who excel in arithmetic may wish to determine the quantity of volts, watts, or amperes used when only

two of these factors are known. Present the formula $A = W \backslash V$. Next to it place $4 = 8/2$. Tell them that these numerals can help them to think through the relationships of the symbols in the formula. Now ask them they can discover a formula that will nine volts, if only watts and amperes known. In a like manner the other quantities may be thought through.

3. Invite a local fireman to class for a talk on safety with electricity. This courtesy is extended by many fire departments as a public service.

4. The class may be interested in determining how electric power bills are calulated by the local power company.

The essentials of the arithmetic involved are to multiply watts times hours, which yields watt-hours. Dividing this figure by 1000 gives the kilowatt-hours. This figure is then multiplied by the kilowatt-hour charge.

Example:

1700 watts for 200 hours = 340,000 watt-hours

340,000 watt-hours = 340 kilowatt-hours

―――――

1,000

340 kilowatt-hours

x 0.05 per kilowatt-hour charge

―――――

$17.00 bill

Electromagnets. In 1820 a professor of physics at Copenhagen made a discovery that opened up for development one of the most useful devices ever conceived: the electromagnet. *Hans Christian Oersted* had believed for years that there was a relationship between magnetism and electricity. In spite of much research, however, Oersted had not succeeded in discovering a useful connection between these phenomena. One day, while lecturing to a class, he noticed that a wire carrying electric current was deflecting a nearby compass needle. Oersted realised immediately that the wire was generating a magnetic field. His subsequent experiments, writings, and lectures helped spread to the world the new concept of electromagnetism.

The telephone, electric motor, and many other indispensable tools of modern living had their origin in Oersted's work and related discoveries. This section of the unit goes into some detail on how several of these devices work. It would be most helpful to the children if the tremendous impact of these inventions on their lives can be discussed as they are studied.

Generalisation V: Electromagnets Can be Made Because a Magnetic Field is Generated Around a Wire Carrying Electricity; Electromagnets Can be Used in Many Ways

Contributing Idea A. A magnetic field is generated around a wire carrying electricity; the strength of the field can be increased in several ways.

Materials: for each child or group a D cell; large iron stove bolt or nail; 8-foot insulated wire (Number 22 enameled magnet wire is best); small box of carpet tacks or brads (small nails).

In this activity, pupils can experiment with electromagnets. It is like a previous investigation in the magnetism unit, except that a more precise measurement technique is used.

Does anyone know how to make a magnet from the materials and how to test it? Chances are that a good portion of the class will. (Remove an inch of insulation from each end of the wire. Leave about a foot of one wire end free, and wrap the rest as needed around the bolt. Touch the wire ends to the D cell and touch the bolt to the brads at the same time. Pick up the brads, *end to end*, then drop them on the table by disconnecting the D cell.)

Discuss possible ways to make an electromagnet stronger. Ask questions such as: How many more brads do you think a twenty-turn electromagnet will pick up compared to a ten-turn one? Thirty turns compared to twenty turns? (Pupils should understand that, since a wire carrying an electric current generates magnetism, wrapping the wire closely around an object concentrates the magnetism into a smaller area and so increases its practical effect.)

Suggest that each team keep a record of the number of turns used, ten turns each time, and the results in brads picked up. (It is important that small objects be picked up *end to end* to counter the effect of "leftover" or residual magnetism, and to have a uniform procedure for assessing power. But let pupils discover these things.)

A graph can easily be made by each group, with number of turns on the horizontal axis, number of brads on the vertical axis. Since a fairly straight-line relationship will be noted after three or four recordings on the graphs, you might ask individual groups if they can predict the results of the next ten-turn trial. (Although a scientifically controlled procedure will show a doubling of power with doubling the turns, children will rarely achieve this finding.)

Look for variations among the teams' results. Help the class analyze why these variations happened. Even though the same number of turns was used by each group, there must have been other variables that were not controlled. Help them isolate and check possible variables:

Were the bolts the same? Used in the same way?

Was the wire the same? Wrapped around the same?

Were the D cells equally strong? Was more than one used?

Were the brads all the same? Picked in the same way?

Was the counting correct? Recording correct?

Is there a way that every group will get *exactly* the same results? This is a challenge that some classes relish. (Probably it will be impossible, especially if the material to be picked up is made smaller and smaller! It might be interesting for your class to learn that greater relative variations may occur as the measurement unit becomes smaller. That is, a variation of *one* nail may be equivalent to *three* brads or *five* small wire staples.)

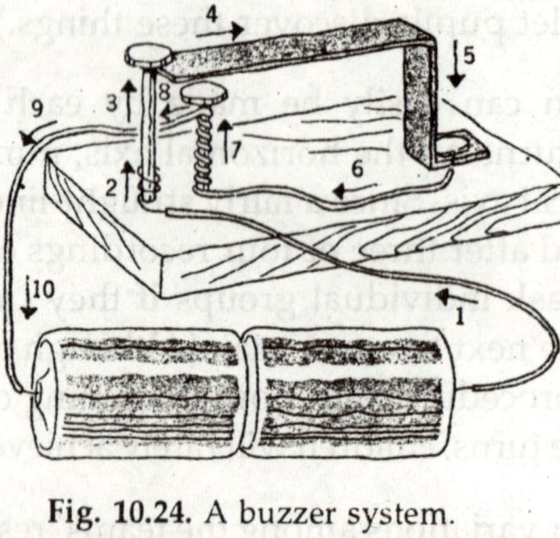

Fig. 10.24. A buzzer system.

Contributing Idea B. Electromagnets may be used in the construction of an interrupted circuit for a bell or buzzer system.

1. *Materials:* for each small group two nails, about 2½

inches and 2-$^3/_4$ inches in length; 10-foot enameled (Number 22) magnet wire; 7- by 3- by 3/4-inch block of wood; large thumb tack, hammer; pliers; 1- by 8-inch bare metal strip. (Cut the strip from a discarded large can with tin shears. Use gloves to avoid cutting fingers on sharp edges. File jagged or sharp parts so that the strip may be safely handled. Scrape or sand away paint or other covering, especially at the ends on both sides. Several fathers of pupils may be willing to prepare a number of strips, given these instructions.)

Have the children build a buzzer to learn how an electromagnet may be used in a circuit. Let them use a projection of Figure 10.24 to build the system and describe how it works. About one hundred turns of wire are needed around the smaller nail to make an electromagnet powerful enough to pull down the strip end. Make sure they understand that this circuit is alternately opened and closed as the contact point opens and closes at the nail head. The end of the metal strip must touch the bottom of the larger nail head. If it does not, tap the nail down with the hammer until it touches.

2. Remove the cover of a door bell. Compare the buzzer and bell. (See Figure 5.25.) Develop that the circuitry is pracically identical. The main differences are a materials used and sounds made.

Contributing Idea C. Telephone receivers contain electromagnets that help change spurts of electrical energy to sound energy; the transmitter uses sound energy to turn on electrical energy.

1. *Materials:* carbon rod from an old dry cell; hammer; two 25-cent pieces; small, clear-glass egg cup; wire; cellophane tape; three D cells; miniature lamp and socket; large sketch or projection of a telephone transmitter and

receiver (Figure 10.27); if possible, a real telephone. (Local telephone companies are usually cooperative in lending many useful materials to schools).

This sequence should give children some understanding of how a telephone works. Begin by asking the pupils if they have ever made a long distance call on a telephone. Bring out distances involved. Cite the case of a person who phones someone 2250 miles away. The two people seem to hear each other instantly. Yet it is known that sound travels about 750 miles per hour, about the speed of some jet aircraft. What is the problem? (How is it possible to hear a person almost instantly when a telephone is used?)

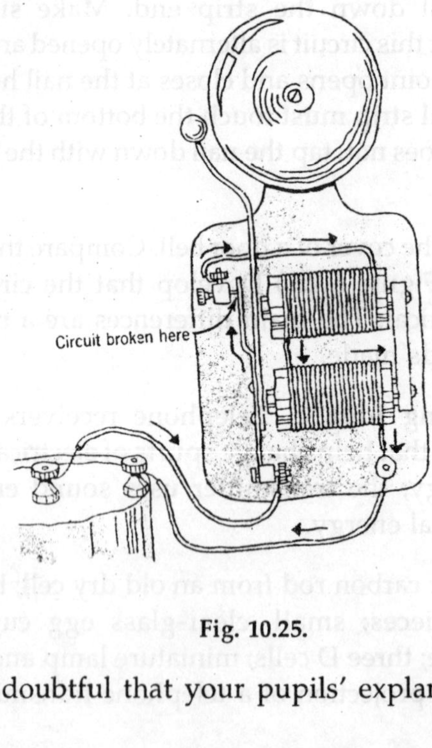

Fig. 10.25.

It is doubtful that your pupils' explanations will be

entirely correct. However, ask which explanation seems most reasonable, then continue. Tell them they now have almost enough background to understand how a telephone works, and will be able to figure out shortly for themselves what happens when a telephone is used.

It will be helpful to begin the sequence with a demonstration. Show that the amount of electrical current sent through a wire can be varied by increasing or decreasing the distance between conductors. Recall the children's previous experience with the nichrome wire rheostat, where length was an important factor in varying the resistance. In the following demonstration with carbon granules, the varying distance of the granules to one another will alter the amount of electrical current that flows in the circuit. This will cause light to burn with varying brightness.

Place the carbon rod on some paper and break it into small pieces with a hammer. Take two large coins, and attach the bared ends of two wires with cellophane tape to the coins. Complete the rest of the circuit as in Figure 10.26, placing the carbon granules between the coins to make a "sandwich." A small, clear-glass egg cup or plastic container will keep the granules from scattering and yet permit observation. Tell someone to press down on the coin gently, then harder. Ask the children to tell what they see and to explain why it happens. (More electricity is conducted when particles are squeezed together; this makes the light brighter. The opposite happens when the particles are not squeezed together.)

2. Have the children recall the ways in which an electromagnet can be made stronger. Emphasise that increasing the current by hooking up more dry cells in series makes an electromagnet more powerful. Ask if an electromagnet would gain or lose power through the same reason that the light's brightness varies. If there is any

difficulty at this point, substitute an electromagnet for the light. Note its varying power of attraction with paper clips as the coins are pressed and released.

3. Place on the chalkboard or project the sketch of a telephone transmitter and receiver in Figure 10.27. Point to the two diaphragms and inform the class that they are made of very thin metal that can *vibrate,* or move back and forth rapidly. Note that the carbon granules or particles in the transmitter are like those used in the coin "sandwich" demonstration. Now ask the class to study the sketch and give an explanation of how the telephone works.

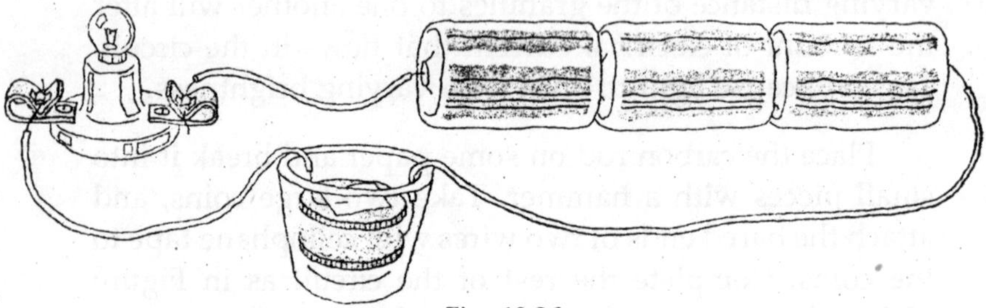

Fig. 10.26.

With a little assistance, it should now be clear to the children why it is possible to hear someone speaking over the telephone almost instantly. Sound vibrations from the voice variably squeeze the carbon granules. This causes the granules to conduct variable electrical impulses, rather than a steady current. The electrical impulses rather than the voice itself are transmitted in the wire. Therefore, they travel thousands of miles almost instantly instead of at the much slower speed of sound. The varying currents or impulses cause the electromagnet in the receiver to set its diaphragm vibrating. This creates the sounds. To summarise, you might emphasise the idea that one kind of energy may be changed to another. In this case, sound energy is

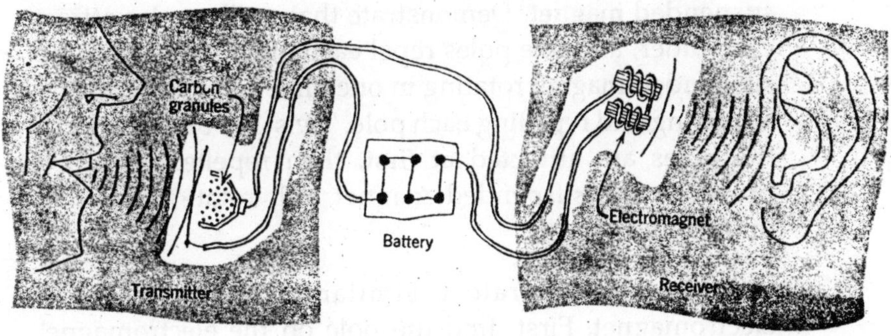

Fig. 10.27. A telephone circuit.

used to provide the electrical energy, which is then used to provide sound energy. For reinforcement of learning, this would be an ideal time for pupils to read a textbook explanation.

If an actual telephone is available for inspection, unscrew the transmitter and receiver. Let pupils compare the parts with those in the sketch.

Contributing Idea D. Electric motors spin because they contain electromagnets which alternately push and pull as their poles change.

1. *Materials:* two bar magnets; string; electromagnet; Number 6 cell or D cell.

Tell the children that one of the most important applications of the electromagnet is electric motors. Draw out names of comon appliances that use electric motors, such as sewing machines, washers, fans, etc. Mention that the class will begin to understand how electric motors function after the following demonstration.

Suspended a bar magnet form a string. Bring the opposite pole of the second bar magnet close to the suspended magnet. Demonstrate that unlike poles attract each other, and like poles repel each other. Now start the suspended magnet rotating in one direction by alternately attracting and repelling each pole. Twist the bar magnet so the poles are attracted at first, then repelled. If timed properly, the suspended magnet will rotate somewhat uniformly.

Now demonstrate a similar technique with an electromagnet. First, find the pole on the electromagnet that is the opposite of the bar magnet's nearer pole. It will attract. Next, reverse terminal connections and the poles will also be reversed. The nearer pole will now be repelled. (See Figure 10.28.) It should be possible to rotate the suspended magnet smoothly by touching the binding posts—first one way, then the opposite way. (A child can do this at a given signal.) Explain that in electric motors there is a device which reverses the current automatically, and thus reverses the poles. The alternating attraction and repulsion of the poles keeps the motor turning.

2. *Materials:* commercially made St. Louis motor; bell wire; dry cell.

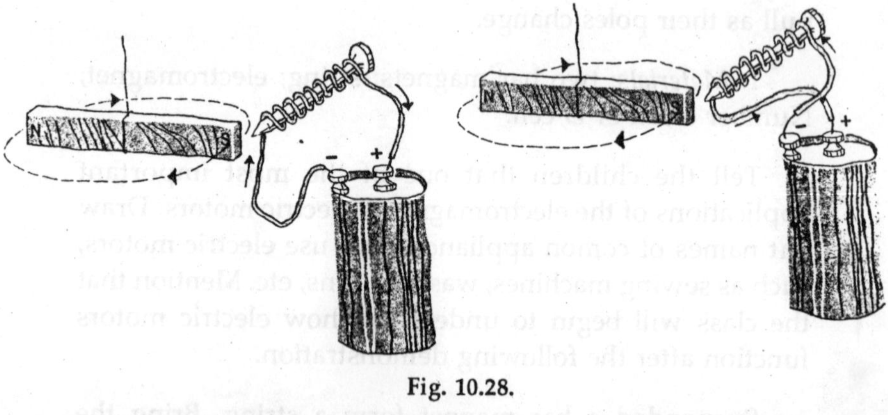

Fig. 10.28.

A St. Louis motor is excellent for illustrative purposes.

(See Figure 10.29.) Point out the main moving part, the *armature,* which is a rotating electromagnet. Show the *commutator.* This device automatically reverses the armature's current- and thus its poles—just as the poles line up with the poles of the *field magnets.* These two permanent magnets are fastened on opposite sides of the armature. Also point out the *brushes,* which enable electricity to flow through the commutator to the electromagnet and back again.

EXTENDING ACTIVITIES

1. Have short reports on contributions of the following men to the technology of communication:

Samuel F. B. Morse (invented the first practical telegraph and code for each letter of the alphabet).

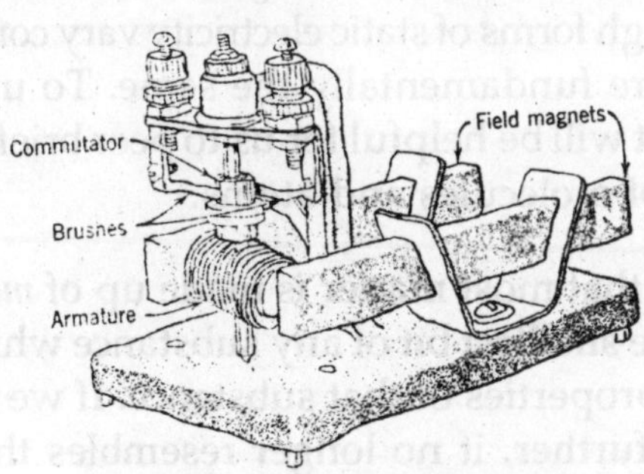

Fig. 10.29. A St. Louis motor.

Cyrus W. Field (major contributor to research information used in laying telegraph cables across the Atlantic Ocean, through which messages called cablegrams are sent).

Guglielmo Marconi (invented the wireless telegraph, making possible transmission of electrical waves through air for communication purposes).

Alexander Graham Bell (invented the first practical telephone).

Hans Christian Oersted (conducted early experiments in electromagnetism).

2. A few advanced pupils may wish to build their own electric motor and demonstrate it. Directions for construction of simple motors may be found in many children's books on electricity.

Static Electricity. Not all electricity is useful. Almost everyone has experienced some form of *static electricity:* the crackling sound of hair when it is combed after having been washed and dried; the slight shock felt when a metal door knob is touched after scuffing across a rug; the flash of lightning that briefly illuminates a darkened sky. In each case an electric charge appears to build up on an object and then stay there (hence the name static) until a conductor provides a route through which the charge can escape. Although forms of static electricity vary considerably, their causes are fundamentally the same. To understand these causes, it will be helpful for us to peer briefly into the composition of molecules and atoms.

We know that most matter is made up of *molecules.* A molecule is the smallest bit of any substance which retains the chemical properties of that substance. If we subdivide the molecule further, it no longer resembles the original substance; we have arrived at the atomic level.

Only two of the particles of which an atom is composed need concern us here: *electrons* and *protons.* Each of these particles has a tiny electric charge that is the opposite of the other. The electron's charge is called a *negative charge* and the proton's charge a *positive charge.*

In their "normal" state, atoms possess as many electrons as protons. Since these particles attract each other with equal force they balance or neutralise each other. The atom is said to be *neutral*, or uncharged. However, electrons are easily dislodged or torn away from atoms by rubbing and by other means. Free electrons, as these dislodged particles are called, may be attracted to another atom. If an atom loses one or more electrons it will have an excess of protons, and hence a positive electric charge. If it gains one or more electrons the atom will have an excess of electrons and a negative electric charge.

When neutral, unlike materials are rubbed together one tends to lose electrons to the other. For example, when a hard rubber rod is rubbed with a wool cloth, the cloth loses some of its electrons to the rod. This gives the cloth a positive charge and the rod a negative charge. When a glass rod is rubbed with silk, however, scientists have found that some electrons leave the glass and go onto the silk cloth. This gives the silk a negative charge and the glass a positive charge. Although almost any unlike materials rubbed together will produce some static electricity, usually these materials—hard rubber and wool, silk and glass-give the best results.

A modern conception of the atom is needed to understand reasonably well the nature of static electricity. But early scientific discoveries helped at least to make it a less mysterious phenomenon than it must have been to primitive man. Benjamin Franklin's contribution to the understanding of static electricity is an interesting example.

To find out if lightning was associated with electricity, Franklin flew a kite during a thunderstorm. Attached to the kite was a metal rod, and at the end of the string a key was fastened. Franklin hypothesised that a spark would jump to the key as electricity traveled down the string. To avoid being shocked, he held the key by means of a silk ribbon. (Silk is a fairly good insulator.) Franklin took the additional precaution of standing under a shelter so the ribbon would remain dry. He realised that moisture increases conduction of electricity. His success with this and other experiments helped prove that lightning was a form of static electricity.

(Discourage anyone from trying Franklin's experiment. We know now that a severe electric charge would have electrocuted him in spite of the silk cloth insulator.)

What causes lightning? Basically, it is produced by friction. A cloud contains varying amounts of dust particles, rain drops, air (gas) molecules, and sometimes ice crystals. When violent air currents occur in clouds, these substances rub together in various combinations. If a huge electric charge is built up, it may be attracted by an oppositely charged cloud, or the ground. When this happens, we see lightning.

Since metals are excellent conductors, usually anyone is safe from lightning in a steel-framed building, or in a building equipped with a lightning rod. If the object is struck, the charge is harmlessly conducted by the metal down into the ground. Electricity always takes the path of least resistance. Lightning rod systems have the extra advantage of permitting excess charges on the ground to leak off the rod into the air, thus lessening the chance of a lightning stroke. Teach children to stay away from tall trees and other tall objects during a storm, especially if these are isolated and wet. The least resistance effect occurs here, too.

Static electricity can be dangerous or annoying in other ways. When spots or stains are rubbed off clothing through use of a flammable fluid, sparks may ignite the explosive vapor. Air inside flour and grain mills is often laden with fine particles of dust. Almost any material is highly combustible if reduced to small enough particles. Again there is danger of a spark causing an explosion.

Gasoline trucks have a strap or chain dangling from the chassis to the ground. This drains off static electricity built up from the gasoline jostling around in the tank. Toll booths on bridges and highways usually have thin metal rods imbedded in the ground immediately before each station. These rods drain off whatever static charges a vehicle has accumulated, thus preventing either driver or attendant from receiving a shock when the toll is paid. In the forthcoming activities, charged objects may be "grounded" (neutralised) by touching them. In the case of a balloon, you may have to touch several parts before it becomes neutralised all over.

Experiments with static electricity may be disappointing unless performed on dry days. Cold days are often ideal, because the air holds less moisture than on warmer days. When there is much moisture in the air, whatever static charges are built up may leak off rapidly into the air and ground.

Generalisation VI: Matter Contains Electrons Which May be Accumulated Through Friction into Electric Charges; Unlike Charges Attract, like Charges Repel Each Other

Contributing Idea A. Matter is made up of atoms which contain tiny particles of electricity called electrons and protons.

1. *Materials:* rubber comb; small bits of tissue paper; wool cloth; new balloon.

Invite a child to rub a comb briskly over some cloth and then place the comb near bits of tissue paper. The two will be attracted. Have another pupil rub a balloon with cloth and then place the balloon against the wall. It usually will stay there. Ask the class what is causing these phenomena to occur. They are almost sure to say "electricity."

Mention that this kind of electricity is called *static* or *frictional* electricity. Briefly, go into the meaning of the two words. Continue by inquiring whether someone has washed his hair a day or so previously. Have him recount what he noticed if he had brushed or briskly combed his hair after it dried. Invite the children to tell of other instances when they have noticed static electricity. They may mention experiences of sparks after rubbing their pets' fur, or sliding across a plastic automobile seat and then touching a metal door handle. Someone may have scuffed across a deeply piled rug and then touched a metal door knob.

After experiences have been told, develop that in each case rubbing one thing against another brought on a charge of static electricity. Now, ask the children where the electricity came from. Some may volunteer an explanation. Perhaps no one can. This will arouse the need for finding out how electric charges are built up on objects.

2. Permit the class to read or view visual materials to find out about the electrical particles of which atoms are partly made. Or your simplified exposition will help. Some ideas to stress are:

a. Everything in the world is made up of atoms. Atoms are very, very tiny. No one has ever seen one. But scientists have formed some ideas about them through their experiments and mathematical cal-culations.
b. Atoms have two different kinds of tiny electrical particles, of equal but opposite forces. One kind is the electron, whose electric charge is called a *negative* or minus (–) charge. The other is the proton, whose electric charge is called a *positive*, or plus (+) charge.

c. Electrons may whirl in many different orbits around the center of an atom. Protons usually stay located in the center of the atom.
d. Different atoms may have different amounts of electrons and protons, but usually they have an electron for every proton. When there is a balance of this sort, the atom is said to be *neutral*, or *uncharged.*
e. Protons usually stay where they are. However, some electrons are rather easily removed from atoms by an outside force, such as rubbing. When that happens, there is no longer a balance of electrical charges.
f. When electrons are rubbed off a neutral object, there are more positive protons left than electrons. The object has a positive charge.
g. A neutral object that gains negative electrons now has more electrons than protons. It has a negative charge.
h. Therefore, objects that have more electrons than usual have a negative electric charge. Those that have fewer electrons than usual have a positive charge. Atoms that have the same amount of electrons have no charge, or are neutral.

Fig. 10.30.

Review to insure understanding. Place on the board the material in Figure 10.30:

Atom A has four electrons but only three protons. What charge, if any, does it have? (Negative.)

What charge, if any, does atom B have? (Positive.)

What charge, if any, does atom C have? (It is neutral, or uncharged.)

Contributing Idea B. Materials which have unlike charges attract each other.

1. *Materials:* glass rod (or piece of glass tubing or test tube or plastic object); piece of silk; hard rubber rod (or comb); piece of wool cloth; new inflated balloon; 18 inch string.

Suspend a balloon by a string from an upturned chair or other support so that it hangs freely. Have someone rub the balloon with a cloth. Explain that wool loses electrons easily and that electrons are going onto the balloon. Ask the class what charge the balloon may now have. (Negative.)

Ask a child to rub a glass rod vigorously with some silk. Explain that silk can remove electrons from a glass rod. Ask what charge the rod now has. (Positive.) Inquire as to what the children think will happen when a positively charged object (glass rod) is brought near a negatively charged object (balloon). After trying it, elicit that the objects tested had unlike charges, and therefore attracted each other.

2. *Materials:* glass rod or substitute; string and clothespin nod holder; silk cloth; rubber rod or substitute; woolen cloth.

Suspend the glass rod from a string. (A wooden spring-type clothespin attached to the string and clamped to the rod makes this easy to do.) Charge it positively with the silk cloth. Let someone charge a rubber rod negatively by rubbing it hard on some wool. Be sure everyone knows the rubber is negatively charged and the glass is positively charged. Have someone explain what is happening to the electrons. Again request the children to predict what will happen when the unlike charges are brought close together. After they find the same result, draw from them the idea that unlike charges attract each other.

Contributing Idea C. Materials which have like charges repel each other.

1. *Materials:* string; inflated balloon; wool cloth; rubber rod or comb.

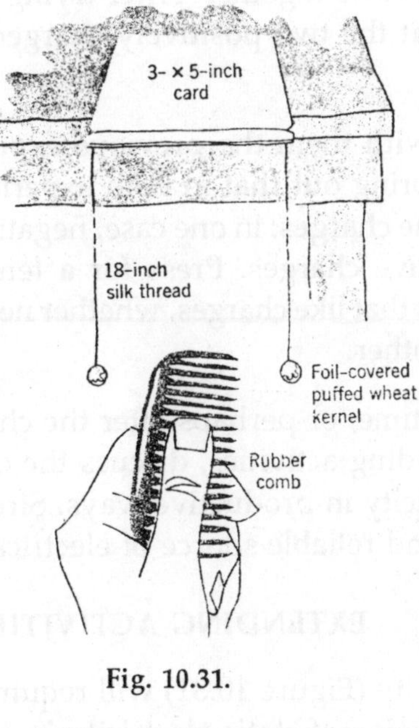

Fig. 10.31.

Allow a class member to suspend the balloon again and recharge it with the wool cloth. The rod should also be recharged with the wool cloth. Make sure that everyone understands both items are negatively charged. Invite predictions as to what will happen if two negative charges are brought near each other. After trying it, draw from the group that the two negatively charged objects pushed or repelled each other.

2. *Materials:* two glass rods or substitutes; silk cloth; string and clothespin rod holder.

Let a glass rod be suspended again. Have both rods rubbed with the silk cloth. If only one-half of each rod is rubbed, make sure that only those parts are brought near one another, as the charge will be built up only on the portion of the rod that is rubbed. Again call for predictions of what will happen when two positively charged objects are brought close together. After trying it, draw from the children that the two positively charged objects repelled each other.

Recall with them the previous experiment. Through questions, bring out that in both experiments the objects had the same charges; in one case, negative charges, in the other, positive charges. Press for a tentative conclusion which states that like charges, whether negative or positive, repel each other.

At this time, or perhaps after the children try several of the extending activities, discuss the difficulty of using static electricity in productive ways. Stress the need for a sustained and reliable source of electrical power.

EXTENDING ACTIVITIES

1. This activity (Figure 10.31) will require pupils to apply their knowledge of static electricity in a problem-solving way. In other words, the previous investigations may be thought of as input for this activity. For this reason, you can also use it for appraisal purposes.

Each child or group will need a 3- by 5- inch file card; one piece each of silk and wool cloth; glass rod or substitute; hard rubber rod or substitute; 2-inch square piece of thin kitchen foil or substitute (chewing gum wrapper foil with paper removed, clean wrapper from Hershey chocolate candy kisses, etc.); 18-inch silk thread; scissors, puffed wheat kernels.

Inform the class that they can make an *electroscope* to figure out some of the strange ways of static electricity. Show them how to assemble the materials as in Figure 10.31. With scissors, make two small nicks in the card about one-half inch from the end. This will keep the thread from sliding off. To suspend each wheat kernel, just put one end of the thread next to the kernel and wrap it in foil together with the kernel. The card will stay secure if about three-fourths of an inch protrudes over a table edge.

Let the children explore for several minutes actions of the suspended pellets as uncharged and charged rubber or glass rods are brought close or allowed to touch them. If needed, help them discover that the pellets may be charged together by touching them with one charged rod; or may be charged separately with opposite charges by holding the strings farther apart and touching each pellet with a differently charged rod. Also, that the pellets may be neutralised by holding them for an instant.

Have them explain why a pellet may be attracted to a rod, touch it, then flit away. (At first, the pellet is either neutral or has an opposite charge from that of the rod. As soon as it touches the rod, it instantly acquires a like charge and is repelled.) Review that rubbing silk on a glass rod produces a positive charge on the rod, and rubbing wool on a rubber rod produces a negative charge. Also, that like charges repel and unlike attract.

Now bring up the problem; perhaps in form of a chalkboard sketch of Figure 10.32 A-E (left side only). Mention that the five sketches show the behavior of the pellets when a rod is put between them. They are to figure out what charge the rod has (if any), and the charge (if any) on the pellets. To make descriptions simple, a code be used: N for neutral or no charge, + for positive, and — for negative charges. (Worksheets here would be ideal for recording findings and evaluative feedback.) Suggest that pupils hypothesise first, then test the hypotheses with their electroscopes.

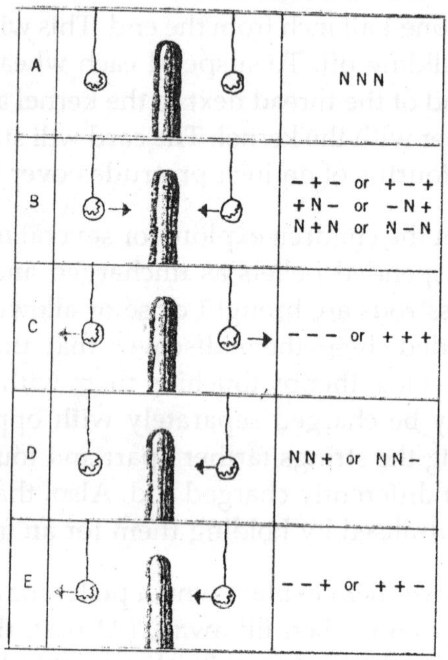

Fig. 10.32.

Treat all findings as tentative until the class seems ready for an evaluative discussion. Then have individual children test before the entire class their ideas about pellet behavior in the five situations. Thirteen combinations of charges and neutral states are possible. Try to bring out the valuable idea that the same phenomenon may have more than one valid explanation.

2. Get a committee to find out what causes lightning and what safety precautions may be taken to protect people and property.

3. Invite someone to report on how Benjamin Franklin experimented with a kite to find out about lightning. Have the class discuss the danger of this experiment and the danger of flying kites near power poles.

4. Draw up two teams. Each team can find out how the following things or places may be affected by static electricity; also, what precautions are necessary to prevent static charges from piling up. Develop with the class criteria for choosing valid and reliable information sources. Illustrative questions to pose before the pupils begin their search will also be helpful.

Dry cleaners	Spray paint shop
Flour mill	Gasoline truck
Automobiles	Highway and bridge toll stations

11

New Developments in Elementary School Teaching

9What are the opportunities for ICT within the core curriculum? What styles of teaching and learning are supported? How do pupils benefit? Are attitudes to learning, and ability to work independently, enhanced? This book explores contexts within Mathematics, English and Science at Key Stages 1 and 2. It considers the role of the computer as 'tutor', enabling teaching focused at developing core skills within these subjects. 'Legacy' software from the dawn of microcomputing in schools has a place, alongside new developments such as multimedia authoring and the World Wide Web. The balance of the book, however, is weighted towards the role of the computer as a tool for problem solving and inquiry, since this is where there appears to be the greatest need for curriculum development. For instance, inspection findings show that the majority of pupils gain some experience of ICT in handling data. However, opportunities to interpret results and draw conclusions are not always taken (Goldstein, 1997).

With rapid developments in multimedia and telecommunications, gaps between 'low-tech' and 'high-tech' learning environments in schools are set to increase. Practitioners may regard the pace of current change with considerable unease. As existing hardware becomes obsolete, will teachers' hard-won ICT capability be declared redundant? There is a real danger that the expertise of a generation of innovators will be discounted and swept aside. It is time to take stock of what we already know about the ways in which IT enhances and enriches teaching and learning. Teachers should look to the new technologies for better ways of reaching established goals. We need to build upon, rather than discard, our existing professional knowledge.

Government initiatives to resource ICT across the curriculum and train teachers are long overdue. As the new Government took office, ministers faced a situation where the classroom computing 'revolution', fuelled by industrial developments in the early 1980s, had run out of steam. Prophecies that IT would change the face of education had not been fulfilled. Government statistics (DfE. 1995a) showed that only two-thirds of primary teachers use IT 'regularly', which could mean as little as twice a week. More than 50% of the computers in schools were at least five years old. Software development was restricted because applications had to run on older machines.

In contrast, technology has brought about irreversible change in the workplace. ICT increasingly impinges on our leisure and social activity. Today's personal computers are well over a hundred times faster and more capacious than the cumbersome machines installed in classrooms in the early 1980s, and are actually cheaper. Due to vastly improved interface design, they are considerably easier to use. The rate of development of new communications technologies has accelerated.

OFSTED inspections confirmed that teachers lack confidence and knowledge of applications (Goldstein, 1997).

Opportunities for integrating ICT across the curriculum are undeveloped (SCAA, 1996a). Many teachers are unsure how to incorporate ICT in lesson planning, and have little experience of assessment and differentiation in IT. Inspection data shows that pupils' achievements in IT are lower than in any other subject. Only one in two schools are meeting IT curriculum requirements.

Nevertheless, OFSTED observed 'much valuable work' in primary classrooms. The challenge and motivational appeal of ICT has been demonstrated. 'Skilful and creative' work with graphics and multimedia has been in evidence. However, many pupils experience ICT in isolation. Opportunities for greater challenge are missed, due to a lack of teacher intervention. Many pupils have opportunities to use new technology to support research, but use is often 'superficial and unstructured'.

Today, a large portion of funding is devolved directly to schools, and the tradition of free help and advice has 'ended. There is a fragmented, commercialised pattern of local support. In any case, local centres were forced to reduce their staffing as 'spotlight' funding was directed onto other targets. Many school managers have been ill prepared for the transition and have not planned strategically for targeting funding at curriculum training. There has been reliance on internal support. Most IT co-ordinators have little or no non-teaching time in which to utilise external sources of support, train colleagues and monitor pupils' progress. A national strategy has been called for in co-ordinating services and improving quality, thus increasing the market through making services more attractive to schools (NCET, 1996a).

Early training courses focused on the workings of the machine. The dominant use of computers in classrooms both in this country and the U.S. in the early 1980s was for instruction in computer 'literacy' (Becker, 1985). Even then, it was recognised that the new literacy 'cannot be founded on the shifting sand of the technology itself (Long-worth, 1981). Pupils need to be taught information skills in the context of authentic tasks modelled on real life.

The rapid advance of the personal computer in the 1980s brought powerful generic tools such as word processors and spreadsheets into the workplace. This innovation had a profound effect on the development of IT in education (Heppell, 1993). The IT Curriculum reflects the predominance of business applications in the curricula of the late 1980s (Ball, 1990). Teachers may feel, with justification, that widely used terms such as 'computer literacy' and 'information skills' have not been adequately defined.

Teachers lack confidence in teaching IT and rate it highly as a training need (Hargreaves et al, 1996). Most teachers feel comfortable using a limited range of applications (Murray and Collison, 1995), and can demonstrate that some aspects of the statutory requirements are being met. There is a unique difficulty in that, as soon as most primary schools have reached a state of relative equilibrium, new technological change drives 'progress'.

Education for the 'information society' has become an urgent Government priority. Yet there is still no clear vision of the role of ICT in education. This can be traced to a lack of shared values and goals, and the failure of national bodies to agree common aspirations. The question of how we should use ICT in schools reaches to the very heart of issues which affect curriculum content, teaching methods and expectations of learners. What should children be taught? What is the nature of computer-mediated experience? How do children learn, and what can they achieve?

We use computers to perform tasks which would require many hours of intensive human activity. In freeing our time, we are given increased opportunities for thinking and reflection. It is the responsibility of educators to empower young people to use these tools purposefully. creatively and responsibly. Teaching, according to Davis and collaborators (1997), must be intentional, and must be informed by understanding of the power of the tool, its generative capacity and of the demands made on the user'.

There may be considerable diversity in the ICT-rich schools of the future. Older machines may be. used for tasks which do not require state-of-the-art functionality, such as planning, note making, writing and redrafting, analysing data, producing graphs and preparing reports. Notebook computers, which can be used at pupils' desks or taken out of doors, may also be used for these tasks. Inexpensive networked computers may become the mainstay in schools of the future. They will derive their capacity not from ever more powerful processors, but from local servers connected via high-volume, two-way, links.

Throughout this book, illustrative use has been made of evidence drawn from close observation of pupils' interaction with ICT. Analysis will assist readers in forming expectations. The author cannot offer universal generalisations from the small-scale studies which formed the basis of her research. It is not possible in a small volume to give complete descriptions of the circumstances in which data was obtained. However, teachers will recognise similarities in the broader context, and be able to judge whether it is likely that their own pupils will respond in similar ways.

This book is not solely concerned with innovative technology. In fact, most of the practical examples in this book were developed on 2Mb Acorn systems. It would be a colossal error to draw a line over all older machines, effectively-consigning them to the skip. Where teachers have made a committed effort to introduce ICT, belittlement of ageing classroom computers must be profoundly discouraging. Our knowledge of the ways in which ICT supports learning, gained through practical experience of teaching with older systems, will be just as valuable and as relevant in years to come. We should look to new technological capability to improve what we are already trying to do, and build upon our existing achievements.

The role of the teacher should be carefully considered. When is explicit IT teaching called for, and what form should it take? An important issue is whether whole-class teaching through the medium of ICT is desirable, or even feasible. In many of the examples in this book, whole-class teaching was an important element of what took place. Metacognitive skills (organising knowledge, identifying goals, planning, checking results and evaluating outcomes) may be modelled by the teacher, then developed through computer group work combined with whole-class discussion and review.

A good example occurs in Chapter 4, where the whole class reviews the graphs of seedling growth produced by groups. Another instance arises in Chapter 6, where many salient teaching points are covered with the whole class rather than repeated nine or ten times.

The Curriculum for ICT in subject teaching (TTA, 1998) requires teachers to be able to employ a range of approaches, including whole-class teaching with ICT. However, it seems hardly worth attempting this when the typical classroom display is a fourteen-inch monitor. I have observed a Year 1 teacher, with her whole class in a circle on the floor, lead an interactive Maths session with the Roamer. She encouraged children to talk though the commands, and everyone could see the outcomes. Later, she reviewed *MyWorld* screens (Chapter 2) on the computer by the door, while the class were lined up for assembly. Even then, not all children could see the screen. No-one would dream of giving a commercial presentation to thirty colleagues using a desktop display, yet this is apparently what we are expected to do in the classroom.

Fortunately, portable data projectors are now available. They are virtually silent in operation and, in a normal classroom, do not require blackout. An alternative is the LCD panel which sits on top of an over-head projector. Used with a portable computer, it may quickly be set up virtually anywhere in school. The drawback is that these displays are costly, although prices are on a downward trend. Whichever option is chosen, schools will have to budget at least £2000 - for one unit! A cheaper alternative is the thirty-four inch Hantarex video monitor, but few primary classrooms have space for this type of equipment. Some LEAs have set aside a portion of NGfL money for a pool of central resources. Provision of data projectors to selected schools, for instance to pilot the use of ICT in Literacy and Numeracy Hours, would be a commendable move.

Applications of ICT in schools are expanding and diversifying. It is impossible in a book of this size to cover every aspect of ICT in primary education. ILS (Integrated Learning Systems) will be viewed by some as an important omission. Sadly, there is no space to review the enabling role of ICT in special education. However, the scope for differentiation through ICT is noted throughout the following chapters, and ways of supporting and extending pupils within the mainstream setting are suggested.

This book provides a unique insight into pupils' development of ICT capability and the wider potential for learning in the core subjects. The case studies themselves are intended to offer exemplars: other practical suggestions and recommendations are made in the light of outcomes. Space does not permit a detailed review of planning, assessment and recording, and ICT management issues. Many current publications offer detailed advice in these areas, and it is not my intention to duplicate these materials.

A number of LEA IT Centres have published high quality guides and frameworks for ICT in cross-curricular planning. Good examples are Oxfordshire's *Progression in IT* and *Opportunities Across the Curriculum* (Oxfordshire County Council, 1996) and *Making IT Manageable* (Hertfordshire Education Services, 1997). NCET's planning tool *Managing IT in Primary Schools* (NCET, 1996b) is strongly recommended. The Primary IT co-ordinator will find further support and a host of planning materials in the NAACE ring binder *Implementing IT* (NCET, 1997).

It or ICT?

To put it simply, IT is the subject. ICT the tools. It pupils use CD-ROM to research a topic in Geography, they are using ICT. If the teacher sets up an overlay keyboard with initial consonant blends to match to pictures, she is Using ICT to support literacy development. Other ICT applications include email, video conferencing and the use of the World Wide Web. In ICT; the focus is on the subject being taught or studied [...] rather than developing pupils' skills with, and knowledge of, the technologies themselves' (QCA, 1998). The QCA framework also refers to the important role of ICT in school management and administration.

On the other hand, IT 'comprises the knowledge, skills and understanding' to make appropriate, productive use of ICT. QCA cites the analogous relationship of literacy to books, journals and reading material. IT (the subject) includes knowledge of how information is structured in a database, and skills of using ICT to communicate ideas and information. .

Teachers may feel the distinction is a very fine one. Whatever the ICT application, it is nearly always possible to identify some potential for the development of IT skills. Multimedia CD-ROMs which provide practice in early number skills such as counting, sequencing and simple addition are good examples. Young children learn to point and click with the mouse, and associate numbers with numerals on the keyboard. It is precisely because teachers need to select such opportunities for developing IT skills that the distinction between ICT and IT is important.

At the same time, it should be recognised that older pupils may use ICT to support learning in a subject, while hardly adding anything to their knowledge of IT. The computer controls the learning environment by presenting manageable tasks and prompting for responses. Steps are repeated if mistakes are made. Curriculum-related software may be a rich resource to support learning in the subject. However, it may do little to develop IT skills because there is too much cushioning against errors. IT capability means being able to cope with, and learn from, errors. Pupils need opportunities to review faulty strategies. They need to develop the confidence to regard mistakes, and their consequences, in a positive light.

Why is ICT Problematic?

As the pace of technological development continues to

exert pressure to innovate, there are many unresolved Questions in teachers' minds. Why use these ICT tools? Are they manageable, in the typical classroom? What may pupils achieve with ICT, and what wider learning is involved? What IT Skills need to be taught and how? What are effective ways of organising opportunities and supporting pupils?.

It is now widely accepted that schools cannot be offered the same solutions as industrial and commercial concerns, since there are critical differences in aims and expectations. A new office computer system may perform highly regulated operations which were previously carried out manually. While the transition may exact a heavy personal toll on employees, there are clear expectations, since routines are modelled on established practice.

The school's ICT objectives, on the other hand, may be unclear. Lack of knowledge of applications is compounded by a virtual absence of established models for new types of learner activity. Computers cannot be used to deliver the traditional curriculum, since an all-embracing range of instructional software does not exist.

Even in schools where ICT is in everyday use, it is difficult for busy teachers to probe beyond surface features. End products (a graph printed in colour, a page downloaded from CD-ROM) rarely lead to further investigation. Most teachers work in comparative isolation, and have not had the opportunity to observe colleagues and pupils in ICT-rich classrooms. Consequently, a body of pedagogic knowledge, grounded in classroom experience and professional practice, developed and communicated within the professional network, scarcely exists. No wonder many teachers find ICT threatening. The introduction of ICT necessitates changes in attitudes, changes in classroom practice and changes in the knowledge base of teachers. In other words, all three dimensions of educational change (Fullan, 1991) are involved.

Both the National Curriculum and NGfL targets make considerable demands on teachers' IT subject knowledge. SCAA have produced leaflets intended to assist teachers in recognising appropriate cross-curricular applications. While slimmed-down guidance, with clear practical exemplars, is welcome, there is a great risk of over-simplification. Faced with the revised Programmes of Study (DfE, 1995b), there is still a great deal of unpacking for practitioners to do. Sophisticated ICT tools present complex teaching and learning environments. It was the desire to gain a better understanding of the nature of ICT, and the demands on teachers and pupils, that prompted the research which led to this book.

Styles of Teaching and Learning

Somekh (1997) defines three ways in which teachers may approach the use of the computer to support learning. At the first level, the machine is used chiefly in *tutorial* mode. The software is designed to teach specific subject content. The learner receives knowledge delivered by the system. However, the computer allows opportunities for interaction, and the learner may have a degree of control (for example, being able to request help). There may be automatic assessment and tracking of progress. Due to the structured nature of the learning environment, there are predictable demands on pupils and learning outcomes. These programmes do not have the potential to transform teaching and learning, but 'do the same things that schools have traditionally done [...] perhaps more systematically and efficiently' (Means et al., 1993).

The second (intermediate) stage is in using the computer

as a *neutral tool.* The pupil has the opportunity to use content-free software, allowing a far greater range of applications. However, the computer activity is modelled on. familiar routines which remain fundamentally - unchanged by the presence of technology. A good example is the use of a word processor to make a 'best copy' of work that has already been drafted and corrected on paper.

Finally, the computer is used as a *cognitive tool* to support inquiry-based research. Pupils are introduced to open-ended applications such as databases, spreadsheets and controlling and monitoring software. However, there may be a high degree of focus in their use. For example, the activity may be driven by questions such as, 'What are the best conditions for growing seedlings?' 'How effectively do various materials insulate a container of water?' In using ICT to store, process and present data, new approaches to teaching and learning are implicit.

Pupils need access to higher order skills: formulating questions, planning, organising, interpreting feedback, testing hypotheses and evaluating outcomes. Al this level, pupils take increasing responsibility for their own learning as they become able to undertake inquiries independently.

Arguments in favour of inquiry-based approaches are based on the recognition that learners acquire process skills through interaction with the environment. Ideas and explanations are accepted, modified or rejected in the light of experience. Pupils actively raise and develop questions, gather information, formulate and test their explanations and ideas, and communicate their findings to others. Pupils are more likely to be motivated to engage in challenging inquiries if presented with authentic tasks, modelled on real-world problems (Sheingold, 1990).

Somekh acknowledges that the step from 'neutral tool'

to 'cognitive tool' is massive. In practice, many teachers edge forward as they gain confidence in using a greater range of ICT applications. With increased familiarity, the teacher is better able to make links with learning in other subjects. Open-ended software may be used for particular tasks. Teaching is planned with the intention of developing pupils' IT skills and knowledge. For example, the teacher shows children how to cut and paste with a word processor, and encourages them to employ these techniques in re-drafting their writing on the screen.

It hardly needs to be said that the development of ICT in supporting pupil-directed inquiry places intensive demands on the teacher, as pupils gain familiarity with skills, concepts and strategies. Official sources do not always recognise that even the simplest 'tutorial' software imposes organisational challenge. The teacher must decide where to incorporate in medium-term planning; how to match to pupils' levels (e.g. by selecting options); how to organise groups; how to integrate into daily planning; how to monitor and record progress. The teacher will also wish to identify opportunities for questioning and review, and plan links with other tasks. At school level, there are immense resourcing demands, especially where there is a plan to use ICT for individualised learning.

Given the rapid emergence of multimedia and new communications technologies, there are new specialist demands, with even deeper implications for changing pedagogy. There are opportunities for teachers, to produce their own interactive teaching materials, using multimedia presentation tools. Given the opportunity, the teacher is able to use communications networks, both as a professional resource and in providing planned access for pupils to curriculum materials on-line. Through electronic link-ups with other schools, the teacher engages in collaborative projects. Distance is immaterial as pupils collaborate with students overseas in tackling research projects of common interest. Classroom groups devise tasks for each other, and co-operate in electronically publishing their findings. The teacher finds that, as an expert in the use of classroom technology, s/he no longer works in isolation but is an active member of an international electronic community. S/he becomes a learner alongside the pupils (Riel, 1990; Means et al., 1993: Davis, 1997).

In the use of open-ended software, the role of the teacher is critical: the mere presence of technology may have little impact on learning. Through informed, sensitive intervention, and through providing appropriate tasks alongside (or away from) the computer, the teacher provides 'scaffolding' (Elliott, 1995). The computer environment provides further structuring and feedback. The teacher passes on models which guide pupils' notions of the type of inquiries they may pursue, and possible strategies. As pupils adapt these models to serve their own ends, they develop higher-order thinking skills. The success of any approach to investigative learning with ICT depends on the extent of the teacher's knowledge, both of the ICT tools themselves and the challenges and opportunities presented to pupils. A further critical factor lies in the quality of the teacher's insight into learners' interactions, and ability to intervene appropriately.

The National Grid for Learning

According to the Government's desired objectives. ICT will be commonplace, and routinely used across the curriculum. By the year 2002, the National Grid for Learning (NGfL) will link all schools with libraries, museums, higher education systems and the home. This will inevitably change the ways in which learning is delivered, but the prospect of a widening gap between ICT 'haves' and 'have nots' must be viewed with concern. OFSTED (Goldstein, 1997) have reported signs of a gulf between schools with good levels of resourcing and those which can only offer limited-ICT access.

The importance of teacher training has been recognised, and will be supported through Millennium Commission funding. All Local Education Authorities have development plans tor ICT, as a precondition for NCET funding. Priority issues are the connection of schools with minimum access charges; the development of curriculum content to be published on the Grid; the overcoming of harriers which currently inhibit the development of ICT in schools.

What are the chances of success? Much depends on the quality of content and the willingness of teachers to explore ways of incorporating resource-based learning opportunities. Teachers who do not already draw on a wide range of resources in the classroom may scarcely be affected. An influential Government adviser anticipates gradual change through 'stepwise' development, with setbacks as well as progress (Stevenson, 1998). Schools will welcome a gradualist approach in a climate where continued funding will very much depend on demonstrable results. Schools should not be penalised for failing to attain targets which initially appeared achievable, provided that every reasonable effort has been made.

A major feature of NGfL is the *Virtual Teachers' Centre* website, which appeared online in January 1998. The development of the VTC is critical to the success of the Grid. Many believe that the VTC was launched too soon, in a prototype form which largely consisted of an archive of official documents and curriculum resources lifted from the former NCET site. The active participation of teachers' groups in developing VTC content is to be hoped for.

Other organisations such as BBC Education and Channel 4 Schools are to provide materials. Pages will be 'badged' as a mark of the high standard expected of the VTC. The chief advantage will be in a single access point to a range of resources covering the full curriculum.

While the VTC will be an asset, materials on their own will not deliver all the teaching. The VTC must not be allowed to become a mere Vehicle for dissemination of worksheets and lesson plans from central sources. We need to consider ways of using on-line sources in the class-room. What skills do pupils need to acquire? How may on-line resources be used to enrich and enhance teaching and learning? Above all, active participation by teachers in sharing experiences and contributing trialled materials will go a long way towards rectifying the prevailing lack of shared professional knowledge of 'what works'...

Summary of Main Sections

Opportunities for ICT in Mathematics

Materials and advice for teachers issued in the early 1980s still have some relevance today. Examples of 'legacy' software illustrate the ways in which ICT may provide an interactive class teaching aid and a tool for pupil-led investigation. Content-free applications with tools for manipulating graphics provide the teacher with opportunities to adapt tasks to meet specific objectives.

Roamers, Pixies and turtles provide early experience of controlling IT systems through sequences of commands. In this section, we look at the opportunities for supporting teaching and learning in numeracy and introducing angular turn. Once children progress to controlling the turtle on the screen, there are many possibilities for enriching knowledge of number, shape and spatial concepts through problem solving and exploration of pattern.

Graphing programmes are a non-threatening and familiar use of ICT. Computer graphs are often regarded as attractive end products, rather than as tools to support further inquiry. Important issues concern interpretation, and the language children use in communicating what their graphs show. In this chapter, we see how spreadsheet tools overcome some of the limitations of simple graphing programmes.

Pupils may find spreadsheets more accessible than databases. Ways of introducing the spreadsheet and developing its use as an investigative tool are explored. Where ICT helps to sheds light on a difficult concept, pupils may experience pleasure, excitement and deep satisfaction. Such experiences not only contribute to effective learning. They help to overcome some of the barriers surrounding the technology itself.

Year 5 pupils created and used a database in Mathematics as part of a study of 2D shapes. This case study shows how, in organising the data initially and in carrying out database searches, pupils developed classificatory skills through identifying attributes. The opportunity appeared to widen their understanding of the properties of plane shapes.

Opportunities for ICT in English

The first chapter in this section identifies ways in which ICT may promote speaking and listening. In particular, we look at opportunities provided by 'adventure' games at Key Stage 1. The role of talking stories and talking word processors in the teaching of reading is discussed. We also see how overlay keyboards may provide a useful teaching aid in developing literacy.

The enabling skills which pupils need in order to make effective use of the word processor at both Key

Stages are identified. Does the medium really serve as an 'ideas processor' for young writers, as has been claimed?, Research, including detailed evaluations by teachers, is reviewed. Opportunities for ICT within the Literacy Framework (DfEE, 1998a) are identified.

At Key Stage 2, pupils may use overlay keyboards in storing and accessing semi-structured texts. There is a strong link with the Literacy Framework in supporting non-fiction text level work. Texts were manipulated on screen, using standard word processor facilities. Pupils found that features of texts originating in other genres (such as pictorial captions) needed adaptation. They began to gain greater awareness of structural features and language patterns.

The contribution of CD-ROM in supporting topic work is investigated. What information handling skills are demanded? How may pupils use downloaded content in the classroom? We also look at the use of multimedia authoring tools by pupils, integral approaches to presentation, in the format of 'topic folders', have been established for many years. What, uniquely, is contributed through the use of ICT?

Finding Out Through ICT

This section begins with a close look at the contribution of databases in pupil-led inquiry. How may teachers identify curriculum contexts? What are the critical issues for managing learning? What skills are demanded, and what are the constraints? All stages of database creation and interrogation can be highly problematic. In making practical recommendations, the chapter draws on extensive observation of pupils engaged in computer group work.

Data logging systems enable pupils to view at first hand the direct plotting of readings obtained by continuous monitoring. Lower-ability pupils encountered some unexpected difficulties, and the experience helped them to come to terms with graphical models. Teaching strategies involving a high level of interaction with real-time displays are explored. We see how Year 6 pupils made extended use of data log-ging equipment in Science investigations.

Control technology is as daunting for teachers as it is exciting for children. We look at opportunities across the curriculum, and see how initial work with the Roamer may lead into sensing and control. Progression is defined and links with work in other subjects are made explicit. There are practical examples showing starting points at a range of levels.

Finally, we explore what is involved in seeking information on the Internet. Strategies that teachers may use in tracking down specific topics are discussed. Independent use by pupils is examined critically. Capable 11 year olds readily acquired on-line navigational skills, and were prepared to compare and evaluate information sources. Pupils' ability to plan an inquiry, and use retrieved information away from the computer, will prove critical. In contrast to CD-ROM, the Internet is open and unfenced, with no integral signposts. What are the implications for the role of the teacher?

12

Opportunities for ICT in Teaching Mathematics

With up to half a day committed to meeting the new Literacy and Numeracy requirements, teachers may feel there is little time for computer group work. How can opportunities for ICT possibly be incorporated, given the current emphasis on whole-class teaching? Before addressing the practical problems, we need to understand the unique benefits of ICT. The final report of the Numeracy Task Force (DfEE. 1998b) is quite clear. A major contribution of ICT lies in teaching, whether to focus on specific aspects of number or to support general demonstration.

Starting with 'Legacy' Software: Number Grids and Factors

To look at how the computer may uniquely support the teaching of numeracy, we begin with a simple programme first distributed - on cassette tape! - in 1982. *Ergo* could hardly look less inviting. The introductory screen is primitive in the extreme. The Acom version which I use can easily be crashed. Printing BBC screen dumps is a long-forgotten skill. Despite these drawbacks, *Ergo* proved its worth when I recently taught a Year 3 class.

The screen shows a 5 x 5 grid, with only one number revealed at the start. Vertical and horizontal patterns underlie the grid. A typical example of a completed grid is shown here:

9	12	15	18	21
7	10	13	16	19
5	8	11	14	17
3	6	9	12	15
1	4	7	10	13

The aim is for children to discover the patterns and use them to complete the grid. The first number which children enter is a guess: they are told if the number is too large or too small. Immediately, this presents a situation where children have to think strategically in order to find the first number.

In teacher-led lessons, there is much scope for interaction at different levels. Can children correctly predict an adjacent number or - for the most able - the numbers at the ends of rows or in the corners of the grid? Pressing D at the start gives a 'difficult' level with bigger numbers and more exacting patterns to discover. At any stage, the teacher may complete the grid by pressing Ctrl-W.

After several demonstrations, I asked children, in pairs, to make grids on squared paper. Each pair played their own game, with one child in the role of the computer while the other tried to work out the hidden pattern. Later, children investigated adding diagonally opposite corners.

The Association of Teachers of Mathematics published *Some Lessons In Mathematics With A Microcomputer* (the SLIMWAM booklets) in the early Eighties. The booklets contain lesson plans for using *Ergo* and similar software, with accounts by teachers of the ways in which activities away from the computer were developed. It is interesting to note that the emphasis is on *teaching* with the computer. Independent group use follows the initial lesson.

For example, a teacher works with a low ability Year 7 class. He pretends to know little more than the pupils about what *Ergo* does. He acts as operator and 'voice' for the machine. Initial discussion focuses on tactics for finding the first number quickly. Discovery of vertical and horizontal patterns leads to pupils looking for diagonal patterns, combining the 'across' and 'up' rules to form a diagonal rule.

Where pupils had difficulty in articulating the rule, it was helpful to ask. What happens when you move to the right?' The related question. What happens when you move to the left?' introduces the idea of inverse operations in algebra. The teacher had prepared sheets with partrally complete grids. Pupils had to identify and record the rules for up, down right and left, then complete the grids.

The unique contribution of the computer was in enabling the modelling of grids in a whole-class lesson. The computer was more than a visual and, in that it gave immediate, accurate feedback in response to pupils' suggestions. Children continued working on the programme in pairs, gaining valuable practice at their own level. As well as practising mental subtraction and addition, they were engaged in identifying patterns and in applying their knowledge to a problem.

Today, spreadsheets may be used in Mathematics for the same purpose. There are advantages in that grids may be printed and patterns in columns may be displayed graphically. Chapter 5 introduces spreadsheets in the context of calculator work and number investigations. We shall sec how valuable this experience is in developing algebraic ideas. Once pupils know how to enter a simple function such as 'subtract two from the value above' and copy it to other cells, they may construct their own grids.

Knowledge of the pattern enables us to construct and manipulate a mental *image* of the grid. Another programme from the eighties, *Monty,* begins by revealing the complete grid, for pupils to discern its structure. The grid is then hidden. A 'python' slithers around the grid, then stops in a random position. Pupils have to find the numbers covered by the python.

It is extremely difficult to retain a visual 'snapshot' of the grid. It can only be reconstructed mentally by applying observed rules, for example, 'It goes up in tens from left to right. It goes down in ones from top to bottom.' In other words, a mathematical description is more efficient, and more easily remembered, than a visual image.

'*Circle* generates patterns on a circle of equally spaced dots, by repeatedly counting a fixed step then joining the start and finish points. Initially, children may be asked to explore freely. Even at this 'play' level, structured teacher intervention is important. In the past, inappropriate 'discovery learning' may simply have masked the fact that teachers were too busy to sit down and explore the possibilities for themselves!

It is important to ask questions such as, 'What patterns can you make? What does the screen always tell you?' From the beginning, the teacher's questions focus pupils' attention on the information on screen. Numbers of points and step size are shown, and the number of rotations is also given. The ultimate aim will be to investigate connections between these values and the type of pattern that is produced.

Pupils may be given a structured series of investigations. For example, they may first be asked to enter a fixed number of points (say 12 or 24) and investigate the range of patterns that the computer will draw. From the beginning, it is important to record the results. On a circle of 12 points, a step of 3 draws a square. Why? What happens with a step of 9? Teachers' questions should focus on the interconnections between the numbers and the patterns produced.

The next step might be to focus on a particular outcome such as a hexagon. Which pairs of numbers give hexagons? Again, it is important to record the data. As soon as the child notices a pattern, prediction should be actively encouraged. (How do we account for the fourth result?)

Number of dots	*Step size*	*Number of Sides*	*Number of revolutions*
6	1	6	1
12	2	6	1
18	3	6	1
6	5	6	5

A more advanced investigation focuses on 'stars'. Can the child discover, for example, five-pointed stars? (10,4), (20,8) are good examples. The pairs (number of dots, step size) are all in the ratio 5:2. Factors, multiples, ratios and equivalence can be extremely difficult to grasp, yet are related concepts. The problems presented by *Circle* broaden the child's experience, in providing opportunities to identify and use numeric relationships.

Fig. 12.1. 'Star' produced by a step size of 4 on a circle of 10 dots.

At an even higher level, the teacher may ask, 'What rules can we use to predict whether the pattern will be a polygon or a star?' The unique contribution of *Circle* is the speed with which it can generate a range of patterns. Capable children may quickly move to a more demanding problem. Unless pupils have some expertise with protractors, it is difficult to space dots evenly on paper. I do recall making similar 'clock races' on a banda master, but I think I would rather use the computer! Unfortunately, software of this vintage does not run in Windows, ruling out the pasting of patterns into other applications and causing printing to be a nightmare.

ICT is not a substitute for practical activities of a concrete nature. The computer is simply one of a range of resources for teaching Mathematics. The ICT application may support or extend work begun away from the computer. It may, for example, be used to extend an ongoing investigation. The computer can do this by readily generating exemplars and providing feedback, as in the case of *Circle*.

Multimedia resources may provide 'scaffolding' through graphics, sound and animation. For example, there are animated sequences controlled by the child which show a ten exploding into ten ones. (*Mighty Maths Carnival Countdown* contains a good example.) CD-ROMs with colourful, appealing graphics may be of particular value in supporting children who do not find it easy to get to grips with mathematical ideas.

For example, some young children find it difficult to grasp concepts of pairing and counting in twos. Much practice is needed and the compute offers another experiencer. For example, *Caterpillar in Tizzy's Toybox* requires the child to match pairs of shoes.

My World Mathematics Activities with Infants

We have looked ways in which ICT may be used in teaching the whole class, and in providing opportunities for investigation. A further advantage of ICT is that it may provide a framework to the teacher who is prepared to spend just a little time in adapting content to meet learners' needs. To illustrate, we look at ways in which *MyWorld* screens may be used in Mathematics at Key Stage 1.

MyWorld features a background on which children may place and arrange graphic images. The graphics are stored on the screen and are of two types, 'one-off' or 'copiable many times'. On some screens there is a text button, enabling pupils to add labels to the background. Unwanted objects may be disposed of in the 'bin'.

Since *MyWorld* is an open-ended *framework* programme, it depends on a good supply of content to serve a range of teaching objectives. The quality and appropriateness of *MyWorld* screens varies widely. Screens developed to meet a particular need - for example, practice in coin recognition for pupils with learning difficulties - may not succeed in another situation. Many teachers have expressed disappointment that there is no feedback. If pupils make incorrect matches, say between objects and captions, there is no response from the system. Screens where there is a 'right answer', such as those featuring time and money, suffer from this drawback, although the teacher may print the correct results for comparison.

Learning outcomes depend on the precise activity. A screen may be used in different ways, as we shall see. Since it is possible to prepare and save screens in advance, the teacher may frame an activity to serve a particular objective. Learning is not confined to Mathematics. In enabling children to arrange pictures on a background, some screens also serve as vehicles for story telling.

It is important to appreciate the open-ended nature of *My World* screens. The most effective screens are those where ther eis no 'right' answer. In the 'Teddies' screens on the *MyWorld Nursery* disc, children may move objects to find the concealed bear, then rearrange the room in any way they like so that the next group has no idea where Teddy is hiding.

Another simple example is *Bricks*, where children may arrange 3D bricks to make their own pictures. A group of low ability Year 2 children agreed to build a 'castle'. Sam could not see which brick was needed to span the top of a door. Steven told him which one to use; he was able to visualise the brick in place, but Sam could not do this. The chance to experiment assisted Sam in discriminating between the bricks. Later, the picture was labelled.

Some activities enable self-checking. The objective may be to make, copy or finish a pattern, or set of objects. Children may check for themselves whether the pattern, or set, is complete. An example is the *Clowns* screen on the *MyWorld Maths* disc. There is an infinite supply of clowns: each may be given a red, blue or green hat, nose and tie. As with all *MyWorld* screens, the activity is essentially open ended: children may arrange the clowns as they please. However, if a rule is made that all clowns must be different, the screen offers a range of combinatorial problems.

A group of three Year 2 pupils set out to find all the clowns. It did not take them long to discover twelve different clowns. There are 27 possible combinations, but the task, becomes much harder as fewer combinations remain unused. Away from the computer, the children made a list on paper of four further clowns. This was a difficult challenge, and it seemed unlikely that they would find any more clowns, due to the amount of checking that was now involved.

There was clearly a need to constrain the number of possible outcomes, by fixing one of the variables. One group chose to make clowns with blue hats. They quickly discovered five, and I asked if they could make any more. They succeeded in making all nine. The approach was one of trial and error, followed by careful checking against clowns already on the screen. There was much use of the bin during this activity.

I posed the problem, 'How many clowns can you make with red noses?' One group showed signs of a systematic approach. They began with three clowns, each with a different hat. But instead of sticking to the same colour tie, they mixed the colours up. Because they had not followed a pattern, finding the ninth clown proved hard. Jenna said, 'He can have a blue hat! You can have a green bow, and he'll be different.' Jenna was not reasoning that, because there were three red and three green hats, there should be three blue hats. She was simply telling the others something she had noticed. In the event, the other children ignored her, and the wrong colour was put on. Jenna seemed to lose track of her idea, but at the end she announced, 'There's three red hats and three green hats and three blue hats!

We made 9 clowns with red noses.

3 clowns have got blue hots.

3 clowns have got red hots.

3 downs have got green hots.

Fig. 12.2. Year 2 children recorded the set of clowns with red noses.

Another challenge is to make a set of clowns, each with three colours. Again, the clowns must all be different. There are six possible combinations. Another Year 2 group could not discover the sixth clown. I prompted the children to tell me about the hats. They noticed that there were two green hats and two blue hats, but only one red. They were then able to solve the problem.

The group next used the *Flags* screen. Six flags were made, each flag containing the three coloured stripes in a different arrangement. Grace, who made the last of the six flags, noticed that there were two with fed at the top and two with yellow at the top, but only one with blue at the top. She reasoned that the sixth flag had to have blue at the top.

Older pupils may be asked to use *Clowns* or *Flags* with the objective of exploring different systematic approaches. For example, all nine clowns with red noses may be arranged in a 3x3 matrix. The pupils may opt to select an attribute (i.e. hat or tie) and vary its colour with each clown in the row.

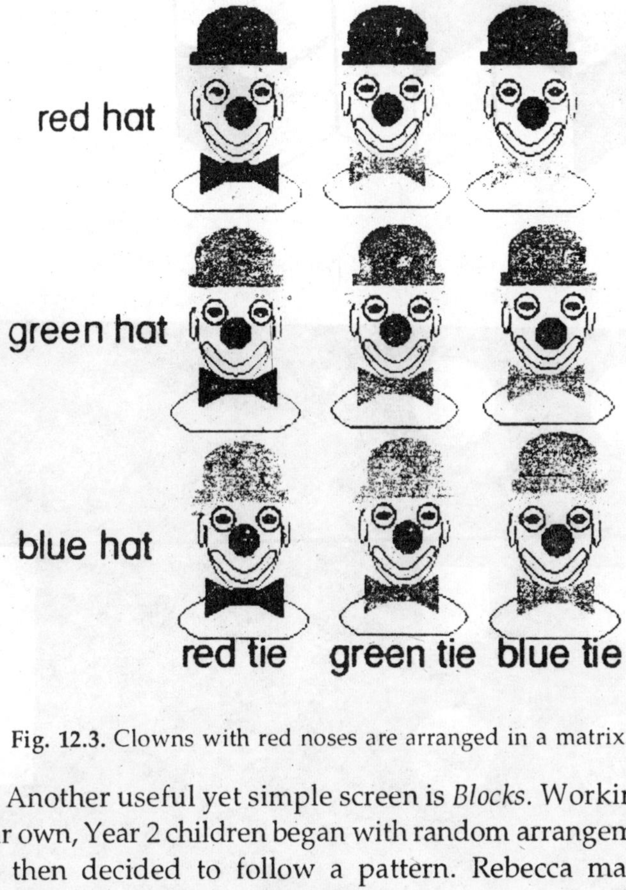

Fig. 12.3. Clowns with red noses are arranged in a matrix.

Another useful yet simple screen is *Blocks*. Working or their own, Year 2 children began with random arrangements but then decided to follow a pattern. Rebecca made a tower with repeating red, yellow and blue blocks. Dean began with a random pattern, then 'binned' blocks as a repeating row began to emerge. Grace made a row of

Fig. 12.4. A Year 2 pupils pattern of blocks

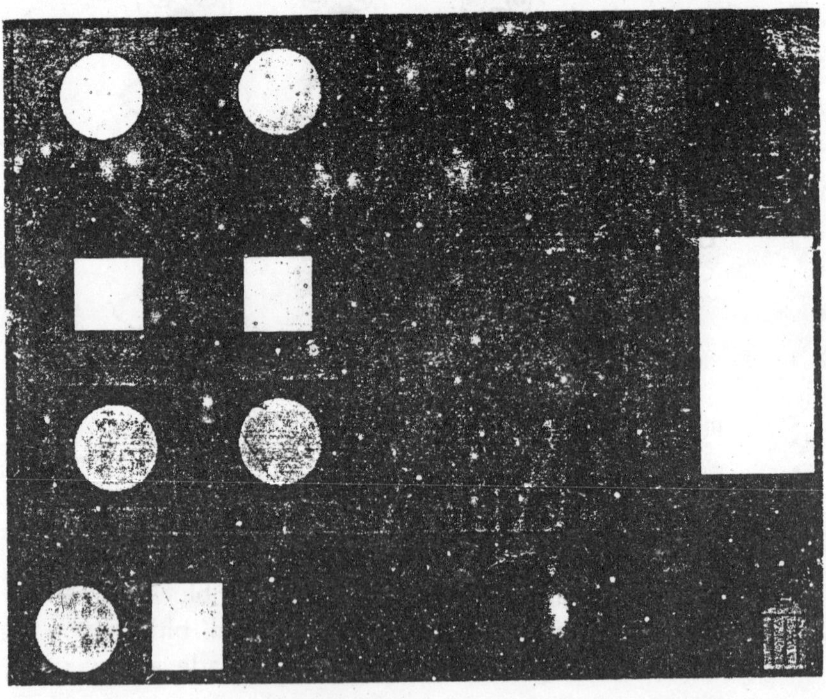

Fig. 12.5. My World Build (Nursery Disc)

three, then extended her pattern into a two dimensional arrangement (Figure 12.4).

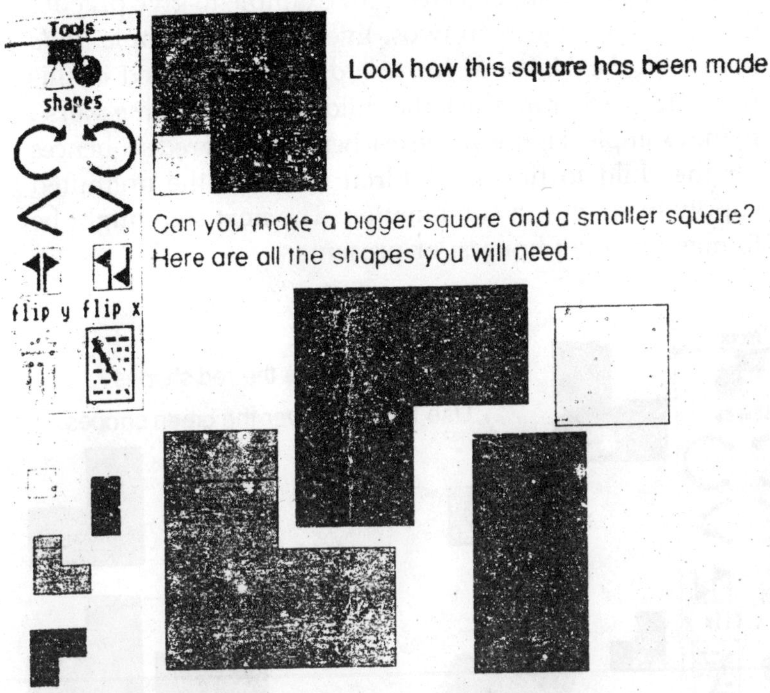

Fig. 12.6. A screen prepared by a teacher using MyWortd2 Tiles

Some *MyWorld* screens provide sets of shapes for tessellation. One Year 2 group began with a pattern of equilateral triangles. When asked, they were unable to identify a hexagon within the tessellation they had made. One girl found a plastic hexagon and this was held up against the screen, to identify the shape. Other pupils needed no help, and made a number of separate hexagons. Children had to think hard about fitting the shapes together. These screens have an advantage over plastic shapes in that the rest of the arrangement is undisturbed while children try to fit a new shape into a gap.

The teacher may prepare and save a *MyWorld* screen to meet a particular objective, for example to give practice in organising objects in twos. Even the very simple *Build* screen on the *MyWorld Nursery* disc may be used in this way. The teacher may ask the child, 'Make me some pairs'. In the example (Figure 4), the teacher has prepared sequences for the child to finish. Children may use the unlimited supply of shapes in combination. The next step might be to make pairs of houses, or presents.

Fig. 12.7. A screen prepared by the teacher. Can children transform the shapes on the right?

The teacher, may set varied tasks for children who do

not always progress readily from one step to the next. The *Tiles* screen and libraries are supplied with *MyWorld2*. Initially, children may choose freely from the four sets of shapes, which appear in a pop-up menu. There are tools which enable the shapes to be enlarged or reduced, flipped horizontally or vertically, and rotated in either direction. Children will discover for themselves what these tools do. However, the teacher may prepare a progression of screens which focus on a particular transformation. Activities may proceed step-by-step, supporting a pupil who has difficulty with the concept.

In Figure 12.6, the child is given the pieces needed to make a smaller and a larger copy of the pattern. Two pieces need to be rotated or flipped in order to fit. The teacher may plan a progression of tasks in which the level of challenge is increased, or support withdrawn, a step at a time. In the preceding task, the child may be asked to match the pattern exactly, with prepared jigsaw pieces. In the follow-up activity, shapes have to be selected from the pop-up menu and manipulated by the child to cover or copy the pattern.

In Figure 12.7 the red shapes on the right have to be manipulated to match the Green shapes on the left. The full range of tools is used and two shapes have to be transformed twice. The red shapes have been pre-selected from the pop-up menu, and the screen saved in advance by the teacher. This saves time, especially where the teacher plans to use this screen in the context of a whole-class interactive session. There is much scope for discussion: 'What do you think will happen? 'Is there another way of making the green shape?' 'Can you describe other things we could do with the red shapes?'

Tasks specially prepared using 'content-free' IT

applications often provide excellent assessment opportunities, because there is a visible end product. In preparing screens such as those above, the teacher may identify the skills, understanding and knowledge demonstrated by a child who completes the tasks successfully.